Contents

Natural
Environment
Research
Council

UNIVERSITY OF
NEWCASTLE UPON TYNE

...or Land Use
...esources Research

Land use change

the causes and

consequences

ITE symposium no. 27

The proceedings of a Conference orga...
Use Research Coordination Committee...
Environment Research Council, with su...
Economic and Social Research Counci...
University of Newcastle upon Tyne

Edited by

M C Whitby

Professor of Countryside Manag...
University of Newcastle upon T...

University of Plymouth Library

Subject to status this item may be renewed
via your Voyager account

http://voyager.plymouth.ac.uk

Exeter tel: (01392) 475049
Exmouth tel: (01395) 255331
Plymouth tel: (01752) 232323

London: HMSO

ACKNOWLEDGEMENTS

The editing of a set of proceedings of this length and complexity, whilst an interesting challenge in itself, is clearly beyond the scope of any one individual, and this volume is no exception. In particular, I must acknowledge the help and encouragement of Professor O W Heal, whose enthusiasm for this Conference and for its eventual outcome has been supportive throughout. The reviewing process to which the papers have been subjected would not have been possible without the generous input from members of the Land Use Research Coordinating Committee. More concretely, I must also recognise the unstinting help of Mrs Karen Leech and Mrs Penny Ward, whose brisk cheerfulness when confronted with yet another set of amendments to incorporate and edit has transformed the job of editing from a chore to a pleasure.

M C Whitby

Professor of Countryside Management
The University
Newcastle upon Tyne
NE1 7RU

The INSTITUTE OF TERRESTRIAL ECOLOGY (ITE) is a component research organisation within the NATURAL ENVIRONMENT RESEARCH COUNCIL. The Institute is part of the Terrestrial and Freshwater Sciences Directorate, and was established in 1973 by the merger of the research stations of the Nature Conservancy with the Institute of Tree Biology.
It has been at the forefront of ecological research ever since. The six research stations of the Institute provide a ready access to sites and to environmental and ecological problems in any part of Britain. In addition to the broad environmental knowledge and experience expected of the modern ecologist, each station has a range of special expertise and facilities. Thus, the Institute is able to provide unparallelled opportunities for long-term, multidisciplinary studies of complex environmental and ecological problems.

ITE undertakes specialist ecological research on subjects ranging from micro-organisms to trees and mammals, from coastal habitats to uplands, from derelict land to air pollution. Understanding the ecology of different species of natural and man-made communities plays an increasingly important role in areas such as monitoring ecological aspects of agriculture, improving productivity in forestry, controlling pests, managing and conserving wildlife, assessing the causes and effects of pollution, and rehabilitating disturbed sites.

The Institute's research is financed by the UK Government through the science budget, and by private and public sector customers who commission or sponsor specific research programmes, ITE's expertise is also widely used by international organisations in overseas collaborative projects.

The results of ITE research are available to those responsible for the protection, management and wise use of our natural resources, being published in a wide range of scientific journals, and in an ITE series of publications. The Annual Report contains more general information.

The context

Introduction to the Conference

D A Trippier

Minister for the Environment and Countryide,
House of Commons, Westminster, London SW1A 0AA

I am delighted to have been invited to open this Conference. It is a timely opportunity to address a major gathering of researchers and practitioners in the increasingly important area of measuring land use change and evaluating its consequences for the economy and the environment. I welcome the drawing together of the interests of the Economic and Social Research Council (ESRC) with that of the Natural Environment Research Council (NERC), which is so evident in the programme for this meeting.

One of my specific remits is the countryside, and I have no hesitation in reaffirming our commitment to enhance the countryside – or the sake of its beauty, its diversity of landscape, and the wealth of its natural resources. Many of us use it for recreation, whilst others use its resources to farm or for other economic activities. The very success of economic activity in rural England has contributed to the changes of recent years. But, in commanding this success, we must not forget that species other than ourselves use the environment, and that they not only contribute to our quality of life but have a right to be there themselves – an argument so central to the maintenance of biodiversity.

The Government White Paper *This common inheritance** was aptly named. It reflects this Government's firm commitment to environmental protection. It sets the environmental agenda for the turn of the century. We all realise the finite nature of the resources of this planet. The land area of our country, small as it is, is renowned for its beauty and diversity, and we need to nurture it. The modern word 'ecology' comes from a Greek word meaning a place to live – we should be maintaining ours and improving it as a fitting inheritance for future generations. It is vital for the aspirations of our society that there is a proper recognition for the sustainability of our environment.

PLANNING

In this country we have a long-established planning system to reconcile priorities and to

*Department of the Environment, 1990. *This common inheritance: Britain's environmental strategy.* (Cm 1200.) London: HMSO.

secure the effective use of land. It has an important part to play in protecting the countryside. We are committed to keeping national Planning Policy Guidance up-to-date, and increasing use is being made of Planning Policy Guidance Notes. The Planning Bill currently (March 1991) in Parliament will move the system fast towards complete coverage of structure plans and district-wide local plans. The Government wants the preparation of these plans to take account of local choices about the pattern of development, and to provide local communities with a greater degree of confidence about where development will and will not be permitted.

Ninety per cent of our population live in urban areas which cover 10% of the land. Recent studies suggest that a further 1% of rural land is likely to be taken into the urban area over the last 20 years of this century. We have an opportunity to ensure that this small but important change occurs in the right locations. The designated land of the Green Belts will continue to provide a buffer. Boundaries should only alter in the most exceptional circumstances.

URBAN AREA

The Government wants to see everyone playing a part in improving the urban and urban fringe environments: local businesses, schoolchildren, voluntary groups, in fact everyone in a local community acting together. The projects of the Groundwork Trusts are excellent examples. We plan to double the number of Groundwork Trusts working mainly in the urban fringe to 50 over the next three years. Trusts have set up partnerships between private and public sectors for the management of land, connecting land management into the planning of what are often neglected areas. In the north-east, the East Durham Groundwork Trust has been active since 1987 in the design and implementation of a variety of tree planting, footpath and reclamation projects.

COUNTRYSIDE

Our theme for the 1990s must be to see economic development advancing hand in glove with the conservation of resources, so that the interests of the

community are properly reconciled. The theme is central to the White Paper and is reflected in the *World conservation strategy**. It is ten years since the strategy was first published. We should be justly proud of what we have done in this country to take a lead in incorporating economic costs and benefits into the policies for the use of land.

INITIATIVES

There has already been significant progress in carrying forward new initiatives in the countryside. Over the past six months my Department has been heavily involved in the development of Nitrate Sensitive Areas, and has been making an input to drawing up Codes of Good Agricultural Practice. We are reviewing the operation of the Countryside Premium Scheme and the extent to which environmental benefits can be made an integral part of the basic Set-Aside Scheme and not just an optional extra. We committed ourselves in the White Paper to a review of the Scheme with a view to it being taken over by the relevant Government Departments.

We have also given the Countryside Commission the green light for the development of the New National Countryside Initiative, referred to in the White Paper. This Countryside Stewardship Scheme is targeted at four types of habitat and landscape that have either declined or are endangered by the changes in land management brought about by the pressures of the last two decades for agricultural intensification. Lowland heaths, water-sides, chalk and limestone grasslands, and possibly some upland areas, will have access to approximately 13 million of extra support over the next three years. This is an exciting new scheme which uses market mechanisms to encourage conservation. In effect, we are saying we will pay X pounds for a new acre of heather on wetland. This is a challenge to the farmers involved; I am sure it will also be a challenge to the research community to determine how best and how economically we might recreate some of these precious habitats.

We have also endorsed the Countryside Commission's objectives for bringing the rights-of-way networks into good order by the end of the century, and revising their policy on Areas of Outstanding Natural Beauty. We will therefore see increased management effort going into these areas of nationally important landscapes.

We have announced a substantial increase in grant-in-aid for the main countryside agencies and the National Park authorities. The reorganised nature conservation agencies established by the Environment Protection Act 1990 will assume their responsibilities on 1 April 1991, fully resourced to undertake their new functions. We have recently

*International Union for Conservation of Nature and Natural Resources. 1980. *World conservation strategy: living resource conservation for sustainable development*. Gland: IUCN.

issued a consultation document on planning controls over Sites of Special Scientific Interest (SSSIs) which proposes strengthening of the need for specific planning permission for temporary recreational uses of land; amplifying the policy on calling in planning applications; and extending the need for local authorities to consult the Nature Conservancy Council on planning proposals adjacent to Sites of Special Scientific Interest. We are strengthening habitat protection signals through our support for the concept of the draft European Directive on Habitat Protection. This Directive provides a real opportunity for the European Commission to ensure environmental concerns are considered throughout the Community on the same sound basis as in the UK.

Our countryside initiatives encourage voluntary action. We provide grant support to a wide range of voluntary groups who take action beneficial to our heritage. We have recently announced a new scheme of support to encourage initiatives linked to the White Paper. We hope that many new ideas will come forward including lots of local environmental initiatives.

AGRICULTURE

Perhaps the most immediate and major effects on our countryside will come from the European Community's efforts to reform the Common Agricultural Policy (CAP). Recently, the European Commission published their outline proposals for the reform of the CAP. We have vigorously opposed these proposals. They discriminate against large and efficient UK farmers, seek to freeze farm structures, and pay little regard to the environmental consequences. What is more, they would increase the cost of the CAP. But reform is in the air, and this will provide us with an opportunity to pursue our White Paper commitment to seek the closer integration of agricultural and environmental policies. My Department will be working closely with the Ministry of Agriculture to bring this about. We all want to see a healthy environment and prosperous countryside with a range of job opportunities.

TREES

There has also been significant progress in carrying forward new initiatives to promote the treescape of this country. We have backed the proposal by the Countryside Commission for a new national forest in the Midlands. We have also lent support to their joint venture with the Forestry Commission to create 'community forests' near the major towns and cities. These are already in an advanced stage of planning. We were delighted to announce in February that work will commence on a further nine areas. One of the first three was the Great North Forest, covering open land in south Tyneside, Sunderland, Gateshead and Chester-le-Street. These schemes will help to enhance the environment and provide important new opportunities for leisure and recreation.

RURAL DEVELOPMENT

The Government is also anxious to maintain a living countryside, with a thriving rural economy. We have had a good deal of success and many rural areas are now doing well. However, there are still many rural communities with problems. The Government is aware of these problems and is taking action to help. For example, my Department sponsors the Rural Development Commission as the Government's main agency for diversifying rural enterprise. To inform policy-making in this area we also carry out research. Two projects have recently been completed – work on the dynamics of the rural economy, and a review of the Rural Development Commission's social programmes. Reports on both will be published in the next two months. Work is in progress on the performance of firms in rural areas, and further work is planned.

NOW BACK TO THE CONFERENCE

I see a real opportunity for the Land Use Research Coordination Committee (LURCC) to 'come out of hiding', to become a real sounding board for the identification of research priorities, working closely with both Government and Research Councils. I am reminded of the success of the Committee on Air Pollution Effects Research (CAPER), in drawing together the scientific community and acting as a forum for peer review when the news first broke of the extent of acidification problems on tree health. It also provided our first expert review groups on acid waters and terrestrial effects.

This is the first LURCC Symposium and I see the subject matter of this Committee's work as being no less important, co-ordinating as it does a very broad mixture of basic, strategic and applied avenues of science, economics and social research.

Already the Committee has played an important role by examining our proposals for a major survey of the countryside, to which I shall return later.

INFORMATION

Changes in attitude, economic pressures and policy have increased the speed and complexity of land use change and altered the relative competitive strengths of different land users. New uncertainties and conflicts have arisen as old problems are resolved. A prerequisite to the resolution of the conflicts and uncertainties is to identify precisely how land use has changed, what effect this has had on its vegetation cover, and what flexibility there may be to cope with change. Do we know how extensive these changes may be in a National Park, a field, a river or a water catchment, and how they will affect other areas of interest?

The Countryside Survey 1990 to which I referred earlier, will be of fundamental scientific value as well as important in informing policy-makers. The cost, which is over £2 million, is being shared equally between my Department and the scientific and technical community. I am excited by the opportunit that this Survey represents for the bringing together of different technologies. It will provide 'broad-brush' census information from satellite remote sensing and connect with it detailed information on the quality of individual habitats obtained by surveying over 500 one kilometre square land parcels throughout Great Britain. This is not all. There is information on over half of these squares, which was obtained earlier in both 1978 and 1984 by the Institute of Terrestrial Ecology. These data will provide, for the first time, guidance on national changes in quantity and distribution of plant species in Great Britain.

We all recognise the special importance of linear features in the countryside. Later in this Conference you will hear some of the first results from Countryside Survey 1990. They confirm the importance of linear features, such as hedgerows, streams and roadside verges, for plant life in the wider countryside, and indicate how they may have been affected by changes in land use over the past decades. The Survey will provide an opportunity to draw together information collected in our SSSIs with that from the wider countryside. The survey methods are consistent, although less detailed, than those used for survey of Environmentally Sensitive Areas (ESAs). The study also offers opportunities for other surveys of a more local nature to be placed in a national context. I will be looking for any important lessons for land managers. I am sure that much of this will be reflected in the meat of the discussion of this Conference.

COUNTRYSIDE RESEARCH

My Department's Countryside Research Programme includes several sectoral studies aimed at increasing our knowledge of the pressures on the environment and understanding how the effects of management operate. An important contribution to beginning to understand these pressures has been our economic modelling project, jointly funded with the Ministry of Agriculture, Rural Development Commission, Nature Conservancy Council, and Countryside Commission at the Centre of Agriculture Strategy (CAS) at the University of Reading. This work has also used the land classification developed by the Institute of Terrestrial Ecology for the Countryside Survey. It seeks to forecast the effects of changes in farm policy and to trace them through to effects on the environment. I endorse the development of this work, which has been taken up by the NERC/ESRC Land Use Programme (NELUP) at the University of Newcastle upon Tyne and is now supported jointly by the Research Councils running this Conference. But there is a long way to go yet, and I look forward to hearing of advances in methodology created by the close links that have been forged.

STATISTICS

Following the publication of its White Paper, the

Government is to produce a new and comprehensive statistical report on the environment, drawing on available data which cover the range of environmental topics. My Department also collects statistics to aid the process of monitoring policies and to keep up to date with understanding demand for land. The main data on the planning system are quarterly returns on the number of planning applications and the time taken to process them. Data on outstanding planning permissions for housing and information on appeals are also collected. Examples of our data are published in the annual digests of environmental statistics*, and include information on urbanisation, derelict land, land cover and vacant land, as well as the Ordnance Survey land use change data. These change data have been collected since 1985, and independent research has underlined the value of the statistics. All such data become so much more valuable when they can be co-ordinated with those from other sources.

I do not underestimate the contribution that can be made from easily accessible and understandable information derived from the data integration process. Shortly we will have the report of one such study undertaken for us by the University of Bristol. I would welcome early and improved access to firm data on the rates of change taking place in order to improve the analysis of what the pressures may be that cause such changes.

PRESSURE FOR CHANGE

Change in the countryside can come from the individual reactions of managers to new production opportunities triggered by change in process or by technical changes; by this I mean the possible introduction of new and novel species as crops, and the manipulation of the genetic make-up of existing species to increase their growth potential. We need to be able to anticipate and forecast the environmental consequences of such changes more accurately in future. You have a key role in helping us to do so. Other reasons for changes in direct management technique can arise from area controls on land, such as nitrate protection zones, indirect discharge limits that affect air pollution, or the standards of use of sewage sludge on soils that may

*Department of the Environment. *Digest of environmental protection and water statistics.* London: HMSO.

be liable to heavy metal contamination. The connection between different uses and how they affect the different parts of our environment is a central theme of our Integrated Quality Control Policy now being developed by the Pollution Inspectorate. I was pleased to hear that integration had been achieved between the technique for land assessment used in the Countryside Survey 1990 and the biological indicators used for river quality assessment that have been incorporated into the National Rivers Authority River Quality Survey of 1990.

CHALLENGES

Your circular introducing this Conference states that your aim is to 'explore' the subject and its 'implications for research and policy'. Mr Chairman, I would like to suggest some objectives that this Conference may wish to explore. First, we need to increase our understanding of the effects which our use of the land has on our environment. Second, we need to find new ways of ensuring the continued economic prosperity of rural areas which also ensure that this precious heritage is passed on in good heart to our children. Finally, there are still too many value judgements made without adequate scientific information.

GOVERNMENT SUPPORT

Sorting out these complex interactions within land-based ecosystems is therefore the challenge to multidisciplinary research. I am pleased that the Department of the Environment has been able to secure an increase in research funding of nearly 20% for the coming year. Our Countryside Programme has been able to share in this increase and, through the application of the customer-contractor principle, I will ensure that these funds support the further understanding of the changes affecting our countryside.

CONCLUSION

Mr Chairman, I wish the Conference well in its deliberations, and hope to hear of a productive outcome that will contribute to our efforts to maintain the continuing prosperity and conservation of rural England.

The research setting

J Knill

Chairman, Natural Environment Research Council
Polaris House, North Star Avenue, Swindon, Wiltshire SN2 1EU

This Conference on 'Land use change' could hardly have been more perfectly timed. We are all aware – from our personal experiences and our professional awareness – of the developing concern in changes to our land: the economic pressures on farmers and foresters, the need to protect water supplies, the loss of species and habitats, the increasing demand for access to the countryside for leisure, and the almost continuous modifications to landscape which seem to form a part of modern life. This interest in how we use our land is expressed at all levels, from the individual rambler through landowners to Government, and, most recently, through Prince Charles' thought-provoking words to the Royal Agricultural Society.

The importance of the subject, and of this Conference, is underlined by the attendance of the Minister for the Environment and Countryside, Mr David Trippier. His presence highlights one of the main issues which no doubt will develop within the formal and informal discussions associated with the Conference – that of land use policy. The Environment White Paper defined many facets of land use and environment on which policy has been, and is likely to be, formulated and implemented. One of the reasons in our being here today is that we all recognise that we will see the enhanced evolution of such policy-making at all scales, from the local to the international.

However, in order that policy can be targeted to identify new opportunities and to solve specific problems, we need effective research, and land use research occupies much of our formal programme over the next three days. There are four topics on which we must focus our attention.

First, the analysis of the cause of change. Possibly as never before we appreciate that we live in an environment which is changing and increasingly driven by man-made influences. Social and economic factors are major determinants of land use change, acting within the physical constraints of topography, climate, geology, and soil conditions created over the millenia. We have a reasonable qualitative comprehension of the effects of individual factors. The challenge that faces us now is to quantify the effects of, and interactions between, social and economic change on land use.

Second, the assessment of the consequences of change. How can we define better the 'knock-on' results of a single change on the total environment? We are not particularly good at this type of analysis, as is too clearly told by the stores of DDT and the CFCs. If an economic incentive results in a major change in farm management, for example, what will be the consequences to richness of habitat and species, water quality, public access, and so on? The environment has the means to both moderate or amplify the transmission of the signal which results from such a change, either delaying responses, or reacting only in particular circumstances, such as drought or flood conditions. Can we improve our ability to predict the consequences of such changes and provide one of the vital tools needed by policy-makers?

Third, the detection of change. Comprehensive data bases exist from agricultural returns, forestry census, conservation surveys, and many other local and national studies. But are we able to integrate these data coherently and efficiently so that we have consistent and compatible measures of rate, type, and scale of change? Can modern methods of remote sensing, networking and computing be applied to make more sense of the data that we already hold; to improve our methods of data capture, processing, and archiving for the future; and to provide wider access and availability?

Fourth, the assessment of land use options. Possibly the greatest challenge is to develop reliable simulations or models which combine research results and knowledge so as to permit both researchers and policy-makers to explore the controls on, and options for, change . . . and thereby to develop decision support systems.

In these four areas of research it is essential that social, economic, land use and environmental scientists work together. It is no accident that this is a genuinely multidisciplinary Conference, as is quite clearly demonstrated by the list of participants. Such a mix of expertise is quite essential to answer the questions raised, to permit communication across disciplinary or functional boundaries, and to relate research to policy.

The theme and approach of the Conference is the brainchild of the Land Use Research Coordination Committee of the Natural Environment Research Council (NERC), a committee which itself covers a wide spectrum of interests, and provides advice to Council on research priorities. In this latter sense, the Conference is of considerable importance to NERC, and to its sister Councils with interests in land use. We see the Conference as identifying the state-of-the-art in the country, and providing some clear signposting for the future. The value of such a Conference is as much to learn about what others are doing as to refocus one's own thoughts and research direction.

NERC has been involved in a surge of research activity in land use in recent years, and much of this has necessarily involved the creation of mechanisms to ensure that organisational boundaries are effectively bridged. These developments include the following:

1. The Joint Agriculture and the Environment Programme, carried out jointly by the Agricultural and Food Research Council, the Economic and Social Research Council (ESRC) and NERC, is focused on ecological change in response to the habitat mosaic of farmland, plant/herbivore relations, and on the opportunities for, and consequences of, multiple income on farms.

2. The Forestry Commission, Department of Environment (DoE) and NERC jointly fund a Special Topic on Farm Forestry.

3. NERC has established an Environmental Information Centre at the Institute of Terrestrial Ecology's Monks Wood Experimental Station, where remote sensing is being used to produce a land cover map of Britain. This is being integrated with the field survey of habitat and ecological change on land and in freshwaters. The Countryside Survey 1990 is, of course, supported by DoE, the Department of Trade and Industry and the Nature Conservancy Council, as well as NERC.

4. NERC and ESRC have joined forces to establish a multidisciplinary land use programme here at the University of Newcastle upon Tyne to explore the development of a decision support system.

As you can appreciate, these initiatives relate closely to the four research themes which I identified earlier. What are our priorities for the future? Should they be directed towards better understanding of the effectiveness of land use policy, to the consequenses of climate change, or to land use interactions within Europe, or what? The Research Councils, and the various Departments represented here, will be listening, and taking careful note of your views.

The Land Use Research Coordination Committee has had the hard work in setting up this Conference. The University of Newcastle is our supportive host. It is now up to you, the speakers and all participants, to use the formal sessions and the informal discussions to full advantage in order to show the way forward. I wish you all an enjoyable and productive meeting.

Land use in the United Kingdom

M L Parry*, J E Hossell*, and L J Wright

Atmospheric Impacts Research Group, School of Geography, University of Birmingham, Edgbaston, Birmingham B15 2TT
*Present address:
Environmental Change Unit, University of Oxford, 1a Mansfield Road, Oxford OX1 3TB

INTRODUCTION

There are 24 million ha of land in the United Kingdom and almost all are used for some purpose. Indeed, the general intensity of land use – a reflection of the limited area per head and the fact that very little land is intrinsically unusable – is a characteristic feature of the United Kingdom. Even in regions of less intensive use, such as the mountains and moorlands, the pattern is complicated by the large number of competing users.

In this introductory address, we will consider how changes in the competition for land have, over the past 50 years, led to changes in activity on the land surface of the UK, and to consequent changes in its land use and landscape. We shall outline the forces that currently, and may in the future, remould present land use patterns, and the policies that we believe are needed to control these forces.

There are two enduring themes in the study of land use in the United Kingdom. The first one of these, which has its origins in the 1930s, is that rural land is scarce and has, for some time, been under pressure from an expanding urban area. The second, and more recent, theme is that the character of the rural landscape is undergoing a radical change due to the modernisation of farming practices. A result has been a shift of concern away from the need to restrict the *quantity* of change in land use (especially of farmland transfers to urban use) toward the need to protect the *quality* of the landscape from the effects of new land users.

PRE-WAR PATTERNS OF LAND USE

Before the marked changes imposed by the Second World War, one-third of farmland in the UK was covered by rough, semi-natural vegetation used largely for extensive grazing by sheep and cattle. In the 1930s the only major transfers of use from grazing were to forestry. These were exceeded by gains due to the invasion of pastures by sedge and bracken, and to the direct reversion of arable to rough pasture (Figure 1).

Within the sector of improved farmland, which

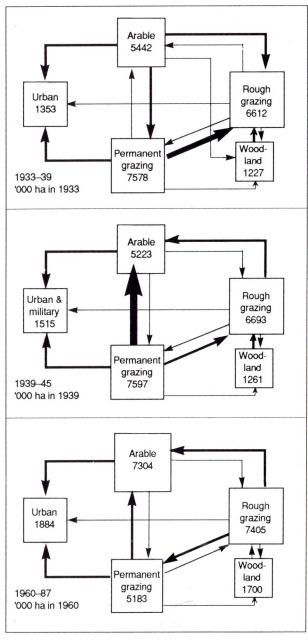

Figure 1. Major land use shifts in the UK in 1933–39, 1939–45 and 1960–87. Arrows are schematic, not quantitative, representations of the land use shifts (source: Parry 1990)

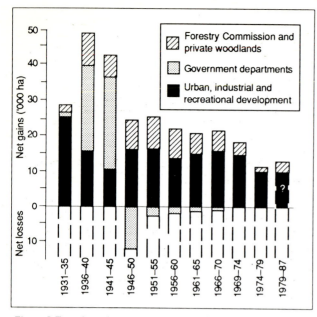

Figure 2. Transfers of agricultural land in England and Wales to urban and other uses, 1931–87 (source: Parry 1990)

covered two-thirds of the agricultural area in the United Kingdom at that time, depressed demand for agricultural products was encouraging the turnover of arable to permanent grass. Moreover, the depressed agricultural land market and the absence of development control, combined with an increased mobility offered by the cheap motor car, led to the rapid suburban development of farmland. As shown by Figure 2, between 1936 and 1939 an average of 25 000 ha of farmland in England and Wales was transferred to urban use every year.

WAR-TIME CHANGES IN LAND USE

The War years saw the most marked and rapid change in UK land use this century – even more marked than those changes in the 1980s. The influence of ploughing grants backed by the compulsory powers of the County War Agricultural Executive Committees led to a reversal in the decline of the arable area. The acreage increased by about 8% in *each year* between 1940 and 1943 (Parry 1990).

Two of these changes were particularly enduring. First, there was the transfer of land, amounting to 1% of improved farmland in England and Wales, to the armed services. More than 140 War-time airfields were constructed in East Anglia alone. Of this national transfer of land, two-thirds represented a permanent change of use: it has not been returned to agriculture.

Second, there was extensive felling of timber. One-fifth of the forest and woodland in Britain had been cut over in the War years. In particular, the extent of mature, and especially broadleaved, woodland was greatly reduced (Parry 1990).

THE MODERN LAND USE STRUCTURE

The present use of land (as shown in Figure 3) – and the resulting landscape – is the product of this country's history, and of myriad decisions by management. Ownership of land in the UK is thus a

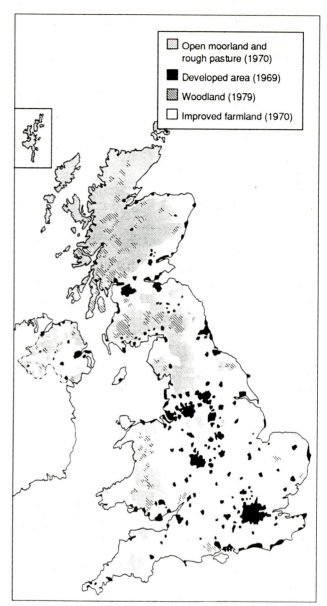

Figure 3. Major land uses in the United Kingdom (source: Parry 1990)

key to its use today. In the rural sector alone, there are about 270 000 separate holdings (Harrison 1977).

About one-half of these farmers are also landowners; the remainder are tenants whose management decisions are constrained by conditions of lease from the owner. There are, therefore, about 400 000 decision-makers involved in the use of rural land in the UK.

AGENTS OF POST-WAR CHANGE

The impression given by official statistics is that the present land use structure of the United Kingdom, if not its landscape, is not substantially different from that in 1930. But this impression is misleading for it is derived from aggregate figures which disguise both major changes in regional pattern and substantial internal adjustments between land use types.

There are four major types of changes in land use at present: the growth of urban areas and their changing composition, changes in the agricultural sector (particularly between roughland and improved land, tillage and pasture), the extension of

the forest and woodland and, finally, the growing competition for rural land from quasi-urban uses (for example, recreation and water-gathering). We shall consider each of these components in turn.

First, and with regard to urban land use, one of the dominant forces for change in post-War British land use has been the growth of the urban area. Although the subject of quite heated debate, the evidence is clear that the UK urban area is advancing at an average rate of about 10% per decade (Best 1981; Parry 1990).

A second cause for concern, particularly in the 1950s, was that the most rapid rates of urban growth continued to occur in the most 'urbanised' regions (eg the east Midlands and the south-east), thus further eroding the already-diminished countryside in these areas. More recently, however, growth has been concentrated in the less 'urbanised' regions and has, in fact, been *least* in the south-east (Best 1981).

A third concern has been for land uses at the urban periphery. Here, urban nuisance and the anticipation of urban growth has led to 'run-down' or 'idle' land. A survey of London's Green Belt in 1979, for example, found that one-third of farmland here exhibited signs of idling or urban nuisance (Munton 1983).

The indications are, however, that there has been no sustained increase in the rate of farmland loss to urban use. The annual average rate is currently about 15 000 ha per year – less than two-thirds of the rate in the 1930s. It *is* true that conversion has occurred in the most productive agricultural regions, but these losses have been more than offset by increases in agricultural productivity: over the past five years, about 0.5% of UK farmland may have converted to urban use, yet agricultural gross output, net of inputs, probably increased by 15% over the same period (Parry 1990).

A corollary of urban growth in the United Kingdom has been the contraction of land in agricultural use. Within this agricultural sector, three major trends are discernible: the intensification of farming, its increasing specialisation by farm and by area, and the increasing scale of farm operations.

Changes in the extent of tillage and grassland

Increasing intensity of use has been reflected in a substantial increase in the area under tillage, with major regional variations of change which have served to enhance the contrast between east and west. Thus, the area under crops has grown over the past 30 years in the corn-growing counties but has contracted in the west (Figure 4). The arable east has become more arable, the pastoral west has become less arable.

Most notable within the tillage has been an increase in the area devoted to barley, as a feed crop for cattle, and a decrease in labour-demanding root crops and a decline in orchards.

In the north and west, the principal trend (though this

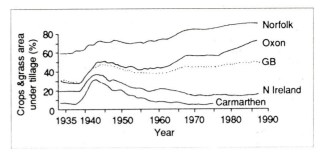

Figure 4. Changes in the area under tillage in the UK and selected area, 1983–87 (source: Parry 1990)

may have been reversed in recent years) has been toward the steady increase in temporary, at the expense of permanent, grassland. The improvement inquality of pasture has been reflected in substantial livestock increases in the grazing counties. Changes to the farming landscape have been less marked here than in the east.

Changes in rough grazing extent

Particularly important for the landscape in the northern and western UK have been recent changes in the extent of rough grazing. Rough grazings cover about 6 million ha or one-quarter of the farmland. They contribute perhaps only 5% of the nation's agricultural product by value, but their aesthetic and ecological value is substantial.

Competition between uses for this land has increased recently. Between 1933 and 1980, about one million ha (15% of the nation's roughland) were transferred to improved farmland. In some areas, reclamation was particularly extensive – eg on the plateau uplands of the east and south-west (the North York Moors, Exmoor, Dartmoor and the Brecon Beacons), where gentle slopes are no obstacle to the plough. About 10% of the primary roughland of the North York Moors was ploughed in the period 1950 to 1980, as illustrated in Figure 5. The increasing rate of roughland reclamation in National Parks was of serious concern in the 1960s and 1970s. However, there are indications from recent surveys in the mid-Wales uplands that the rate of reclamation has diminished substantially since about 1982, following the reduction in incentives for cereal production under the EC Common Agricultural Policy (CAP) (Parry & Sinclair 1985).

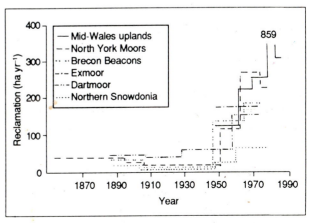

Figure 5. Average annual rates of roughland reclamation for agriculture in five National Parks (source: Parry 1990)

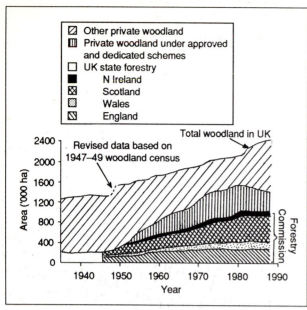

Figure 6. Changes in the area under woodland in the UK, 1935–88 (source: Parry 1990)

Changes in woodland extent

Of course, not all land converted from agricultural use has been urbanised. More than one-third of the land lost to farming has been converted to forestry, at an increasing rate and increasingly by private plantings. But with less than 10% of the land surface covered by woodland, the UK is still one of the least-wooded countries in Europe.

Nevertheless, the UK area under woodland has almost doubled since the 1940s, so that in several conservancies it amounts to more than 10% of the land. Private planting, encouraged by changes in taxable status of woodland, has seen a marked increase in the 1980s. Figure 6 illustrates the extent of woodland changes between 1935 and 1988.

Changes in rural landscape

The changes in land use described above have been reflected in marked changes in landscape. Declines in broadleaved woodland, semi-natural vegetation, and grasslands were largely accounted for by the expansion of cultivated land use by 25% between 1945 and 1980. An estimated 22% of hedgerows had been lost in England and Wales from 1947 to 1985 (Westmacott & Worthington 1984), 50% of all ancient broadleaved woodlands, 50% of lowland fens and marshes, 60% of heathlands, 80% of chalk grasslands, and perhaps over 95% of herb-rich lowland grasslands (Lowe *et al.* 1986). Perhaps it is no wonder, therefore, that in the early 1980s the farmer's traditional role of landscape conservator was being questioned.

The Government response to threats to the UK landscape has been to extend the areas covered by statutory protection. Since March 1987, Environmentally Sensitive Areas (ESAs) have been designated in areas noted for landscape and wildlife quality (Ministry of Agriculture, Fisheries & Food 1989), and, since 1982, the reform of CAP price support, combined with oversupply in agriculture,

has turned the tables in the cereal market. Now the search is for viable alternative uses through, for example, the Farm Diversification Grant Scheme (MAFF 1988a), which supports enterprises such as farm shops, craft workshops or tourist activities, together with the Farm Woodland Scheme (MAFF 1988b), which introduced annual payments to plant trees on farmland, and the launch of the Set-Aside Scheme (MAFF 1988c), whereby farmers may be paid compensation for transferring land from crop production to permanent fallow, rotational fallow, woodland planting or non-agricultural purposes.

FORCES FOR CHANGE IN THE FUTURE

Agricultural and forest landscapes

Agricultural land uses and landscapes will continue to change but, at least in the short term, possibly at a less dramatic rate. It will remain more profitable to farm efficiently, and there are demand limits for diversification enterprises. But policy revisions are shifting the balance away from intensification so that more traditional landscape features survive and more trees are planted. The arable area is likely to decrease whilst reductions in livestock subsidies may affect hill farm viability and create upland management problems.

Forestry is undergoing transition just as much as agriculture. The original objective of timber production will remain but, over the last 30 years, the Forestry Commission has increasingly considered potential multipurpose values. The aims of national subsidies are changing, with the first national forest planned around Staffordshire and Leicestershire, and three community forests to be planted in east London, south Staffordshire and south Tyneside. Recreation, visual amenity, wildlife and now carbon dioxide fixing are regarded as legitimate arguments for afforestation, as well as substitution for surplus agricultural land. Amenity and ecological emphasis will favour broadleaved species. New grants for the Farm Woodland Scheme and Set-Aside woodlands, for example, are biased towards the planting of deciduous, broadleaved species. This trend could result in the gradual return to a more wooded appearance to the British countryside.

Landscapes of conservation and recreation

In England and Wales, the ten National Parks, and the similarly administered Norfolk Broads, cover 9% of the land and the 38 Areas of Outstanding Natural Beauty about another 11% (Countryside Commission 1989). In Scotland, the 40 national scenic areas now extend over 12.9% of the land area. Voluntary organisations in England and Wales, of which the National Trust is by far the largest landowner with over 200 000 ha, are a considerable force for conservation and will remain so in the future. The National Trust for Scotland now owns some 35 000 ha. In addition, common lands total over 600 000 ha in Britain, frequently preserving semi-natural ecosystems.

The current indications are that these non-market conservationist forces will strengthen rather than diminish. Additional designations of Nature Reserves and Sites of Special Scientific Interest are likely in response to the growing environmental awareness of the public, and recreation demands. Sites protected by voluntary organisations are likely to increase in number gradually.

New forces for land use changes

Over the next two or three decades, we suspect that some new and potent forces for change may become more influential. For example, water catchment conservation, and inter-urban transport will probably place increasing demands on traditional rural uses. Mineral extraction demands, especially for the construction industry, will also pose further planning problems. But possibly the most important of these new agents of change could be long-term changes in climate, which could shift the resource base of vegetation and agricultural land uses that characterise our landscape. The impact of this change will be examined in more detail in the next section.

THE POTENTIAL EFFECT OF CHANGES IN CLIMATE

Assuming a 'business-as-usual' scenario for greenhouse gas emissions, the current best indication is that summer temperatures for the UK will increase by perhaps +1.5°C by the year 2030 and winter temperatures by 1.5–2.5°C (Department of the Environment 1991).

Changes in precipitation patterns are much less clear. In summer the percentage change is expected to be very small, and under higher temperatures this implies that less moisture could be available. Winter, spring and autumn totals for rainfall may increase, perhaps by 5% by 2030.

Changes in growing potential for crops

There are, of course, enormous uncertainties surrounding these numbers. Nevertheless, it is also relevant to note that any changes in climate of the scale and at the rate mentioned above would have a noticeable effect on plant growth. Increases in temperature would generally lengthen the growing season in northern Europe but shorten it in the south. This could lead to a northward shift of crop potential in the European region, with major implications for land use policy in the European Community.

To illustrate, the current distribution of sunflowers in Europe is closely related to the thermal limit for successful ripening. Under a range of general circulation model 2 x CO₂ scenarios (which produces a temperature rise of 3–6°C across the area), the northward shift of the growing limit for this crop can be seen in Figure 7. It must be noted that the current limit of the crop is due as much to high humidity levels as temperature. However, if humidity were to decrease, sunflowers could become a feature of the

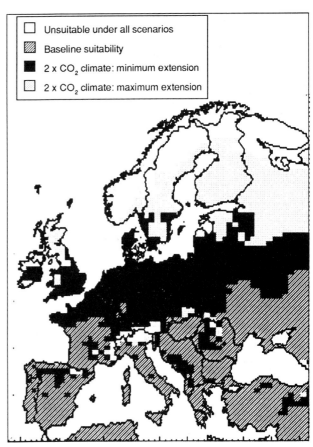

Figure 7. The shift in potential sunflower limits for a range of GCM 2 x CO₂ climate scenarios (source: Carter, Porter & Parry 1991)

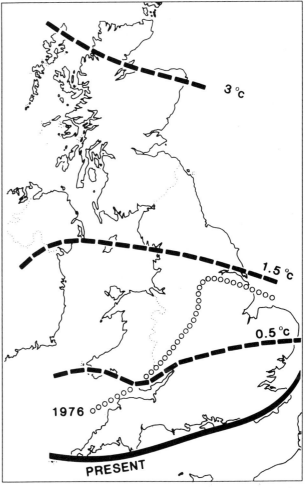

Figure 8. The potential distribution of grain maize in the UK under several warming scenarios (source: Parry, Carter & Porter 1990)

11

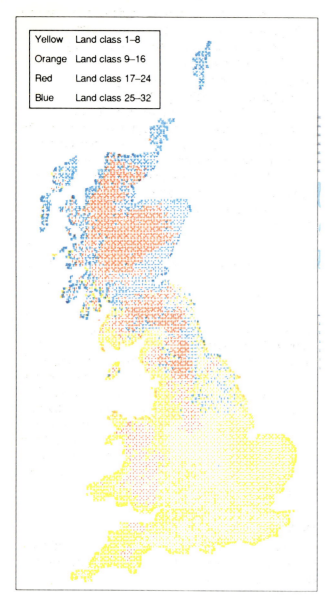

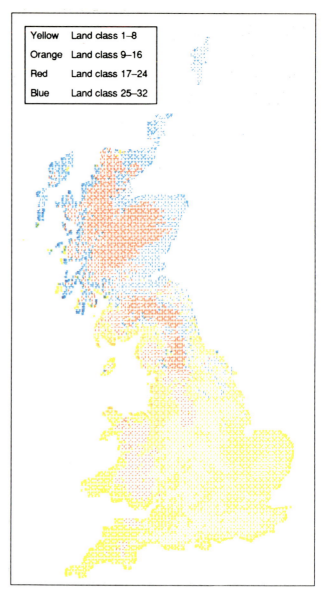

Figure 9. The pattern of British land use based on the ITE land classification scheme for the baseline climate 1941-70 (source: J E Hossell)

Figure 10. The distribution of the land classes in Britain under a 1°C increase in temperature +2.5% precipitation (source: J E Hossell)

landscape of southern England in the future, just as they are in the Paris Basin today (Carter, Porter & Parry 1991).

However, whilst new crops or new varieties of crops may be viable in the future over much of Europe, the yields of current crop types might be adversely affected by higher temperatures. For example, excluding the direct effect of CO_2 fertilisation, the yields of varieties of winter wheat grown at present in the south-east of England would be expected to decrease as a result of more rapid maturation in a warmer climate – and the positive effects of CO_2 could be negated by temperature increases above 4°C (Squire & Unsworth 1988).

Effects on vegetation

While agriculture has an ability to adapt to quite a wide range of climatic conditions, this is not true for all types of natural vegetation. Changes in climate would be likely to shift thermal limits to vegetation in the order of 300 km of latitude and 200 m of altitude

per °C. Several familiar mountainous and northern landscapes could disappear as a result of relatively small changes in temperature and rainfall. The current landscapes of Great Britain can be divided into 32 land classes, under a climatic baseline period 1941–70, as illustrated in Figure 9. This division is based on the Institute of Terrestrial Ecology's classification at the one kilometre square resolution (Bunce, Barr & Whittaker 1981). Arbitrary changes in monthly mean and extreme temperature and rainfall have been imposed on this data base to examine its sensitivity to possible changes in climate. As may be seen from Figure 10, a uniform increase of just 1°C and +2.5% rainfall is sufficient for over one-third of the 6025 squares studied (a 1:45 sample) to be reassigned to other land classes. These changes indicate the potential retreat of the associated northern vegetation types to higher altitudes, and the loss of lower sites to alternative land uses.

The effect of a 3°C increase in temperature and a 7.5% rise in rainfall, shown in Figure 11, is more

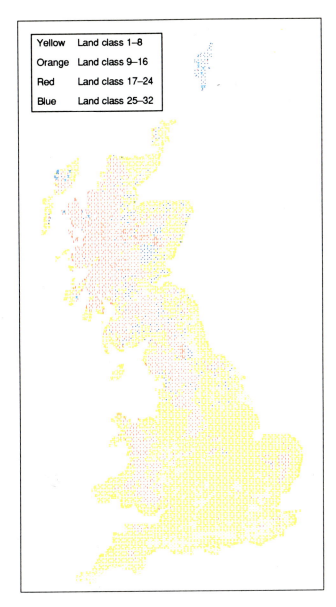

Yellow	Land class 1–8
Orange	Land class 9–16
Red	Land class 17–24
Blue	Land class 25–32

Figure 11. The distribution of the land classes in Britain under a 3°C increase in temperature +7.5% precipitation (source: J E Hossell)

substantial. Under this change, more than 80% of the squares are reassigned to a different land class or fail to have squares allocated to them. For one of the current southern land uses, land class 1, this represents a northward shift of its northern limits of around 700 km. If a 3°C increase, as projected under the Inter-Governmental Panel on Climate Change 'business-as-usual' scenario, occurred around 2050, this translates into a rate of northward movement of the land class of 100 km per decade. These shifts imply substantial changes in British land use – and new policies of land use will surely be needed to encourage adaptation without dislocation.

CONCLUSIONS

While we cannot predict with any accuracy what future forces will mould the pattern of UK land use, we should make an attempt to guess them. We should certainly aim to observe closely what changes are occurring now. We wish to close, then, with a plea (first) for the monitoring of land use and landscape change, both as an indication of regional changes that are important in their own right and as early indicators of possible long-term global changes caused by changes of climate.

To monitor effectively, however, requires a knowledge of the (unchanged) base-case, and to characterise this we need more data. Thus, second, we conclude with a plea for integrated data bases, for geographical information systems to utilise these on the national scale, and for bench sites to enable empirical analysis of changes in the field. These data should enable us to pursue three equally important types of research: on the underlying processes that affect land use, on changes to these processes, and on policy responses to combat undesirable changes.

Finally, research policies should be encouraged to enable this research to be pursued in a coherent manner. The combination of integrated research programmes, such as NERC's Terrestrial Initiative in Global Environmental Research (TIGER), and new centres of environmental research, such as those at the Universities of Oxford, Newcastle and at Imperial College, should be a source of great encouragement to those concerned with land use management. With the further strengthening and development of these initiatives, we are more confident now than we were (say) five years ago that we can improve our ability to monitor, measure and explain current changes in land use and to design appropriate land use policies to respond to these changes.

ACKNOWLEDGMENTS

The work undertaken by J E Hossell was funded by a CASE award from the Natural Environment Research Council, based at the University of Birmingham.

REFERENCES

Best, R.H. 1981. *Land use and living space.* London: Methuen.

Bunce, R.G.H, Barr, C.J. & Whittaker, H.A. 1981. *Land classes in Great Britain: preliminary descriptions for users of the Merlewood method of land classification.* (Merlewood research and development paper no. 86.) Grange-over-Sands: Institute of Terrestrial Ecology.

Carter, T.R., Porter, J.H, & Parry, M.L. 1991. Climatic warming and crop potential in Europe: prospects and uncertainties. *Global Environmental Change,* **1,** 291-313.

Countryside Commission. 1989. *Directory of Areas of Outstanding Natural Beauty.* Cheltenham: Countryside Commission.

Department of the Environment. 1991. *The potential effects of climate change in the United Kingdom.* (A report prepared by the Climate Change Impact Review Group.) London: HMSO.

Harrison, A., Tranter, R.B. & Gibbs, R.S. 1977. *Landownership by public and semi-public institutions in the UK.* (CAS, paper no. 3.) Reading: Centre for Agricultural Strategy, University of Reading.

Lowe, P., Cox, G., MacEwan, M., O'Riordan, T. & Winter, M. 1986. *Countryside Conflicts.* Aldershot: Temple Smith/Gower.

Ministry of Agriculture, Fisheries and Food. 1988a. *Capital grants for farm diversification.* London: HMSO.

Ministry of Agriculture, Fisheries and Food. 1988b. *The farm woodland scheme: a general introduction.* London: HMSO.

Ministry of Agriculture, Fisheries and Food. 1988c. *Set-aside.* London: HMSO.

Ministry of Agriculture, Fisheries and Food. 1989. *Agriculture in the United Kingdom.* London: HMSO.

Munton, R. 1983. *London's green belt, containment in practice.* London: Allen and Unwin.

Parry, M. L., Carter, T.R. & Porter, J.H. 1990. The greenhouse effect and the future of UK agriculture. *Journal of the Royal Agricultural Society of England,* **150,** 120-131.

Parry, M.L. 1990. The changing use of land. In: *The changing geography of the United Kingdom,* edited by R.J. Johnston & V. Gardiner, 7-34. London: Routledge.

Parry, M.L. & Sinclair, G. 1985. *Mid Wales uplands study.* Cheltenham: Countryside Commission.

Squire, G.R. & Unsworth, M.H. 1988. *Impacts on agriculture and horticulture.* (Report to Department of the Environment.) Sutton Bonington: School of Agriculture, University of Nottingham.

Westmacott, R. & Worthington, T. 1984. *Agricultural landscapes: a second look.* Cheltenham: Countryside Commission.

Forces driving land use change

The social, economic and political context

R J C Munton, P Lowe and T Marsden

Rural Studies Research Centre, Dept of Geography, University College London, 26 Bedford Way, London WC1H 0AP

INTRODUCTION

A high population density, rising standards of living, and widespread personal mobility mean that rural land in Britain is subject to numerous competing demands on its use. These conditions have led to a long-standing concern over *who* should regulate the use of land and *how* that should be done, contributing to strongly held views about the distribution of property rights. There is no evidence of any weakening of this debate, especially now with the breakdown of the post-War consensus over which land uses should prevail. More specifically, the dominant position accorded to agricultural production is giving way to a more varied range of activities which place a higher priority on consumption-oriented land uses[1].

It is over the last decade especially that the privileged position of agriculture both as an activity and as a land use has been progressively undermined. It has occurred from within by declining returns to traditional farming activities, and from without by growing disunity within the political system as to how much and in what form public support should be given to farmers. In land use terms, the production imperative, itself a by-product of post-War strategic thinking concerning national food security and the search for improved farming efficiency through industrial methods, has been challenged, raising serious but unresolved questions about the amount of land that should remain in agricultural use (Carruthers 1986; North 1988; Potter 1991). Furthermore, the decline in farming incomes has encouraged the search for new land uses and new means of farm support in a context of surplus capacity and an international challenge to production-oriented supports (Marsden & Murdoch 1990a). The search has coincided with a renewed surge in demand for country living, for recreation and leisure activities in a rural setting, and for environmental 'goods'. Together, they have created new market opportunities for those with proprietorial rights over rural land.

In terms of area, the exclusive needs of these activities may prove to be modest, but they will have to be met in large part from land that is currently in agricultural use. Much more significant is the manner in which the remaining land will be farmed in the face of continuing economic difficulty, the imposition of more stringent pollution standards, and greater environmental demands. Similarly, other production interests, including mineral extraction and forestry, will also be confronted by a growing rural population, both resident and visiting, espousing quite different values and expectations of rural life. These, Mormont (1990) suggests, are based less on a sense of belonging to a particular place and more on the varying levels of opportunity that rural areas afford.

The means by which such social and economic demands are being regulated are central to an understanding of the future of rural areas, and they represent the key theme of this paper. Given the rapidity of recent legislative change, no attempt will be made to review all recent policy initiatives. Instead, a synoptic overview of the current style of regulation and its relationship to the social and economic forces affecting the British countryside will be presented before returning to the substantive issue of land use change. First, a brief comment is required on how the analysis of land use is viewed in this context.

LAND USE AS AN OBJECT OF STUDY

Over and above the intrinsic importance of being able to measure, record and categorise change in the use of land, a substantial problem in its own right, the land use pattern can be taken as an expression of the social and economic pressures which bear upon it. In this sense, the pattern at any point in time may be seen as a proxy for the past and present forces leading to changes in use. It is a manifestation of the ways in which these pressures interact with existing productive forces. Thus, the pattern is neither an inert feature nor a dependent variable. The particular form it takes will have impacts on the physical and biological environment and on the attitudes of different segments of society towards the appropriate management of land. These impacts, in turn, will lead to pressures for and constraints on further change. But, as a proxy, the pattern may not be a useful guide to the process of change.

It is more pertinent to see land use as an activity or as an integral part of the land development process. This more dynamic perspective immediately brings into focus the causal factors in the integration of land into wider social, economic and political forces for change. The concern is not so much with the use itself, although that is important, but with the changing valuation placed upon it by different interests. This leads to the realisation that almost all land uses produce an array of benefits and disbenefits at one and the same time, and in this sense each constitutes a form of multiple use (see Whitby 1990). Through the same activity, agriculture produces (and destroys) landscapes as well as food, for example. Some of these benefits will be material, others not; some will be private (ie captured by individuals or concerns which hold the appropriate beneficial property rights), while others are public or collective, over which the recipients may have little control. It follows that, as the range of demands on the countryside widens and as the priority accorded to each alters, so the social value attributable to each use will change. The debate should not, therefore, be about how much land is in agriculture, or any other use for that matter, but about the combination of products that society expects land users to produce. For example, in Britain we have farming areas in which the production of food is seen increasingly as a by-product of the environment created, as in Sites of Special Scientific Interest (SSSIs), National Parks and Environmentally Sensitive Areas (ESAs), but elsewhere we have zones of intensive agricultural production directed primarily towards the provision of a secure food supply. It is a question of what the balance should be, how it should be achieved, and among whom (producers and consumers) the benefits should be distributed.

Other questions automatically follow. Should the balance be locally determined or strategically driven? What importance should be accorded to the market? What property rights should private owners be allowed to retain?

As previously argued, over most of the post-War period, priority has been given to industrialised farming methods, which means that the quality and quantity of the other benefits derived from the countryside have been largely determined by agricultural practice. But that is now changing, even if it will be some time before the shift in emphasis is fully evident in the land use pattern. Fixed investments in existing activities introduce rigidity, attitudes are often slow to change, and today's policy signals, it will be suggested, are often confusing and contradictory. Together, these conditions lead to widely differing individual responses on the part of those who control rural property rights, creating the opportunity for them to affect the rate of change, if not its general tendency, and to reinforce the spatial unevenness of rural development in a period of transition.

REGULATORY STYLE[2]

Most Government policies in one form or another affect land use directly or indirectly, and throughout the post-War period most policies for rural areas have been implemented via the land base. Considerably more capital has been invested in agriculture through price support and grant aid, and therefore has had to be realised largely through land-based production, than in welfare policies directed at social deprivation in rural areas (see Cloke 1988, Ch2). This has continued in recent years, even if, at the level of rhetoric certainly, and in terms of practice less consistently, the last decade has seen a marked shift in regulatory style. This shift has coincided with changing demands on the countryside, but for reasons only partly related to the change in style. At the risk of oversimplification, change in four aspects of domestic policy style relevant to rural land development can be identified:

1. the attempt to restrain public expenditure;
2. the encouragement of market forces through the privatisation of public assets and services, support for entrepreneurialism, and extension of commodity relations;
3. the promotion and protection of private property; and
4. attempts to price the environment.

These aspects often overlap and are illustrative of a broader ideological position which links together apparently disparate and unrelated policy changes. The most significant thrust is contained in the encouragement being given to the commodity form (commoditisation), or the extension of market forces into areas that previously stood outside them or on their margins. Good illustrations of this tendency are provided by the development of a heritage industry, in which access to our past increasingly has to be paid for; the shift of public and private (including tied) rented housing into owner occupation; the privatisation of the water authorities with their extensive land assets and the sale of land from such diverse sources as the Forestry Commission's (FC) estate and local authority smallholdings; and the extension of the management agreement principle to the protection of rural areas we value. Placing a price in this way on aspects of the rural environment involves a profound shift in the principles governing access to the benefits, from paternalistic provision based on welfarist notions of social need to market-oriented provision based on consumer demand.

The consequences of the shift are thus bound to be socially selective, in that some groups of consumers are more easily able to participate than others and, as with past policies such as farm price support, they strongly favour those who hold, or can afford to acquire, the appropriate private property rights. Moreover, attention is often diverted towards the technical calibration of how such 'market prices' should be set and away from analysing the intensity and spread of benefits brought about by the resulting rearrangement of property rights.

Change has not always been as radical as some free marketeers would have liked, not least because of contradictory positions held within the Conservative Party. It is also important not to underestimate continuities of *administrative practice* (see Healey *et al.* (1988), for example, with reference to the planning system), and the ability of groups disadvantaged by the changes to use their political resources to resist. Shifts in domestic style have also been shaped by the changing international context, including obligations arising from membership of the European Community (EC). These external influences are at least partly beyond the British Government's ability to determine or deflect, and some have been embraced enthusiastically and others resisted. They include the internationalisation of financial markets, progress towards European economic integration, and a growing weight of EC legislation affecting regional policy, agriculture and environmental standards.

As far as the future use of rural land is concerned, among the more important developments have been attempts by the British Government to contain spending under the Common Agricultural Policy (CAP) and on agricultural research and development, the privatisation of forestry land and public utilities, efforts to streamline the land use planning system, the deregulation of housing finance and the 'right-to-buy' scheme, promotion of farm diversification and 'rural enterprise', and an approach to solving disputes between farmers and environmentalists which involves valuing the environment in terms of loss of farming income. Some of these issues are given more attention below. More generally, however, the impact of the changes in regulatory style depends upon the ability of those who are expected to implement them to respond, and the degree to which those opposed to the changes are able to resist.

REGULATORY STYLE, POLICY AND PROPERTY RIGHTS

Policy development is closely related to regulatory style, but the term 'policy development' needs unpacking in order to avoid ascribing too much significance to it under a democratic political system, however imperfect that system might be. As an instrument of the state's intentions, there are always limits to its effectiveness. This is not to underestimate its importance in creating a context for local action, but any attempt to treat its effects deterministically should be viewed sceptically.

There are three main reasons. First, change in policy does not emerge from an independent policy, for it then to be imposed on a passive set of recipients. The state is but part of the social and economic system over which it has jurisdiction. Individuals, families or economic organisations, and more importantly the bodies which seek to represent their interests, may actively engage in defending the existing policy framework and, if change is beyond their ability to achieve or prevent, try to influence its pace so that it more adequately meets their requirements. Within particular sectors, the British political system is characterised by numerous corporatist relations between Government at all levels and mainly producer interests. Between sectional interests, the ability to influence is very uneven and fluctuates in response to new social concerns and with changes in administration.

In the area of rural land use there are numerous examples. Much has been written about the close links between the Ministry of Agriculture, Fisheries and Food (MAFF) and the National Farmers' Union (NFU), although this relationship has lost much of its former importance in a context in which agricultural policy is determined more in Brussels than in Whitehall, and in which the political imperative is no longer to raise output but to curb surpluses and public expenditure (Cox, Lowe & Winter 1986). Another illustration is provided by the involvement of the House Builders' Federation in the preparation of Joint Housing Land Availability Studies alongside local planning authorities, providing it with what appears to be a privileged position in the planning process. In the context of mineral exploitation, one can point to the composition of the Regional Aggregates Working Parties, responsible for establishing regional estimates of demand, of which membership is restricted to County Planning Officers, representatives of mineral companies and officials of the Department of the Environment (DoE).

It is not easy to demonstrate the financial gains that accrue to the members of these different producer interests from these arrangements, but, where their participation has been sustained, it is reasonable to suggest that they think they are worthwhile. Beyond the local level, much closer political links have traditionally existed between Government and producer interests than between Government and consumer interests, but this position will not be sustainable where the countryside is concerned if the Government is to take public concern over the environment, food hygiene, and animal welfare more seriously.

Second, partly in response to the complexity of modern society and partly as a reflection of the width of official involvement in its regulation, the institutional structure of Government is complex and fragmented. Moreover, as will already be evident, there are always areas of control and responsibility that are undergoing alteration. This means that branches of the state apparatus are regularly engaged in defending their own vested interests, while seeking to expand the area of their remits. The result is an endemically fractured bureaucracy exhibiting overlapping functions, internal disagreements over policy, and different

links with producer and consumer interests (Rhodes 1988).

In these circumstances, power can be widely diffused, making it possible for interest groups to exploit the incoherence to their own advantage, as some established environmental groups have done, for example, in playing off policy differences between the agriculture and environment departments.

Third, policy-making is not simply a top-down process. It is much more complicated. A top-down perspective is encouraged by tendencies towards the centralisation of authority, brought about in part by the increasing internationalisation of the economy and the development of supra-national structures in response. The importance of these tendencies should not be underestimated but, at the same time, their significance should not be accepted uncritically. To do so would be to underestimate the power of local resistance and the transaction costs incurred by ever larger bureaucracies where their remits extend over increasingly varied local circumstances. It would also overlook the ability of a decentralised administration to deflect, or even overturn, central initiatives. Demands for a partial renationalisation of the CAP, or the wish to retain almost complete national discretion over the implementation of particular policies, such as agricultural extensification, are but one reflection of this tension at the supra-national level, while the break up of the Nature Conservancy Council (NCC) into separate 'regional' agencies (ie for England, Wales, Scotland and Northern Ireland) is an example at the intra-national level.

These apparently contradictory trends are also reflected in more general changes to the structure and functioning of the economic system. We are confronted simultaneously by the globalisation of the economy and the concentration of production in fewer corporate hands *and* by evidence of growing responsiveness to local conditions (Piore & Sabel 1984; Allen & Massey 1988; Marsden & Murdoch 1990a). These trends, it is argued, are a response to the higher profit margins that can be realised from a series of short-run production lines aimed at niche-markets and made possible by computer-aided production techniques, rather than from traditional, mass-production methods. An organisational consequence among some companies is the devolution of authority to maximise local responsiveness. Moves in this direction are bound to be uneven and, depending upon the nature of particular production processes and the attitudes of consumers, may never penetrate some sectors of the economy (for a critical review of some of these arguments, see Amin & Robins 1990).

In terms of those sectors that bear most evidently on rural land use, processes of concentration in the corporate structure of house-builders, food

processors and retailers, mineral operators and those supplying industrial inputs to agriculture still dominate. In the case of house-building, this means the emergence of a small number of house-builders who largely control national and regional markets (Ball 1983)[3], while the foodchain has an increasingly oligopolistic structure which is increasingly internationally oriented (Ward 1990). At the same time, most of these concerns reveal an increasing sensitivity to local conditions and consumer susceptibilities as they seek to expand their market share. This change can be observed in more flexible housing production strategies, in the environmental sensitivities of large mineral companies, in more sophisticated food marketing, and even in the policies of Food from Britain which has encouraged farmers and farming groups to market local and regional food specialities to an increasingly discerning consumer[4]. The development of all these markets, local and global, are structured to varying degree by the regulatory styles outlined previously. As market structures change, new modes of regulation are demanded.

All these trends point to a complex process of interaction between policy-making and regulatory style, and between policy-makers and the interests to be regulated. The discussion is not intended to suggest that local actors have an inordinate freedom of action; they often do not. But it does argue for seeing them in a constant process of interaction with central and even local policy-making processes, and from time to time creating specific or even general precedents that lead to changes in policy (see, for example, Lowe *et al.* 1986).

The ability to resist locally, perhaps by dividing the agents of Government, is no more evident than in the numerous examples where local interests have been able to mobilise opinion through the planning system against what they regard as undesirable development. There is, therefore, much more to 'policy' and its implementation than what is contained in, say, the Government's Planning Policy Guidance Notes, White Papers, and agricultural price support settlements. These provide powerful signals and justifications to those taking land use decisions, but they do no more. Indeed, the use of land arises from numerous decisions taken by a wide range of individuals. The challenge is to find a way of linking their decisions to the wider processes of social and economic change and the style of regulation. An analysis of the shifting distribution of property rights[5] is one way of doing so, assuming that a suitably broad perspective on the nature of property rights is adopted. Two matters are central to such a perspective: the social construction of property rights, and their nature and divisibility.

Property rights are socially constituted and subject to change (see MacPherson 1978). The notion of property consisting of a 'bundle of rights' is

analytically powerful, provided that the rights are understood as embodying social and economic relationships and do not simply refer to legal or physical objects. Their existence depends upon the character of the socio-political system and the regulatory functions of the state, including the law, for their affirmation and maintenance. It follows that particular rights are continuously being created, dissolved and combined. What is crucial is the degree of recognition accorded to particular rights and whether this is seen as vulnerable to challenge. In discussing this point, Harrison (1987) suggests that:

> any time... there are degrees of recognition of rights claims. Some are backed fully by law, others by administrative custom, and others only by assertions about morality... Furthermore, some claims are not often expressed formally, yet seem implicit in widespread material conflicts of interest, as "submerged" rights claims to which parts of the political system may be under pressure to respond' (pp37–38).

The key point is that interests in property are, at any one time, more than the legal rights held by owners and beneficiaries. Indeed, current environmental concern throws the question of access to property rights into sharp relief, challenging the historical individualism of property rights in land, and it comes as no surprise that existing property rights are regularly contested by third parties in a variety of arenas, such as the planning enquiry, even though the rights of restraint which objectors claim over others' property would not at that moment be upheld in a court of law. However, the opportunity to dispute injects a dynamic element into the distribution of rights because new claims may receive statutory backing in due time, or come to be recognised as legitimate by the courts, or existing owners may make concessions of their own accord.

Another key feature of property rights in countries such as Britain is their range of divisibility. Freehold ownership bestows considerable freedom of action, providing rights of use, occupancy and ownership (alienation). It is perfectly normal for these rights to be divided between different legal entities (landlords and tenants, farmers and mineral extractors, financial institutions and forestry companies, etc) and for the divisions to vary between parties on different parts of the same property (in ownership terms). The freedom to combine and recombine rights to mutual economic advantage is of crucial importance to the use and development of land, especially as production processes vary qualitatively in their requirements of land (for example, between house-building, mining and farming). It is this flexibility, combined with the use of rental, royalty and option payments, that facilitates the use and development of land (see

Whatmore, Munton & Marsden 1990). A central question, and one which reflects on the dominant regulatory style, concerns the definition of which rights should be 'public' or 'common' and freely accessible, and which should be private. More specifically, how should this distinction be treated when public money is used to encourage a particular combination of products from the land? This question is the contemporary version of a historical debate in British society concerning the legitimate balance between the rights and obligations of private property.

FROM PRODUCTION TO CONSUMPTION: RURAL LAND IN BRITAIN

Taking the case of demands upon the development of rural land in Britain, there are three main aspects to the current pattern of change. The first concerns the economic health of the farming industry and its consequences; the second relates to the evolving demographic and social structure of those resident in rural areas; and the third centres upon recent amendments to the land use planning system. In certain respects change in all three is a function of contemporary shifts in regulatory style, but in others it reflects the contradictory pressures which lie behind each and the varying abilities, from issue to issue and place to place, of competing interests to promote their positions.

The retreat of agriculture

The post-War strategy of agricultural development has been characterised by the application of industrial methods to farming. The major aim has been to increase agricultural productivity to ensure secure supplies of quality food at falling real prices. This strategy dominated the policy statements of the Ministry of Agriculture until the end of the 1970s (see MAFF 1975, 1979) and was not seriously challenged within the EC until the Dublin Summit of 1984 (Moyer & Josling 1990). Its aims have been achieved but at the expense of other public policy objectives. For example, as the share of the Gross Domestic Product contributed by the farming industry has declined, so public spending on agriculture has continued to rise; but, as spending has risen, farmers' incomes have fallen in spite of a continuing reduction in their numbers, most of the benefits accruing to other, more powerful, economic interest in the foodchain (Munton, Marsden & Whatmore 1990); and, as greater productivity has contributed to larger 'unwanted surpluses', so the natural environment has, in the public mind, been viewed as being 'destroyed'.

Temporarily, at least, and in the absence of a major food shortage probably for the longer term, farm production interests have failed to sustain their political authority. One illustration of this is the current debate over farmers' incomes. While most analysts would now accept that the industry's net

income from farming has declined by about 60% in real terms since 1975, that land values have fallen by about 40% since 1980, and that interest repayments on farm debt are now equivalent to about 40% of the industry's income, this decline has not been condemned as unacceptable except by farming interests. Instead, it has led to considerable controversy on, *inter alia,* the importance of off-farm earnings (Gasson 1988), relative living standards between occupations (House of Lords Select Committee on the European Communities 1990), and the importance of landed wealth (Hill 1990). So far, it has not led to major changes in policy designed to reverse the fall in farmers' earnings (Cox, Lowe & Winter 1989).

In these unpropitious circumstances, it could be argued that those representing the interests of British farmers have been effective at tactics while rarely ever being able to take the initiative. Some solace has been derived from the resistance to radical change to the CAP exerted by many of Britain's EC partners and their farming lobbies, but, at home, farmers have been confronted by an administration committed to cutting public spending and encouraging market forces. Farmers now need new skills. To the still necessary technical, financial and fiscal skills, invested in so heavily since the 1950s, must be added entrepreneurial flair and a willingness to look for new markets. Farmers are being presented with conflicting signals, those emanating from the food system which still emphasise technological advance, sectoral integration within the foodchain and concentration of production, and those from a more diversified set of markets demanding flexibility of response and new marketing skills (Marsden & Murdoch 1990b).

The policy signals favouring the latter are increasingly evident but fragmented, flowing from two Government departments (MAFF and DoE) and several public sector agencies (eg NCC, FC, Countryside Commission, Rural Development Commission). The most comprehensive attempt to address the issue of farm business diversification is contained in the Alternative Land Use and Rural Economy (ALURE) initiative (MAFF 1987) and the 1988 Farm Land and Rural Development Act, but financial support for this change has been limited, at least by comparison with the sums dispensed on price support through a still largely unreformed CAP (House of Lords Select Committee 1990). For example, a mere 5 million per annum initially was allocated to the Farm Diversification Grants (FDG) Scheme under the ALURE proposals, and, not surprisingly, uptake under the Scheme during its two first years (up to March 1990) was limited (1634 approved grants) to 1% of all significant farm holdings (for more general discussions, see Halliday 1989; Shucksmith *et al.* 1989).

Other modest changes – more important in terms

of principle than in the allocation of resources – are reflected in the attention being given to the putative 'land surplus' (see Potter 1991) and through the promotion of environmental benefits of types of land management (Cox, Lowe & Winter 1990). The one scheme aimed primarily at limiting agricultural production and intended to work through the land base[6] is the 'Extensification' Scheme introduced under EC Regulation 1094/887. In 1989-90, it cost 11 million to implement in the UK, creating a theoretical saving of up to 30 million on intervention purchase, storage and disposal of surplus grain (see Robinson 1991). Initial evidence on uptake suggests a very cautious approach right across Europe, although the actual level is partly a function of the differing terms offered by national governments (Jones 1991). By October 1990, 3800 farmers were participating in the UK (though many more had registered for possible participation at a later date), contributing 132 000 ha of cereal land to the reserve, or approximately 3% of the land in cereal production (MAFF 1990). The additional number of participants in the Scheme has declined each year, and most of their land has been placed in short-term, rotational fallow so that it can be readily brought back into production after three or five years, if thought appropriate (Ilbery 1990).

A more promising long-term prospect lies in measures taken to promote environmental benefits from farmland. Among the more significant have been the Wildlife and Countryside Act 1981 on habitat protection (see Cox & Lowe 1983; Cox, Low & Winter 1985), the introduction of Environmentally Sensitive Areas (see Baldock *et al.* 1990), Nitrate Sensitive Areas (NSAs) and Nitrate Advisory Areas, and the current promotion of the new national forest and 12 community forests by the Countryside and Forestry Commissions (for a brief description of all of these initiatives, see DoE 1990, Ch7). Individually, they will make only a small impact on the land use pattern but, collectively, their effect may well prove significant. For example, the 19 ESAs cover 7900 km[2], and the area designated for the community forests approximately 2400 km[2]. These areas have to be added to environmental designations of much longer standing and much greater extent, including National Parks (13 500 km[2]), Areas of Outstanding Natural Beauty (AONBs) (20 000 km[2]), SSSIs (16 270 km[2]) and Nature Reserves (1650 km[2])[8]. Much more important is the wider effect these schemes are intended to have on public perceptions of the purpose of the countryside and the contribution of landholders - whom society may or may not wish to term farmers - to national welfare, and this point will be driven home by the new Countryside Stewardship Scheme being implemented by the Countryside Commission. The Scheme will provide financial incentives to enhance or restore certain valued landscapes and habitats and to improve public access to them. It will apply to anyone with a controlling interest in land - a farmer, landowner,

voluntary organisation or local authority - and, significantly, will be open to part-time farmers who are usually barred from agricultural grant schemes.

Three main conclusions can be drawn from the nature of these initiatives.

First, farming interests have been able to persuade Government that land-based policies remain a major way forward, privileging the current holders of property rights. This is most evident in the 'surplus land' and 'alternative land use' debates in which it is suggested that it is 'agricultural' land that is in surplus and for which new production-oriented uses managed by farmers are required (Cox *et al.* 1987). These debates allow more politically sensitive issues, such as the need to withdraw capital and full-time farmers from the industry, to be sidelined.

Second, the Government has adopted the role of enabler, rather than provider, of environmental benefits. Private property rights are to be respected and the environment given a value determined by reference to the profitability of competing uses, usually food production, which are publicly supported, as occurs in the case of ESAs and NSAs, for example. Participation in most environmental initiatives remains permissive, with compensation to cover additional management costs and the net loss, or anticipated loss, of income incurred through participation, effectively reversing the 'polluter pays' principle (Cox, Lowe & Winter 1988; Lowe *et al.* 1990). Additions to the supply of environmental goods, and even to the protection of *existing* goods, are being acquired at prices being determined by the needs of other policy objectives.

Third, at a more fundamental level are the economic pressures on farming which promise less intensive systems of production in due course, and will themselves play an important role in the supply of environmental benefits. The real level of fixed capital stock in agriculture, after due allowance for depreciation, has been falling since 1980, even if the pattern of decline is uneven between businesses and farming sectors. Many fixed investments necessary for an industrialised system of production have a long life, which means that the impact of the decline of the capital stock on husbandry methods and land use will be slow to emerge, but may well be evident by the turn of the century. In addition, many landowners are attempting to develop their properties, for recreation or through the conversion of 'redundant' buildings to industrial or residential uses (Watkins & Winter 1988), and are often doing so without any incentive provided by a specific policy initiative. Success in such ventures often depends in the first instance on obtaining planning permission, and the development control system is much more open to local contestation than broad areas of public policy in the agricultural and environmental fields. It is, therefore, to the two linked areas of the changing

composition of the rural population and opportunities for development provided by changes to the planning system that the paper now turns.

Rural social change

Annual estimates by the Office for Population and Census Surveys (OPCS) repeatedly suggest continuing growth in the numbers living in the countryside, with the greatest increases in the outer south-east of England, south-west England and East Anglia, even if the rate of growth may prove to be slightly less in the 1980s than it was in the 1970s (Champion & Townsend 1990)[9]. The increase is primarily the result of in-migration, especially in remoter rural areas which are still experiencing an excess of deaths over births. At the district scale, OPCS estimates for the period 1981-86 record an increase in every rural district, except for six in northern and western Scotland. These gains are consistent with more varied patterns at the parish scale, in which many of those parishes with the smallest populations still reveal a picture of decline (Weekley 1988; Rowsell 1989). This is a result, it is argued, of falling average household size, tight planning restrictions on housing development outside the larger settlements in much of the countryside, as well as the relentless decline in primary sector employment.

Those migrating to rural areas are doing so primarily for retirement or residential reasons. In the orbit of major cities, especially London, increasing numbers of rural residents are engaged in medium- and even long-distance commuting. In the remoter rural areas, most incomers are either retirees or what have been termed 'economically active pre-retirement migrants', who are often leaving managerial occupations and seeking to establish local businesses (Perry, Dean & Brown 1986). The fashionable practice of 'tele-working' may be on the increase, but it is by no means the driving force behind rural demographic change. The main motivation is the search for affordable housing located in environmentally pleasant surroundings.

The social characteristics of incomers are now accepted to be more complex than the stereotypes identified in Pahl's pioneering work of more than a quarter of a century ago (Pahl 1965). The idea that incomers constitute a homogeneous middle-class group in constant conflict with an indigenous rural working class has long since been refuted (for discussion, see Cloke & Thrift 1990), and even the more specific term 'service class', introduced to represent the growing numbers of professional and managerial workers (see Cloke & Thrift 1987; Savage & Fielding 1989), runs the risk of underestimating the social diversity of migrants and the intra-class conflicts that arise from their differing consumption interests.

In particular, the term deflects attention from the cleavages within this 'class' and which frequently arise from the property rights they do, or do not, hold in rural areas. Collectively they may want, for example, quality housing in quiet surrounds, new rural pursuits, and greater access to the countryside, and many of them may also pursue these demands through membership of those national bodies established to press these claims; but exactly *where* and *how* these claims are to be promoted remains a source of dispute, most evident between those who live in the countryside, those who work there, and those who do neither. New rural residents have made it their concern to influence the local political agenda in order to ensure the continued exclusivity of their particular piece of rural space. Quality housing is a case in point, but it also spills over into local opposition to new rights-of-way and 'obtrusive' leisure pursuits, as well as to the expansion of some established rural activities, such as mineral working and intensive livestock husbandry.

One possible indicator of the effect of such local action is the relatively low level of loss of agricultural land to urban uses in the 1980s. Figures for England and Wales indicate a loss of only 5000 ha per annum in the mid-1980s, or little more than one-third of the level recorded for the 1950s and 1960s (Blunden & Curry 1988). This trend is backed up by data collected by the County Planning Officers' (CPO) Association. The data show that housing land requirements have been scaled down recently in the great majority of counties following revisions to their structure plans (CPO Association 1989), and this evidence coincides with that from DoE which reveals an increasing proportion of new building taking place within urban areas (the proportion is now estimated to be half; DoE *et al.* 1990).
Surprisingly, perhaps, this trend has occurred against a background of attempts to *reduce* the protection afforded agricultural land from development.

Following Circular 16/87 (DoE 1987), the countryside was to be protected 'for its own sake', and not just for its agricultural value. What, precisely, was meant by this terminological change has never been made clear, although the replacement of a specific agricultural objection to development based on the productive quality of farmland by a wider set of grounds for refusal – and just when agricultural landowners were looking increasingly desperately for new ways of exploiting their property assets to compensate for falling farming returns – could have the opposite effect to what was probably intended (Flynn, Lowe & Cox 1990). Some of the distributional consequences of a reduced rate of loss have received considerable publicity. The most notable is the debate surrounding house price inflation and the inability of local, and especially young, people dependent upon traditional low-wage industries in rural areas, such as farming, tourism, catering and

food processing, to gain access to affordable housing (Archbishop's Commission on Rural Areas 1990; SERPLAN 1990; Shucksmith 1990).

The most important conclusion to be drawn from this discussion is that the continuing change in numbers and social composition of the rural population is creating a local context in which land use change will be increasingly mediated by a politically sophisticated constituency. This constituency will not necessarily oppose all change, neither can it impose its local position indefinitely. It will be responsive to some local concerns (eg low-cost housing needs), whilst being unable to diminish the larger social and economic forces leading to greater demands for consumption-oriented land uses. It will, however, have the ability to affect aspects of the timing and nature of change, resulting in a more locally differential pattern of rural development. Its scope for influencing change locally will depend in part on whether there are contradictions in central Government guidance, and the priority given by Government to *voluntary* participation by landowners in rural land management schemes, but above all on the evolving powers and policies of local planning authorities.

Land use planning

In the area of land use planning policy there has been a tension throughout the 1980s between two recognisable constituencies within the Conservative Party (for a fuller review, see Flynn *et al.* 1990). One has sought to encourage rural enterprise and to reduce the restrictions imposed upon change by the operation of the planning system. The other has been primarily concerned to protect and promote the amenity and conservation value of the countryside.

This has led to reversals of policy or significant amendments to the content of consultation papers. On the one hand, several steps have been taken to streamline the planning system as a whole, and to increase the freedom of action of landowners. For example, permitted development under the General Development Order has been increased, the range of permissible activity under individual Use Class Orders has been extended, and measures have been taken to speed up the processing of planning applications (see, for example, DoE 1985). Moreover, an increasing number of planning applications have been sent to DoE for decision on appeal, and the rate of success has risen. On the whole, however, National Parks, SSSIs and other designated areas have been exempted from these relaxations.

On the other hand, there has been an intense debate over the scope of agricultural and forestry operations, partly because these have lain largely beyond planning control for a long time and have been an obvious target for environmental protest.

However, in the initial version of its Planning and Policy Guidance Note *Rural enterprise and development* (DoE 1988), the Government expressed a wish to go further and to relax controls over the conversion of farmland and farm buildings to certain other uses in order to assist farm diversification, especially in the area of recreational development. In the face of strong protest from environmental groups, these proposals were withdrawn and even replaced by the suggestion that planning controls might be extended over certain agricultural operations. Evidence of this is signposted in the White Paper (DoE 1990), where the Government expressed its intention to extend control over the siting, design and external appearance of farm buildings across the whole countryside (ie extending the tighter rules over permitted development rights already in operation in National Parks), and to impose full development control procedures on all buildings on agricultural holdings of less than 5 ha (paras 6.15–6.16). Introduction of these changes was announced in June 1991. The Government has also been forced to increase controls on tipping on farmland and the siting of intensive livestock units, and recent proposals have been issued to tighten development control over SSSIs.

Of greater long-term significance are the proposals contained in the 1991 Planning and Compensation Act which could considerably strengthen planning control in rural areas. Among the Act's key provisions are its new arrangements for development plans. County councils will be required to prepare single structure plans for the whole of their areas and will have the power to approve these plans themselves. Non-metropolitan district councils will be required to provide single district-wide local plans[10]. Structure plans are to be reprieved and their preparation and approval streamlined, and the whole of the country covered by local plans. In 1988, only 54 of the 333 non-metropolitan districts had local plans, either on deposit or adopted, which fully covered their areas (DoE 1988). Today, approximately three-quarters of rural England by population are without an adopted local plan and only one county (Hertfordshire) has complete coverage, although the District Planning Officers' Society estimates that 80% of all districts will have adopted district-wide development plans by the end of 1992. This represents the most profound extension of the planning system to the countryside since 1947 and, indeed, at long last, completes what was then claimed to be a *comprehensive* land use planning system.

One consequence will be to place district planning authorities ever more at the centre of contentious conflicts over land development, testing severely their capacity to mediate consistently and in ways acceptable to local and national political opinion. In its discussion of the future plan system in the White Paper *This common inheritance,* the Government argues that the changes proposed would:

> 'make the development plan simpler and more responsive, reducing costs for both the private sector and local authorities. Removing excessive detail from plans at the county level will leave a larger range of matters of local concern to be dealt with through local plans' (DoE 1990, para 6.28, p85).

Another view would be that the change in responsibilities is not so much one of public economy but of redistribution of effort from the counties to the non-metropolitan districts. This raises two questions. Are there sufficient qualified staff resources at the district level to do this work effectively, especially in smaller rural districts? Will the change lead to increased tensions between county and district? In the case of the former, the number of staff allocated to development plan work has declined during the last ten years in response to Government attempts to streamline and simplify the process. Many staff have left local planning offices for jobs in the private sector, not only denuding the public sector of experience and talent but contributing to the increasingly sophisticated negotiating skills of the larger development interests. Any attempt to improve matters may well fall foul of tight local authority budgets.

As for the latter question, the Act revives in a small way the flagging fortunes of the counties by retaining structure plans, albeit in a less detailed form. At the same time, the requirement to prepare area-wide district plans is in keeping with the Government's general policy of placing much of the real power in the hands of the districts. This could exacerbate existing county/district tensions, especially as the counties can approve their own plans. Would disagreement between a county and one or more of its districts over aspects of the structure plan provide a *prima facie* case for the Secretary of State to call in the plan, retaining almost endless opportunity for central Government interference in local planning? Furthermore, district councillors will not readily relinquish the additional power which recent policy has devolved upon them. It is *the* crucial area in which they can be seen to be acting (or not) in favour of their constituents' interests, and they are often quick to criticise county council decisions (eg over minerals) and policy statements, such as those arising out of the housing land availability exercises, to which they have not been fully party.

However, with this additional power goes greater responsibilities. The whole thrust of our earlier argument about the changing functions of the countryside, the widening range of interests and values held by rural residents, and their increasing ability to express them through development decisions seems bound to raise the level of difficulty in resolving local conflicts. This is no mere

procedural question amenable to technical fixes; it is a clash of values between groups with quite different ideologies as well as material interests. At least the competing claims of foresters, farmers and developers shared a profit motive, whatever the secondary arguments. Newer interests, while by no means immune from such considerations, frequently will not accept a financial pay-off matrix as the basis of decision-making. Such conflicts raise the importance of local politics and the managerial skills of planning staff in seeking consistency and social justice from their negotiations over development proposals. Their importance cannot be underestimated in a climate in which local planners and politicians may feel a loss both of control over events and of professional status, if decisions frequently go to appeal.

Furthermore, one of the less appealing consequences of the social restructuring of the countryside in recent decades has been the tendency among residents to 'put up the shutters'. While the extent and nature of this tendency can be exaggerated, and can be the result of developers using an initial planning permission as the basis for successive applications rather than an inherent hostility to all forms of development, it presents another difficulty for local planners whose interpretation of the public interest may be more broadly based than the interests of middle-class incomers. Compromise may be readily achieved where the case for development is based on meeting small-scale local needs, but the planners' negotiating skills can be tried to the limit over large schemes when confronted by local objection, on the one hand, and vague national guidance, on the other.

CONCLUSIONS

The range of social demands on rural land is both growing and constantly changing, but this has not altered one important element of continuity in British rural policy, the attempt to realise objectives through the land base. This approach has afforded a privileged position to the holders of property rights, and recent changes in regulatory style have merely reinforced their position. In this context, it is essential to explore how different interests promote their representations of the 'rural' as a means of legitimating their access to land. Only then can a better understanding of the land development process be achieved and some sense made of the changing land use pattern.

A frequently repeated word in the White Paper (DoE 1990) is integration, especially at the interface between agricultural practice and the environment, and considerable space in the White Paper is devoted to policy initiatives in this area. A shift in Government thinking is being expressed but the transitional nature of the present is also evident. For example, while the comprehensive listing of initiatives is welcome, the White Paper reveals little about how policy is being contested or how institutions and agencies are being reorganised in order to carry the project forward. The discussion rarely reaches down to the practical level of implementation, such as the need for integrated farm management plans (see Countryside Policy Review Panel 1987), neither does it address the contradictory pressures contained in the present situation. Farmers are receiving conflicting signals, unsure whether they can or must remain on the technological treadmill in order to meet the demands of agribusiness, or whether they should venture into the much more uncertain markets offered by diversification (see Marsden & Murdoch 1990b).

Perhaps it is the role of White Papers to retain a lofty detachment; but, even here, some response to European thinking would have been helpful. What of moves to switch from an agricultural to a rural policy, as proposed in the EC's Green Paper *The future of rural society* (Commission of the European Communities 1988; see also the analysis contained in House of Lords Select Committee 1990)? Is such thinking to be disregarded simply because most of the real money remains in the CAP? Does the notion of social sustainability no longer have much resonance in British policy for rural areas? Given the social recomposition of much of rural Britain in recent years, our understanding of social sustainability may be just as far removed from the European conception promoted by the Commission as is the structure of our farming industry from the other agricultures of western Europe. Nonetheless, we need to recognise that the search for a sustainable relationship between agriculture and the environment lies embedded within larger social and political structures, local and national, a perspective that the EC is now beginning to promote and which reflects national policies long held on the Continent. It would, however, be more in the British tradition to retain our focus of attention on the land base, given that most rural land will continue to be farmed for the foreseeable future. There is only a putative land 'surplus'.

Estimates of 'surplus' land are at best dependent upon the variable levels of commodity surpluses and speculations over future average yields as realised by farmers. The central question, one around which considerable uncertainty exists, concerns the extent to which modifications to policy will stimulate uneven falls in the patterns of land use *intensity* as farmers, the predominant occupiers of the rural estate, are pressured to provide a wider range of goods and services.

In terms of traditional land use categories, this does not mean that the *rate* of change will necessarily be much greater than in the past. What will continue to change are the economic and social values placed on the products which each use supplies, and thus

the likely *direction* of change. Moves towards a new pattern of land use will develop unevenly, both regionally and locally, and will challenge the exclusive occupation of large swathes of countryside by an industrialised agriculture directed primarily towards food production. It is perfectly reasonable, however, to anticipate extensification and intensification going on side by side, on neighbouring farms and even on parts of the same farm. A more variegated land use pattern will emerge as owners and occupiers revalue their property assets and seek incomes from beyond their farms and estates.

These tendencies will create additional analytical and interpretative problems for those measuring land use change. The difficulties of addressing multiple use are well recognised, but they seem likely to become more awkward. Although a more spatially fragmented pattern of land use is a problem amenable to technical resolution, in the absence of ground surveys engaging both producers and consumers, the presence of multiple use may be difficult to establish and its significance even more problematic to evaluate and explain.

ACKNOWLEDGEMENTS

This paper takes its themes from research being undertaken by the London Countryside Change Centre located at University College London as part of the ESRC's Countryside Change Initiative. The authors wish to acknowledge ESRC's financial support and the contributions made to the paper by Andy Flynn, Julie Grove-Hills and Jonathon Murdoch, research officers to the programme.

Footnotes

[1] The consumption/production dichotomy is itself problematic in the case of land use. For example, housing development may be treated as a production activity while housing occupance a form of consumption, and agriculture produces both food, largely for consumption within urban areas, and landscapes for consumption in rural areas.

[2] As used here, the term 'regulatory style' should not be confused with the theoretical notion of the 'mode of regulation' as employed in the work of the French 'regulationist school' (see Liepitz 1988; Aglietta 1979), in which 'the mode of regulation is defined as the ensemble of institutional forms, networks and norms which assure the compatibility of behaviour in the framework of a regime of accumulation' (Liepitz 1988, p13). The term 'regulatory style' is used in an empirical sense to mean the broad ideology of Government in its mediation between production and consumption interests. It merely calls upon the theoretical notion by drawing attention to the similarities of perspective that may be evident across a range of quite different policy areas and because it is much wider in concept than policy *sensu stricto* in that it engages directly with the economic, political and social. On the notion of national styles of regulation, see Vogel (1986).

[3] In the UK, for example, in 1978, 89 companies built more than 250 houses (1% of registered builders), constituting 47% of total housing output. In 1988, only 63 companies built more than 250 houses. Their output made up 55.3% of the total, while that of the largest nine (more than 2500 houses) 28.6%.

[4] As an industry dominated by small firms, agriculture reveals similar but not identical trends. For example, although the

mean size of farms rose by 55% between 1939 and 1989 (from 42.3 ha to 66.5 ha), the mode only rose by 7% (Allanson 1990). These findings suggest a growing dualistic size structure, but uncritical acceptance of this trend is questioned by Munton and Marsden (1991).

[5] In this discussion, property rights always refer to landed property.

[6] Other more important mechanisms have been introduced in recent years through the CAP designed to limit further increases in production. These include production quotas, as in the case of milk quotas introduced in 1984, and budgetary stabilisers for grain and beef.

[7] Although termed an 'Extensification' Scheme when introduced by the EC, to all intents and purposes it is a Set-Aside Scheme in that its operation leads to land not being farmed. It contributes to an extensification of agricultural land use only in the trivial sense that it leads to less output *overall* from the land (see Harvey & Whitby 1988). As a means of reducing production and producing conservation benefits (Ervin 1988), or as a means of reducing the cost of agricultural support (Koester 1989), land diversion (set-aside) has been seriously questioned. One response to these criticisms has been the attempt by the Countryside Commission to link production controls more directly with environmental benefits through the introduction of a Countryside Premium Scheme in seven counties in eastern England, where additional payments can be made to farmers who manage set-aside land specifically for the benefit of wildlife, landscape and the community.

[8] These designations cannot be simply equated or aggregated because they carry different functions and powers, confer variable public rights, and physically overlap to some extent.

[9] Until the results of the 1991 Population Census are published, detailed and up-to-date information on the characteristics of the rural population will be unavailable.

[10] Special provisions are to apply in relation to minerals plans and to local plans for National Parks (see also the recent report of the National Parks Review Panel 1991).

REFERENCES

Archbishop's Commission on Rural Areas. 1990. *Faith in the countryside*. Worthing: Churchman.

Aglietta, M. 1979. *A theory of capitalist regulation: the US experience*. London: New Left Books.

Allanson, P. 1990. *The evolution of the size distribution of agricultural holdings*. (ESRC Countryside Change Initiative working paper 11.) Newcastle upon Tyne: Countryside Change Unit, University of Newcastle upon Tyne.

Allen, J. & Massey, D., eds. 1988. *The economy in question*. London: Sage.

Amin, A. & Robins, K. 1990. The re-emergence of regional economics? The mythical geography of flexible accumulation. *Environment and Planning, D: Society and Space,* **8**, 7-34.

Baldock, D., Cox, G., Lowe, P. & Winter, M. 1990. Environmentally Sensitive Areas: incrementalism or reform? *Journal of Rural Studies,* **6**, 143-162.

Ball, M. 1983. *Housing policy and economic power*. London: Methuen.

Blunden, J. & Curry, N. 1988. *A future for our countryside*. Oxford: Blackwell Scientific.

Carruthers, S.P., ed. 1986. *Alternative enterprises for agriculture in the U.K.* (CAS report no.11.) Reading: Centre for Agricultural Strategy, University of Reading.

Champion, A.G. & Townsend, A.R. 1990. *Contemporary Britain: a geographical perspective*. London: Edward Arnold.

Cloke, P. 1988. Britain. In: *Policies and plans for rural people: an international perspective,* edited by P. Cloke, 19-46. London: Unwin Hyman.

Cloke, P. & Thrift, N. 1987. Intra-class conflict in rural areas. *Journal of Rural Studies,* **3**, 331-333.

Cloke, P. & Thrift, N. 1990. Class and change in rural Britain. In: *Rural restructuring: global processes and their responses,* edited by T. Marsden, P. Lowe & S. Whatmore, 165-181. London: Fulton.

Commission of the European Communities. 1988. *The future of rural society.* (COM (88) 501 final.) Brussels: CEC.

Countryside Policy Review Panel. 1987. *New opportunities for the countryside.* (CCP 224.) Cheltenham: Countryside Commission.

County Planning Officers' Association. 1989. *Structure plans and housing land.* Hertford: CPO Association.

Cox, G. & Lowe, P. 1983. A battle not the war: the politics of the Wildlife and Countryside Act. *Countryside Planning Yearbook,* **4**, 48-76.

Cox, G., Lowe, P. & Winter, M. 1985. Land use conflict after the Wildlife and Countryside Act 1981: the role of the Farming and Wildlife Advisory Group. *Journal of Rural Studies,* **2**, 173-183.

Cox, G., Lowe, P. & Winter, M. 1986. From state direction to self regulation: the historical development of corporatism in British agriculture. *Policy and Politics,* **14**, 475-490.

Cox, G., Lowe, P. & Winter, M. 1988. Private rights and public responsibilities: the prospects for agricultural and environmental controls. *Journal of Rural Studies,* **4**, 323-337.

Cox, G., Lowe, P. & Winter, M. 1989. The farm crisis in Britain. In: *The international farm crisis,* edited by D. Goodman & M. Redclift, 113-134. London: Macmillan.

Cox, G., Lowe, P. & Winter, M. 1990. *The voluntary principle in conservation: a study of the Farming and Wildlife Advisory Group.* Chichester: Packard.

Cox, G., Flynn, A., Lowe, P. & Winter, M. 1987. *Alternative uses of agricultural land in England and Wales.* (IIUG report 87-16.) Berlin: Research Unit Environmental Policy, University of West Berlin.

Department of the Environment. 1985. *Lifting the burden.* London: DoE.

Department of the Environment. 1987. *Development involving agricultural land.* (Circular 16/87.) London: DoE.

Department of the Environment. 1988. *Rural enterprise and development.* (Planning policy guidance note 7.) London: DoE.

Department of the Environment. 1990. *This common inheritance: Britain's environmental strategy.* (Cm 1200.) London: HMSO.

Ervin, D.E. 1988. Cropland diversion (Set-Aside) in the US and UK. *Journal of Agricultural Economics,* **39**, 183-196.

Flynn, A., Lowe, P. & Cox, G. 1990. *The rural land development process.* (ESRC Countryside Change Initiative working paper 6.) London: Countryside Change Centre, University College London.

Gasson, R. 1988. *The economics of part-time farming.* Harlow: Longman.

Halliday, J. 1989. Attitudes to farm diversification: results from a survey of Devon farms. *Journal of Agricultural Economics,* **40**, 191-202.

Harrison, M.L. 1987. Property rights, philosophies and the justification of planning control. *In: Planning control: philosophies, prospects and practice,* edited by M.L. Harrison & R. Mordy, 32-58. London: Croom Helm.

Harvey, D. & Whitby, M. 1988. Issues and policies. In: *Land use and the European environment,* edited by M. Whitby & J. Ollerenshaw, 143-177. London: Belhaven Press.

Healey, P., McNamara, P., Elson, M. & Doak, A. 1988. *Land use planning and the mediation of urban change.* Cambridge: Cambridge University Press.

Hill, B. 1990. *Farm incomes, wealth and agricultural policy.* Aldershot: Avebury.

House of Lords Select Committee on the European Communities. 1990. *The future of rural society.* (HL paper 80.) London: HMSO.

Ilbery, B. 1990. Adoption of the arable Set-Aside Scheme in the UK. *Geography,* **76**, 69-73.

Jones, A. 1991. The impact of the EC's set-aside programme: the response of farm businesses in Rendsburg-Eckernforde, Germany. *Land Use Policy,* **8**, 108-124.

Koester, U. 1989. Financial implications of the EC Set-Aside programme. *Journal of Agricultural Economics,* **40**, 240-248.

Liepitz, A. 1988. *Mirages and miracles: the crisis of global fordism.* London: Verso.

Lowe, P., Cox, G., McEwen, M., O'Riordan, T. & Winter, M. 1986. *Countryside conflicts: the politics of farming, forestry and conservation.* Aldershot: Gower.

Lowe, P., Cox, G., Goodman, D., Munton, R. & Winter, M. 1990. Technological change, farm management and pollution regulation: the example of Britain. In: *Technological change and the rural environment,* edited by P. Lowe, T. Marsden & S. Whatmore. 53-80. London: Fulton.

MacPherson, C.B., ed. 1978. *Property: mainstream and critical positions.* Oxford: Blackwell Scientific.

Marsden, T. & Murdoch, J. 1990a. *Restructuring rurality: key areas for development in assessing rural change.* (ESRC Countryside Change Initiative working paper 4.) London: Countryside Change Centre, University College London.

Marsden, T. & Murdoch, J. 1990b. *Agriculture in retreat: implications for the changing control and development of rural land.* (ESRC Countryside Change Initiative working paper 9.) London: Countryside Change Centre, University College London.

Ministry of Agriculture, Fisheries and Food. 1975. *Food from our own resources.* (Cmnd 6020.) London: HMSO.

Ministry of Agriculture, Fisheries and Food. 1979. *Farming and the nation.* (Cmnd 7458.) London: HMSO.

Ministry of Agriculture, Fisheries and Food. 1987. *Farming and rural enterprise.* London: MAFF.

Ministry of Agriculture, Fisheries and Food. 1990. *Set-Aside: third year take-up.* (Press release 397-90.) London: MAFF.

Mormont, M. 1990. Who is rural? or how to be rural: towards a sociology of the rural. In: *Rural restructuring: global processes and their responses,* edited by T. Marsden, P. Lowe & S. Whatmore, 21-44. London: Fulton.

Moyer, H.W. & Josling, T.E. 1990. *Agricultural policy reform: politics and process in the EC and USA.* London: Harvester Wheatsheaf.

Munton, R. & Marsden, T. 1991. Dualism or diversity in family farming? Patterns of occupancy change in British agriculture. *Geoforum,* **22**, 105-117.

Munton, R., Marsden, T. & Whatmore, S. 1990. Technological change in a period of agricultural adjustment. In: *Technological change and the rural environment,* edited by P. Lowe, T. Marsden & S. Whatmore, 104-126. London: Fulton.

National Parks Review Panel. 1991. *Fit for the future.* Cheltenham: Countryside Commission.

North, J. 1988. *Future land use in the UK.* Cambridge: Department of Land Economy, University of Cambridge.

Pahl, R.E. 1965. *Urbs in Rure.* London: Weidenfeld and Nicolson.

Perry, R., Dean, K. & Brown, B. 1986. *Counterurbanisation: international case studies of socio-economic change in the rural areas.* Norwich: Geo Books.

Piore, M. & Sabel, C. 1984. *The second industrial divide: prospects for prosperity.* New York: Basic Books.

Potter, C. 1991. *The division of land: conservation in a period of farming contraction.* London: Routledge.

Rhodes, R. 1988. *Beyond Westminster and Whitehall: the sub-central governments of Britain.* London: Unwin Hyman.

Robinson, G.M. 1991. EC agricultural policy and the environment: land use implications in the UK. *Land Use Policy,* **8**, 95-107.

Rowsell, A. 1989. Rural depopulation and counter-urbanisation: a paradox. *Area,* **21**, 93-94.

Savage, M. & Fielding, A. 1989. Class formation and regional development: the service class in south east England. *Geoforum,* **20**, 203-218.

SERPLAN (The London and South East Regional Planning Conference). 1990. *Access to affordable housing in the south east.* (RPC 1720.) London: SERPLAN.

Shucksmith, D.M. 1990. *Housebuilding in Britain's countryside.* London: Routledge.

Shucksmith, D.M., Bryden, J., Rosenthall, P., Short, C. & Winter, M. 1989. Pluriactivity, farm structures and rural change. *Journal of Agricultural Economics,* **40**, 345-360.

Vogel, D. 1986. *National styles of regulation.* Ithaca & London: Cornell University Press.

Ward, N. 1990. A preliminary analysis of the UK food chain. *Food Policy,* **15**, 439-441.

Watkins, C. & Winter, M. 1988. *Superb conversions? Farm diversification – the farm building experience.* London: Council for the Preservation of Rural England.

Weekley, L. 1988. Rural depopulation and counter-urbanisation: a paradox. *Area,* **20**, 127-134.

Whatmore, S., Munton, R. & Marsden, T. 1990. The rural restructuring process: emerging divisions of agricultural property rights. *Regional Studies,* **24**, 235-245.

Whitby, M. 1990. Multiple land use and the market for countryside goods. *Journal of the Royal Agricultural Society of England,* **151**, 32-43.

Land use change and the environment: cause or effect?

M B Usher*

Dept of Biology, University of York, Heslington, York YO1 5DD
*Present address:
Nature Conservancy Council for Scotland, 2/5 Anderson Place, Edinburgh EH6 5NP

INTRODUCTION

The title of the session in which this paper was presented is *Forces driving land use change*. It is relatively simple to understand that human economic and social conditions will influence patterns of land use, and that technological innovation will also affect how land is managed. These are all changing facets of human societies that affect the way land is used for the benefit of individual owners or for the members of the society. Conceptually, it is much more difficult to understand how 'the environment' may influence land use change; until recently, the environment tended to be seen as unchanging, and to be characterised by quoting long-term means of temperature, precipitation, etc. In other words, the environment tended to be viewed as 'stable'. If the environment is unchanging, or even if it fluctuates randomly about a mean, how can it influence land use change? The environmental factors will determine what form of land use is possible, but an unchanging environment cannot itself drive changes in land use. It is only changes in these environmental factors that can themselves drive land use change.

There are three aims to this paper. The first aim is to explore the spatial and temporal context of land use. Patterns of land use in a geographical area at one time, or the patterns at one site over time, may give hints as to how changes in the environment may drive changes in land use. The second aim is to explore some of the environmental determinants that are causing change. It is now more widely appreciated that climate is not invariant (cf Parry, Carter & Porter 1989; Hekstra 1991), and hence climatic factors need to be considered. The soil supports plant life, and there are long-term changes here that influence the ability of that soil to support different kinds of vegetation. There are also demands made on land, one of which is the increasing public awareness of wildlife conservation. The role of conservation is, therefore, another factor that can influence change in land use, though this is closely related to sociological perceptions. Although climate, soil and conservation are not the only three environmental factors driving land use change, they are taken to act as three important specimen factors.

The third aim is to investigate the complex inter-relationships between some of the environmental influences and the form of land use; for example, the type of soil determines a broad class of possible land uses, but the actual form of land management may alter the soil, thereby changing the potential of that soil to support its previous range of land uses. Biological systems are dynamic, but it is this dynamic nature of the systems that is so hard to understand and to model.

THE SPATIAL AND TEMPORAL CONTEXT

One of the most striking examples that I have met of the spatial variation in land use was on the North York Moors. On Bridestones Moor, the expanse of heather (*Calluna vulgaris*) gives way to cross-leaved heath (*Erica tetralix*) in the wetter depressions. However, at an altitude of about 215 m, this gives way to an almost circular patch, *c* 140 m in diameter, of grassland, with buttercups (*Ranunculus* spp.), thistles (*Cirsium* spp.) and daisies (*Bellis perennis*). An ancient earth-work around the area indicates that it has been used for herding grazing stock, although there is now substantial bracken (*Pteridium aquilinum*) encroachment of this zone. Reference to the geological map (see Figure 1) indicates that calcareous rocks crop out in this area of moorland. The contrast between the sandstones, passage beds and peat, which all give rise to the acid heather moorland, and the very impure limestone, giving rise to the grassland, is immense.

The contrast may, however, be exaggerated. If the area of limestone was chosen for herding grazing stock because it was better drained, then the soil improvement may have been due in large measure to the repeated applications of dung and urine from those grazing stock. Land use differences relating to small environmental differences may thus have magnified the effects of the latter.

This example is not isolated. Raven and Walters (1956) make a similar point when describing the scenery just north of Inchnadamph: 'On his right is white rock and green grass, on his left grey rock, heather and peat. And if he wants to see the rare plants of the district, of which there are many, he will thereafter cling firmly to the former'. The important

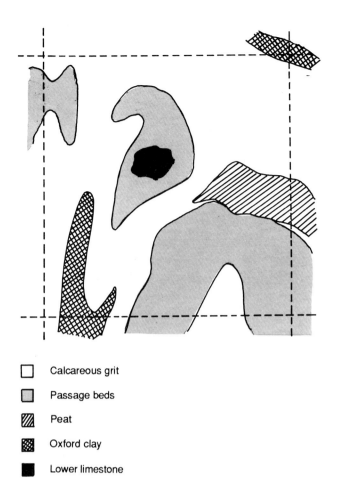

Calcareous grit

Passage beds

Peat

Oxford clay

Lower limestone

Figure 1. A section of Bridestones Moor, North York Moors National Park, showing the geological variability within a one km square (square SE8791 of the National Grid)

point from these examples is that geological variability is reflected in soil variation, leading to changes in the natural vegetation, and thence to differences in the form of land use. Historically, the soil factors have determined the form of land use within spatial scales of fractions of kilometres or tens of kilometres, except where altitudinal variation introduces a climatic element over shorter distances. Enclosures, and hence the delineation of fields as we see them today, often reflect local variation in the soil. Ecological studies at such scales fall within the general subject of 'landscape ecology', defined by Turner (1989) as emphasising 'broad spatial scales and the ecological effects of the spatial patterning of ecosystems. Specifically, it considers (a) the development and dynamics of spatial heterogeneity, (b) interactions and exchanges across heterogeneous landscapes, (c) the influences of spatial heterogeneity on biotic and abiotic processes, and (d) the management of spatial heterogeneity'. Much of Turner's analysis seems appropriate when considering land use and its change, for it adds an extra dimension to conventional thinking. Ecological studies are often undertaken on a single site, perhaps a piece of semi-natural vegetation or a field of winter cereal, without reference to the surrounding habitat types. The extra dimension introduced by landscape ecology is that the surrounding habitats interact with the habitat being studied. No field, forest or stream should be studied in isolation; it is a 'land unit'

(Zonneveld 1989), an ecologically homogeneous tract of land at the scale being studied, that is part of a two-way interactive process with all surrounding land units. As a discipline, landscape ecology is still in its infancy in the United Kingdom: its relevance to studies of land use change has still to be proven and is clearly an area that demands further research.

On spatial scales, it is important to move from descriptive studies of landscapes to predictive models. A useful example is the prediction of *Eucalyptus* species in eastern Australia. Early work (Austin, Cunningham & Good 1983) modelled the probability of occurrence of six species in 100 m altitudinal zones; altitude, rainfall, a radiation index and aspect, as might be predicted, were important variables, as was geology. The work was extended (Austin 1987) to investigate species' responses to environmental gradients; the important finding is that smooth, bell-shaped curves are not universally found for a species' response (probability of occurrence) to a range of environmental variables. Of value to land use studies is not so much the prediction of single species but more the aggregation of such data for modelling community attributes. This has been attempted by Margules, Nicholls and Austin (1987), who have predicted the diversity of *Eucalyptus* species on 0.1 ha plots. The basis of the prediction is a generalised linear model developed on a data set of observations on 4977 plots. This series of Australian studies is important because it demonstrates (i) the need for a large data set, (ii) the power of generalised linear models, (iii) the eventual need for only a limited number of factors (rainfall, temperature and solar radiation), and (iv) the application of predictive models to a landscape characterised by factors that can be either measured or predicted from existing maps. Such models, fitted using ranges of environmental data, enable the effects of changes in these environmental factors to be incorporated into simulations; what will happen to *Eucalyptus* species richness if, say, temperature increased by 2°C, if annual rainfall decreased by 100 mm, or if solar radiation was reduced by 5%? The spatial collection of data, and their incorporation into a suitable predictive model, is a powerful tool.

Considerably less use seems to have been made of temporal data. Long-term data sets may be rare, but there are many monitoring studies (eg chapters in Goldsmith 1991) that are potentially important. Too frequently the data are used only *a posteriori* to show that change has occurred, though at times the data may be used to assess the success of conservation management (cf the butterflies on a National Nature Reserve reported by Pollard 1991). Analysis of the data has traditionally been used to detect cycles and trends (Usher 1991) or to compile series of index numbers that convey the year-to-year (or long-term) changes (the calculation of such index numbers is reviewed by Crawford 1991). However, little attention has been paid to using monitoring data to make predictions. On the basis of a Markovian

model, Usher, Crawford and Williams (1992) used data collected annually from 1973 to 1988 to predict the likely distributional changes in the red and grey squirrels *(Sciurus vulgaris* and *S. carolinensis)* in Great Britain. However, the model did not incorporate environmental data, and its predictions over five-year periods were 'smoother' than the actual distribution patterns found in the surveys carried out by Forestry Commission staff. There remain many unused data in monitoring programmes, but the analytical techniques needed to incorporate such data into efficient predictive models probably still require further development.

A consideration of the spatial and temporal contexts leaves a question that is difficult to resolve. Are the observed vegetation patterns the ecological consequences of land use change (cf Bunce & Heal 1990), or can one deduce from the patterns the environmental forces driving such change? The two aspects of this question are not mutually exclusive, and they will be addressed in greater detail in the following sections.

THE ENVIRONMENTAL INFLUENCES

Climatic factors

Climate change has recently been rediscovered! Lamb (1969) analysed changes in the British climate from the late 1600s until the 1960s. His data showed that there can be quite marked changes in climate; for example, in the 40 years from the 1690s the mean annual temperature increased by about 2°C. Usher (1973) suggested that these data, together with windiness data, were factors for consideration in conservation management. However, it was not until the mid-to-late-1980s that serious attention was paid to climatic change and the influence that this will have on land use (Brouwer & Chadwick 1991), conservation (Holdgate 1991), etc.

The implications of climate change for agriculture have been extensively documented (eg Parry *et al.* 1989). For other forms of land use, the documentation is possibly not so extensive. For forests in north-western Canada, Wein (1990) has foreseen a scenario of drier and warmer weather leading to a greater incidence (frequency and intensity) of wildfires. Stress, caused by the warmer temperatures, could lead to some trees dying, and hence to the availability of more fuel for the fires, which themselves would yield large quantities of CO_2 to the atmosphere. More generally, foresters seem less concerned with the kinds of timber crops that will be grown, and more concerned with the contribution that forests will make in storing carbon. For example, Freer-Smith (1990) argues that the UK's afforestation programme (the planting of 4.4×10^4 ha yr^{-1} for the next 25 years) will provide a net carbon flux from the atmosphere of 1×10^5 t yr^{-1} (or 7×10^5 t yr^{-1} for the afforestation programmes throughout the European Community (EC)). Foresters perceive that forestry, as a land use, is an important means of storing carbon (either in the trees or as timber products) that would

otherwise contribute to global warming, and hence a change of land use in the direction of a greater extent of forests is a practical ameliorative step.

The predictions of rapid changes in climate, particularly temperature (Holdgate 1991), have considerable implications for the conservation of natural and semi-natural vegetation, as well as the microbial and animal species associated with these vegetation types. Palaeobiological research has shown how species responded to global warming in the Quaternary (Graham & Grimm 1990); the important result is that individual species respond individually, as demonstrated for the different speeds and directions of spread of beech *(Fagus)* and hemlock *(Tsuga)* in eastern North America. Wein *et al.* (1990) introduced a further factor into the uncertainties – that of stress. They quote the example of Krkonose National Park in Czechoslovakia where there is considerable damage to, and death of, white spruce trees *(Picea abies)* due to atmospheric pollution. Given such existing stress, how will the species respond to changes in climate? There are also likely to be major geographical differences, with perhaps the greatest effects of climate change being experienced in the polar regions (Spicer & Chapman 1990). This may not only affect the geographical movement of species already existing in polar and extreme temperate regions, but it may also make many polar ecosystems vulnerable to invasion by a whole series of temperate weed species. Usher (1988) considered that the only conservation areas currently without invasive species were those in Antarctica; even the island of South Georgia has a large alien component in its vegetation (Greene 1964), with annual meadow-grass *(Poa annua)* as a primary colonist of newly exposed glacial moraine. With all of these uncertainties, ameliorative action for the managers of natural and semi-natural vegetation will be difficult to find (Wein *et al.* 1990), yet it is essential for the long-term conservation of biodiversity.

Perhaps one of the more useful side effects of the increasing CO_2 levels, and the potential of this and other gases to increase global temperatures, has been to focus attention on the need for predictive modelling. This need has been reflected in the development of computer models (reviewed by Shugart 1990) with increasing sophistication for modelling the effects of global warming on other climatic factors, such as ocean currents, precipitation and windiness. All of these factors will affect land use, either by changing the potential of land to support different crop species (eg the discussion about grain and silage maize in UK by Parry *et al.* 1989, and in Europe more generally by Brouwer and Chadwick 1991), by changing the genetical basis of some of the species being managed (eg the probability of needing different provenances of north-western American coniferous species in British forestry), or by gradual and possibly unpredictable changes in the communities of microbes, plants and animals in

land used for wildlife conservation. However, so many facets of climate change are still speculation that there is far from universal agreement about the effects, let alone the consequences.

Soil factors

Soil is 'what plants grow in' (Jacks 1954), and hence it is a fundamental aspect of land use. In some instances soils change through natural processes (eg salinisation), in others through remote human activity (eg acidification), and in others through direct human intervention(eg the establishment of Nitrate Sensitive Areas). These three examples will be explored in greater detail for their effects on changing patterns of land use, though it could have been possible to review other aspects of soil change such as erosion or degradation (see the chapters in Brouwer, Thomas & Chadwick 1991).

In western Australia, the deep groundwater is saline (Main 1987). There is a close relationship between the form of land use, the salinity of the environment, and the occurrence of sheet flooding. Native vegetation has a higher evapotranspiration rate than crops and pastures; land cleared of native vegetation has increased quantities of water percolating into the soil, and hence ultimately raising the groundwater table. Movement down gradients leads to salt water emerging as springs and seepages, killing the surface vegetation over large areas, and radically altering the potential of that land for any further use. The balance between areas of native vegetation and land used for crops and pasture is one of fundamental importance in Australia (Main 1987; Loyn 1987), both economically and for the conservation of biodiversity.

It has been postulated that man-made emissions of gases such as SO_2 and NO_x have led to increased soil acidity (United Kingdom Review Group on Acid Rain 1990). In Wales, the pH of a series of soils was measured in the mid-1950s and the measurements were repeated in 1990 (Kuylenstierna & Chadwick 1992). The results are striking; all soils had become more acid over the period of approximately 33 years (Figure 2). No average increase in acidity can be given because there is a curvilinear relationship with the least acid soils changing most. However, the extent of this acidification can be visualised from the fact that soil with a pH of 5–6 in 1957 had a pH of 4–5 in 1990, ie it had become about one pH unit more acidic. This change may have been natural (acidifying processes associated with plant succession, or the natural deposition of acid substances) or man-induced (land use change, or SO_2/NO_x deposition). Kuylenstierna and Chadwick (1992), quoting other work in Britain, incline to the view that the wet deposition of man-made emissions was largely responsible. What is not recorded in this study is the effect on the soil fauna. Satchell (1967) showed that soil pH has a profound effect on earthworm species. In a survey of 35 Lake District woodlands, *Allolobophora* spp. were found in 12 of the 13 soils with a pH of 5.0 or greater, and in no soil

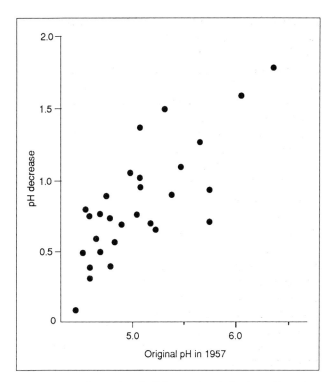

Figure 2. The change in soil pH for a series of sites in north-west Wales sampled in 1957 and resampled in 1990 (source: Kuylenstierna & Chadwick 1992)

with a pH of 4.5 or less. *Lumbricus terrestris* occurred in ten soils in each group, whereas *Bimastos eiseni* occurred in only one of the less acid soils and in 18 of the 22 more acid soils. These figures, however, disguise the community differences, which indicate a species-rich community with large earthworm biomass when the soil is only slightly acid to neutral (pH of 5 and above) and a species-poor community with extremely low earthworm biomass when the soil is acid (Edwards & Lofty 1972; Satchell 1983). Many of the Welsh soils were only marginally suitable for earthworm activity in the 1950s, and had virtually all become too acid for the majority of earthworm species by 1990. This will clearly have an effect on decomposition of dead plant materials, which in turn will affect the soil structure and processes. The important point is, however, that a small change in pH may cause a soil to cross a threshold, thereby having a profound effect on the decomposition process, and hence on the potential of that soil to support different types of land use.

The third example concerns soil nitrates, arguably a social influence rather than a direct environmental influence due to the designation of Nitrate Sensitive Areas (NSAs). The situation is potentially serious in areas of lowland England (Brown 1989) where the drinking water nitrate limit of 50 ppm is already exceeded. Inevitably, there will be a debate about restricting the use of nitrogenous fertilizers. From the agricultural side, there is clearly scepticism about any enforced reduction in the use of fertilizers (Luers 1990), thereby leading to a perceived production inefficiency. From the public health side, as reflected in national and EC legislation, there is an interest in ensuring that the slow process of nitrates entering groundwater is made even slower. As with global

warming, there is a case for afforestation in NSAs (Whiteley 1990a, b). If trees are planted in fertile arable soils, there is an initial nitrate flush, with nitrate in drainage water reaching levels of 100–200 ppm. However, in the longer term, there could be distinct advantages, with drainage water from broadleaved and coniferous woodland having 2–10 ppm and less than 2.5 ppm of nitrate, respectively.

These three soil examples – salinisation, acidification and nitrate leaching – are all clearly related to environmental influences that affect and change land use. There are two general principles that would seem to emerge from these examples. The first relates to biological thresholds. It may be that a gradual change in soil conditions has a gradual effect on the biota of the site, and hence that a small change in an input variable has a small change in an output variable. However, this cannot be relied upon to occur always. A change in pH of 0.5 of a unit, from 5.5 to 5.0, may have little effect on an earthworm community, perhaps with six to eight species persisting and with biomass remaining virtually constant. However, a similar change, from 5.0 to 4.5, may have a profound effect, reducing the number of species to two and reducing the biomass by perhaps 70–90%. Thresholds have to be expected.

The second general principle relates to the mosaic of habitats in the landscape. Patches of native vegetation in the western Australian wheat belt are important in reducing water tables, and hence at slowing the process of salinisation. Patches of woodland in lowland England, once they have been established, could lead to an overall reduction of nitrate reaching the groundwater reserves. Once again, land use needs to be considered at the scale of the landscape, rather than at the scale of the individual field.

Conservation and designation

It could be argued that wildlife conservation is a factor determined by human societies, and is therefore not an environmental factor driving land use change. However, the human concern is expressed either in terms of designating areas of land whose primary use is wildlife or in terms of incorporating conservation objectives as secondary management aims in other forms of land use. Protection of the wildlife resource can, therefore, be seen as an environmental factor that influences land use policy, and hence that may cause land use change.

The criteria for selecting areas whose primary use is wildlife conservation have been reviewed by several authors (see Usher 1986), but foremost are the extent of a candidate site, its diversity (usually measured as species richness), and the rarity of species or habitats occurring on the site. Leader-Williams, Harrison and Green (1990) have reviewed the design of protected areas, arguing that a buffer zone may be an integral part of the protection of the area. Such zones may be needed so as to give a degree of protection to the minimum viable population of one or more of the

larger species, or it may be a useful interface between the needs and aspirations of human societies and the needs of the fauna and flora to be protected.

Protection of an area does not imply that no further changes take place. Jefferson and Usher (1986) have considered several examples where conservation management aims to protect successional communities of plants and animals; such conservation needs very considerable management input to be successful. However, in apparently more nearly climax ecosystems, changes will usually occur. In the Ouse Washes, Cambridgeshire, there have been extensive changes in five grassland types over a 16-year period (Burgess, Evans & Thomas 1990); both the reed-grass *(Glyceria maxima)* swamp and the fiorin/marsh foxtail *(Agrostis stolonifera/Alopecurus geniculatus)* inundation grassland have more than doubled their extent (from 750 ha to 1670 ha), whilst three other grassland and swamp types had been reduced to less than one-quarter of their 1972 extent by 1988. Similarly, in a desert site in Mexico, there have been remarkable changes in the population sizes of the woody perennial species, with 50–90% decreases in some species matched by a 200-fold increase in another (Turner 1990). Even in protected sites such as these in Mexico or England, changes must be expected, caused by climatic factors (either gradual change or extreme events) and by variations in management.

There is, however, the question of multiple land use. The Sonoran Desert example may be an area where complete protection is possible, but in the Ouse Washes some of the grassland is cut for hay whilst other areas are grazed. It is these traditional systems of low-intensity agriculture that are responsible, at least in part, for the current wildlife conservation interest of the sites. As Olson (1990) says, 'In reality, most environmental resources are developed for some form of production . . . The most important factor to be considered in the allocation of environmental resources is the nature of society's preferences over alternative uses for the environment'.

Society's preferences are often shown by some form of land designation, eg Nitrate Sensitive Areas, Environmentally Sensitive Areas (ESAs), Sites of Special Scientific Interest (SSSIs), Areas of Outstanding Natural Beauty, Heritage Coasts, the proposed Natural Heritage Areas in Scotland, etc. In reality, these designations of land affect the form of land use, either by encouragement (eg the payments for voluntarily agreeing to low-intensity management practices in ESAs) or with a degree of legal backing (eg the lists of Potentially Damaging Operations for SSSIs). They do not prevent land use change, but generally aim to ameliorate that change so that some environmental benefits accrue.

Each year the Nature Conservancy Council (NCC) lists damage to SSSIs; the details are given in Table 1 and are testimony to the fact that SSSIs are not fully

Table 1. Data on the number of Sites of Special Scientific Interest (SSSIs) and on the damage to these sites for five years (data abstracted from the 12th–16th Annual Reports of the Nature Conservancy Council; data on area only included in the 16th Annual Report)

	1986	1987	1988	1989	1990
Total number of SSSIs at 31 March					
Number	4842	4729	4996	5184	5435
Area (x 10^6 ha)	1.43	1.52	1.58	1.64	1.71
SSSIs lost or partially lost in year to 31 March*					
Number	2	24	21	21	7
Area (ha)	-	-	-	-	112
SSSIs with long- or short-term damage in year to 31 March**					
Number	172	212	146	220	317
Area (x 10^3 ha)	-	-	-	-	91.6

* Categories included damage that will result in the denotification of whole or part of the SSSI

** Categories include damage causing a lasting reduction in the special interest or from which the special interest could recover

protected (eg NCC 1990). In a detailed study of one county, Shropshire, there is a figure of 1% loss of the natural and semi-natural habitats per year (Shropshire Wildlife Trust 1989). This figure is based on a ten-year period from 1978–79, but it obscures considerable variation between habitats (see Table 2). Although the survey methods used can be criticised, the Shropshire study gives a general indication that, even with designated land, about 1% of the best wildlife sites in the county have been converted each year into use by agriculture (64% of the change), by forestry (21%) or for development (15%).

Figures such as these raise the question: is designation of land effective? If such large changes can take place when designation is aiming to obtain an environmental enhancement, are there better

Table 2. Data on the change of natural and semi-natural habitats in Shropshire over a ten-year period (data abstracted from Shropshire Wildlife Trust 1989)

Habitat	1978–79 situation		1989 situation		Reduction in area (%)
	No. of sites	Area (ha)	No. of sites	Area (ha)	
Woodland	483	6019	388	5476	9.0
Grassland	466	4553	299	3630	20.3
Heathland	43	2790	29	2621	6.1
Wetland (bog, swamp, fen & open water)	476	2189	49	2142	2.1
Other habitats (tall herb, rock & quarry)	151	1428	123	1344	5.9

mechanisms available? Such a debate is inevitably going to continue, with case studies pointing one way or the other. In mid-Wales, Higgs and Bracken (1990) found major changes between 1957 and 1985. In an analysis of the Somerset Levels ESA, Baldock *et al.* (1990) have stressed the positive features of the ESA policy, but they stress the need for greater co-ordination and for consistency of policy. The Nature Conservancy Council's own review of the ESAs in England states '. . . ESAs have resulted in significant benefits for nature conservation' (Merricks 1990), but the report goes on to make a series of recommendations for improving the conservation delivery of the ESA policy.

Designation of land is clearly a tool that can be used by the policy-maker for influencing land use. If wildlife conservation benefits are to be gained, with general public support for the conservation objectives, it is increasingly clear that the designation must provide incentives for positive management of the land so that the conservation objectives are achieved. In this sense, conservation and the designation of areas of countryside are environmental influences acting to cause land use change.

DISCUSSION

Three strands can be identified as running through this review of the environmental factors driving land use change.

The first relates to the dynamic nature of ecosystems. It is not always clear whether an environmental factor is responsible for causing the change or whether it is a consequence of the change. Often, as in the Ecological Consequences of Land Use Change (ECOLUC) project, the latter is assumed (Bunce *et al.* 1991), whereas it is possible that there is often an interaction between land use and the environment, especially the soil environment, so that the distinction between cause and effect is blurred. An excellent example relates to vegetation change and grazing patterns (Figure 3). Under low grazing pressure, Miles (1988) showed that the predominant direction of vegetation succession in north-east Scotland was from grassland to heathland, and on to scrub and woodland. However, if the grazing pressure was increased three-fold, the direction of the succession was reversed. Miles (1988) categorised these changes in terms of density of sheep; Watson (1989) has implicated browsing by red deer *(Cervus elaphus)* in a similar manner. Shetland shows many examples of the change of vegetation due to grazing pressures (eg Birnie & Hulme 1990), compared to the herb-rich stands in the few areas protected from grazing (Spence 1979). Once again, the present-day use of the land will affect the soil, which in turn will have an influence on the future use of that land. The balance between acidification and de-acidification, implicit in Miles' (1988) work on vegetation change under grazing pressures, is of importance in understanding the dynamic nature of the association between land use and the environment.

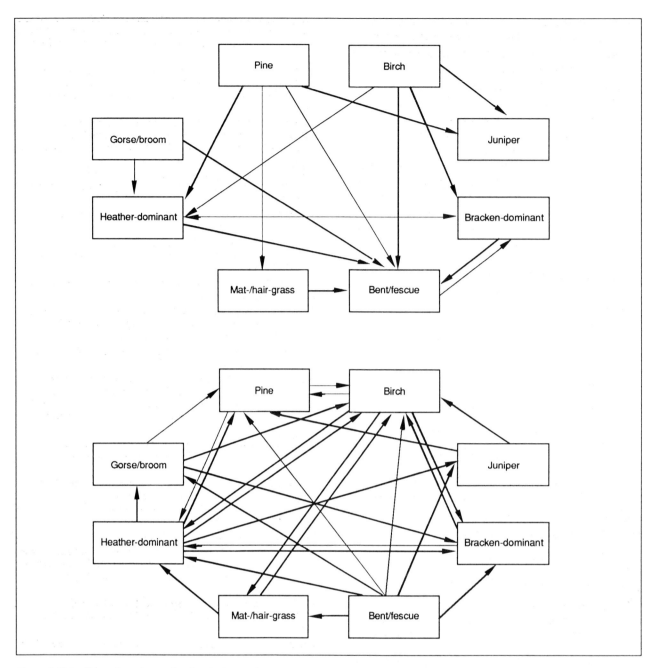

Figure 3. The effects of grazing on the development of vegetation, and hence potentially land use, in north-east Scotland (source: Miles 1988). The top diagram indicates light grazing (less than one sheep equivalent ha^{-1} yr^{-1}), and shows a general successional movement to scrub and woodland. The bottom diagram indicates heavy grazing (2–3 or more sheep equivalents ha^{-1} yr^{-1}), and shows the general movement towards grassland. More frequent transitions are shown as bold arrows. The vegetation types are arranged so that those on the left of each diagram tend to podzolise or acidify the soil, with the opposite process on the right of the diagrams

The second strand in this review relates to the scale of any research or planning study. The concepts of landscape ecology have already been invoked to indicate that the component units of a landscape may interact with each other. Scales may be small, such as the marauding predatory birds from coniferous plantations (Cadbury 1987) or marauding kangaroos from remnants of natural woodland (Arnold, Steven & Weeldenburg 1989). Scales may be large, such as the Environmentally Sensitive Areas or Nitrate Sensitive Areas. Whatever the scale, it is important for any study to concentrate on the appropriate scale. Murphy (1989) castigated conservationists with his provocative paper 'wrong species, wrong scale, wrong conclusions'!

The final strand relates to prediction. If there is a good understanding of the system and if good data are available (Starfield & Bleloch 1986), then good predictive models can be built. The problem with land use change is that the systems are often insufficiently understood so that approximations need to be made; one example is the linking together of an economic model and a data base of land use and its relationships with habitat composition (described by Bunce & Jenkins 1989). The inclusion of simple analytic models (eg Bunce *et al.* 1984) and the need for extensive data bases of biological information (eg Avery & Riper 1990) will inevitably underpin much predictive modelling for the foreseeable future. An inventory approach will also be needed to determine the gross movement of parcels of land between different use classes (eg Bunce & Barr 1988).

Whatever sort of modelling frameworks are used, they will be influenced to a greater or lesser extent by the overall policy in relation to land use and to the frequent changes in that policy. The White Paper (Department of the Environment 1990) sets out a framework within which policy is likely to be developed. However, changes in policy are both nationally and internationally determined, and operate on a totally different timescale to the environmental factors being considered here. In any predictive modelling, whilst it is important to get the spatial scale correct, it is also important to consider the temporal scales which are bound to differ between the policy framework and the environmental factors that may drive changes in land use.

ACKNOWLEDGEMENTS

I should like to thank Professor M J Chadwick both for making unpublished data available and for useful discussions. Thanks are also due to the Land Use Research Coordination Committee, in the context of which this paper has been prepared.

REFERENCES

Arnold, G.W., Steven, D.E. & Weeldenburg, J.R. 1989. The use of surrounding farmland by western grey kangaroos living in a remnant of wandoo woodland and their impact on crop production. *Australian Wildlife Research*, **16**, 85-93.

Austin, M.P. 1987. Models for the analysis of species' response to environmental gradients. *Vegetatio*, **69**, 35-45.

Austin, M.P., Cunningham, R.B. & Good, R.B. 1983. Altitudinal distribution of several eucalypt species in relation to other environmental factors in southern New South Wales. *Australian Journal of Ecology*, **8**, 169-180.

Avery, M.L. & Riper, C. van. 1990. Evaluation of wildlife-habitat relationships data base for predicting bird community composition in central California chaparral and blue oak woodlands. *California Fish & Game*, **76**, 103-117.

Baldock, D., Cox, G., Lowe, P. & Winter, M. 1990. Environmentally Sensitive Areas: incrementalism or reform? *Journal of Rural Studies*, **6**, 143-162.

Birnie, R.V. & Hulme, P.D. 1990. Overgrazing of peatland vegetation in Shetland. *Scottish Geographical Magazine*, **106**, 28-36.

Brouwer, F.M. & Chadwick, M.J. 1991. Future land use pattern in Europe. In: *Land use changes in Europe: processes of change, environmental transformations and future patterns*, edited by F.M. Brouwer, A.J. Thomas & M.J. Chadwick, 49-78. Dordrecht: Kluwer.

Brouwer, F.M., Thomas, A.J. & Chadwick, M.J., eds. 1991. *Land use changes in Europe: processes of change, environmental transformations and future patterns.* Dordrecht: Kluwer.

Brown, G. 1989. Cash for cutting nitrate leaks. *Daily Telegraph*, 10 May.

Bunce, R.G.H. & Barr, C.J. 1988. The extent of land under different management regimes in the uplands and the potential for change. In: *Ecological change in the uplands*, edited by M.B. Usher & D.B.A. Thompson, 415-426. Oxford: Blackwell Scientific.

Bunce, R.G.H. & Heal, O.W. 1990. Ecological consequences of land use change (ECOLUC). *Annual Report of the Institute of Terrestrial Ecology 1989-90*, 19-24.

Bunce, R.G.H. & Jenkins, N.R. 1989. Land potential for habitat reconstruction in Britain. In: *Biological habitat reconstruction*, edited by G.P. Buckley, 81-91. London: Belhaven.

Bunce, R.G.H., Tranter, R.B., Thompson, A.M.M., Mitchell, C.P. & Barr, C.J. 1984. Models for predicting changes in rural land use in Great Britain. In: *Agriculture and the environment*, edited by D. Jenkins, 37-44. (ITE symposium no. 13.) Cambridge: Institute of Terrestrial Ecology.

Bunce, R.G.H., Howard, D.C., Hallam, C.J., Barr, C.J. & Benefield, C.B. 1991. *The ecological consequences of land use change overview report.* Grange-over-Sands: Institute of Terrestrial Ecology.

Burgess, M.D., Evans, C.E. & Thomas, G.J. 1990. Vegetation change on the Ouse Washes wetland, England, 1972-88 and effects on their conservation importance. *Biological Conservation*, **53**, 173-189.

Cadbury, C.J. 1991. The calculation of index numbers from wildlife monitoring data. In: *Monitoring for conservation and ecology*, edited by F.B. Goldsmith, 225-248. London: Chapman and Hall.

Crawford, T.J. 1991. The calculation of index numbers from wildlife monitoring data. In: *Monitoring for conservation and ecology*, edited by F.B. Goldsmith, 225-248. London: Chapman and Hall.

Department of the Environment. 1990. *This common inheritance: Britain's environmental strategy.* (Cm 1200.) London: HMSO.

Edwards, C.A. & Lofty, J.R. 1972. *Biology of earthworms.* London: Chapman and Hall.

Freer-Smith, P.H. 1990. Climate change: the contribution of forestry to response strategies. *Forestry Commission Research Information Note*, no. 189,1-3.

Goldsmith, F.B. 1991. *Monitoring for conservation and ecology.* London: Chapman and Hall.

Graham, R.W. & Grimm, E.C. 1990. Effects of global climate change on the patterns of terrestrial biological communities. *Trends in Ecology and Evolution*, **5**, 289-292.

Greene, S.W. 1964. The vascular flora of South Georgia. *British Antarctic Survey Reports*, no. 45, 1-58.

Hekstra, G.P. 1991. Climatic change and land use impact in Europe. In: *Land use changes in Europe: processes of change, environmental transformations and future patterns*, edited by F.M. Brouwer, A.J. Thomas, & M.J. Chadwick, 177-207. Dordrecht: Kluwer.

Higgs, G. & Bracken, I. 1990. Statutory designation and land-use changes – a case study from mid-Wales. *Journal of Rural Studies*, **6**, 279-290.

Holdgate, M.W. 1991. Conservation in a world context. In: *The scientific management of temperate communities for conservation*, edited by I.F. Spellerberg, F.B. Goldsmith & M.G. Morris, 1-26. Oxford: Blackwell Scientific.

Jacks, G.V. 1954. *Soil.* London: Nelson.

Jefferson, R.G. & Usher, M.B. 1986. Ecological succession and the evaluation on non-climax communities. In: *Wildlife conservation evaluation*, edited by M.B. Usher, 69-91. London: Chapman and Hall.

Kuylenstierna, J.C.I. & Chadwick, M.J. 1992. Increases in soil acidity in north-west Wales between 1957 and 1990. *Ambio.* In press.

Lamb, H.H. 1969. The new look of climatology. *Nature*, **223**, 1209-1215.

Leader-Williams, N., Harrison, J. & Green, M.J.B. 1990. Designing protected areas to conserve natural resources. *Science Progress, Oxford*, **74**, 189-204.

Loyn, R.H. 1987. Effects of patch area and habitat on bird abundances, species numbers and tree health in fragmented Victorian forests. In: *Nature conservation: the role of remnants of native vegetation*, edited by D.A. Saunders, G.W. Arnold, A.A. Burbidge & A.J.M. Hopkins, 65-77. Chipping Norton, NSW: Surrey Beatty.

Luers, H. 1990. Nitrate debate: blanket cut-back, not the answer. *The Agronomist*, 1990 (1), 8-10.

Main, A.R. 1987. Management of remnants of native vegetation – a review of the problems and the development of an approach with reference to the wheatbelt of Western Australia. In: *Nature conservation: the role of remnants of native vegetation*, edited by D.A. Saunders, G.W. Arnold, A.A. Burbidge & A.J.M. Hopkins, 1-13. Chipping Norton, NSW: Surrey Beatty.

Margules, C.R., Nicholls, A.O. & Austin, M.P. 1987. Diversity of *Eucalyptus* species predicted by a multi-variable environmental gradient. *Oecologia*, **71**, 229-232.

Merricks, P. 1990. *A review of Environmentally Sensitive Areas in England, volume I: main report.* Peterborough: Nature Conservancy Council.

Miles, J. 1988. Vegetation and soil change in the uplands. In: *Ecological change in the uplands*, edited by M.B. Usher & D.B.A. Thompson, 57-70. Oxford: Blackwell Scientific.

Murphy, D.D. 1989. Conservation and confusion: wrong species, wrong scale, wrong conclusions. *Conservation Biology*, **3**, 82-84.

Nature Conservancy Council. 1990. *Sixteenth report, covering the period 1 April 1989-31 March 1990.* Peterborough: NCC.

Olson, L.J. 1990. Environmental preservation with production. *Journal of Environmental Economics and Management*, **18**, 88-96.

Parry, M.L., Carter, T.R. & Porter, J.H. 1989. The greenhouse effect and the future of UK agriculture. *Journal of the Royal Agricultural Society of England*, **150**, 120-131.

Pollard, E. 1991. Monitoring butterfly numbers. In: *Monitoring for conservation and ecology*, edited by F.B. Goldsmith, 87-111. London: Chapman and Hall.

Raven, J. & Walters, M. 1956. *Mountain flowers.* London: Collins.

Satchell, J.E. 1967. Lumbricidae. In: *Soil biology*, edited by A. Burges & F. Raw, 259-322. London: Academic Press.

Satchell, J.E. 1983. Earthworm ecology in forest soils. In: *Earthworm ecology: from Darwin to vermiculture*, edited by J.E. Satchell, 161-170. London: Chapman and Hall.

Shropshire Wildlife Trust. 1989. *Losing ground in Shropshire.* Shrewsbury: Shropshire Wildlife Trust.

Shugart, H.H. 1990. Using ecosystem models to assess potential consequences of global climatic change. *Trends in Ecology and Evolution*, **5**, 303-307.

Spence, D. 1979. *Shetland's living landscape: a study in island plant ecology.* Sandwick, Shetland: Thule Press.

Spicer, R.A. & Chapman, J.L. 1990. Climate change and the evolution of high-latitude terrestrial vegetation and floras. *Trends in Ecology and Evolution*, **5**, 279-284.

Starfield, A.M. & Bleloch, A.L. 1986. *Building models for conservation and wildlife management.* New York: Macmillan.

Turner, M.G. 1989. Landscape ecology: the effect of pattern on process. *Annual Review of Ecology and Systematics*, **20**, 171-197.

Turner, R.M. 1990. Long-term vegetation change at a fully protected Sonoran Desert site. *Ecology*, **71**, 464-477.

United Kingdom Review Group on Acid Rain. 1990. *Acid deposition in the United Kingdom 1986-1988: third report.* Stevenage: Waren Spring Laboratory.

Usher, M.B. 1973. *Biological management and conservation.* London: Chapman and Hall.

Usher, M.B., ed. 1986. *Wildlife conservation evaluation.* London: Chapman and Hall.

Usher, M.B. 1988. Biological invasions of nature reserves: a search for generalisations. *Biological Conservation*, **44**, 119-135.

Usher, M.B. 1991. Scientific requirements of a monitoring programme. In: *Monitoring for conservation and ecology*, edited by F.B. Goldsmith, 15-32. London: Chapman and Hall.

Usher, M.B., Crawford, T.J. & Williams, J.L. 1992. An American invasion of Great Britain: the case of the native and alien squirrel *(Sciurus)* species. *Conservation Biology.* In press.

Watson, A. 1989. Land use, reduction of heather, and natural tree regeneration on open upland. *Annual Report of the Institute of Terrestrial Ecology 1988-89*, 25-26.

Wein, R. W. 1990. The importance of wildfire to climate change – hypotheses for the taiga. In: *Fire in ecosystem dynamics*, edited by J.G. Goldammer & M.J. Jenkins, 185-190. The Hague: SPB Academic Publishing.

Wein, R.W., Hogenbirk, J.C., McFarlane, B.L., Schwartz, A.G. & Wright, R.A. 1990. Protection strategies for parks under predicted climate change. *Parks*, **1**, 17-22.

Whiteley, G.M. 1990a. Extensive re-afforestation of arable farmland in eastern England: the potential for groundwater protection in Nitrate Sensitive Areas. *Belowground Ecology*, Summer, 10-11.

Whiteley, G.M. 1990b. *Forestry as an alternative land use in Nitrate Sensitive Areas.* (Information sheet). Leeds: University of Leeds.

Zonneveld, I.S. 1989. The land unit – a fundamental concept in landscape ecology, and its applications. *Landscape Ecology*, **3**, 67-86.

Production technology forces driving land use change in Sweden

B Johnsson

Dept of Economics, Swedish University of Agricultural Sciences, Box 7013, S-750 07 Uppsala, Sweden

INTRODUCTION

Changes in agricultural production technology have had a great impact on land use patterns in Sweden. One direct effect has been yield increases, allowing farmers to produce the same volume of products with less resource input. Simultaneously, an extensive substitution of fertilizers and other capital goods for land has taken place, in the sense that more capital inputs are used per hectare.

Considerable structural changes have also been made. In general, mechanisation has increased the competitiveness of large farms in the most productive regions, at the expense of smaller farms in less productive areas. The transition from horse power to tractor power and from ruminant to non-ruminant livestock has reduced the need for pasture and, consequently, several hundred thousand hectares have become available for producing grain and other crops.

The introduction of new technology is greatly influenced by prevailing agricultural policy and other socio-economic factors outside agriculture. During the post-War industrial period of the 1950s and 1960s, there was a strong demand for labour in other sectors, and consequently there was a rapid substitution of machinery for manual labour on farms. In the 1970s and the 1980s, technology for increasing output was favoured, making it possible for the remaining labour on the farm to secure a reasonable family income.

Foreseeable technological and demand changes will probably continue to reduce the need for land to

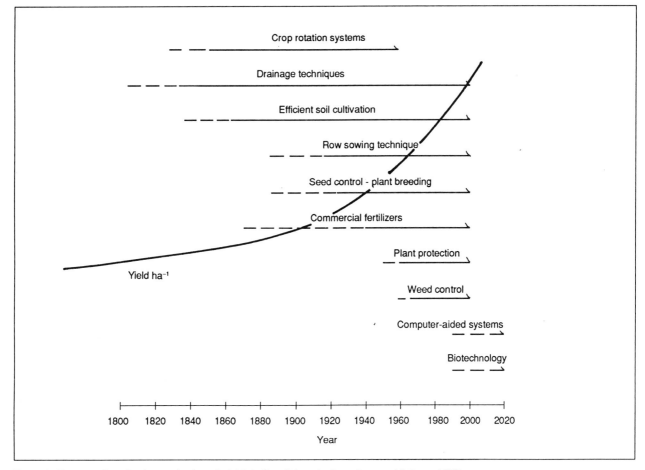

Figure 1. Changes of production methods and yields in Swedish agriculture (source: Mattsson 1978)

produce food. Together with fewer market regulations, this will lead to a reduction in land use for agriculture throughout northern Sweden and in the forest regions of southern and central Sweden. Possible alternatives to agricultural production include fuel-crop cultivation, agroforestry and forestry, depending upon their relative profitability. From technical and biological points of view, none of these alternatives would preclude a future reconversion to food production, if market conditions were to change in that direction.

Although falling land prices and environmental and landscape considerations may retard this process of change, they probably cannot prevent it. Low-input agriculture, eg organic farming, may develop under specific market conditions, but present knowledge suggests that it will not play a dominant role in the future.

To protect arable and pasture land of great environmental and aesthetic value, specific management practices will be encouraged by offering financial incentives to farmers. In other areas, less intensive farming will be promoted to protect the open landscapes.

A HISTORICAL PERSPECTIVE

Impressive changes in the productivity of land and other inputs have taken place during the last few centuries. Yields per hectare have increased through improvements in technology and production methods, as demonstrated in Figure 1. In Sweden, new cropping systems, drainage techniques and ploughing methods were introduced early in the 19th century, making it possible to cultivate and use the heavy clay soils and lowland areas subject to spring flooding, which are now our most fertile soils. Early in the 20th century, the introduction of new varieties and artificial fertilizers led to considerably increased yields of arable land. Since the end of the Second World War, there have been great increases in the use of pesticides for the control of insects, diseases and weeds. The rapid introduction of these new products and techniques resulted from improvements in research and information transfer, especially teaching.

During the post-War industrial period, extensive mechanisation has also occurred. This has greatly increased *labour productivity*, making it possible for one person to manage an area that would have previously required a large labour force.

These two major changes and their consequences for land use in Swedish agriculture are the focus of this paper. Possible future changes and their implications are also presented.

BASIC CONCEPTS

The introduction of new production technology usually leads to a shift in the production function (1) of agricultural products:

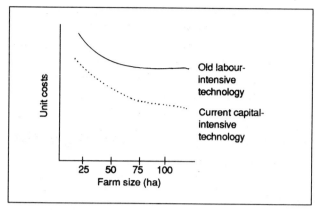

Figure 2. Production technology and economies of size

$$Y = f(A, L, C) \tag{1}$$

where Y = output, A = input of arable land, L = input of labour, and C = input of capital goods.

For a specified combination of factors, new technology will allow output to increase while inputs remain constant, or the same output may be obtained with less inputs. Assuming constant factor prices, the unit cost of production will decrease and, generally speaking, it has been profitable to introduce new technology.

In most cases, new technology changes the relationship between inputs so that the marginal substitution rates* between them adjust. For instance, new seed varieties have increased the marginal productivities of fertilizers and chemicals used for weed and pest control. A substitution of the other inputs (fertilizers, etc) for land has taken place, often strengthened by the fact that the relative factor prices have developed in favour of these inputs (Crosson 1986). The relative importance of land as the key factor for agricultural production has quantitatively decreased, and will probably continue to do so in the future. The qualitative aspects of the land resource, especially in its environmental value, may become more important in the future. Increased labour costs have stimulated the development of new and improved machinery which has been substituted for farm labour.

The importance of the above changes during the post-War industrial period is discussed below. Here, it is enough to note their structural implications. Machinery-intensive agriculture requires heavy capital investments, which has important consequences for economies-of-size (Figure 2). The indivisibility of machinery and organisational costs often mean that more land is needed per farm to utilise fully the capacity of each farm's equipment. Such structural changes can easily occur in the plain areas, but are much more difficult to achieve in forest regions with topographical limitations. By lowering

*Marginal substitution rates measure the rate at which one factor (eg capital) might substitute for another (eg labour) for a given level of output. The fact that substantial substitution of capital for labour has occurred indicates a high marginal substitution rate, one for the other.

unit costs, ease of mechanisation will thus favour agricultural concentration on the plains.

New technology, eg machinery, may also change the relative competitiveness of alternative farm products or enterprises. For instance, much of the machinery developed in the last few decades, with the introduction of improved methods for weed and pest control, has favoured grain production at the expense of grass and legumes, which are difficult to mechanise in the rather wet climate of Scandinavia. This, in turn, has led to regional specialisation: most of the grain is now produced on large farms on the plains, whereas grass crops and livestock production will be largely restricted to regions less favourable for cropping.

In addition to its direct effects, technological change often has indirect consequences. For example, high-yielding dairy cows require higher-quality hay and silage than standard breeds. Thus, the area of high-yielding feed crops on fertile arable land will increase at the expense of hay-making and grazing on marginal meadows and forested pasture.

Changes in production technology may also occur in the processing and use of agricultural products. Many countries currently favour an energy policy emphasising renewable energy resources, such as biomass fuels. Some of these crops, eg energy grass, can be grown on less productive land with limited alternative opportunities. Others, such as oil seed, are most competitive on fertile soils.

Environmental considerations will probably lead to great technological changes in future agricultural production systems. The type and extent of the changes required are still under debate. Systems that rely heavily on recirculation and local production, such as small-scale, diversified farms (eg organic farming), offer one viable alternative (Petrini 1990). However, there is also a strong trend towards highly specialised, large-scale farm production, based on sophisticated, resource-saving technology which employs biotechnology and computer-aided systems (Office of Technology Assessment (OTA) 1986; Sylvan et al. 1990; Hjelm 1991).

As pointed out by Hayami & Ruttan (1985), the character of agricultural development and the type of technology chosen are largely determined by the relative availability of land and labour. Differences between the USA and Japan provide a good example: in the USA, which has ample land resources but a relative scarcity of labour, low-intensive land use predominates. By contrast, in Japan, land is scarce while labour is easy to come by, favouring a highly intensive production system. The relative scarcity of resources may, however, shift over time, owing to technological development or changes in demand.

SOME SWEDISH EXPERIENCE

In Sweden 2.9 million ha of arable land are divided up among some 100 000 farms. Most of these farms are family enterprises of moderate size, but only 40 000 of these families derive a large part of their income from agriculture. Incomes from forestry and other non-farm occupations are of great importance to most of the farmers. Part-time and hobby farmers are two increasing groups.

Some 3% of the total labour force in Sweden is engaged in primary agricultural production, which accounts for about 1.5% of the Gross National Product. Forestry-related income is of great significance, especially to small-scale farmers in the forest regions. About 4 million ha of forest land is owned by farmers, and another 4 million ha is owned by small forestry firms with less than 2 ha of arable land. Many of these owners live in urban areas and the farmstead is used mainly for recreation.

By promoting surpluses of agricultural products, technological improvements have been followed by declining profitability. Because forestry offers scope for the conversion of land from agriculture, it has featured increasingly in policy debates.

The major changes in Swedish agriculture during the post-War period are summarised in Table 1, in support of the above argument.

Table 1. Proportional structural and productivity changes within Swedish agriculture, 1950–90 (source: Kungl. Skogs- och lantbruksakademien 1989)

Number of farms	$-2/3$
Arable land	$-1/4$
Labour	$-3/4$
Total resources	$-2/5$
Production	$+1/3$
Productivity	x2

Considerable change in the structure and productivity of Swedish agriculture has occurred since 1950. Total resource input, for example, has decreased by 40%, mainly by reducing the labour force (– three-quarters) and taking land out of production (– one-quarter). This decrease took place in the 1950s and 1960s, with almost no change in the total volume of production. The replacement of manual labour by machinery was the key driving force in that period. Arable land taken out of production, mainly small farms in less productive regions, has been partially converted to forest. Much of the land was left unmanaged (eg wetland areas in southern and central Sweden) or used for part-time or hobby farming; a small amount was used for roads and urban development.

In the 1970s and 1980s, following a shift in agricultural policy, the total input of resources remained unchanged, while the output of agricultural products increased, leading to the current surplus of agricultural commodities. In the early 1970s many farmers were faced with deciding whether to give up farming or to increase their enterprise. Most of the mechanisation possibilities had already been exploited to the full, and the manager remained as

the sole working force on the farm. The only way for the full-time farmer to provide a satisfactory income for his family was to buy or lease more land, or to intensify production. Naturally, changes in agricultural policy encouraged these trends by increasing profitability.

Considerable structural change has also occurred. Specialisation has increased, and much agricultural production has been concentrated in the major agricultural regions of southern and central Sweden. In addition, the average size of the commercial farm, especially those producing grain on the plains, has increased. Even so, Swedish farms remain smaller than British ones, on average.

Two changes that had a great influence on land use patterns were the substitution of tractor power for horse power, and the transition from ruminant to non-ruminant (pigs and chickens) livestock, the latter being much more efficient feed transformers. The number of horses has decreased from some 450 000 in 1950 to about 120 000 at present. The majority of horses are now used for sport and recreation. Over the same period, dairy cows and sheep have decreased in number by almost 66%, whereas the numbers of pigs and chickens have more than doubled. As a result of these changes, roughly 0.5 million ha of farmland have been made available for

other uses, and most livestock production is now concentrated in large units.

Total productivity (output per unit of all inputs) has doubled during the last 40 years. Studies by Uhlin (1985) indicate that most of this increase can be attributed to improvements in production technology and an increase in the efficiency with which farm resources are organised. Contrary to expectations, economies-of-size have played a less dominant role.

Between about 1950 and 1980, it was comparatively easy to compensate for rising costs, especially for labour, by increasing mechanisation and intensifying the use of cheap fertilizers and other chemicals. The marginal cost of production could, therefore, be reduced, making it possible (and profitable) to farm poor land. Later in this period, however, these easy strategies for increasing productivity had been exhausted, and rising input prices and environmental considerations increased the marginal cost of production. Poorer land was abandoned (Jonasson & Uhlin 1990): a trend which will probably continue for many years.

Land quality factors and their influence on land use and land rent have been studied by Hasund (1986). Some of his conclusions are given in Figure 3. First, economic land rent (the net returns to land after paying all other costs) seems to be normally distributed among land quality classes. Zero land rent seems to appear (cultivation becomes unprofitable) at the level of 3 million ha of arable land, surprisingly (or maybe not) close to the current level of land use for crops. A comparison of the distribution curves for 1968–69 and 1983 reveals a striking change in the shape of curves, with a much steeper slope for 1983. In 1968–69, land classes had similar rent values, whereas changes in price conditions and technology over the next 15 years created a situation in which land rent values were much more sensitive to differences in the quality of land. Hasund suggested that this increased sensitivity reflects the fact that some of the new technologies can only be applied on the productive soils of the plains.

Several studies (eg Andersson 1989) indicate that, although a traditional economic approach helps to explain changes in land use, a more comprehensive explanation requires additional factors to be taken into account. Larsson (1991), for example, has considered changes over time in the land use attitudes and expectations of farmers, as well as other more psychological factors.

WHAT IS GOING TO HAPPEN IN THE FUTURE?

The development and introduction of new technology will certainly continue. Imminent new techniques in microbiology, biotechnology and information-handling are indicated by OTA (1986), Sylvan et al. (1990) and Hjelm (1991). These changes are likely to improve the productivity of land, but not equally for all types of land. Large firms on the most productive

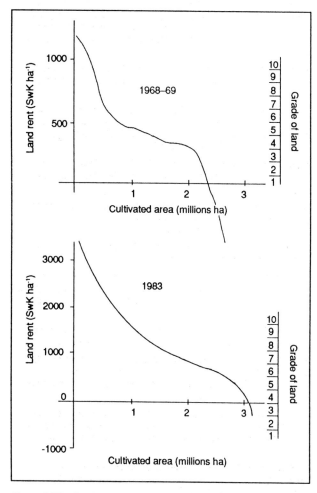

Figure 3. Distribution of land values in Sweden, 1968–69 and 1983 (source: Hasund 1986)

land of the plain areas will probably benefit most from these changes, because the new techniques will be restricted in availability and require high-quality management.

Technological change and a decreasing market for food will probably lead to the continued abandonment of farmland, especially in northern Sweden and in the forest regions of southern and central Sweden. New agricultural policies that favour a less regulated domestic market for food will strengthen this trend (Jonasson & Uhlin 1990). Thus, about one-third of the currently farmed area, or more than 1 million ha, will probably become available for uses other than food production. In certain regions, such changes will alter the current open landscape with its pleasant mixture of agricultural land, pasture and forest.

The increased prices and the environmental effects of fertilizers, pesticides and other chemicals will favour less intensive use of arable land. These changes may retard the rate of land withdrawal. However, the price elasticities for these inputs are low; ie high input taxes will be required if usage rates are to decrease considerably. In addition, changes in these factor prices, together with lower product prices, may have a disproportionately strong effect on less productive marginal land; ie the land rent of marginal land will fall below zero.

Various interest groups in Swedish society have demanded a decrease in the intensity of land use for agriculture. Their concerns range from protecting the environment and enhancing its sustainability to maintaining regional balances and preserving the countryside landscape (Petrini 1990; Drake 1989). Recirculating crop nutrients and other inputs within the farm and between urban and rural locations are major themes in this debate. Organic farming has some characteristics that may partially satisfy these demands. Studies to date (Petrini 1990) indicate that the potential for introducing such agricultural systems on a large scale is severely restricted. The obstacles are both economic and structural in nature.

Current agricultural policy supports financial incentives for encouraging the preservation of arable land and pasture of great natural or aesthetic value, but the budget provides only for an area of 0.1–0.2 million ha.

Much emphasis has been placed on developing methods for producing non-food commodities on agricultural land, eg fuel crops, such as willow *(Salix)*, and raw materials for industrial use, such as starch, oil seed and fibre crops. Current plans include the establishment of 0.1–0.2 million ha of willow species before 2000 AD. Agricultural crops for industrial use (eg starch and fibre crops as a substitute for wood in the pulp and paper industry) require a long lead time to change the processing systems in these industries, even if the conversion is profitable. In addition, international competition in the production of cheap fibre and wood substitutes has to be considered. So far, only limited research has been directed to the development of non-food agricultural products.

All of the above-mentioned land use alternatives have to be considered. For economic reasons, however, a large-scale conversion from agricultural production to forestry or perhaps agroforestry seems inevitable. Agroforestry may offer one way to preserve the aesthetically pleasing countryside landscape, as well as the management flexibility to respond effectively to an uncertain future (Kumm 1989; Kumm & Andersson 1991).

REFERENCES

Andersson, Y. 1989. *Markpriser i jordbruket. En teorserisk studie belyst med svenska data.* (Report 15.) Uppsala: Department of Economics, Swedish University of Agricultural Sciences.

Drake, L. 1989. Swedish agriculture at a turning point. *Agriculture and Human Values,* **6,** 117-126

Crosson, P. 1986. Agricultural development - looking into the future. In: *Sustainable development of the biosphere,* edited by W.C. Munn & R.E. Munn, 104-135. Cambridge: Cambridge University Press.

Hasund, K.P. 1986. *Jordbruksmarken i ett naturresursekonomiskt perspektiv.* (Report 269.) Uppsala: Department of Economics and Statistics, Swedish University of Agricultural Sciences.

Hayami, Y & Ruttan, V. 1985. *Agricultural development.* Baltimore: Johns Hopkins University Press.

Hjelm, L. 1991. *Jordbrukets strukturella och driftsmässiga utveckling.* Stockholm: Lansforsakringsbolagens Forskningsfond.

Jonasson, L. & Uhlin, H.E. 1990. Consequences of changed agricultural policy - a microeconomic approach. In: *European agriculture in search of new strategies, VIth European Congress of Agricultural Economists, The Hague, The Netherlands. September 1990.* Uppsala: Department of Economics, Swedish University of Agricultural Sciences.

Kungl. Skogs-och Lantbruksakademien. 1989. *Research strategies for agriculture and forestry.* (Report 41). Stockholm: KSLA

Kumm, K.I. 1989. Economic possibilities for agroforestry in Sweden. In: *Programme abstracts. International conference on agroforestry. Principles and practice. July, 1989, Edinburgh.* Edinburgh: University of Edinburgh.

Kumm, K.I. & Andersson, R. 1991. *Skog på Jordbruksmark ekonomi och miljö.* Aktuellt från lantbruksuniversitetet nr. 394. Ekonomi, Uppsala.

Larsson, G. 1991. *Den foretagsekonomiska utvecklingen inom jordbruket.* (PM 5, 1990-08-10.) Stockholm: Lansforsakringsbolagens Forskningsfond.

Mattson, R. 1978. *Jordbrukets utveckling i Svierge.* Aktuellt fran lantbruksuniversitet nr 258, Allmant. Uppsala.

Petrini, F., ed. 1990. *Toward an agriculture under sustainable conditions and environmental considerations.* (Report 28.) Uppsala: Department of Economics, Swedish University of Agricultural Sciences.

Petrini, F. 1990. *Mark - några naturresursekonomiska aspekter.* (Småskriftserien nr 39.) Uppsala: Institutionen for Ekonomi.

Sylvan, P., Herbertsson, C., Johnsson, H. & Tamura, E. 1990. *Bioteknikens frontlinjer.* (Utlandsrapport från Sveriges tekniska Attacheer.) Stockholm: Sveriges Tekniska Attacheer och Institutet for framtidsstudier.

Uhlin, H.E. 1985. *Concepts and measurement of technical and structural change in Swedish agriculture.* PhD thesis, Department of Economics and Statistics, Swedish University of Agricultural Sciences.

US Congress Office of Technology Assessment. 1986. *Technology, public policy and the changing structure of American agriculture.* Washington: OTA.

Social analysis of land use change: the role of the farmer

P Lowe, N Ward and R J C Munton

Rural Studies Research Centre, University College London,
26 Bedford Way, London WC1H 0AP

INTRODUCTION

Without doubt, the analysis and resolution of pressing environmental problems call for a multidisciplinary approach, and not just within the natural sciences but embracing the social sciences too (Newby 1990, 1991). Natural scientists may be increasingly well equipped to identify, describe and monitor such problems in all their complexity, but their causes lie ultimately in human action or inaction, as do possible solutions. The potential demands upon social scientists are daunting, and it is only recently that they have begun to rise to the challenge in any number. One consequence is that a great deal more is known about physical changes to the rural environment and land use in Britain than about the social factors underlying them, leaving considerable scope for a greatly enhanced role for social analysis. In particular, additional attention must be paid to the precise role of human agency and to means of evaluating options for policy and change.

The central actor in rural land use change is the farmer, on whom many instruments of policy, as well as general economic and social pressures, are focused. As the most extensive user of land, agriculture is the primary social and economic activity creating and recreating the physical environment. Farming remains a form of activity based largely on family labour and family-based units of production, and this distinctive form of organisation poses challenges for the steering of rural land use change, challenges to which social analysis must be sensitive.

In this paper, we seek to present briefly the traditions of social science investigation of the role of farmers in land use change, before reviewing the evolving sociological approaches to farm survey work and assessing the findings of such work. Finally, we return to the theme of the possible future contribution of social survey and social analysis to the study of land use change.

TRADITIONS OF SOCIAL SCIENCE ANALYSIS

Britain has long been an urbanised society, and its major social science disciplines have traditionally had a strong urban orientation. British sociology and political science, in particular, have been preoccupied with class and occupational issues which are urban and industrial in their context and which, until recently, have marginalised rural and environmental problems (Lowe & Bodiguel 1990). In certain other disciplines, notably geography and history, study of the rural world has always been more in evidence, but only one has consistently adopted a rural focus – agricultural economics. Created, in part, by the Ministry of Agriculture (MAFF), largely to help provide a scientific rationale for the modernisation of the agricultural sector, departments of agricultural economics were set up in a number of universities from the 1930s onwards, and today constitute the sole institutionalised rural discipline (Whetham 1981).

Unlike most other countries in Europe, Britain has never developed a distinct rural sociology, largely because of its lack of a substantial rural population dependent upon farming. It is now more than a century since 10% of the working population gained their livelihoods directly from the land. For those countries, such as France, with a sizeable peasantry until a generation or two ago, post-War agricultural modernisation has involved not only massive technical and structural change in farming, but also the absorption of the rural population into civil society. This has caused widespread social upheaval, with political reverberations that could not be ignored. Agricultural modernisation could not possibly be conceived simply as a technical exercise in the management of markets and the promotion of new technologies. To help understand and ease the wider social changes involved, European rural sociology developed as a sister discipline to agricultural economics, and alongside the agricultural sciences, establishing and sustaining an area of academic enquiry into the rural world of longer standing and greater status than has existed in Britain.

Post-War politics in Britain has been more concerned with the agricultural sector than earlier in the century. The focus has been on food security and the strategic role of the industry, rather than the

social changes accompanying industrial modernisation. The subdisciplines to be fostered were those that had a direct role to play in boosting agricultural productivity and efficiency, creating the illusion that agricultural and rural concerns were essentially one and the same, while encouraging the development of particular aspects of agricultural economics, such as farm policy and econometric studies of production. The more 'rounded' perspectives of the early leaders of the Agricultural Economics Society, as reflected in their presidential addresses published in the Society's journal, gave way to a more analytical style corresponding to the 'farming as a business', rather than 'farming as a way of life', approach to agricultural development, being promoted by Government and other off-farm industrial interests.

Major studies of social change on the farm were conducted (eg by Nalson 1968; Gasson 1973, 1974; Williams 1963), but not as a part of an institutionalised research tradition, and often by academics, including anthropologists, geographers and sociologists, well removed from agricultural policy circles. In consequence, there arose a marked intellectual and institutional divide between an agricultural economics profession committed to developing the tools of analysis to promote the production and market efficiency of British agriculture, and a fitful succession of critical studies of the social relations and consequences of agricultural change.

This divide was accentuated by differences in the techniques and objects of study. With the branching-off of the more practical and behavioural subdisciplines of farm management and agricultural marketing, mainstream agricultural economics became preoccupied with micro-economics, rooted in neo-classical theory, and applied through the development of econometric models. Such models, largely based upon and tested against market as opposed to individual behaviour, proved powerful tools in the quantitative analysis of economic policy. But, given that they were built upon assumptions of conformity to market rationality, what such models were not designed to do was to explore or clarify the variability of farmer (or consumer) responses. In contrast, those who, from other disciplinary perspectives, brought out the role of social factors in mediating and differentiating agricultural change tended to draw much more on qualitative data derived from interviews, case studies, and detailed social surveys. These enquiries often failed to make detailed reference to the farming economy, focusing instead on key life events, such as marriage, succession, mobility, family structure and, more latterly, on the wider social relations of agricultural production. In doing so, they often emphasised the specificity of the circumstances of individual farm families and remote rural localities divorced

from mainstream agricultural development.

Reviewing these two divergent perspectives in 1978, and calling for a dialogue between them, Newby (1978, p25) concluded that 'sociological variables have largely been relegated to residual factors by agricultural economists, while much rural sociology has been carried out in almost total isolation from a consideration of the economic context of modern agriculture'. Since then, there has been some convergence. On the one hand, following Newby's lead, social scientists have become more interested in studying the interaction between economic and social factors in the choices made by farm families. On the other hand, the emergent budgetary and overproduction crisis of the Common Agricultural Policy (CAP) has induced a change in the research agenda in agricultural economics, to embrace such issues as rural employment, environmental conservation, and alternative land uses, as well as a new openness towards multidisciplinary collaboration.

One consequence of the previous isolation of economic and sociological perspectives was a lack of systematic attention to farm-level decision-making, save for a minor socio-psychological tradition in farm management studies focused on the positivistic measurement of farmers' expressed goals and values. This was despite the resources allocated each year to the Farm Business Survey (FBS), termed the Farm Management Survey for the first 50 years of its life (1936–86). Indeed, the FBS is itself a classic illustration of the main argument. It has been conceived of narrowly as a means of estimating changes to farmers' incomes and that of the industry in aggregate, and not as a way of monitoring either the changing social relations of production on farms, or, until recently, farm family incomes and well-being, where these incorporate income and wealth derived from sources other than producing food.

By and large, agricultural economists have preferred much higher levels of aggregation – typically they either deal with market rather than individual relationships and responses, or have been restricted to an exploration of farmer behaviour purely from the perspective of a rational economic producer. Such an emphasis may have been justified by a policy and market preoccupation with efficient production and balance of payments. However, as public attention has shifted to the production of environmental goods by the industry, and as markets have developed in favour of 'greener' products, so the emphasis on average or aggregate economic performance has become less useful. A much more disaggregated level of analysis sensitive to the variability of farm-level decision-making, and the local contexts in which it is cast, is needed to inform effective regulation and provide effective analysis of emerging policy and market issues. In the past, it mattered little to policy-makers that

some farmers produced lower yields of a crop than others, and econometric models ignored variations in farmers' performance due to sociological factors that did not impact on aggregate market behaviour.

The environment is a different type of product. One farmer's environmental vandalism is not necessarily compensated for by another's conservation zeal. The environmental risk from a farm with inadequate slurry storage on the banks of a trout stream is not offset by another farm with adequate facilities elsewhere. Likewise, in a particular beauty spot or Site of Special Scientific Interest, it is the actions of particular farmers which either mar or enhance the environment. Of course, farming activities in aggregate can have significant environmental impacts, for example in the diffuse contribution they make to water pollution. But farming activities also produce and destroy unique local environments. As policy-making and regulation increasingly come to grips with this reality, then the need for a richer, empirical understanding of farm-level decision-making and its variability will be apparent. As Hamilton has commented, 'until the advent of the environmental agencies and organisation in recent years there has not been a "demand" for rural sociology in the UK' (Lowe & Bodiguel 1990, p228).

EVOLVING SOCIOLOGICAL APPROACHES TO RURAL LAND USE CHANGE

Interest in the processes of land use change has long been central to the work of geographers, but has been fuelled more widely in social science by environmentalists' claims about the damaging impact of modern agriculture on the countryside, and the accumulating scientific evidence of the extensive change to the farmed landscape in the period since the Second World War (see, for example, Westmacott & Worthington 1974, 1984; Barr et al. 1986; Hunting Surveys and Consultants Ltd 1986). Despite the technical problems of providing consistent and irrefutable data, and the difficulties of making direct comparisons between the many studies available, the evidence of extensive change is now overwhelming and generally accepted. As this body of scientific evidence has increased, so the way the relationship between agriculture and the environment has been conceptualised has also evolved. A series of approaches to the *explanation* of rural land use change during the 1970s and 1980s can be traced, and these we now turn to.

The Maverick thesis

The first response from the farming lobby to the growing evidence of land use and landscape change was to seek to deny any particular responsibility for environmental damage. What were termed the farming 'mavericks' were blamed for the deterioration of the farmed landscape (Cox & Lowe 1983, p65). Farming interests preferred to

draw attention instead to the good stewardship of most farmers and the economic and technological progress of the industry as a whole, and argued that scientific evidence demonstrating both the rate and universality of change was still inadequate to prove the environmentalists' case. This led to studies of stewardship, both as an active principle of farm management and as a political defence of farmers' relative freedom from environmental controls (Cox, Lowe & Winter 1990).

Attitudinal studies

As the rate and scale of land use changes became evident, the notion of 'maverick' or 'black sheep' farmers as solely responsible for the conflict with conservation interests was soon discarded with the recognition that environmental change was a general feature of agricultural modernisation. The individualistic orientation was retained, though, in a series of studies of farmers' attitudes to conservation and land use change (Agricultural Development and Advisory Service 1976; LeVay 1979; Worthington 1979; Social Research Consultancy 1982; Macdonald 1984; MAFF 1985; MORI 1987). Some studies were little more than opinion surveys, but others were in keeping with a socio-psychological tradition of farm survey work in Britain. Investigators implicitly accepted that attitudes determine behaviour, and that, within farming, there was a basic divide between modern (or progressive) farmers and traditional (or conservative) ones. Survey results that revealed a discrepancy between attitudes and behaviour, with many farmers regretting the environmental changes they made but feeling that they had little alternative, shifted attention from individual behaviour to structural factors (Newby et al. 1977).

The policy thesis

The role of agricultural policy in instigating change then began to receive considerable attention. Some investigators focused their attention on the Common Agricultural Policy and agricultural pricing (eg Body 1982; Baldock 1986), while others took a broader view, including capital investment incentives, taxation reliefs and the advisory system (eg Bowers & Cheshire 1983; Eldon 1988). The central tenet of the 'policy thesis' was that agricultural policy has provided farmers with access to guaranteed markets, fixed prices, capital grants and other less visible means of support, including an advisory service and a relatively favourable tax situation. These conditions created confidence, encouraging, *inter alia,* the specialisation and regional concentration of production, increased output, the substitution of capital for labour, and high land prices. In turn, these developments led to a more intensive use of farmland and, indirectly, to fewer, larger businesses, owned and occupied by a more profit- and asset-conscious generation of farmers who adopt environmentally damaging practices, not wantonly

but because the policy framework has made such practices irresistibly attractive.

Despite broad agreement in the social sciences on these main points, determining the *precise* significance and contribution of agricultural policy measures to land use change has proved much more difficult. Cheshire (1986) and Harvey *et al.* (1986) drew attention to the lack of detailed, empirical enquiry capable of sustaining this thesis, and a number of other criticisms can also be made. First, among those emphasising the importance of agricultural policy, there has been little recognition of the wider social and economic conext within which the limits to, as well as the importance of, public policy need to be critically assessed. Within a capitalist economy, the competitive forces associated with the circulation of capital will, of themselves and irrespective of public policy, tend to restructure the ownership of capital within the industry, and encourage fewer full-time farm businesses (Marsden *et al.* 1986). It has been argued, for example, that none of the major long-term trends evident in the UK farming industry in the 1960s have been altered to any significant degree by our entry into the European Community (EC) (Capstick 1983). Certain prominent trends, such as labour shedding, are long-standing features of British agriculture which first emerged under 'laissez-faire' conditions. Second, advocates of the policy thesis often presume a mechanistic response on the part of farmers to the economic signals provided by regulated markets, and then proceed to make assumptions about the causes of landscape change on this basis. Third, the role of technological change within the policy thesis has remained a neglected area of study. Although agricultural policy may have created the conditions under which environmental change would take place, the social relations of the uptake of new agricultural technologies, often the instruments of change, have been of crucial importance.

The farming style thesis

An attempt to chart a mid-way course between the individualistic approach of attitudinal surveys and the macro-approach of the policy thesis could be described as the 'farming style thesis'. The origins of such work into agriculture and the environment lay with Newby *et al.'s* typology of farmers' attitudes to conservation (Newby *et al.* 1977). Such a Weberian approach to class and market situations, with its focus on attitudes and its use of an ideal-type methodology, proved to bea marked conceptual development. Similarly, building upon the 'policy thesis', Potter (1986) has argued that a macro-perspective based on policy context, general profitability and the technological treadmill should be accompanied by farm-level perspectives on land use change, including 'family processes' such as succession which may drive farm adjustment,

adaptability, and the sets of values held by farmers. For example, Potter (1986, p149) suggests that 'environmental damage may result from behaviour which is conditioned by investment norms and notions of what makes good farming practice'. Commencing from this position, Potter categorises farmers on the basis of their investment style, discriminating between those who make systematic and programmed investments in land improvement and those who have an incremental, often *ad hoc,* style of investment. He suggests that the propensity for land use change and the scale of that change will vary according to the different types of investment style identified. For those familiar with the wide variety of conditions existing on farms, these arguments represent a valuable palliative to the public policy thesis, but what Potter leaves inadequately developed are the *relations* between the individual, the farm business, and the family household, and the macro-economic and technological context within which farming takes place.

The modified political economy thesis

Such a perspective has been pursued by Munton, Marsden and Eldon (1987a,b), and draws upon the reconceptualisation of the farm as a complex of internal and external production relations (see Whatmore *et al.* 1987a,b). It focuses on the interactive relationship between the economic, technological and political forces that surround the individual farmer (and they are themselves inter-related) and the internal family and financial circumstances of the business. Farmers manage their businesses within a range of constraints beyond their control, but they do exercise options within this range. The investment styles identified by Potter may be real enough, and capable of being distinguished in terms of the different consequences each holds for the landscape, but they remain *descriptions* of behaviour. In themselves, they cannot account for why a farmer adopts one particular investment strategy rather than another. The political economy approach, in contrast, focuses on the *processes* that lead to agricultural change (for a fuller discussion, see Marsden *et al.* 1986).

The approach involves integrating sets of structural conditions associated with policy and economy which bear down upon farm families, with a focus upon the internal nature of those families with respect to household composition and business organisation. The description of the structural context in operation, until the mid-1980s at least, is a familiar one. Economic and policy conditions have demanded lower unit costs, and these have been achieved largely through more capital-intensive systems of production. Most farmers have thus been obliged to participate on a 'technological treadmill', whereby they have, within limits, continuously had to adopt new cost-reducing

technologies to offset falls in real prices (Munton, Marsden & Whatmore 1990). These new technologies have often required substantial fixed investment and are best exploited as a package, making withdrawal from the treadmill – leading to a return to less-intensive systems – difficult to achieve in the short term. They have also tended to increase the scope for economies of scale, placing a premium on business enlargement, and have required expertise that is beyond the ability of the average farmer to provide. A growing set of dependencies on outside agents – the suppliers of credit, advanced technologies, and so on – have tended to reduce the autonomy of the individual farmer while gradually weakening the economic position of the industry as a whole within the food system. Farming households that do not depend upon their farming incomes for a substantial part of their livelihoods, large farm businesses with a range of enterprises, and those with low debts *may* be able to avoid such commitments and pay more regard to their farm environments. But the distribution of such farms may bear little relation to those areas valued highly by society for their natural beauty or wildlife.

RESEARCH FINDINGS ON RURAL LAND USE CHANGE AND THEIR POLICY IMPLICATIONS

What have such approaches to the study of farmers and the environment told us so far about the key determinants of rural land use change?

Farm occupancy change and land use

In spite of technological advances which seek to reduce the dependence of food production on the land base, land remains an essential means of production for a wide range of farming enterprises. It is not surprising, therefore, that the changing distribution of property rights, and the control that occupiers can exert over them, have been viewed as important influences on the way rural land is used, provided their role is investigated in conjunction with the wider economic and technological forces for change, and the interactions between these and the structures of individual farm families and businesses (see Whatmore, Munton & Marsden 1990).
The current pattern of property rights is very complex, and only fairly crude analyses have been possible beyond the case study method. Nonetheless, in a study of change on more than 250 farms in lowland England over the period 1970–85, Munton and Marsden (1991) have established, *inter alia,* that landscape changes associated with agricultural intensification have occurred at faster rates on land which has changed hands than on land which has remained within the same business. Moreover, landscape change is especially associated with a range of 'occupancy events' (eg a new occupier, new business structure, etc), so that

n 50% of cases a change in occupancy leads directly to alterations in the farmed landscape. The facts that landscape change is associated directly with only half the events identified, and that the ability of the researchers to predict which ones is limited, reveal that occupancy change is best viewed as providing 'the opportunities and incentives for radical change' (p673) rather than acting in a more deterministic way. Such work has identified the need for policy measures aimed at reducing the loss of landscape features to be incorporated within occupancy change processes, with advice being given *during* the discussion and planning which precede management and landscape changes (Marsden & Munton 1991). The need for such a pro-active approach becomes all the more pressing with mounting evidence that, for a growing proportion of farms, the *conditions* for family continuity are not being met and, more generally, the *commitment to* family continuity - once seen as one of the key traditional values underpinning farming– is weakening (Symes & Appleton 1986; Hutson 1987). At the same time, locally specific responses to broader policy and economic changes can often be identified (see Ward, Marsden & Munton 1990), and it is plausible that, as the ethos underpinning the policy framework is transformed and the move towards a 'post-productivist' model continues, so divergent local responses will become more marked. While this would support arguments for *geographically* targeted policies, the growing *social* differentiation of farming has raised unanswered questions about the environmental consequences of greater differentiation.

Farmer decision-making and the role of advisors

 Another area where evidence is becoming available on the nature of the relations between agriculture and the environment is that of the role of external advice in farmers' decision-making. The shifting pattern of advice which farmers seek and receive is underpinned by differing and potentially conflicting ideologies. On the one hand, the increasing technological and financial complexity of modern farming has accentuated many farmers' dependence on private sector sources where economic considerations are paramount (Tait 1978, 1985; Eldon 1988; Carr 1988), while, on the other, voluntary and state sectors are emerging as among the most significant sources of conservation advice (Cox *et al.* 1990).

The extent of contact between farmers and source of conservation advice remains patchy, and farmers' views of its relevance to the management of their businesses are variable and selective (Carr 1988). A recent evaluation of farm conservation advice demonstrated the tendency even of receptive farmers to select such advice and modify it according to their own perceptions of appropriate

conservation practice (Centre for Rural Studies 1990). For many farmers, this is taken to imply habitat creation, classically through tree planting and digging ponds, with farm conservation advisers reporting difficulties in persuading farmers of the importance of managing or retaining existing semi-natural features, or of the need to integrate conservation into general farming practices and plans.

Such findings are in keeping with other survey work which suggests that the most important source of influence on farmers' practices are those within the farming community itself (including the family, neighouring farmers, and the landlord) or closely associated with it, like the Agricultural Development and Advisory Service (ADAS). Even with regard to environmentally sensitive practices such as straw burning, hedgerow removal, tree planting and pesticide use, these sources remain the most salient, and conservation organisations even then are typically ranked below other sources of advice, such as the farming media, the National Farmers' Union, and commercial representatives (Carr 1988). The limited and selective impact of conservation advice is compounded by biases within that advice which, with its preoccupation with nature and landscape conservation, has typically neglected pollution and wider health and ecological concerns.

In contrast, farmers' growing dependence on private sector sources of advice is particularly apparent in relation to pesticide use. In one survey of fruit and vegetable growers in East Anglia, 62% favoured a commercial source of advice, generally the pesticide salesman (Tait 1978). Subsequent surveys of cereal, sugar beet and oil seed rape growers indicated an even greater reliance on commercial advisers, with a majority having their fields monitored frequently in spring and early summer by a pesticide salesman (Tait 1985; Lawson 1982). Under these circumstances, 'the monitoring and forecasting information generated in the non-commercial sector was reaching the farmer almost exclusively through the commercial sector' (Tait 1985, p232). In a broader study, farmers revealed a considerable willingness to pay for technological or professional advice where it was directly linked to their business (Fearne 1990). At the point of *action,* it reveals that personal contact remains very important, and this undermines the otherwise laudable suggestion for a small farm conservation support unit put forward by Clark and O'Riordan (1989), designed to overcome the tendency to institutional fragmentation where advice to farmers on the environment is concerned.

Types of farmers, land use and conservation

Debate has also focused on the relative environmental merits of part-time as against full-time farmers and of smaller as against larger farmers. In neither cases, though, does the

available evidence support prevailing popular or political prejudices. Here, we will briefly review these debates and outline other models of farmer types which centre on orientation towards conservation schemes and grants, and towards risk. Such models can often be inherent in policy proposals without being explicitly examined. For example, the McSharry proposals to the EC, contained in *Com (91) 258 Final* (European Commission, 11.7.91), for reform of the CAP would appear to be based on the notion that small farmers are better protectors of the rural environment.

Part-time versus full-time farmers

Convincing evidence is lacking that part-time farmers are likely to be better conservators of the farmed landscape. The issue depends very largely on the objectives of the occupier. If part-time farming is conceived as a strategy for accumulating capital, then it will tend to result in a similar impact on the farmed landscape to that of full-time farms. Hobby farmers earning an incidental proportion of household income from farming may, however, be more likely to manage their land in a way that protects and enhances the farmed landscape (Munton, Whatmore & Marsden 1989). This finding provides some support for Gasson (1983), who also found evidence that those less dependent upon farming for a living were more sympathetic to nature conservation, and were more likely to have taken positive action to conserve the environment. Likewise, Sinclair (1983) found that farmers who held, or had held, non-farming jobs were more sympathetic to conservation than others. Effectively, the possible impacts of part-time farming vary according to the type of income diversification pursued by the farm household. In the majority of cases, there is neither environmental enhancement, through the switching of labour from production and attuning the management of the farm to the likely demands of tourists for a pleasant environment, nor, conversely, environmental destruction prompted by an injection of capital derived from tourist income. Diversification into game management might be expected to be more beneficial, and a number of surveys of farmers have found positive attitudes towards wildlife and habitat conservation amongst those with an interest in shooting and other field sports, whether as a hobby or a commercial activity (Westmacott & Worthington 1974; ADAS 1976; Piddington 1981; MAFF 1985).

Small versus large farmers

Large farmers may have attracted more criticism from environmentalists because they adopted the means to alter the landscape earlier and with more extensive effect than smaller operators. But it was only large private landowners that Newby and his colleagues (1977) found in East Anglia could afford to retain a traditional landscape, if they so chose.

Otherwise, once farmers become engaged with the technological treadmill, most, if not all, will begin initiating significant alterations to the landscape. Moreover, there is some evidence that more profitable operators are more likely to alter the farmed landscape. In their study, Munton, Eldon and Marsden (1987b) allocated farm businesses to 'economic status' categories on the basis of the general trajectory of the farm's financial viability (ie the ability of the business to reproduce itself economically), in terms of the farming enterprise alone. It was farms in the 'accumulator' category (ie farm businesses that had provided a steady and often increasing profit since 1970, often in association with an increase in business size) that had most frequently changed key aspects of the farmed landscape. What the study could not elucidate, however, was whether the more marginal enterprises were unable or unwilling to make changes that would affect the environment.

Conservation scheme adopters versus non-adopters

In a context in which participation in conservation programmes is voluntary and conservation advice-giving is reactive, the characteristics of those farmers who choose to take part is significant. Potter (1986, 1987) noted how farmers tend to become interested in voluntary conservation schemes only after major programmes of farm improvement have been undertaken, and this fact has been supported by evidence from Munton et al. (1987b). There is also a marked tendency for farmers to regard conservation practices as merely an adjunct to farm management, to be implemented on economically marginal parts of their farms, and as a source of income loss for which they need to be compensated. The needs of business security and family income have to be met first, and this has major implications for the operation of environmental policies. Typically, those most prepared to engage in environmental projects:

> 'have already modernised their businesses, and altered landscapes...and seek... to use grants *after the event* to replace individual features... with the effect that... conservation grants appear to be less useful in protecting *existing* vulnerable landscapes, with policy generally being unable to direct attention to damaging farm practices at the time of their occurrence' (Marsden & Munton 1991, p673).

In terms of this experience, the designation of spatial policies, such as Environmentally Sensitive Areas (in which farmers receive payments for farming in a traditional and sympathetic manner), makes sense but leaves much of the countryside vulnerable to further environmental damage.

Other research indicates that it is the initiation of conservation practices, however modest, which are crucial to longer-term adjustments in farm management. Those farmers who have significant areas of semi-natural habitat or woodland on their farms are most willing to entertain the diversion of further land from intensive agricultural production. This is not to suggest, however, that such operators are persuaded more generally of the merits of less intensive systems of production. Conservation simply has its place within a carefully zoned property. Multiple use may be exhibited at the level of the farm, but be strikingly absent at the field scale. In their study of the potential responsiveness of farmers to land diversion, Gasson and Potter (1988) also demonstrated quite clearly the finacial filter through which conservation practices have to pass. Not only do levels of compensation need to be competitive with the returns from existing farming enterprises, but they suggest that:

> 'those who are most sympathetic to the idea of diverting land to conservation uses, and who are willing to offer most acres would in fact be offering a smaller share of productive capacity than less willing and able participants... such schemes are likely to meet with considerable resistance from small-scale, financially constrained farms. Far from redistributing income, any payments are likely to be channelled mainly to the better off' (pp349–350).

Risk-averse versus risk-taking farmers

An important issue in determining the social processes behind land use change is the farmers' assessment of different kinds of risk within a farm management strategy, and how they may be traded off (Lowe et al. 1990). Tait (1978, 1982, 1983), for example, has examined farmers' use of pesticides in relation to their attitudes to the risks involved. Though many farmers expressed strong conern over the environmental and personal health hazards, this concern was not often correlated with pesticide usage. The attitude to financial risk, though, was significantly correlated with behaviour, with farmers who were more risk averse using more pesticides than others. Clearly, such trade-offs depend upon the information available to farmers, their changing financial circumstances, and other pressures (including, with regard to pollution incidents, the chances of detection).

The assessment of risk is not an identical technical exercise for every farmer: there is no optimum or generalisable solution when such a broad range of factors interplay. For example, one farmer's high risk strategy, such as investment in high-cost pollution technology with no guarantee of correspondingly increased returns, might be a matter of low risk for another farmer, if undertaken as part of a planned expansion in business. A farmer's attitude to investment and borrowing is crucial here, and on this attitude hinges much of the variation in farm adjustment strategies over the medium term. What are the factors, for example, which persuade farmers to use particular kinds of pesticide, and what determines the way in which they apply them? What factors influence a farmer's judgement on the

suitability of weather or soil conditions for particular agricultural operations? Are these really questions of technical or economic competence, as they have traditionally been viewed, or, as now seems more likely, are they in essence questions of sociology and psychology (Tait 1978, 1985; Carr 1988)? And, under these circumstances, to what kinds of regulation (or incentive) will the farmer be sensitive?

By and large, the response of farmers to environmental issues and concerns is much less significant than the environmental effects of their responses to agricultural production policy. Indeed, a number of studies have shown that, whatever the attitudes of farmers towards nature or landscape conservation, their behaviour tends to be dominated by economic and farming considerations (Newby et al. 1977; Carr 1988). Even some responses to reduced levels of production may have adverse environmental consequences. For example, adaptations to husbandry induced by milk quotas, particularly a reduction in the purchase of bought-in feed, have led to an increase in the intensity of grassland management and silage-making (Halliday 1988). In eastern England, concerned that similar kinds of quota might be introduced to control cereal output, cereal producers expanded their acreage in the mid-1980s on to more marginal land, and the fact that this form of supply control now seems most unlikely to be introduced cannot repair the environmental damage done thereby (Munton et al. 1987b). In other words, until we understand more fully farmers' risk-taking behaviour, in what is an uncertain period for them, then the unintended consequences of changes to farm production policy, such as less regulated markets, may undermine all the progress on environmental protection achieved under existing initiatives.

FURTHER RESEARCH NEEDS

The demands placed by society on the countryside are in a period of flux. On the one hand, the demands for recreational and living space are growing while the expectations of amenity and wildlife interest continue to rise. On the other, the high cost of agricultural support has dented the political legitimacy of post-War agricultural policy. It seems inevitable that the expectations of agriculture, as the dominant rural land use, must continue to adjust. Most rural land will remain in some form of agricultural use, but the manner in which it is farmed will become increasingly sensitive to new markets beyond the food system and to tighter environmental controls. How such a process of adjustment will be regulated, and to what degree different parts of Britain will be encouraged along alternative development paths, is beyond the scope of this paper. It is, however, increasingly clear that the kinds of information we will need to collect about the farming industry have

to be changed, and it is to this issue that we now turn.

In certain respects, there is plenty of information about agriculture, much of it collected regularly by MAFF and its designated agents, and some acquired over a long period (see, for example, MAFF 1968). It can be argued that this effort has been worthwhile in a period of expansion, providing evidence on the pattern of enterprise change (the annual and comprehensive Agricultural Census) and levels of profitability (the annual sample Farm Business Survey). These sources have been directed towards informing Government and other economic interests of changes in production and profitability. They have not helped, however, to answer questions regarding the changing social character of the industry to any great extent. For example, they have not directly addressed the social relations of production, the distribution of wealth as opposed to income, the extent and nature of pluriactivity, and the impact of farming on the environment. This point is not made to criticise established surveys for not doing what they were not intended to do, but to question their continued relevance under the new sets of circumstances. Unfortunately, they have been resistant to change in content and organisation, and have tended to monopolise the resources available for survey work. An illustration is provided by the Northfield Committee (1979). In its report, the Committee observed that:

> 'The lack of data on agricultural land ownership and occupancy is in sharp contrast to the wide range of statistics upon which agricultural support policy is based. Yet Government fiscal policy may well affect the industry more fundamentally than annual changes in support prices' (p113).

The Committee proceeded to make some modest proposals for change to the annual census form to close the gap in our knowledge, but little has happened.

Given the spatial specificity of the environment and its management needs, and the growing social and economic variation in the circumstances of individual farms, the case for more socially oriented surveys directed towards an improved understanding of farmers' decision-making is urgent. It is essential, for example, that surveys are made more sensitive to the fact that, in spite of 50 years of increasingly industrialised production, well over 90% of all farm enterprises remain essentially *family* businesses. It is unacceptable to argue that farms are now businesses and then to ignore their family basis as if this made no difference to their goals and operational objectives (for a review, see Gasson et al. 1988). Moreover, both in the Agricultural Census and the FBS, it no longer makes sense, if it ever did, to focus data collection, and therefore our statistical understanding, very

largely on the farm enterprise *sensu stricto,* as if it existed in a social vacuum detached from the wider family interests to which it belongs, and from the rural society of which it is part. A regular social survey of a sample of farm households, perhaps an additional questionnaire to those taking part in the FBS, would constitute a sensible starting point. A reluctance to participate, the usual first line of defence against such a proposal, sits uneasily with an industry that accepts large sums of public money and regularly claims it could do with more. What better way of addressing the real difficulties of the industry, and the need for public monies to ameliorate them, than for some of the most pressing problems of the day to be addressed through a properly conducted social survey?

REFERENCES

Agricultural Development and Advisory Service. 1976. *Wildlife conservation in semi-natural habitats on farms: a survey of farmer attitudes and intentions in England and Wales.* London: HMSO.

Baldock, D. 1986. The CAP price policy and the environment: an exploratory essay. In: *Can the CAP fit the environment?* edited by D. Baldock & D. Conder, 55-74. London: Institute of European Environmental Policy and Council for the Protection of Rural England.

Barr, C., Benefield, C., Bunce, B., Ridsdale, H. & Whittaker, M. 1986. *Landscape changes in Britain.* Abbots Ripton: Institute of Terrestrial Ecology.

Body, R. 1982. *Agriculture: the triumph and the shame.* London: Temple-Smith.

Bowers, J. & Cheshire, P. 1983. *Agriculture, the countryside and land use.* London: Methuen.

Capstick, C. 1983. Agricultural policy issues and economic analyses. *Journal of Agricultural Economics,* **34,** 263-278.

Carr, S. 1988. *Conservation on farms: conflicting attitudes, social pressures and behaviour.* PhD thesis, Faculty of Technology, Open University.

Centre for Rural Studies. 1990. *Farmers and conservation advice.* (Occasional paper no.9.) Cirencester: Centre for Rural Studies.

Cheshire, P. 1986. The environmental implications of European agricultural support policies. In: *Can the CAP fit the environment?* edited by D. Baldock & D. Conder, 9-18. London: Institute of European Environmental Policy and Council for the Protection of Rural England.

Clark, A. & O'Riordan, T. 1989. A case for a farm conservation support unit. *Ecos,* **10,** 30-35.

Cox, G. & Lowe, P. 1983. A battle not the war: the politics of the Wildlife and Countryside Act. In: *Countryside planning yearbook,* Volume 4, edited by A.W. Gilg, 48-76. Norwich: Geobooks.

Cox, G., Lowe, P. & Winter, M. 1986. *Agriculture, people and policies.* London: Allen and Unwin.

Cox, G., Lowe, P. & Winter, M. 1990. *The voluntary principle in conservation.* Chichester: Packard.

Eldon, J. 1988. Agricultural change, conservation and the role of advisers. *Ecos,* **9,** 14-20.

Fearne, A. 1990. Communications in agriculture: results of a farmer survey. *Journal of Agricultural Economics,* **41,** 371-380.

Gasson, R. 1973. Goals and values of farmers. *Journal of Agricultural Economics,* **24,** 521-542.

Gasson, R. 1974. Socio-economic status and orientation to work: the case of farmers. *Sociologia Ruralis,* **14,** 127-141.

Gasson, R. 1983. *Gainful occupations of farm families.* Wye: Department of Rural Economics, Wye College.

Gasson, R. & Potter, C. 1988. Conservation through land diversion: a survey of farmers' attitudes. *Journal of Agricultural Economics,* **39,** 340-351.

Gasson, R., Crow, G., Errington, A., Hutson, J., Marsden, T. & Winter, M. 1988. The farm as a family business: a review. *Journal of Agricultural Economics,* **39,** 1-41.

Halliday, J. 1988. Dairy farmers take stock: a study of milk producers' reaction to quota in Devon. *Journal of Rural Studies,* **4,** 193-202.

Harvey, D., Barr, C.J., Bell, M., Bunce, R.G.H., Edwards, D., Errington, A.J., Jollans, J.L., McClintock, J.H., Thompson, A.M.M. & Tranter, R.B. 1986. *Countryside implications for England and Wales of possible changes in the Common Agricultural Policy.* Reading: Centre for Agricultural Strategy, University of Reading.

Hunting Surveys and Consultants Ltd. 1986. *Monitoring landscape change.* Borehamwood: Hunting Surveys and Consultants Ltd.

Hutson, J. 1987. Father and sons: family farms, family businesses and the farming industry. *Sociology,* **21,** 215-229.

Lawson, T. 1982. Information flow and crop protection decision. In: *Decision making in the practice of crop protection,* edited by R. Austin. (Monograph no. 25.) Croydon: British Crop Protection Council.

LeVay, C. 1979. Farm viability in mid-Wales. *Town and Country Planning,* **48,** 197-198.

Lowe, P. & Bodiguel, M., eds. 1990. *Rural studies in Britain and France.* London: Belhaven.

Lowe, P., Marsden, T. & Whatmore, S., eds. 1990. *Technological change and the rural environment.* London: Fulton.

Lowe, P., Cox, G., Goodman, D., Munton, R. & Winter, M. 1990. Technological change, farm management and pollution regulation: the example of Britain. In: *Technological change and the rural environment,* edited by P. Lowe, T. Marsden & S. Whatmore, 53-80. London: Fulton.

Macdonald, D. 1984. A questionnaire survey of farmers' opinions and actions towards wildlife on farmlands. In: *Agriculture and the environment,* edited by D. Jenkins, 171-177. (ITE symposium no.13.) Cambridge: Institute of Terrestrial Ecology.

Marsden, T. & Munton, R. 1991. Occupancy change and the farmed landscape: implications for policy. *Environment and Planning A,* 23, 663-676.

Marsden, T., Munton, R., Whatmore, S. & Little, J. 1986. Towards a political economy of capitalist agriculture: a British perspective. *International Journal of Urban and Regional Research,* **10,** 498-521.

Ministry of Agriculture, Fisheries and Food. 1968. *A century of agricultural statistics: Great Britain 1866-1966.* London: HMSO.

Ministry of Agriculture, Fisheries and Food. 1985. *Survey of environmental topics on farms in England and Wales.* (MAFF statistical notice no. 244/85.) Guildford: Government Statistical Service.

MORI. 1987. *Farmers' attitudes towards nature conservation: a report on qualitative research prepared for the NCC.* London: MORI.

Munton, R. & Marsden, T. 1991. Occupancy change and the farmed landscape: an analysis of farm level trends, 1970-1985. *Environment and Planning A,* **23,** 499-510.

Munton, R., Marsden, T. & Eldon, J. 1987a. *Occupancy change and the farmed landscape.* Unpublished report to the Countryside Commission.

Munton, R., Eldon, J. & Marsden, T. 1987b. Farmers' responses to an uncertain policy future. In: *Removing land from agriculture: implications for farming and the environment,* edited by D. Baldock & D. Conder, 19-30. London: Council for the Protection of Rural England and Institute of European Environmental Policy.

Munton, R., Whatmore, S. & Marsden, T. 1989. Part-time farming and its implications for the rural landscape: a preliminary analysis. *Environment and Planning A,* **21,** 523-536.

Munton, R., Marsden, T. and Whatmore, S. 1990. Technological change in a period of agricultural adjustment. In: *Technological change and the rural environment,* edited by P. Lowe, T.K. Marsden & S.J. Whatmore, 104-26. London: Fulton.

Nalson, J. 1968. *The mobility of farm families.* Manchester: Manchester University Press.

Newby, H. 1978. The rural sociology for advanced capitalist societies. In: *International perspectives in rural sociology,* edited by H. Newby, 3-30. London: Wiley.

Newby, H. 1990. Opening the door to social scientists. *New Scientist,* 8 September, 26.

Newby, H. 1991. One world, two cultures: sociology and the environment. *Network (Newsletter of the British Sociological Association) no. 50.*

Newby, H., Bell, C., Saunders, P. & Rose, D. 1977. Farmers' attitudes to conservation. *Countryside Recreation Review,* **2**, 23-30.

Northfield Committee. 1979. *Report into the requisition and occupancy of agricultural land.* (Cmnd 7599.) London: HMSO.

Piddington, H. 1981. *Land management for shooting and fishing.* (Occasional paper 13.) Cambridge: Department of Land Economy, University of Cambridge.

Potter, C. 1986. Investment styles and countryside change in lowland England. In: *Agriculture, people and policies,* edited by E. Cox, P. Lowe & M. Winter, 146-159. London: Allen and Unwin.

Potter, C. 1987. Processes of countryside change in lowland England. *Journal of Rural Studies,* **2**, 187-195.

Sinclair, G. 1983. *The upland landscapes study.* Martletwy: Environmental Information Services.

Social Research consultancy. 1982. *Demonstration farms project: monitoring and evaluation programme. Conclusions document.* Oxford: Social Research Consultancy.

Symes, D. & Appleton, J. 1986. Family goals and survival strategies: the role of kinship in an English upland farming community. *Sociologia Ruralis,* **26**, 345-363.

Tait, E. 1978. Factors affecting the usage of insecticides and fungicides on fruit and vegetable crops in Great Britain. *Journal of Environmental Management,* **6**, 143-151.

Tait, E. 1982. Farmers' attitudes and crop-protection decision making. In: *Decision making in the practice of crop protection,* edited by R. Austen, 43-52. (Monograph no. 25.). Croydon: British Crop Protection Council.

Tait, E. 1983. Pest control in brassica crops. *Advances in Applied Biology,* **8**, 121-188.

Tait, E. 1985. Rationality in pesticide use and the role of forecasting. In: *Rational pesticide use,* edited by K. Brent & R. Aitken, 225-238. Cambridge: Cambridge University Press.

Ward, N., Marsden, T. & Munton, R. 1990. Farmed landscape change: an analysis of trends in upland and lowland England. *Land Use Policy,* **7**, 291-302.

Westmacott, R. & Worthington, T. 1974. *New agricultural landscapes.* Cheltenham: Countryside Commission.

Westmacott, R. & Worthington, T. 1984. *Agricultural landscapes: a second look.* (CCP168.) Cheltenham: Countryside Commission.

Whatmore, S., Munton, R., Little, J. & Marsden, T. 1987a. Towards a typology of farm business in contemporary British agriculture. *Sociologia Ruralis,* **27**, 21-37.

Whatmore, S., Munton, R., Little, J. & Marsden, T. 1987b. Interpreting a relational typology of farm business in southern England. *Sociologia Ruralis,* **27**, 103-122.

Whatmore, S., Munton, R. & Marsden, T. 1990. The rural restructuring process: emerging divisions of agricultural property rights. *Regional Studies,* **24**, 235-245.

Whetham, E. 1981. *Agricultural economics in Britain, 1900-1940.* Oxford: Institute of Agricultural Economics.

Williams, W.M. 1963. *A West Country village, Ashworth: family, kinship and land.* London: Routledge.

Worthington, T. 1979. *The landscapes of institutional landowners: a study for the Countryside Commission.* Cheltenham: Countryside Commission.

Measurement and perception of change

Field monitoring of environmental change in the Environmentally Sensitive Areas

A J Hooper

Agricultural Development & Advisory Service, Ministry of Agriculture, Fisheries & Food, Room 208, Nobel House, 17 Smith Square, London SW1P 6JU

INTRODUCTION

The concern about changes which have occurred in the countryside, which is reflected in the theme of this Conference, is not new but has gathered pace in the past two decades. Attention has focused, in particular, on the role of agriculture as an agent of change. Although there are many other factors at play, the attention given to farming is not surprising, as 75% or more of the land is under some form of agricultural management, and agricultural policies have influenced land use from mountain to coastal marsh and from dry heath to wetland.

After several decades of unprecedented technical development and agricultural investment, which has generally seen an intensification of agricultural production methods, we have entered a new phase. Measures are being introduced to moderate agricultural output. There is increasing emphasis on the use of more environmentally friendly and sustainable farming methods, and on steering agriculture towards practices which ensure the survival and enhancement of an attractive, unpolluted countryside rich in wildlife.

Awareness of the impact that agriculture has been having on land use has partly been stimulated by recent surveys of land use change. There have been historical analyses of change in sample areas using archival aerial photography, such as the Monitoring Landscape Change project (Hunting Surveys & Consultants Ltd 1986) and the National Countryside Monitoring Scheme (Nature Conservancy Council 1987). Despite some of the statistical uncertainties about the results obtained in such surveys, they have served to indicate the types and magnitudes of change which have been occurring.

There has also been acceptance that there is a need to monitor change in a forward-looking sense. Such monitoring involves establishing a baseline record and repeating the surveys at intervals. This is the concept behind work undertaken by the Institute of Terrestrial Ecology (ITE) since the mid-1970s, using the land classification system (Bunce, Barr & Whittaker 1983), exemplified by the present Countryside Survey 1990 project (Bunce, Barr & Fuller 1992).

Appreciation of the need to monitor and assess the environmental impact of policies can be demonstrated by reference to a number of survey and evaluation programmes now being carried out by the Ministry of Agriculture, Fisheries and Food (MAFF). Foremost amongst these is the monitoring programme established in the Environmentally Sensitive Areas (ESAs) which were designated in 1987 and 1988. Such monitoring programmes present new technical and logistical challenges to those who are charged with detecting, measuring and appraising any changes which are occurring. This paper considers some of the practical issues and problems that have arisen in the ESA environmental monitoring programme which are of wider relevance to the monitoring of countryside change.

ENVIRONMENTALLY SENSITIVE AREAS

Environmentally Sensitive Areas were first designated in 1987, through the powers given to the Minister of Agriculture by the Agriculture Act 1986 (MAFF 1989). The aim of the ESA scheme is to conserve and enhance the wildlife, landscape and historic interest in areas at particular risk from changes to the more traditional farming practices which have helped to form or preserve their character. In these areas, farmers receive payments in return for farming in a less intensive way and maintaining the environmental interest. Nineteen ESAs have been designated in the UK, of which 12 are in England and Wales, as listed in Table 1.

Table 1. ESAs in England and Wales

Designated 1987	Designated 1988
Broads	Breckland
Cambrian Mountains	Lleyn Peninsula
Pennine Dales	South Downs (West)
South Downs (East)	North Peak
Somerset Levels and Moors	Shropshire Borders
West Penwith	Suffolk River Valleys
	Test Valley

The approach adopted in the ESAs can be illustrated by reference to the Pennine Dales ESA. The objectives of this ESA are to:

● maintain or improve the floristic richness of meadows and pastures;

● maintain or improve the landscape and ecological interest of wet pastures and rough grazings of the allotments (enclosed moorland);

● maintain and upgrade landscape and historic features such as dry stone walls, hedges, stone field barns, archaeological earthworks and semi-natural woodland.

Farmers who enter the scheme are required to follow a set of prescriptions concerning their management practices. The prescriptions vary according to the specific requirements of each ESA. In the Pennine Dales ESA, examples of the prescriptions can be summarised as follows.

Grassland – no ploughing, levelling or reseeding

      – no grazing seven weeks before cutting

      – earliest cutting date specified

      – no new drainage

      – no pesticides or lime

      – fertilizer, manure and herbicide use limited

Wall and hedges – must be maintained, if stockproof

Stone barns – must be maintained, if weatherproof

Historic features – must not be damaged

The concept of the scheme is, therefore, to provide protection to a wide area by operating a general set of prescriptions for all farms, rather than by formulating a different set of prescriptions for each farm. For following the management prescriptions, farmers are paid a specified amount per hectare. In some ESAs there are two sets of prescriptions, the second 'tier' placing greater management obligations on farmers, who then receive a higher rate of payment.

It is important in such schemes to assess the impact which is being achieved within the designated area. This importance was recognised from the outset, and Section 18, subsection 8 of the Agriculture Act 1986 requires that 'the Minister shall arrange for the effect on the area as a whole of the performance of the agreements to be kept under review and shall from time to time publish such information as he considers appropriate about these effects'. Both environmental and socio-economic evaluations are required, to establish whether the ESA objectives are being achieved and whether the scheme is providing value for money. The following section of this paper describes briefly the scope of the ESA environmental monitoring programme and some of the practical issues which have arisen during its development and operation.

ESA MONITORING

The environmental monitoring programme in the ESAs is designed to identify any significant changes to wildlife, landscape or historic features which occur after designation. There is an overall, national strategy for monitoring which includes some flexibility to allow adaptation according to the character and objectives of each ESA. The basic concept has been to establish a record of characteristics and features of importance at, or close to, the time of designation, to provide a baseline for comparison with later resurveys and against which any changes can be measured.

When devising the monitoring programme, it was important to keep in mind a number of key issues, many of which apply to other similar types of monitoring activity. These include:

● ensuring that the questions needing to be answered are anticipated, and that these, and the objectives for the monitoring are identified clearly and unambiguously;

● taking account of the type, scale and rate of changes which might occur;

● considering the timescale on which results are to be produced, which for ESAs means initial resurvey after only three or four years;

● in light of the above, and with the monitoring techniques available, assessing the feasibility of measuring the changes which might occur, within reasonable limits for manpower and other resources;

● taking care that the monitoring activity is carried out in such a way as to avoid antagonising and disrupting the farmers on whom the success of the scheme depends.

The task of devising and implementing the environmental monitoring programme for ESAs was given to the Agricultural Development and Advisory Service (ADAS), a part of MAFF. This has given rise to another important consideration, namely the need to ensure that the methods used are credible to those outside MAFF with an interest in the results obtained. In particular, much attention has been given to assessing the sensitivity and accuracy of the data being collected and analysed. Some aspects of this work are described later in this paper.

The approach in ESA monitoring has been to use a combination of census of the whole area for some surveys and a sampling strategy for others. The basic source of information for land cover and linear feature change at the general level is aerial photography. This is an efficient means for gathering information about the extent, quantity, presence or absence of features, and has the advantage that it provides a universal permanent record for reference at any time in the future. It is generally less suited for monitoring the quality or condition of features. Field survey, therefore, has a vital role in the monitoring process, including the checking of aerial

photographic interpretation. It is often assumed that field survey is more accurate than other methods, and surprisingly little has been published about the reliability or consistency of field methods in, for example, botanical survey. The ESA experience suggests that this aspect merits much closer attention when the results are to be used to describe the changes which are thought to be occurring.

When devising a monitoring programme, it is particularly important to consider the timescale over which it is to operate, relative to the rate at which the various changes are likely to occur. If the timescale is short, as is often the case with the evaluation of new schemes, then the monitoring needs to be sufficiently detailed and sensitive to detect small changes. Even then, it may be very difficult to be confident about the significance or reality of some detected changes. If, on the other hand, the monitoring is to continue over a long period, the challenge is to adopt procedures that can be repeated consistently by different personnel. With finite resources, this means there is often a balance to be struck between quantity and quality of data collected.

Field survey methods have been used in a variety of ways in ESA monitoring, but the remainder of this paper will concentrate on four elements of the work, namely:

- surveys of management practices
- accuracy assessments of aerial photographic interpretation
- landscape change assessment
- botanical survey

The botanical survey work will be considered in most detail, but the other elements will be described briefly.

SURVEYS OF MANAGEMENT PRACTICES

The fundamental aim of the ESA scheme is to influence and, if necessary, modify the management practices used by the farmers. Some changes will be immediate and visible, such as conversions between arable and grass. But, as noted above, it can take a considerable amount of time for other effects to become apparent. This is the case, for example, with the response of the meadow flora to reduced fertilizer inputs or controls on grass cutting dates, as applies in the Pennine Dales and some other ESAs.

An interim measure of scheme impact can be provided by monitoring the practices being used. The most objective way to collect information about these practices is by direct observation. This is practicable with activities such as grass cutting or hedge trimming because the visual evidence persists long enough to allow it to be surveyed. It is less feasible or objective with activities like fertilizer application, as the surveyor is not likely to be present when it happens and cannot reliably judge what has happened from the subsequent appearance of the land.

Cost usually prevents frequent aerial photographic surveys, but some practices, such as new drainage or reseeding, can persist long enough to be detectable. The practicalities are such that the data collected in this way provide useful intelligence rather than systematic survey data.

Grass cutting date surveys have been carried out in the Pennine Dales ESA for three years (MAFF 1991). For farmers in the scheme, dates are specified before which hay or silage must not be cut. Comparisons have been made between cutting dates on 141 fields under ESA agreement and 200 fields not entered into the scheme. The fields were selected randomly and were inspected at weekly intervals over the critical two-month period.

The results obtained from this work are summarised in Figure 1, which shows the cumulative percentage of fields that had been cut by particular dates. There is a clear difference in cutting dates between agreement and non-agreement fields, with an initial delaying effect on agreement fields. It can be seen, however, that once cutting is permitted, the grass cutting proceeded at a faster pace on agreement fields and that virtually all fields had been cut within six weeks. It remains to be seen what effect this timing has on the floristic quality of the meadows but, in the meantime, this basic type of field survey work is helping MAFF to understand how farmers are responding to the new prescriptions.

A similar approach has been adopted for assessing hedgerows in the Shropshire Borders ESA, where one of the aims is to encourage more positive hedgerow management. Observations are being made at randomly selected sites to record the extent and type of hedgerow treatments being carried out. Such information also contributes to the landscape evaluations which are made in ESA monitoring.

Other useful information about management practices has been obtained during botanical surveys, when background data are collected about

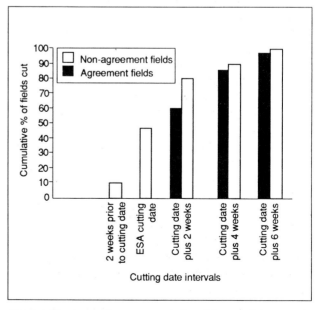

Figure 1. Meadow cutting progress in four dales; results averaged from three survey years (1988–90)

the management history of fields being sampled. Intelligence also accumulates from the ESA project officers, who are regularly visiting farms in their area. It is important to be aware, for example, of any shifts which are occurring between hay-making and silage-making or between hay-making and grazing that may be in response to ESA management prescriptions. Where necessary, this feedback has been followed up by systematic field surveys.

ASSESSING ACCURACY OF AERIAL PHOTOGRAPHIC INTERPRETATION

Aerial photography is an important tool in monitoring, having the advantage that complete cover of large areas can be obtained quickly and providing a permanent record which can be compared with photography obtained subsequently.

It is often assumed by the uninitiated that land cover or habitat can be mapped easily and very accurately using aerial photographs. It also seems that it should be straightforward to recognise and classify features such as hedges and walls. It is an unfortunate fact of life that it can be difficult to identify and delineate features of interest consistently, the degree of difficulty depending on a whole range of factors, such as time of year, land management, type of photography, and interpreter skill.

For many purposes, it may not matter if there are errors in the map produced; for example, when it is required simply to provide a general picture of an area. The situation can be very different in monitoring, where it is important to know, when comparing survey results at different dates, whether the recorded changes are real or the result of interpretation errors. For this reason, systematic procedures have been adopted in the ESA work for assessing the accuracy of land cover and linear feature maps derived from aerial photographic interpretation.

The accuracy assessments have been based on ground surveys in sample areas, selected using a systematic unaligned random sampling technique (Berry & Baker 1968). This technique ensures that the sample units are selected without bias, but distributed throughout the survey area. There has to be a compromise between number of sample areas, size of sample areas, statistical accuracy, and the affordable time and cost. Research into previous work on this subject (including Curran & Williamson 1985; Fitzpatrick-Lins 1981; Rosenfield, Fitzpatrick-Lins & Ling 1982; and Taylor 1989) led to a decision to set the minimum total sample area at 3% and the minimum number of sample units at 30. This level of sampling should meet the required limit of the 95% confidence interval for the more extensive of commonly occurring categories. It has to be accepted that the sample cannot be large enough to assess the rare categories.

The sample areas vary in size according to the size and configuration of the ESA, but are commonly one

kilometre square. A grid of suitable density is placed over each sample square, the intersections of which provide the sample points to be inspected on the ground. Thus, a 5 x 5 grid produces 25 sample points at 200 m spacing in a 1 km x 1 km square. A surveyor visits each point and assigns it to a class, using the same class descriptions as were used during aerial photographic interpretation. The results obtained on the ground are compared, point-by-point, with those on the map. The paired values are entered into a confusion matrix, from which various accuracy coefficients can be calculated. ADAS has adopted the Kappa coefficient for this purpose (Rosenfield & Fitzpatrick-Lins 1986).

The results from such analyses are invariably illuminating. They indicate the degree of agreement between the ground observations and the map being assessed, and are valuable for identifying those classes that have been identified inconsistently. Where appropriate, classes can be amalgamated or modified to produce classes which can be mapped with acceptable accuracy. The results in ESAs and elsewhere (Taylor 1989) indicate that final map accuracies of between 85% and 90% are the norm in this type of work.

A lesson learned in the ESA work has been not to assume that the field observation has always given the right answer. It might be more appropriate to regard the findings as indicating differences between the results, rather than absolute accuracies. Misclassification between closely related classes can occur in the field and, in marginal situations, different ground observers may opt for different classes. Sometimes the distinction is more easily and reliably made on the aerial photograph, especially where class boundaries are not clear when viewed at close range. Furthermore, it is not always easy to locate accurately a sample point on the ground, especially in semi-natural vegetation.

It follows, therefore, that the ground elements of accuracy assessments need to be planned and carried out with care and skill if the results are to be used meaningfully. Comprehensive descriptions of classes that can be clearly understood by the interpreter and ground surveyor are essential. Many apparent mapping errors have been found to be due to different interpretations of class definitions, rather than true photo-interpretation error. The ground surveyor needs to have stringent rules for locating sites and deciding what to record in marginal situations, such as where the sample point falls on a boundary between classes. The ground survey needs to be carried out as close as possible to the date of the aerial photography. It is axiomatic that the classes ultimately defined must be meaningful, in terms of the types of change being monitored.

The method described above is suitable for assessing separately the accuracy of baseline or resurvey maps. To date, no meaningful way has been developed for assessing the accuracy of the maps of change that are obtained after the baseline and

resurvey maps have been combined. Areas where change has been recorded can be visited and checked; the problem is to know the extent to which changes have occurred that have not been detected. This is an area of accuracy assessment which requires further development.

LANDSCAPE CHANGE ASSESSMENT

Changes which occur to the distribution of land cover types or the presence or absence of features such as hedges and walls are clearly very important for assessments of landscape change in an area, but they do not provide a complete picture. Some of the changes that affect the quality of a landscape are more subtle, local, and concerned as much or more with the quality and condition of the elements of the landscape. They often occur slowly rather than dramatically and, if they are to be identified over a short time period, require the use of ground survey techniques.

There have been few documented attempts to monitor these more qualitative changes on a large scale. As mentioned in the previous section, the classification of landscape elements on the ground can be subjective and inconsistent. This applies even more to the description of the condition or detailed characteristics of those elements, which must be done in a way that allows the area to be revisited at a later date and any changes that have occurred to be positively identified.

This problem has led ADAS to develop and use a method for monitoring based on ground photography in some ESAs. Each ESA has been divided into landscape types, the key characteristics of which have been described (MAFF 1990). Where ground survey methods are being used for landscape assessment, sample areas have been selected, stratified by landscape type. The technique involves photographing landscape features (commonly linear features like hedges and walls) at close to medium range from carefully selected viewpoints. The locations and view directions are carefully logged so that the site can be revisited and the photography repeated.

An advantage of this method is that a large number of sites can be visited and recorded quite rapidly by relatively unskilled staff. The interpretations of changes are made from the photographs by professional staff, who can then direct their attention to those sites where significant change is thought to have occurred and where their skills can be used to best effect. Whilst there is an unavoidable element of subjectivity in the interpretation of the data, it is small by comparison with relying entirely on a written historic record.

BOTANICAL MONITORING

In common with the landscape monitoring in ESAs, the botanical monitoring involves both full area survey and detailed ground-based studies. The overall distribution of some habitat types can be monitored using methods based on aerial photographic survey, but field methods are essential to assess the effect of ESA prescriptions on the botanical quality of habitats.

Detailed botanical survey is labour-intensive, and it has been necessary to target the work on key habitats. There is a substantial programme which covers grasslands, lowland heaths, moorland, woodland and ditches. In each case, a detailed protocol for the work has been set down and agreed with English Nature (MAFF 1987). The general approach is to select sites as objectively as possible on agreement and non-agreement land, so that floristic changes can be compared.

Some botanical change can be very rapid, for example as a result of cultivation, the use of herbicides, or maintenance of ditches. Some changes are large but temporary, as is often the case after moorland burning. But much of the change with which ESA management is concerned is slower and less obvious, and therefore presents problems for reliable detection. Changes occur naturally at this more subtle level, in response to factors such as weather conditions. They also occur in response to changes in farming practices, and a principal aim of the monitoring is therefore to detect any such changes.

Because the changes which might occur are often small in relation to the existing dynamics of the plant communities investigated, a great deal of emphasis has been placed from the outset on estimating the reliability of the data collected. The remainder of this section will describe some of the steps taken to provide quality control and gauge accuracy, with particular reference to grassland monitoring during the first three years of the scheme. It will concentrate on field procedures rather than questions of sample design.

The botanical observations are collected by visual estimates using quadrats. The key variables being measured are presence or absence of species and the abundance or cover of species. Recording is carried out by experienced field botanists working under the supervision of ADAS specialists.

A number of factors which do not have a causal relationship with the ESA but which can influence the results of the botanical monitoring have been identified. These include:

- quadrat location
- time of year
- climatic conditions
- observer performance

The effect that small changes in the location of a quadrat will have on the record obtained depends on the variability of the habitat. The effect may be negligible in a very uniform grass sward, but can be large if the vegetation is more variable. This factor could be overcome by increasing the sample size,

but with obvious consequences for manpower requirements in the longer term. A decision was therefore taken to remove or minimise this variable by fixing the location of quadrats, mostly by means of buried metal markers but sometimes by intersecting compass bearings.The ease and accuracy with which plant species can be recorded vary with the time of year. Early summer is generally considered to be the best time for grassland, although, for logistical reasons, the survey work may need to continue beyond this period. As an attempt to minimise the effect of time of year on the results, resurveys of sites have generally been timed to be within one week of the original survey date.

This care with timing provides only partial protection against seasonal variation, as weather and therefore plant growth vary from year to year. A particular problem encountered in the ESA work has been the occurrence of the two very warm and dry years, 1989 and 1990. Little can be done to avoid this problem other than to take the factor into account when interpreting the data.

A very important factor which has received a surprisingly modest amount of attention in the literature is observer performance. Being human, observers vary in the consistency, accuracy and precision with which they make their observations, and the results of some simple tests carried out as part of the ESA work are instructive. The investigations have sought to quantify performance in terms of observer bias and random error. Bias, which occurs, for example, if an observer tends usually to estimate high or low or to misclassify in a particular way, is the more serious problem and can invalidate results. There are, however, steps that can be taken to avoid or mitigate this problem, and these will be discussed.

The tests described were carried out during grassland monitoring in five ESAs (with two sets in one ESA) and involved skilled botanists working singly or in pairs. Although not exhaustive or fully replicated, the tests provide some indication of degree of variation to be expected in such surveys. It should be noted that, in this work, relative accuracy has been assessed by comparing the results obtained from different observers, rather than by comparison with a fixed or absolute standard.

The arrangement for the tests is indicated in Table 2.

Table 2. Observer performance tests

Survey area	No. of quadrats	Average no. of species per quadrat	Observers	Visits
A	4	24	2 pairs	1
B	5	29	4 pairs	1
C	3	36	2 pairs	1
C	5	36	2 pairs	2
D	6	14	3 pairs	2
E	6	19	3 singles	2

Various statistical procedures were applied to the data to test for bias between observers. They will not be described in detail, but the results have been summarised in Table 3. They indicate that, for species recognition, the level of bias was not significant when records were made by pairs of observers, but that there was significant bias for observers working alone. Estimates of species cover using Domin scores were, as might be expected, more susceptible to bias.

Table 3. Summary of results of tests for systematic observer bias

	Significance of bias for:	
Variable	paired observers	single observers
No. of species per quadrat	Not significant	Significant
Presence/absence of individual species	Not significant	Significant
Domin score	Significant (2 sites) Not significant (2 sites)	Significant

The results of the analysis of the amount of agreement between observers for the number of species in a quadrat are shown in Table 4.

Table 4. Percentage of agreement between observers for the number of species in a quadrat

Survey	Pair-wise comparisons	Complete agreement	Within 1 species	Within 2 species	Within 3 species
A	8	25%	75%	100%	-
B	60	10%	40%	50%	80%
C	6	33%	100%	-	-
D	72	25%	75%	92%	100%
E	72	11%	39%	61%	64%
A–D (mean)		23%	72%	85%	95%

The results indicate that, for quadrats averaging about 25 species per quadrat and ranging up to 36 species per quadrat, it is exceptional for there to be complete agreement between observers when attempting to identify all species present. Performance was much better for observers who worked in pairs (Surveys A to D), and such pairs could achieve agreement within two or three species most of the time.

Analysis was also carried out to assess the variation which occurred in the identification of species if observers repeated their observations for a quadrat. The results are shown in Table 5. Once again, it is unusual for there to be complete agreement, but encouraging that paired observers (Surveys C and D) came within one or two species of their original list.

Table 5. Variation in number of species recorded by observers during two visits to a quadrat

Survey	Pair-wise comparisons	Complete agreement	Within 1 species	Within 2 species	Within 3 species
C	10	40%	100%	-	-
D	36	11%	78%	100%	-
E	36	11%	39%	72%	78%
C–D (mean)		26%	89%	100%	100%

The data were also analysed to assess the extent to which the recorded presence or absence of individual species is independent of the observer used, as shown in Table 6.

Table 6. Agreement between observers in the recorded presence or absence of individual species

Survey	Pair-wise comparisons	Agreement (both record present)
A	216	78%
B	1992	85%
C	220	98%
D	1206	86%
E	1848	63%
A–D (mean)		87%

The final analysis for this particular set of data examines the degree of agreement between observers for cover estimates made using Domin scores (Table 7). The average results achieved by observers working in pairs indicate that, although there was complete agreement only half of the time, there was agreement within one score 85% of the time and virtually all observations were within three scores.

Table 7. Agreement between observers – Domin scores

Survey	Pair-wise comparisons	Complete agreement	Within 1 Domin	Within 2 Domin	Within 3 Domin
A	216	28%	65%	91%	95%
B	1992	44%	87%	96%	100%
C	220	81%	100%	-	-
D	1206	55%	89%	95%	98%
E	1848	29%	64%	85%	95%
A-D (mean)		52%	85%	95%	98%

A number of useful conclusions about our ability to collect botanical data can be drawn from these analyses and from other experience gained in the ESA surveys. There are very clear advantages for accuracy in using pairs of observers, as there is a chance that what one observer misses, the other will see. Accuracy and consistency are significantly worse if observers work alone.

Observer bias can be kept within acceptable limits, but rigorous quality control measures are essential throughout the survey. These start by ensuring that the surveys are carried out by experienced field botanists of proven competence. Training and calibration tests are essential before survey starts, and discipline should be maintained by means of regular accuracy assessments.

The pairings should be changed regularly, preferably at least daily. In a long field campaign, the welfare of the surveyors should be considered, ensuring that they receive proper logistical and moral support.

Given these measures, a reasonable level of agreement between observers can be attained (results in the order of 80% to 90% are good), but the available, less resource-intensive field methods are relatively imprecise; this fact should be remembered when the data are analysed. There are clear indications that indices of change based on presence or absence of species, such as species richness, are less susceptible to observer bias than indices that incorporate cover estimates.

CONCLUSIONS

This description of ESA environmental monitoring has highlighted some ways in which field survey has been used and some of the problems that have been encountered. In other circumstances, these problems may not have been so significant. The need in this case to be able to detect and report objectively the changes which might be occurring, on a relatively short timescale, has provided a strong incentive to address the issue of data quality control. The conclusion is that such measures are essential, despite the fact that they absorb resources that could otherwise have been used to increase the amount of data collected. The alternatives, both unsatisfactory, may be to draw wrong conclusions or to have to discard data as unusable.

The work has also revealed that there are significant gaps in knowledge about methods for assessing the accuracy of change detection and measurement in the land use field. Given the increasing interest in environmental monitoring, this is a subject which seems to merit further research.

ACKNOWLEDGEMENTS

This paper has drawn heavily on the work and advice of many colleagues in ADAS and a valuable dialogue over many years with researchers in the Institute of Terrestrial Ecology. I am particularly indebted to Simon Poulton of ADAS for supplying the botanical data, and to David Askey, Robert Blakeman, Ian Condliffe, Michael Silverwood, Ann Tarran and Mark Watson, also in ADAS, for their assistance.

REFERENCES

Berry, B.J.L. & Baker, A.M. 1968. Geographic sampling in spatial analysis. In: *Spatial analysis,* edited by B.J.L. Berry & D.F. Marble, 91-100. Englewood-Cliffs, NJ: Prentice-Hall.

Bunce, R.G.H., Barr, C.J. & Whittaker, H.A. 1983. A stratification system for ecological sampling. In: *Ecological mapping from ground, air and space,* edited by R.M. Fuller, 39-46. (ITE symposium no. 10.) Cambridge: Institute of Terrestrial Ecology.

Bunce, R.G.H., Barr, C.J. & Fuller, R.M. 1992. Integration of methods for detecting land use change, with special reference to Countryside Survey 1990. In: *Land use change: the causes and consequences,* edited by M.C. Whitby, 69-78. (ITE symposium no. 27.) London: HMSO.

Curran, P.J. & Williamson, H.D. 1985. The accuracy of ground data used in remote sensing investigations. *International Journal of Remote Sensing,* **6**, 1637-1651.

Fitzpatrick-Lins, K. 1981. Comparison sampling procedures and data analysis for a land-use and land cover map. *Photogrammetric Engineering and Remote Sensing,* **3**, 343-351.

Hunting Surveys and Consultants Ltd. 1986. *Monitoring landscape change.* Borehamwood: Hunting Surveys and Consultants Ltd.

Ministry of Agriculture, Fisheries and Food. 1987. *Environmentally Sensitive Areas. Biological survey and monitoring in England and Wales, national guidelines.* (MAFF internal document.) London: MAFF.

Ministry of Agriculture, Fisheries and Food. 1989. *Environmentally Sensitive Areas.* (First report.) London: HMSO.

Ministry of Agriculture, Fisheries and Food. 1990. *Environmentally Sensitive Areas. Pennine Dales. Landscape assessment for monitoring.* London: MAFF.

Ministry of Agriculture, Fisheries and Food. 1991. *The Pennine Dales Environmentally Sensitive Area,* 13-16. (Report of monitoring.) London: HMSO.

Nature Conservancy Council. 1987. *Changes in the Cumbrian countryside.* (Research and survey in nature conservation no. 6.) Peterborough: NCC.

Rosenfield, GH., Fitzpatrick-Lins, K. & Ling, H.S. 1982. Sampling for thematic map accuracy testing. *Photogrammetric Engineering and Remote Sensing,* **48**, 131-137.

Rosenfield, G.H. & Fitzpatrick-Lins, K. 1986. A co-efficient of agreement as a measure of thematic classification accuracy. *Photogrammetric Engineering and Remote Sensing,* **52**, 223-227.

Taylor, J. 1989. *Monitoring landscape changes in the National Parks.* (First interim report.) Cheltenham: Countryside Commission.

Remote sensing and the detection of change

P M Mather

Dept of Geography, University of Nottingham, Nottingham NG7 2RD

INTRODUCTION

One of the immutable properties of ecosystems is that they are subject to change, whether natural or human-induced. Changes in the characteristics of ecosystems have an effect on climate, which in turn influences land use. A major challenge facing ecologists and biogeographers in the 1990s is to determine where and how land use patterns are changing, in which direction, and at what rate. Terrestrial ecosystems vary in scale from the global to the local, and it is at global, continental and regional scales that monitoring and detection of change encounter difficulties if conventional methods of observation and recording are used. It is at these scales that observations of the earth from space become an important source of information. The need for consistent, large-scale, and temporally frequent coverage of the earth's surface features to provide input to global climate models has led to significant national and international investment in earth-observing systems that are planned for the coming decade. Europe's first earth resources satellite (ERS-1) is to be launched in 1991, with a successor planned for 1994. The International Geosphere–Biosphere Programme's (IGBP) study of global change (1990) will depend on remotely sensed sources for much of its data input. These sources will include the international Columbus programme/earth observing system (EOS) which will, in the later part of the 1990s, provide multi-sensor systems carried on two polar-orbiting satellites. The data acquired from these systems will have a range of resolutions, both spatial and temporal, that will suit a variety of applications.

> 'The IGBP needs space-derived data for three overriding reasons. These are (i) document precisely global-scale changes in key variables to assess the way the planet as a whole is evolving with time; (ii) measure the long-term trends in the forcing functions of global change; and (iii) simultaneous measurements of several parameters to study the interactive forces which regulate the earth system' (IGBP 1990, pp10–13).

There is, therefore, little doubt that earth observation data, whether from international programmes such as Columbus/EOS and ERS or from existing systems such as Landsat, the satellite pour l'observation de la terre (SPOT) and the marine observation satellite

(MOS), will become widely available during the 1990s, offering regional and global coverage at a variety of spatial resolutions (Townshend & Justice 1988). The decision of the US Government to supply EOS data at low cost to scientists throughout the world will, no doubt, add to their appeal. These data will be used in a variety of applications, to observe changes in such properties as land and sea ice extent, cloud patterns and dynamics, near-surface winds, surface topography, sea surface temperatures, expansion of desert areas, and vegetation cover.

Data acquisition is but the first step toward the solution of problems such as the monitoring of change. Significant administrative, technical and financial problems must be overcome if useful data are to be made available to the research and user communities in an organised and timely way. In the first part of this paper, the nature of different types of image data derived from space-borne sensors are described (including those operating in the solar, thermal and microwave wavelengths of the electro-magnetic spectrum), together with a survey of the technical problems that must be resolved if such data are to be used routinely in land cover mapping. The second part of the paper is concerned with the use of remotely sensed data to extract land cover information, and to monitor change at scales ranging from the regional to the global, stressing the need for data integration within an information system.

PRINCIPLES OF REMOTE SENSING OF VEGETATION

Types of image data

Multispectral remotely sensed images are made up of measures of spectral radiance collected over an area of interest. Sensors operate in different parts of the electro-magnetic spectrum, which can conveniently be divided into the solar (0.4–2.5 µm), thermal (3–100 µm), and microwave regions (centimetre wavelengths). Imaging sensors operating in the *solar spectral region* collect reflected solar radiation. The nature and geographical distribution of earth surface materials can be inferred from the distribution of reflected energy in this spectral region. Most remote sensing studies of vegetation to date have employed images collected in the 0.5–1.1 µm region, covering the visible and short-wave infra-red regions of the

spectrum, which contains important information concerning the type of vegetation, its stage of development, extent of stress, biomass, areal cover, and canopy architecture. Other information is also present in the signal, which may be contaminated by soil reflectance as well as being affected by the atmosphere. The principal satellite systems carrying imaging sensors which operate in the solar region of the electro-magnetic spectrum are the US Landsat and the National Oceanographic and Atmospheric Administration (NOAA) satellites, the French SPOT, and Japan's MOS-1. The characteristics of these sensors are summarised in Table 1.

The polar platforms, the first of which has a launch date of 1998, are intended to carry a range of imaging and profiling instruments which will produce data that can be used synergistically. Three such instruments are of interest in land cover monitoring: the high-resolution imaging spectrometer (HIRIS), the moderate-resolution imaging spectrometer (MODIS), and the multi-angle imaging spectro-radiometer (MISR).

The HIRIS instrument (National Aeronautics and Space Administration (NASA) 1987a) is intended to acquire simultaneous images in 192 spectral bands in the wavelengths of the solar spectrum (0.4–2.5 µm) at a sampling interval of 10 nm. The ground resolution will be 30 m over a 30 km swath, and the instrument will be capable of being pointed up to +60/–30° down-track and ±24° across-track. This will permit the study of bidirectional reflectance properties and variations in atmospheric attenuation with viewing angle. The

ability to point the sensor will allow multiple viewing opportunities over the 16-day repeat cycle. High spectral resolution imagery will make possible the study of biochemical processes in, and properties of, vegetation canopies. A prototype instrument (airborne visible/infra-red imaging spectrometer, or AVIRIS) has already been flown, and first results reported (Vane 1987). HIRIS has been selected to fly on the second or third US polar platform. MODIS and MISR will form part of the first polar platform pay load. Like HIRIS, MODIS and MISR are pointable sensors whose features are summarised in Table 2.

Sensors operating in the *thermal region* of the spectrum measure emitted terrestrial heat. Only the spectral regions around 3.5–4 µm and 8–14 µm are useful for surface imaging because of atmospheric absorption. Profiling instruments carried on-board satellites use the 4–8 µm and 14–100 µm wavebands to acquire information about the temperature and humidity of the atmosphere, which is used in weather forecasting and climate models. Thermal infra-red data are, in theory, capable of providing information about the ability of the surface to support evaporation and transpiration which can be inferred from surface temperature and from the day–night temperature range. However, remote sensing of vegetation at these wavelengths is not currently operational, though research is ongoing (Price 1989). For example, Becker and Li (1991) describe the derivation of a vegetation index using coarse-resolution thermal imagery from the advanced very high-resolution radiometer (AVHRR) (Table 1). Thermal infra-red

Table 1. Characteristics of imaging sensors operating in the solar and thermal regions of the spectrum

Platform	Sensor	Wavebands (µm)	Repeat cycle	Overpass time	Spatial resolution
NOAA	AVHRR	0.58 – 0.68 0.725 – 1.1 3.55 – 3.93 10.5 – 11.5 11.5 – 12.5	12 hours	1430/0230 1930/0730	1.1 km
Landsat	MSS	0.50 – 0.60 0.60 – 0.70 0.70 – 0.80 0.80 – 1.10	16 days	0945	80 m
Landsat	TM	0.45 – 0.52 0.52 – 0.60 0.63 – 0.69 0.76 – 0.90 1.55 – 1.75 2.08 – 2.35 10.4 – 12.5	16 days	0945	30 m
SPOT	HRV (MSS)	0.50 – 0.59 0.62 – 0.66 0.77 – 0.87	26 days	1030	20 m
	HRV (PAN)	0.51 – 0.73			10 m
MOS-1	MESSR	0.51 – 0.59 0.61 – 0.69 0.72 – 0.80 0.80 – 1.10	17 days		50 m
	VTIR	0.50 – 0.70 6.00 – 7.00 10.5 – 11.5 11.5 – 12.5			900 m 2.7 km

Table 2. Polar platform instruments

The US EOS and European Columbus programmes will include a series of polar-orbiting earth satellites (polar platforms), one set to be provided by the USA and others by the European and Japanese Space Agencies. Two satellites will be in orbit at any one time; one will have an equatorial crossing time of 1000 and the other of 1330. Each platform will carry a suite of instruments giving a range of spectral, temporal, and radiometric resolutions. The first of the polar platforms, called EOS-A, is planned for launch in 1998. The imaging instruments to be carried on EOS-A were announced in January 1991. They are described below.

MODIS	Moderate-resolution imaging spectrometer. MODIS is an imaging spectrometer for the measurent of biological and physical processes. MODIS-T has an off-nadir tilt capability
	MODIS-T: 0.4–1.04 µm spectral range, 64 bands, 1 km resolution across a 1800 km swath.
	MODIS-N: 0.47–2.13 µm, 3.47–4.56 µm and 6.7–14.2 µm spectral ranges, in 40 bands, with 250 µm, 500 µm or 1 km pixel size across a 1800 km swath.
ASTER	Advanced spaceborne thermal emission and reflection, formerly the intermediate thermal infra-red radiometer. This is a Japanese instrument covering the spectral ranges 0.85–0.92 µm, 1.60–2.26 µm and 3.53–11.7 µm at a resolution of 15 m (near- and short-wavelength infra-red) and 90 m (thermal infra-red)
MISR	Multi-angle imaging spectro-radiometer. This instrument will obtain global observations of the directional characteristics of reflected light. This information is needed for studying the bidirectional reflectance of vegetation. The instrument consists of four identical CCD cameras pointing at viewing angles of 25.8°, 45.6°, 60° and 72.5° respectively, looking both fore and aft, giving eight different viewing directions at two different sun azimuth angles. Images will be acquired simultaneously in four narrow spectral bands centred at 440, 550, 670 and 860 nm

The high-resolution imaging spectrometer (HIRIS) will be carried on-board the second and third polar platforms. HIRIS will cover the spectral ranges of 0.4–1.0 µm and 1.0–2.5 µm in about 200 bands at a resolution of 30 m. It has along-track and across-track pointing capability.

Other instruments currently being considered for the US and European polar platforms include the following.

EOS-SAR	This instrument is a three-frequency (l, C and X-band) multi-polarisation sensor, with selectable incidence angles of 15° to 55°. Its spatial resolution can be varied from 30 m (30–50 km swath), 50–100 m (100–200 km swath), and 200–500 m resolution (up to 700 km swath)
MERIS	Medium resolution imaging spectrometer with selectable number of narrow (5–20 nm) spectral bands in the range 0.40–1.05 µm. The swath width of 1500 km and global coverage will be provided every two days at a spatial resolution of 250–500 m
POLDER	Polarisation and directionality of reflectances. This narrow-band six-channel instrument is designed to measure the bidirectional properties of ocean and land targets in six spectral bands spanning the range 0.435–0.880 µm at viewing angles of up to 50° both along- and across-track
AMI	Active microwave instrumentation will be a development of the ERS-1 SAR. It will operate in the C band and will have selectable look angles of 23° and 30–45°. The EOS-SAR will provide similar information

remote sensing is, like remote sensing in the solar region of the spectrum, limited by cloud cover. However, unlike remote sensing in the solar region, thermal infra-red sensing can be carried out at night. Current satellite-borne thermal infra-red sensors are AVHRR, the thematic mapper (TM) and VTIR. An advanced space-borne thermal emission and reflection instrument (ASTER) is to be carried on the first polar platform mission.

An imaging *microwave* (radar) sensor was carried by Seasat in 1978; it operated for less than 100 days and produced useful images, particularly of oceanic phenomena. Since that date, no civilian imaging radar instrument has been carried into orbit, apart from the shuttle imaging radar in the mid-1980s. The European Space Agency's (ESA) ERS-1 satellite, which is scheduled for launch in May 1991, will carry a synthetic aperture radar similar to Seasat's, which operated at a wavelength of 23.5 cm and generated images with a spatial resolution of 25 m. The Japanese JERS-1 and the Canadian Radarsat are intended to carry similar instruments, and synthetic aperture radars (SARS) will be part of the pay load of later polar platform missions. Microwave imaging sensors are active devices in that they provide their own source of energy, rather than passively measuring energy that is

reflected or emitted by the target. Their operation is thus not limited by the availability of an external source of energy, neither are they sensitive to atmospheric conditions. Microwaves provide information about surface physical conditions (topography, morphology and roughness) and dielectric properties. Important parameters of a microwave sensor system are the polarisation of the incident and back-scattered radiation, the frequency of the incident wave, and its angle of incidence (Elachi 1987). The SAR carried by ERS-1 will have an incidence angle that is optimised for ocean rather than land applications, but – like its Seasat predecessor – it will still produce valuable information for terrestrial scientists. The principal biophysical parameters that SAR will be capable of providing include canopy water content, canopy structure, and soil moisture. Multispectral SARs, such as EOS-SAR (Table 2), will be capable of providing greater detail. The applications of microwave remote sensing to vegetation studies are considered in European Space Agency (ESA 1985) and NASA (1987b).

Although sensors operating in the solar, thermal and microwave regions of the spectrum have been described separately, it should be borne in mind that the images they produce can often be combined

beneficially, so that information concerning colour, temperature and texture are viewed simultaneously. Rast, Jaskolla and Arnason (1991) give an example of the combined use of data collected in the optical and microwave spectral regions. Several satellite systems, notably the Landsat TM and the NOAA AVHRR, collect image data in both the solar and thermal infra-red regions, so that images at these wavelengths from a single sensor system can be merged without difficulty.

Problems in the use of remotely sensed images
Overview

It has already been noted that remote sensing at solar and thermal wavelengths is weather-dependent. Cloud cover limits remote sensing of many humid temperate and tropical regions of the world (see Legg 1991 for a study of Landsat multispectral scanner (MSS) image availability over the UK, 1976–88). The advent of sensors with the capability to look off nadir helps to alleviate the problem, which is most severe for platforms with a long orbital repeat cycle. Landsat, for example, returns regularly every 16 days, giving approximately 23 viewing opportunities per year. Nevertheless, in some regions, for example the north of Scotland, only one or two cloud-free images are serendipitously available over a period of several years. Microwave sensors are weather-independent, and are also capable of operating at night, so that a clear image of a target area will be obtained on every overpass. Experience in the interpretation and use of microwave images is, however, not as great as that which has been built over almost 20 years with images collected in the solar region of the spectrum. As the number of remote sensing platforms of different types increases, and with the advent of EOS, it is expected that a greater number of images of a target area will be acquired for a given time period. Nevertheless, significant research problems remain. These problems are considered in more detail in this section. They relate to the need for sensor calibration, correction for atmospheric, illumination and viewing geometry effects and georeferencing of imagery. A valuable recent critique is provided by Duggin and Robinove (1990).

Radiometric calibration

Passive image sensors carried by orbiting satellites collect upwelling radiance from the earth's surface in one or more spectral bands for each of a large number of areas (or pixels) on the ground or sea surface. The output of the sensor is a voltage, Q, which is proportional to the spectral radiance, L_λ; the relationship between input and output is approximately linear so that Q is a function of L_λ and the spectral responsivity of the sensor. Asrar (1989 pp6–7) shows that this relationship is, in fact, more complex, that Q is a function of several variables, and that, in order to compute the mean radiance for a given spectral band, the gain and offset of the sensor must be known as well as the band pass limits. The gain and offset of the sensor are found initially by pre-launch calibration, and are estimated over the effective lifetime of the instrument by in-flight calibration or by means of measurements made over known targets. Details of pre-launch calibration are normally given in instrument manuals, and in-flight calibration results are stored in the header records of data tapes. The data provided on the tapes are integer counts derived from analogue to digital conversion of the voltages output by the sensor. For example, in the first three spectral bands of Landsat's MSS, which cover the spectral range 0.5–0.6 μm, 0.6–0.7 μm and 0.7–0.8 μm respectively, the output voltages are passed through non-linear amplifiers and and then quantised on a 6-bit (0–63) scale. These values are transmitted to the ground station, where the counts are linearly decompressed on to a 0–127 scale, using look-up tables derived from a knowledge of the characteristics of the non-linear amplifier and the gain and offset of the system (Freden & Gordon 1983). Thus, it is difficult to convert from counts in the range 0–127 back to radiances. This point is of considerable significance in the context of change measurement, for any particular count cannot represent a constant spectral radiance from one time to another as the sensor gains and offsets change. If such comparisons cannot be made, then change detection becomes impossible. Furthermore, counts derived from different sensor systems or from different bands of the same image set cannot be compared quantitatively, unless they are converted to equivalent spectral radiance values. Radiometric properties of US-processed Landsat MSS data are considered in detail by Markham and Barker (1987).

Radiometric calibration of image data is an essential first step in studies of change. Data derived from different sensors, or from the same sensor at different times, are supplied in terms of quantised counts, which must be converted to physical values ($wm^{-1} sr^{-1}$) if they are to be used in modelling or in studies of change. This is necessary in order to ensure consistency and comparability over time (Singh 1989).

Atmospheric correction

Solar radiation incident upon the earth's surface must pass through the atmosphere. Equally, reflected or emitted radiation passes through and is, in turn, spectrally modified by its interactions with the atmosphere. It was noted earlier that the nature of the ground surface cover was inferred from the changes in the spectrum produced by the interaction between incident solar irradiation and surface cover materials; hence it is important to realise that atmospheric interactions also modify the signal. This may not be an important consideration if relative differences between ground surface materials at one point in time are the object of study. However, if images are to be compared over time and inferences made concerning changes in the type, vigour or other property of vegetation, then such changes cannot be reliably confirmed if the effects of the atmosphere are not taken into consideration. Atmospheric constituents (gases and aerosols) scatter and absorb solar radiation. Kaufman (1989) notes the following effects produced

by interaction with the atmosphere:

- variation in the severity of the effect with wavelength, which may affect discrimination between stressed and unstressed vegetation;

- alteration in the spatial distribution of reflected radiation, affecting the spatial resolution of the system;

- changes in apparent brightness of a target, affecting measurements of albedo and reflection;

- generation of spatial variations in the apparent surface reflection through the effect of subpixel-sized clouds.

Several methods for the atmospheric correction of remotely sensed images have been reported in the literature; none is universally applicable. As Kaufman (1989, p402) notes:

'The basic philosophy of the atmospheric correction is to obtain information about the atmospheric optical characteristics and to apply this information in a correction scheme. One way to describe this information is by the aerosol optical thickness, phase function, the single-scattering albedo, and the gaseous absorption. For high-resolution imagery, some information about the aerosol vertical profile is also required. The problems in the atmospheric correction are due to the difficulty in determining these characteristics'.

In the absence of information about the state of the atmosphere at the time of imaging, some authors, eg United States Geological Survey (1979), use the minimum value in the image histogram as a global estimate of 'haze' or atmospheric path radiance. This value is subtracted from all pixel values in the image. It is acceptable only if the target producing this minimum reflectance is constant from image to image. A similar method, based on the very low surface reflectance of deep clear water in the red wavelengths of the visible spectrum, has been found to be acceptably accurate over oceans (Gordon *et al.* 1983). A more comprehensive approach to the problem of atmospheric correction is described by Hill and Sturm (1988), which uses the histogram minimum method to estimate atmospheric path radiance, and obtains estimates of optical depth for each spectral band from aerosol phase functions describing the scattering characteristics of various aerosol types. Corrections for absorption by ozone, carbon dioxide and water vapour are derived from the LOWTRAN model (Kneizys *et al.* 1983). An approximation to the inherent target reflectance can then be derived for each spectral band, as described by Megier, Hill and Kohl (1991). Until a reliable and generally applicable method of correcting images from the solar and thermal wavebands is developed, then change detection using remote sensing will remain qualitative rather than quantitative.

Correction for illumination and viewing geometry

Table 1 lists remote sensing systems which are currently operational. Each platform has its own orbital characteristics, so that images from Landsat and SPOT, for example, are collected at 0945 and 1030 respectively. The overpass times of the two NOAA satellites, which carry the AVHRR sensor, are 0230, 0730, 1430, and 1930. For daytime passes of these satellites, solar elevation angles will vary depending on the time of day. The sensors themselves have differing optical characteristics. Landsat TM and MSS sensors have a narrow nadir-pointing field of view, whereas AVHRR has a field of view of 57°. SPOT's high-resolution visible (HRV) sensor is pointable, and can be tilted up to ±23° from nadir. When these variations are considered in conjunction with characteristics such as the slope and aspect of the land area being surveyed, it is clear that the different sensors are not measuring upwelling radiance under the same conditions. Even if the effects of topographic shadow are excluded from consideration, and even if the land cover type is constant, variations in illumination and viewing angle, together with variations in surface slope and aspect, still lead to substantial differences in the levels of recorded radiance. Reflection of electro-magnetic radiation from plant canopies is direction-dependent; both viewing and illumination directions must be considered, hence the term 'hemispherical bidirectional reflectance factor' (BDRF). This is the distribution, over the hemisphere, of the ratio of radiant exitance to irradiance for a discrete set of viewing and illumination angles. In the case of a specular reflector, angles of incidence and reflection or scattering are equal, whereas for a Lambertian scatterer the distribution of radiant exitance is isotropic. Vegetated surfaces may for convenience be treated as Lambertian, but in practice this is rarely, if ever, the case. Hence, correction of image data is needed to take account of variations in solar zenith angle (for repetitive viewing from the same platform), view angle variations both within an image and from one image to another, and topographic effects (Baker *et al.* 1991).

Kowalik and Marsh (1982) describe a method for adjusting image pixel values for variations in solar zenith angle. They find a linear relationship between pixel value and the cosine of the zenith angle. Royer, Vincent and Bonn (1985) use data from an airborne system with a ±37° scan angle range; they report a significant variation in detected radiance with view angle. These variations are not symmetrical about the nadir and are affected by solar zenith angle. Holben and Justice (1980) consider the effects of ground surface slope angle and aspect variations. The magnitude of the effects was found to depend on the solar zenith angle, the orientation of the slope, and its inclination. They conclude that '... the topographic effect on (Landsat) data can produce a wide variation in the radiances associated with a given cover type' (Holben & Justice 1980, p1199). It is clear that

comparisons between images acquired at different times must be corrected for solar illumination effects, while corrections should be applied to images collected by different sensors to take account of view angle and slope effects, if realistic estimates of change over time are to be made. This point is taken up again in the next section.

Georeferencing

In geographical studies, the location of an object, both absolute and relative, is generally as important as the properties of that object. A knowledge of the location on the earth's surface of a given pixel is needed, if the purpose of the study is to measure changes in the properties inferred from the multispectral pixel values at that location. Remotely sensed images are not maps; their co-ordinate system (the scan line and row, using matrix conventions) has, in general, only a weak correspondence with latitude and longitude. Given a knowledge of the orbital geometry of the platform and of the time of imaging, it is possible to compute the latitude and longitude of any pixel in the image, to a level of precision depending on the completeness of knowledge and the spatial resolution of the sensor. Precise orbital positions are not available for the current generation of polar-orbiting satellites, though the orbit of the NOAA satellites is known sufficiently well for the approximate calculation of the latitude and longitude of the rather coarse AVHRR pixels, which range in size from 1.1 km at nadir to 5 km or more at the edge of the image. Even so, accurate georeferencing of AVHRR images requires the use of methods which relate points on the image to points with a known location on the earth's surface. These latter points are known as ground (or geodetic) control points, and their positions can be found either from maps or from the use of satellite position fixing systems, such as global positioning systems (GPS). The same technique is used to perform geometrical transformations on medium-resolution images, such as those acquired by Landsat and SPOT; it is described by Mather (1987).

The motivation for georeferencing in studies of land use change lies primarily in the need to relate image pixel values referring to the same ground surface position but collected at different points in time, so that – after adjustment for sensor calibration, atmospheric effects, and viewing/illumination geometry variations – changes in earth surface materials can be inferred from changes in pixel values. There is, however, a second justification. Remotely sensed data alone rarely provide the full answer to a given question. Field data are needed in order to correlate image pixel values and cover materials, and precise location of the field data sampling points is a necessity. Furthermore, the information contained in remotely sensed images can most beneficially be extracted if it is combined with other types of spatial data, such as soil maps, vegetation and land cover maps. This combination is normally carried out within the context of a geographical information system (GIS).

A further link between remote sensing and GIS is demonstrated by the use of digital elevation models (DEMs) in the correction of satellite data for illumination effects, which were described earlier. The amount of reflected energy from a target that is received by the sensor is dependent upon the angles of view and illumination, as well as on the spectral reflectance properties of the target. Solar zenith and azimuth angles at the time of imaging can be obtained from the header information on the data tape, while details of ground slope and aspect are derivable from the DEM. Unless a first-order correction for illumination variations is made, then (i) image data for the same pixel will not be comparable over time, and (ii) similar land covers at different pixel locations in an image of a hilly area will have different apparent reflectances. For southern Britain, DEMs at a scale of 1:50 000 can be purchased from the Ordnance Survey. Cover for the rest of Britain will be released over the next year or so.

THE MEASUREMENT OF CHANGE

The measurement of change requires accurate observations of the conditions of interest at two or more points in time. Change may be natural (such as seasonal variations in vigour) or it may be exogenously induced through alterations in climate. In order accurately to extract the properties of land cover from remotely sensed images, the corrections detailed above must have been carried out, at least to a first approximation, in order to ensure that extraneous information incorporated in the signal collected by the sensor is removed, and to place the data on a common geographical base. Once that is done, the multispectral image set can be processed to extract land cover information. The most obvious way of determining the location, nature and extent of the change is to obtain thematic maps from the multispectral imagery collected at different times, and to subtract these image maps in a pair-wise fashion. An alternative is the production of ratio images which correlate with properties of the vegetation, and the use of image subtraction techniques to detect change. Alternative methods use two or more georeferenced image sets simultaneously; thus, a thematic map can be derived from multitemporal imagery to delineate static categories (forest, water, grassland) and categories representing change. The use of principal component analysis (PCA) is one method which can isolate a dimension of change. Finally, image transforms which extract linear combinations of selected spectral bands correlating with properties such as 'greenness' and 'wetness' can be applied to each image set, and the resulting indices plotted for particular sites. Nelson (1983) and Singh (1989) provide further details of the methods described in the following sections.

Methods based on image subtraction

The subtraction of digital images forms the basis of most approaches to the measurement of change using

remotely sensed data. Three types of derived image are considered in this section:

- classified images showing the distribution of the various categories of land cover,
- ratio images which correlate with vegetation vigour, and
- the products of orthogonal image transforms which relate to properties of greenness and wetness.

It is beyond the scope of this paper to provide a detailed survey of supervised and unsupervised methods of image classification (Mather 1987). In general terms, the procedure involves three steps. First, regions on the image corresponding to known land cover types are identified; these are termed training areas. Second, a decision rule (usually of a statistical nature) is applied to give a correlation or probability measure which associates each pixel in the image with every training area. The pixel is allocated to that class with which it has the highest correlation or probability of belonging. Third, the accuracy of the classification is evaluated against further field data. One drawback of this method is that many land cover classes will change in terms of their spectral reference properties, if imagery from different seasons of the year is used to generate the classified image. It has been found (Fuller & Parsell 1990) that the use of summer and autumn images together gives improved accuracy. However, if raster-format thematic maps can be generated for two or more points in time, they can be subtracted on a pixel-by-pixel basis as each land cover class is allocated a digital identifier. 'No change' is indicated by a zero result. Pixels that have changed class between the times of imaging can readily be detected, and their distribution can be mapped.

A similar procedure can be employed with ratio images. The spectral response of vegetation in the visible and near-infra-red regions of the electro-magnetic spectrum is well known, and differences between vegetation types, as well as changes in vigour or leaf area index, correlate with changes in the shape of the reflectance spectrum. Clark, Steven and Malthus (1991) discuss the ratios, which can be considered as 'vegetation indices'. Ratio images, in which each pixel value is a ratio value, can be subtracted and differences in the magnitude of the ratio can be displayed and interpreted in terms either of seasonal change in land cover or change in the type of land surface cover.

Vegetation indices are normally based upon two spectral bands; for example, the widely used normalised difference vegetation index is computed from (SWIR − R)/(SWIR + R), where SWIR and R are the short-wave infra-red and red reflectances respectively for a given pixel. However, the information present in other bands is not utilised by these methods. Linear transformations, based on all available visible and reflective infra-red channels, have been developed, in particular the tasselled cap transform, originally developed for Landsat MSS data by Kauth and Thomas (1976) and extended to Landsat TM by Crist (1983). Each linear transform is defined such that it correlates as closely as possible with a property of interest. MSS data, for example, appear to have a dimensionality of two; the corresponding tasselled cap functions are 'brightness' and 'greenness'. The additional infra-red bands of the TM provide a third dimension, which is found to be associated with 'wetness'. Each transform is defined a priori by a set of coefficients, one for each band, so that two (MSS) or three (TM) tasselled cap indices can be defined for each pixel. Plots showing the trajectory of a pixel over time have been found to be valuable in studying changes in agricultural crops during the growing season. It is the shape of these plots that gave rise to the name 'tasselled cap'.

Methods based on multitemporal analysis

The methods described in the previous section require separate analysis of image data collected at discrete points in time, and the comparison of the results of these analyses, usually by subtraction of two sets of results. It is also possible to apply methods such as supervised classification to a multitemporal image set consisting of all, or a selection of, the bands forming the two images. The training data used to calibrate the classification are selected by visual analysis of the images, backed up by field observation. The categories output by the classifier will include those that are constant from one time period to the next, plus categories which have changed class during the time interval between the images.

A second method of detecting change using a multitemporal image set is the use of principal component analysis, which identifies the main dimensions of change in a correlated data set. Reference has already been made to the dimensionality of Landsat MSS and TM data; this property of the data is manifested by the results obtained from PCA. For an image set relating to a single time period, two significant principal components are generally identified in Landsat MSS imagery, and three in Landsat TM. If two image sets of a given area are co-registered and subjected to PCA, then common dimensions are subsumed in a single component, and dimensions will emerge that are interpretable in terms of change.

Principal component analysis (Mather 1976, 1987) is a method of partitioning the variance of a multivariate data set. In a multitemporal, multispectral image set, the total variance is the sum of the variances of the individual bands. The spatial distribution of variability correlates across images, and as such can be represented by 'dimensions of common variance', which form the basis of factor analysis. Other components of variance represent differences between images, and these also are represented by specific principal components. Each component is a linear combination of spectral bands, and can be

evaluated at each pixel position. Thus, principal component images are calculable. They can be identified in terms of real-world properties by analysis of the correlations between the individual principal components and the spectral bands making up the multitemporal data set.

Examples of change detection

Existing archives of remotely sensed data are now being used to document changes occurring in land cover and land cover characteristics on scales ranging from the regional to the global. Hall *et al.* (1987) study successional dynamics in the boreal forest of northern Minnesota using Landsat MSS images collected in 1973 and 1983 and a Markov-type analysis of transitions between key life cycle states. Their work shows that, over the ten-year period of observations, considerable changes took place in an ecosystem that had been stable over a long period. Tucker *et al.* (1985, 1986) study the relationship between dry biomass and the normalised difference vegetation index (NDVI) for the Sahel area, and find a strong correlation. Wickland (1989) comments that 'these studies demonstrate the utility of the coarse-resolution AVHRR for monitoring rangeland productivity patterns and providing synoptic information on the progression of regional drought'. More recent reports of the use of coarse-resolution remotely sensed data in monitoring the Sahelian environment can be found in a special issue of the International Journal of Remote Sensing for June 1991. Pilon, Howarth and Bullock (1988) examine the use of Landsat MSS images spanning a nine-year period for an area of sub-Sahelian Nigeria. Because annual variations in precipitation can be as high as 50%, variations in vegetation cover can be considerable, even if images for the same season of the year are used. Human-induced change (in this case, the construction of a dam) also add complications. The multi-component approach developed by Pilon *et al.* (1988) was found to be both simple and effective. Malingreau and Tucker (1987) also use AVHRR data, both in the solar reflectance region and in the short-wave thermal infra-red wavebands, to study change in the southern part of the Amazon basin for the years 1982, 1984 and 1985. They are able to demonstrate a near-exponential increase in the rate of deforestation in the region. A survey of the role of terrestrial vegetation in the global carbon cycle, edited by Woodwell (1984), contains further elaboration of the material in this section.

At a local scale, the detection of land cover change at the urban fringe is described by Quarmby and Cushnie (1989), who use Landsat TM and SPOT HRV images in a study of change detection at two sites, Crawley and Reading. Their approach involves the transformation of digital counts (as read from the data tapes) to radiance values, using the sensor gains and offsets provided with the image data. A second adjustment is made to account for differences in solar zenith angle, which would affect the magnitude of the down-welling solar irradiance. Each image is geometrically corrected, and then image pairs are subtracted. The difference images are thresholded, a procedure which is claimed by the authors to remove atmospheric effects. However, problems result from the fact that the image pairs were not acquired at the same season of the year, hence areas showing seasonal variations in vegetation vigour were recorded as being subject to 'change'. Change detection at the rural/urban fringe is also studied by Martin and Howarth (1989). Using SPOT HRV imagery in photographic hard copy and digital form, these authors find that visual analysis and supervised classification of multitemporal images provide the best overall classification, with accuracies of about 80% (although simpler change/no change assessments produced accuracies of over 90%). Although this level of accuracy is below that achieved with Landsat MSS, the higher spatial resolution of the SPOT HRV means that changes in much smaller land parcels can be observed. Fung and LeDrew (1987), Jensen and Toll (1982), and Martin (1989) provide additional examples of the use of remote sensing to study land use change at the rural/urban fringe, while Ehlers *et al.* (1990) consider the problem in the context of local planning.

Other recent studies of land cover change detection are provided by Milne and O'Neill (1991), who use both analogue (photographic) and digital methods of change detection based on multitemporal Landsat MSS images for a World Heritage site in New South Wales, Australia. Legg (1989) used Landsat TM data to monitor the expansion of waste dumps associated with china clay workings in Cornwall. An approach to land use mapping of areas of agriculturally marginal areas in Europe using expert systems is outlined by Wilkinson, Hill and Megier (1990). Their approach is not based simply on the spectral characteristics of an area as measured by a remote sensor; they incorporate local geographical knowledge within an expert system in an attempt to improve their identification of land use types.

REFERENCES

Asrar, G. 1989. Introduction. In: *Theory and applications of optical remote sensing*, edited by G. Asrar, 1-13. New York: Wiley.

Baker, J.H., Briggs, S.A., Gordon, V., Jones, A.R., Settle, J.J., Townshend, J.R.G. & Wyatt, B.K. 1991. Advances in classification for land cover mapping using SPOT HRV imagery. *International Journal of Remote Sensing*, **12,** 1071-1085.

Becker, F. & Li, Z. 1991. Temperature-independent thermal infra-red spectral indices and land surface temperature determined from space. *Paper presented at the Remote Sensing Society's TERRA-1 Conference, Winchester, Hampshire, March 1991.*

Clark, J.A., Steven, M.D. & Malthus, T.J. 1991. Achievements and unresolved problems in vegetation monitoring. *Paper presented at the Remote Sensing Society's TERRA-1 Conference, Winchester, Hampshire, March 1991.*

Crist, E.P. 1983. The TM tasselled cap – a preliminary formulation. *Proceedings of the Symposium on Machine Processing of Remotely Sensed Data, Purdue University, West Lafayette, Indiana,* 357-364.

Duggin, M.J. & Robinove, C.J. 1990. Assumptions implicit in remote sensing data acquisition and analysis. *International Journal of Remote Sensing,* **11,** 1669-1694.

Ehlers, M., Jadowski, M.A., Howard, R.R. & Brostuen, D.E. 1990. Application of SPOT data for regional growth analysis and local planning. *Photogrammetric Engineering and Remote Sensing,* **56,** 175-180.

Elachi, C. 1987. *Introduction to the physics and techniques of remote sensing.* New York: Wiley.

European Space Agency. 1985. Microwave remote sensing applied to vegetation. *Proceedings of an EARSeL Workshop, Amsterdam, 10-12 December 1984.* (SP-227.) Paris: ESA.

Freden, S.C. & Gordon, F.Jr. 1983. Landsat satellites. In: *Manual of remote sensing, 2nd ed., vol. 1: theory, instruments and techniques,* edited by R.N. Colwell, 517-570. Falls Church, Va: American Society of Photogrammetry.

Fuller, R.M. & Parsell, R.J. 1990. Classification of TM imagery in the study of land use in lowland Britain: practical considerations for operational use. *International Journal of Remote Sensing,* **11,** 1901-1917.

Fung, T. & LeDrew, E. 1987. Land cover change detection with Thematic Mapper spectral/textural data at the rural/urban fringe. *Proceedings of the 21st International Symposium on Remote Sensing of the Environment, Environmental Research Institute of Michigan, Ann Arbor, Michigan,* 783-789.

Gordon, H.R., Clarke, D.K., Brown, J.W., Brown, O.B., Evans, R.H. & Broenkow, W.W. 1983. Phytoplankton pigment concentration in the middle Atlantic bight: comparison of ship determination and CZCS estimates. *Applied Optics,* **22,** 20-36.

Hall, F.G., Strebel, D.E., Goetz, S.J., Woods, K.D. & Botkin, D.B. 1987. Landscape pattern and successional dynamics in the boreal forest. *Proceedings of the International Geoscience and Remote Sensing Symposium (IGARSS'87), Ann Arbor, Michigan,* 473-482.

Harrison, B.A. & Jupp, D.L.B. 1989. *Introduction to remotely-sensed data.* Canberra: CSIRO Division of Water Resources.

Hill, J. & Sturm, B. 1988. Radiometric normalisation of multi-temporal Thematic Mapper data for the use of greenness profiles in agricultural land cover classification and vegetation monitoring. *Proceedings of the EARSeL 8th Symposium: Alpine and Mediterranean areas, Capri, Italy, May 1988,* 21-40.

Holben, B.N. & Justice, C.O. 1980. The topographic effect on spectral response on nadir-pointing sensors. *Photogrammetric Engineering and Remote Sensing,* **46,** 1191-1200.

International Geosphere–Biosphere Programme. 1990. *The initial core projects.* (Report no. 12.) Stockholm: IGBP.

Jensen, J.R. & Toll, D.L. 1982. Detecting residential land-use development at the urban fringe. *Photogrammetric Engineering and Remote Sensing ,* **48,** 629-643.

Kaufman, Y. 1989. The atmospheric effect on remote sensing and its correction. In: *Theory and applications of optical remote sensing,* edited by G. Asrar, 336-428. New York: Wiley.

Kauth, R.J. & Thomas, G. 1976. The tasselled cap – a graphic description of the spectral–temporal development of agricultural crops as seen by Landsat. *Proceedings of the Symposium on Machine Processing of Remotely Sensed Data, Purdue University, West Lafayette, Indiana,* 4, B41-B51.

Kneizys, F.X., Chetwynd, J.H., Selby, J.E.A., Clough, S.A., Shettle, E.P. & Abreu, L.W. 1983. *Atmospheric transmittance/radiance: computer code LOWTRAN 6.* (AFGL-TR-83-0187.) Massachusetts: Hanscom Air Force Base, Air Force Geophysics Laboratory.

Kowalik, W.S. & Marsh, S.E. 1982. A relation between Landsat digital numbers, surface reflectance, and the cosine of the solar zenith angle. *Remote Sensing of Environment,* **12,** 39-55.

Legg, C.A. 1989. Updating thematic maps of the mining districts. An operational demonstration of remote sensing in the south-west of England. In: *Remote sensing for operational applications: technical contents of the 15th Annual Conference of the Remote Sensing Society, 1989,* compiled by E.C.Barrett & K. A Brown, 243-248. Reading: Remote Sensing Society.

Legg, C.A. 1991. A review of Landsat MSS image acquisition over the United Kingdom, 1976–1988, and the implications for operational remote sensing. *International Journal of Remote Sensing,* **12,** 93-106.

Malingreau, J.P. & Tucker, C.J. 1987. The contribution of AVHRR data for measuring and understanding global processes: large-scale deforestation in the Amazon basin. *Proceedings of the International Geoscience and Remote Sensing Symposium (IGARSS'87), Ann Arbor, Michigan,* 443-448.

Markham, B.L & Barker, J.L. 1987. Radiometric properties of U.S. processed MSS data. *Remote Sensing of Environment,* **22,** 39-71.

Martin L.R.G. 1989. Accuracy assessment of Landsat-based visual ch nge detection methods applied to the rural–urban fringe. *Photogram metric Engineering and Remote Sensing,* **55,** 209-215.

Martin, L.R.G. & Howarth, P.J. 1989. Change-detection accuracy assessment using SPOT multispectral imagery of the rural–urban fringe. *Remote Sensing of Environment,* **30,** 55-66.

Mather, P.M. 1976. *Computational methods of multivariate analysis in physical geography.* Chichester: Wiley.

Mather, P.M. 1987. *Computer processing of remotely-sensed images.* Chichester: Wiley.

Megier, J., Hill, J. & Kohl, H. 1991. Land-use inventory and mapping in a mountainous area: the Ardeche experiment. *International Journal of Remote Sensing,* **12,** 445-462.

Milne, A.K. & O'Neill, A.L. 1991. Mapping and monitoring land cover in the Willandra Lakes World Heritage Region. *International Journal of Remote Sensing,* **11,** 2035-2049.

National Aeronautics and Space Administration. 1987a. *HIRIS (high resolution imaging spectrometer). Science opportunities for the 1990s. Earth observing system. Vol.IIc: Instrument panel report.* Greenbelt, Md: NASA.

National Aeronautics and Space Administration. 1987b. *SAR (synthetic aperture radar). Earth observing system. Vol IIf: Instrument panel report.* Greenbelt, Md: NASA.

Nelson, R.F. 1983. Detecting forest canopy change due to insect activity using Landsat MSS. *Photogrammetric Engineering and Remote Sensing,* **49,** 1303-1314.

Pilon, P.G., Howarth, P.J. & Bullock, R.A. 1988. An enhanced classification approach to change detection in semi-arid environments. *Photogrammetric Engineering and Remote Sensing,* **54,** 1709-1716.

Price, J.C. 1989 Quantitative aspects of remote sensing in the thermal infra-red. In: *Theory and applications of optical remote sensing,* edited by G.Asrar, 578-603. New York: Wiley.

Quarmby, N.A. & Cushnie, J.L. 1989. Monitoring urban land cover changes at the urban fringe from SPOT HRV imagery in south-east England. *International Journal of Remote Sensing,* **10,** 953-963.

Rast, M., Jaskolla, F. & Arnason, K. 1991. Comparative digital analysis of Seasat SAR and Landsat TM data for Iceland. *International Journal of Remote Sensing,* **12,** 527-544.

Royer, A., Vincent, P & Bonn, F. 1985. Evaluation and correction of viewing angle effects on satellite measurements of bidirectional reflectance. *Photogrammetric Engineering and Remote Sensing,* **51,** 1899-1914.

Singh, A. 1989. Digital change detection techniques using remotely-sensed data. *International Journal of Remote Sensing,* **10,** 989-1003.

Singh, S.M. 1989. Comparison of TM, HRV and AVHRR-derived vegetation indices: a simulations study for sensor inter-calibration. In: *Remote sensing for operational applications: technical contents of the 15th Annual Conference of the Remote Sensing Society, 1989,* compiled by E.C. Barrett & K.A. Brown, 381-386. Reading: Remote Sensing Society.

Townshend, J.R.G. & Justice, C.O. 1988. Selecting the spatial resolution of satellite sensors required for global monitoring of land transformations. *International Journal of Remote Sensing,* **9,** 187-236.

Tucker, C.J., Vanpraet, C.L., Sharman, M.J. & van Ittersum, G. 1985. Satellite remote sensing of total herbaceous biomass production in the Senegalese Sahel: 1980–1984. *Remote Sensing of Environment,* **17,** 233-249.

Tucker, C.J., Justice, C.O. & Prince, S.D. 1986. Monitoring the grasslands of the Sahel 1984–1985. *International Journal of Remote Sensing,* **17,** 1571-1581.

United States Geological Survey. 1979. *Landsat data users handbook.* Sioux Falls, South Dakota: Eros Data Center.

Vane, G. 1987. Airborne visible/infra-red imaging spectrometer (AVIRIS). A description of the sensor, ground data processing facility, laboratory calibration, and first results. (JPL-PUB-Publication no. 87-38.) Pasadena, Ca: Jet Propulsion Laboratory.

Wickland, D.E. 1989. Future directions for remote sensing in terrestrial ecological research. In: *Theory and applications of optical remote sensing,* edited by G.Asrar, 691-724. New York: Wiley.

Wilkinson, G., Hill, J. & Megier, J. 1990. Development programme for operational land use inventories in European marginal areas using expert systems. In: *Remote sensing for operational applications: technical contents of the 15th Annual Conference of the Remote Sensing Society, 1989,* compiled by E.C.Barrett & K.A. Brown, 435-441. Reading: Remote Sensing Society.

Woodwell, G.M., ed. 1984. *The role of terrestrial vegetation in the global carbon cycle: measurement by remote sensing.* New York: Wiley.

Integration of methods for detecting land use change, with special reference to Countryside Survey 1990

R G H Bunce[1], C J Barr[1] & R M Fuller[2]

Institute of Terrestrial Ecology
[1]Merlewood Research Station, Grange-over-Sands, Cumbria LA11 6JU
[2]Monks Wood Experimental Station, Abbots Ripton, Huntingdon, Cambs PE17 2LS

INTRODUCTION

Although Great Britain is not, in European terms, a large country, it has a complex mosaic of different land uses, cover types, and ecological systems. The present rural land use patterns have been determined by the interaction of man with the vegetation cover and in response to the changing climate since the ice age. Initially, the patterns were determined by the natural environment. Since the Industrial Revolution, however, other pressures have modified the basic pattern and, although many of the underlying correlations between land use and the physical environment still exist, they have been highly modified by industrial, technological, and socio-economic factors.

In recent years, with greater control of development and planning, there has been an increasing interest in the composition of the British countryside. This has been partly in response to public perception of environmental matters, but also because of a recognition of the importance of Government policies in determining the patterns and changes taking place in the landscape.

In recent times, a variety of information-gathering projects has been undertaken by Government agencies in response to the perceived increase in rate of change in the countryside.

One basic problem is that the rural land has a wide variety of demands upon it, and there are conflicts between, for example, agriculture, forestry, urban expansion, industrial development, wildlife conservation, and amenity and recreation. To a large extent, rural land use is outside statutory planning procedures, although urban planning does impinge on the countryside. There is, therefore, a requirement not only at a local level, but also nationally, for examining the patterns in the countryside and the likely changes which are taking place. There are four main requirements:

1. resource assessment, which involves an estimation or measurement of the overall resources of the region, or country, concerned;

2. an indication of the broad regional pattern of these resources: a knowledge of their distribution throughout the region is essential for planning;

3. a measure of the changes taking place: many changes in land use may seem small by themselves but together may have incremental effects on the landscape;

4. estimation and prediction of land use potential and scenarios of change, in order to compare policy options which may affect the patterns and land uses present in the countryside.

Whilst there are many independent detailed studies of particular processes and land uses, these are often unco-ordinated. This paper reviews the studies which have been completed at the present time, then goes on to describe the integration which has taken place to date, and finishes with a description of the approach which has been developed within the Natural Environment Research Council (NERC) to describe the countryside and its changing patterns.

The main purpose of this paper is to describe and discuss the approaches used to monitor changes in land use, as a basis for policy implementation.

METHODS FOR DETECTING LAND USE CHANGE

Field survey

The traditional means of obtaining information about the ecological characteristics of land is to carry out field surveys. These vary in methodology and objectives, but are often based upon observing vegetation, and mapping in the field. From this early approach, the associations of species have been recorded in phytosociological units (eg Rodwell 1991), assessing the association between them. In land use terms, until Sir Dudley Stamp set out to obtain a land use statement in England and Wales in the mid-1930s (Stamp 1937-47), there had been no comprehensive recording of these areas since the Domesday Book of 1066. Stamp's land use statistics have been augmented by the mapping activities of the UK Ordnance Survey and by a survey described by Coleman (1961). In addition, there have been

extensive and repeated field surveys by the Forestry Commission and by the Ministry of Agriculture, Fisheries and Food and the Department of Agriculture and Fisheries for Scotland. The Soil Surveys of England and Wales, and of Scotland, also completed detailed maps recording the distribution of major soil series in Great Britain.

Aerial photography

Ever since the advent of readily available aerial photography in the early 1950s, it has been realised that it represents an important additional source of land use information. The first national survey using aerial photography was the Monitoring Landscape Change (MLC) project in 1986 (Hunting Surveys and Consultants Ltd 1986). This project used a stratified sample, based on the Forestry Commission census strips from soil series, by county, and recorded land cover and landscape features from a series of sites in England and Wales, to obtain national estimates of the nature and extent of these categories. More recently, the National Countryside Monitoring Scheme (NCMS), for the Nature Conservancy Council, has used a comparable approach within counties in Great Britain (Budd 1989). The Macaulay Land Use Research Institute (MLURI), commissioned by the Scottish Office, has also been involved in mapping vegetation throughout the whole of Scotland based on aerial photographic coverage, flown in 1988–89, (Aspinall Miller & Birnie 1991). Over many years, the Ordnance Survey (OS) has been involved with land cover, principally by studying the expansion of urban areas, and has produced quantitative national estimates within GB (eg Department of the Environment (DoE) 1992).

Satellite imagery

It has taken several years for the technical development of satellite imagery to reach a stage where applications have been encouraged. Recent studies have been successful in producing outputs, in the form of maps and statistics, rather than in detailing technical potential. Fuller, Jones and Wyatt (1989), for example, described the application of imagery to obtain regional estimates of land cover types in Cambridgeshire.

Local and regional surveys

There have been many regional surveys of varying levels of detail. For example, habitat surveys of the type devised by the Nature Conservancy Council (NCC) have been carried out in many counties (eg Moreau 1990). The Countryside Commission has funded detailed interpretations of National Parks in England and Wales (Countryside Commission 1991), and Highland Regional Council also carried out regional studies as a basis for land use planning (Highland Regional Council 1984).

Thematic surveys

National surveys have been carried out of the individual features which make up the landscape, and

estimates of change have been made. Thus, Hooper (1968) described hedgerows, Whitbread (1985) ancient woodlands, Fuller (Fuller, Barr & Marais 1986; Fuller 1987) lowland grasslands, and Bunce (1989) heather in England and Wales.

Socio-economic surveys

A wide range of socio-economic surveys have been carried out, both at individual points and also to follow trends, such as the population census and various recreational studies (eg Lowe, Ward & Munton 1992).

To date, there has not been any true integration of methods or of the data sets which have resulted from these various surveys. They have been determined largely by the individual requirements of the agencies concerned. There is, therefore, a strongly disparate nature of much of the information available for the basic description of the environment and land use in Britain; the wide range of approaches used to analyse the information further complicates the final picture.

DATA INTEGRATION

Full data integration does not depend entirely upon the methods, although these are inextricably linked. It is necessary to produce the final estimates involving and overlaying the various data in order that they are on a consistent basis to improve the accuracy of estimates, and also to show the correlation between the various data streams. The importance of such integration has been recognised for many years, and has its basis in the 'sieve technique' much employed by planners, where sets of different requirements for the countryside are successively overlain using different maps, and their interactions assessed (eg Bunce *et al.* 1984).

With the development of increased computing power and sophistication of mapping procedures, there has been a range of attempts to establish comprehensive data bases. The first and most extensive of these was the Rural Land Use Information System (RLUIS) project based in the Lothian region (Coppock & Gebbett 1978). This study focused on the acquisition of comprehensive sets of information, and was successful in showing that computing systems could enable such data to be stored and manipulated for specific requirements, at the regional level. This approach was extended to other parts of Scotland, but was not successfully followed up elsewhere in Britain because of the difficulties involved in handling such large data bases consistently at the national scale, data bases which were collected for a variety of purposes and at different scales. An early attempt to integrate large numbers of mapped environmental data was made by the Institute of Terrestrial Ecology (ITE) in a project called ECOBASE (Molineux 1978), but, again, lack of computing and data base design technology meant that the approach did not achieve its full potential.

Within the European Community (EC), a further example of integration is provided by the CORINE (Co-ordinated environmental information in the European Community) programme where a variety of data sources have been co-ordinated (Moss *et al.* 1991). Here, again, a major limitation has been the inconsistency of data between countries, but a degree of comparability has been obtained and summaries have been produced for the whole of the EC. In Britain, the agricultural land classification represents a different approach, where data on climate, soil, and potential crops are integrated into a single index to define the potential of land for growing crops. At a regional level, the 'sieve map' approach has been adopted by several regional authorities. Lancashire County Council (1991) and Highland Regional Council (Bunce & Claridge 1985) have both developed systems for identifying areas of conflict within their regions. On the Continent, this approach has proceeded further, and the use of the information is actually fundamental to the planning process, as described by Schaller and Haber (1988) in Bavaria, and by de Veer and de Waal (1988) in The Netherlands. Elsewhere, the ecological land classification projects in Canada (eg Lopoukhine, Prout & Hirvonen 1978) and in Australia (Austin & Margules 1984) have developed comparable approaches, and show the way in which modern computing power can be used in such integrated systems.

True integration provides the basis for planning purposes, and geographical information systems (GIS) provide the tool to enable such data integration to be automated using powerful new computer systems. There are four primary areas in which GIS can be used:

1. to develop a flexible method of mapping, showing the geographical distribution of required features;

2. to enable overlaying of competing land uses or potential land uses;

3. to allow the testing of policy options and scenarios, through modelling, in order to examine the likely outcomes;

4. to analyse pattern and examine the relationships of spatial features to each other and to other elements in the landscape.

PREVIOUS WORK INVOLVING INTEGRATION OF METHODS

Satellite imagery, aerial photography, and field survey are the principal ways in which land use data can be collected. Satellite imagery has the advantage of synoptic coverage but at a relatively low level of detail. Aerial photography is able to provide more detail at a local level, whereas field survey, whilst expensive and time-consuming, provides detailed information which will allow analysis of species composition. Thus, the first two approaches are primarily powerful for estimating quantities, and the

latter for estimating the quality of the features concerned. There is a strong synergistic effect in combining these approaches.

Field survey is used routinely in remote sensing studies as 'ground truthing', but rarely feeds back directly to modify the definitions of land classifications determined from satellite images or aerial photography. It is primarily used for ground checking and validating, as in part of the MLC project. In a similar way, soil survey procedures use aerial photography to help in the mapping of soil units; the OS projects use aerial photography to assist the mapping of urban spread.

Some studies have, however, proceeded to develop further the method of full integration. In a study in south Wales, Haines-Young (1992) showed how terrain information and land classification could improve the accuracy of mapping and estimation of features in the countryside, and how they could be used to detect change. Work on Islay (Bignall, Curtis & Matthews 1988) showed how integration could be used to obtain sophisticated estimates of bird populations and to assess their relationship with the environment and with land cover. However, full integration, whilst possible, has not involved modification of the classes produced by interpretation of satellite imagery, in terms of their more detailed composition.

COUNTRYSIDE SURVEY 1990: AN INTEGRATED APPROACH TO LAND USE DATA COLLECTION

The approach described below has been jointly developed by the authors, in association with other staff in NERC and DoE, and others subcontracted to work with ITE. Other organisations, including the Department of Trade and Industry (DTI), the British National Space Centre (BNSC), and NCC, have contributed funding to current work.

The basis of the approach was developed from an ITE project called Ecological Consequences of Land Use Change (ECOLUC) (Bunce & Heal 1990), and was further described by Griffiths and Wooding (1989a). In that study, satellite imagery was used to obtain the distribution and extent of land cover and landscape features, and the incorporation of ground survey data added detail about their ecological characteristics.

The integrated approach pioneered within the ECOLUC project has been fully developed in the Countryside Survey 1990. Five principles, learned from earlier work, were vital in the planning of the Survey.

1. The methods should be objective and reproducible.

2. It should be possible to link data at a variety of scales, eg quadrats at a one metre square level on the one hand, with satellite imagery showing features at perhaps one kilometre or even 10 km· levels.

3. Statistical accuracy of the data, both in space and time, should be quantified and expressed.

4. Land cover definitions should be compared, in order to understand the degree of similarity between different approaches and to ensure that the results of the methods are fully understood, in terms of strengths and limitations.

5. It should be possible to modify the outputs from any one part of the project, by reference to those from other components.

Although the Countryside Survey 1990 project is very much an integrated programme, it is simplest to describe the work under its component parts: field survey; mapping land cover from satellite images; data from other sources; and integration.

Field survey

The field survey element of Countryside Survey 1990 also forms the third in a series of national (GB) sample-based surveys undertaken by ITE, following those of 1977–78 and 1984. In each case, sample units of one km square were drawn from a particular stratification framework, the ITE land classification. With funding from DoE, this system has classified all (approx 250 000) one km squares in GB into 32 environmental strata, termed land classes (Bunce et al. 1991); these classes represent an integrated description of the overall environment, and generate a dispersed sample to ensure, as far as possible, that the ecological variability within the country is covered, as well as the principal land cover types. The statistical aspects of this sampling approach are discussed by Brandon et al. (1989).

In the 1977–78 survey (Bunce 1979; Bunce & Heal 1984), eight one km squares were visited in each of 32 land classes, giving a sample total of 256. This survey was intended to provide a statement on the ecological resource of the countryside, and included the recording of a number of vegetation quadrats and soil pits at each site. As a secondary activity, land cover was mapped and landscape features were recorded.

In the second survey (Barr et al. 1986), the same 256 one km squares were visited and, additionally, four new squares were surveyed in each class, giving a total sample of 384 squares. The main objective of the survey was to provide data on change in land cover and landscape features; no vegetation quadrats were recorded.

In the 1990 survey (Barr 1990), the sample size was increased further, but, having established a statistically viable minimum size in each class, the 124 new squares were allocated to classes in proportion to the overall class fequency in GB. In addition, as part of a separate land use project, 25 one km squares which had been rejected from what is essentially a countryside survey because of their urban character, were surveyed. Thus, the total number of squares visited in 1990 was 533, of which 508 were primarily countryside squares.

In each of the 508 Countryside Survey 1990 squares, two-person survey teams mapped land cover and landscape features throughout the whole square, using OS 1:10 000 base maps. These maps had been updated with information on new and removed boundaries, and with semi-natural vegetation boundaries, interpreted from aerial photographs. Each land cover parcel and landscape feature element was described using a pre-determined list of coded attributes, including details of species and percentage cover, management, and land use. The 313 codes, used in combination, allowed great detail to be attached to each recorded feature. A fuller description of the methods is provided by Barr et al. (1985).

The land cover and landscape features were mapped thematically under five headings:

1. physiography – covering the underlying structure of the land and including details of coastal features, rivers, inland cliff, and rock outcrops;

2. agriculture and semi-natural vegetation – to include all agricultural crops, grassland, moorland, and bog;

3. forestry, woodland and trees – including information on species, age, and management;

4. urban, built-up and recreation – including all man-made features in rural and urban areas alike (eg roads, factories, bridges, farmhouses, and recreational facilities);

5. boundaries – including hedges, fences, banks, and walls, together with details of height, management, and species (in the case of hedgerows).

In addition, to provide detailed ecological information (as had been done in the 1977–78 survey when vegetation and soils were recorded in each square), vegetation was recorded in up to 27 quadrats in each square, as follows.

- Five 200 m^2 plots were placed at random throughout the square.

- 1 m x 10 m linear plots were placed along hedgerows (x 2), streamsides (x 5) and roadsides (x 5) (where these features were present).

- A further 1 m x 10 m linear plot was placed at the nearest boundary to each of the five 200 m^2 plots, allowing comparisons to be drawn between 'open' country and linear habitats.

- Five further plots (4 m^2) were located in areas of semi-natural vegetation which was not adequately represented by the large random plots.

Within each quadrat, all species of flowering plants and grasses, and lichens and bryophytes from a restricted list, were recorded, together with a visual estimate of their cover, in 5% classes. The vegetation plots were permanently marked and photographed

for relocation.

To complete the above schedule of work in a four-month period between mid-June and mid-October, each square took between two and six days to survey by a trained team of two. All surveyors were selected from ITE staff or were botanists employed for the task. Quality control was rigorous, with a demanding two-week training course for all surveyors, followed by field supervision and frequent mixing of team members. A quality assurance exercise was undertaken whereby a subsample of one km squares was resurveyed.

The mapped land cover data are being converted into computer-readable form (digitised), and all data will be entered into a computer-based GIS allowing automatic calculations of areas, lengths, and numbers of features in the sample squares (Howard & Barr 1991). It will also enable the 1990 maps of the squares to be overlain by those of previous surveys to compute changes. Analyses of the plant data will enable changes to be determined from the records made in 1978, and also detailed comparisons of linear features with the remaining open countryside. In addition, the relationship of boundary features to the surrounding vegetation will be determined.

As described above, the field survey is based on a sample of one km squares. By using the known ITE land classification composition of any major region of GB, it is possible to 'gross up' from mean values obtained from the samples, and to make estimates for any surveyed feature within such regions. Further, the statistical accuracy of these estimates can be expressed. The size of any such errors will depend on a variety of factors, including:

- frequency of field samples within strata;
- distributions of features between strata;
- frequency of strata within region of interest;
- spatial characteristics of features, eg small but widespread (small woods); large but relatively uncommon (conifer plantation).

Typically, the statistical errors for the most widespread land cover types in GB, based on a sample of 508, might be 5%. The smaller the geographical region of interest, or the rarer the feature, then the greater will be the error associated with the estimate. However, by linking the detailed information from the sample squares with land cover data for all one km squares, the usefulness of the field data increases.

MAPPING LAND COVER FROM SATELLITE IMAGES

The land cover of Britain is being mapped from Landsat thematic mapper (TM) images. The work of Griffiths and Wooding (1989b) started to develop and demonstrate the strengths of combining the detailed, sample-based approach of the field survey with a generalised census from satellite mapping. A pilot study (Fuller et al. 1989; Fuller & Parsell 1990) showed how combined summer and winter Landsat data could be computer-classified to give accurate maps of land cover.

Landsat's TM records digital numbers, representing the scores for reflected light from 30 m cells on the ground. The spectrum is divided into seven wavebands between the blue and thermal wavelengths. By scanning the landscape from side to side, as the satellite makes forward progress, a full array of reflectance data is collected for a 185 km swath. By means of different orbits, full cover of the earth is obtained every 16 days. The data are supplied as digital tapes, representing 185 km-long sections of a path, called scenes.

The procedure of analysis takes three bands (red, near- and middle-infra-red) of a summer scene (May–July), and, by defining ground control points, geographically registers the data to the British National Grid, using 25 m output cells. The same bands of a winter scene (October–March) are registered to the summer image. Thus, six-band, summer/winter composite scenes result, each with oblique 25 m cells.

An image can be displayed on a visual display unit, using any permutation of three out of the six bands (or a mathematical combination thereof). Each 25 m ground cell is represented as a pixel on the display, so the term 'pixel' is usually used to describe such ground cells in analysis.

Sample areas of different cover types are identified in the field, and outlined interactively on the image analysis system. Where a cover type has several subclasses (for example, wheat, barley and potatoes might be subclasses of arable land), the subclasses are defined separately. From the outlines, the system extracts the pixels in each waveband, and calculates the statistical properties of reflectances for each subclass. A maximum likelihood classifier is then made to allocate each pixel to the nearest subclass (in statistical terms), and subclasses can be aggregated into target classes.

In the project to map all of Britain, 25 cover types are targetted (Figure 1), and are believed to represent a classification which can be provided consistently for the whole of Britain. The classes have been made to correspond to those of other surveys, as far as is possible, and have been agreed after consulting other surveyors and end-users of the maps.

Various knowledge-based correction procedures refine the cover maps. For example, a coastline is drawn and any confusion between maritime and terrestrial cover types is corrected; upland masks are fitted around areas of extensive upland cover, and misclassified pockets of lowland are removed; masks of urban cover types are used to remove erroneous arable patches in towns. A filtering procedure removes any isolated pixels in a 3 x 3 pixel region, on the basis that the most unique pixels are errors of classification, hence noise.

The classification is a hierarchical one, in which users

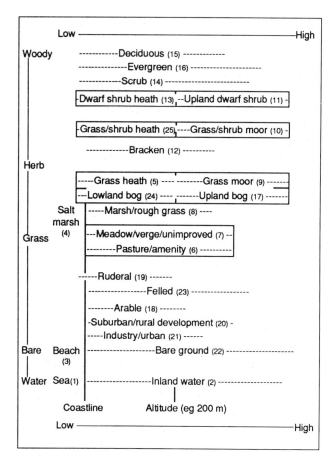

Figure 1. A suggested Landsat classification of Great Britain into land cover classes. Classes which are boxed together are those where spectral separation may be unreliable. In some cases, problems of spectral confusion (eg between beaches and other bare ground) is overcome by knowledge-based correction (eg using digital coastline): in these circumstances, the classes are not boxed. Elsewhere (eg the use of altitude in separating 'lowland grass heath' from 'grass moors') the dividing line is less clear and could present difficulties, at least outside of a GIS environment, so the classes are boxed together

can combine cover types to simplify the classification. Some users may, for example, only want to distinguish between vegetated and bare surfaces. A more simple aggregation might amalgamate the upland and lowland variants of targetted grasslands, and so users can make their own definitions based on altitude, or perhaps an ITE land class. The more detailed subclass data also remain available for specialist consultation, though consistency of subclass interpretation cannot be guaranteed.

Two levels of accuracy assessment are made. First, the cover maps are scored, field-by-field, against a sample of cover data. For 5720 land parcels, results so far show that 85% were correctly identified by the classification. However, the field sample, which was selected to identify unusual features, was not representative of the whole, and the result under-represents the accuracy associated with more common features. A more rigorous procedure will compare the Landsat maps with digitised cover data from the 533 field survey squares. Comparisons will be made pixel-by-pixel, with separate assessments for boundary pixels: summary information at the one km level will also be compared.

The final maps will be available at full 25 m resolution and summarised as one km data. At either level, they

can be integrated with the field survey information and the 32 land classes. At one km resolution, there is the obvious potential to examine squares by land class and by cover type. The Landsat map data (corrected for systematic error) will give revised mean cover values for the full population of squares in each land class. It will be possible to use the cover maps to provide information for local and regional studies, where a study population of one km squares may differ from the average.

Data from other sources

Directly associated with Countryside Survey 1990, and the field survey in particular, are surveys of freshwater biota and of soils. Samples of freshwater biota have been collected from each of the ITE field sample one km squares (where present): those from running waters as part of a larger project of the Institute of Freshwater Ecology (Wright *et al.* 1989), and those from static water as part of collaborative work with the University of Newcastle (Luff *et al.* 1992). Integrating data on the occurrence of freshwater animals and plants, and relating these to local land use and environmental factors, will provide useful indices of pollution, especially in the context of eutrophication and acidification.

Soil surveys of the ITE sites are being undertaken by the Soil Survey and Land Research Centre (SSLRC) and by the Macaulay Land Use Research Institute (MLURI). In due course, data and outputs from a wide range of studies which relate to land use change, and which may be geographically referenced or linked to specific habitats, can be integrated into the system. Work being carried out in other NERC Institutes, such as the Institute of Hydrology and the British Geological Survey, which relates to land use issues, can also be integrated in this way.

There is interest among socio-economists in collaborative work to find out more about the reasons underlying land use change. It is hoped that work in the ITE field survey squares by Warnock and Bell (1987) and Potter and Gasson (1988) will be further developed, so that the causes and consequences of land use change may be better understood.

Because Countryside Survey 1990 operates at the one km scale, many other data may be integrated through the use of the ITE land classification. The benefits of these links are becoming apparent in a project being carried out by ITE to develop a countryside information system, which operates at the one km square level, and is designed to provide an integrated package of land use information on any one geographical area, for countryside planning and management purposes.

Integration

As part of the principal integration programme, land cover maps of Great Britain will be enhanced by use of field data, through the ITE land classification system. The 25 land cover categories derived from satellite imagery can be broken down by the detailed

composition of species from the ground survey samples. For example, coniferous woodland, as defined by the classification of satellite data, can be broken down into its more detailed species composition of pine *(Pinus)*, spruce *(Picea)*, larch *(Larix)* and other species, on a probabilistic basis, from field survey data. In addition, the power of the satellite imagery to display distributions throughout the country will enable categories of the satellite image to be modified by the composition of the field survey squares.

Thus, the cover maps can only give direct information on those cover types which were mapped, but they can give indirect information on other features. For example, the cover of unimproved grassland is not available from the Landsat maps. However, the area of unimproved grassland is clearly related to total grassland cover, and the proportion will have been estimated, by land class, in the field survey. Hence, the Landsat maps can identify the grass cover in a study area, and the land classes can estimate the proportion which is unimproved. The resulting prediction will be much more accurate than would be the case if the user assumed all squares of a land class were identical. The map data can also be used at full resolution; for example, the cover map could show the grassland patterns at a 25 m grid, with probability weightings for unimproved grass cover.

Even the estimates for point and linear features, or plant species distributions, can be improved using the cover map. If the number of ponds, say, is proportionate to the cover of grassland, field-based estimates and Landsat cover can be used to predict pond distribution and density. The number of oak *(Quercus)* trees will relate to the area of woodland and to the land classes of an area; hence, their distribution and density could be estimated. By using other data, such as soil maps, it is possible to further refine estimates, eg of fenland or chalk grassland species. Integration with, say, climatic data would allow development of models which relate cover, land class, species, and climate, and thence the prediction of changes in the event of climate change. A variety of applications is already under development (see later section).

There will be three principal outputs from the integrated approach:

1. the 'stock' of the major land cover categories for every one km square in GB and, from the field survey, estimates of the detailed ecological characteristics of each cover type within each square;

2. by reference to earlier survey data (ITE: 1977–78, 1984; and MLC: 1940, 1970 and 1980), summaries of changes which have taken place over the last three decades, by geographical regions (as far as differences in definitions will allow);

3. a data base, to be used as a definitive statement on the countryside in 1990, with known levels of accuracy and extent, as a baseline for future monitoring.

FUTURE WORK

Countryside Survey 1990 is largely a data collection, integration and comparison project. There is now a need to realise the potential of the investment made, and to initiate further research. Future work might involve the following principal activities.

- Interpretation of the basic information derived from the statistical analyses of the data described above. This will include pattern analysis of spatial features and their relationship with detailed species composition, and an understanding of the processes and structure of changes in the countryside.

- The development of a knowledge-based information system to store the data and enable them to be accessed readily by policy advisers. This work has already proceeded within the Ecological Consequences of Land Use Change project, and has been shown to have considerable potential for further development. In the prototype information system, the characteristics of the land classes and the associated land use and land cover features for which census data were available, together with other predictions described above, were made available within a single computer model. The system is compatible with various other models predicting changes, and any data which are held by one km square can be incorporated. A wide variety of other data, eg on the changes in moth populations or from the MLC project, can be incorporated into this common framework. As it is held within the land classification system on an OS grid, further data can be readily incorporated.

- Further data flows are also involved, eg soils, socio-economics, freshwaters, hydrology, geology, archaeology and phytosociology. It is planned to incorporate these data sets using the same process of integration as described above, in order to demonstrate the interactions between them. For example, archaeological remains can be strongly threatened by changes in land practice.

- The potential for modelling, both in the static and dynamic sense, is considerable. A variety of modelling approaches have been adopted in the past. For example, the land availability study for wood energy plantations (Bunce, Pearce & Mitchell 1981) showed how forestry for energy purposes could be developed in Britain, by overlaying the potential of forestry on to the basic land cover maps. At a more local level, other models have been developed; for example, Maxwell, Sibbald and Eadie (1979) examine the potential for integrating farming and forestry. Smith and Budd (1982) provide an example of a

complicated linear programming model, developed to examine forestry and farming strategies in the Sedbergh district of Cumbria. Other comparable studies have been carried out by Dane, Meadow and White (1977) and Miron (1976). Apart from the models described above, other techniques such as checklists, matrices, networks, and flow diagrams have been widely used to formalise intuitive assessments of future change.

- More recently, models are being developed to formalise the changes taking place in the countryside, and to quantify them, as in the Reading model (Harvey *et al.* 1986) where the consequences of changes in the Common Agricultural Policy have been modelled in terms of agriculture, socio-economics, and ecology.

- Landscape design and habitat creation are necessary measures to repair past damage to the rural environment. The development of interactive systems based on computer landscapes is becoming readily available. In this way, the average landscapes determined by the Survey can be used as a standard against which observed landscapes in development control areas can be tested and compared. In addition, modern interactive methods enable new features to be drawn on to existing landscapes by use of screen technology.

- Ideas are now being developed towards setting environmental quality objectives for land (Peters 1992). The results from Countryside Survey 1990 provide an objective description of the land surface, against which required and desired prescriptions can be measured. They provide a well-described starting point for the planning process.

- The ability to use the above framework as a way of assessing policy options in the landscape, eg support for maintenance of heather *(Calluna vulgaris)* or for tree planting, is readily available.

Immediate uses of Countryside Survey 1990 data, some of which have already been initiated, are:

Estimation of animal populations
Animal range and habitat evaluation
Island biogeography studies
Ecological change detection
Landscape management planning
Environmental impact assessments
Water quality modelling
Critical loads mapping
Hazard impact assessment
Carbon budget assessment
Predicting impacts of climate change
Potential for alternative energy

CONCLUSIONS

The scientific study of the interactions of land uses, with each other and with other factors, is a relatively new research area (although individual elements have been studied for many years). An essential prerequisite to such studies is the availability of reliable, representative, current, and accessible land use data. While the relative advantages of field survey, aerial photography and satellite imagery, as sources of such data, have been recognised and debated for a long time, the current trend is towards an integrated approach.

The work by ITE and others, exemplified in Countryside Survey 1990, is designed to optimise between (i) producing a genuine scientific understanding of the processes involved in interaction between land use change and its environment, and (ii) providing a basis for policy-making, as described in the introduction.

Countryside Survey 1990 is the first project of its type, where national land use data sets, from different sources, have been collected at the same time, in a planned and integrated way. The strengths of both remote sensing and field survey have been combined in an integrated system, specifically designed to provide information on land use change. The data are being collected according to a common format, but can be expressed at a variety of scales and can be linked to other data sets. The outputs provide more extensive and comprehensive information than would be practicable using any single method. The approach can be used for regular monitoring of the land, to provide both quantitative and qualitative information.

The ITE approach allows a full comparison of actual and potential land uses (using data which can be regularly updated), and will provide a fundamental understanding of the causes and consequences of land use change.

ACKNOWLEDGEMENTS

Countryside Survey 1990 was funded by the British National Space Centre, Department of the Environment, Department of Trade and Industry, Natural Environment Research Council, and (former) Nature Conservancy Council.

The authors would like to take this opportunity to acknowledge the support and encouragement given to land use integration studies by staff within the funding organisations, and especially to thank Mr John Peters (DoE) who was largely instrumental in setting up the Countryside Survey 1990 project.

REFERENCES

Aspinall, R.J., Miller, D.R. & Birnie, R.V. 1991. From data source to database: acquisition of land cover information for Scotland. In: *Remote Sensing of the Environment – Proceedings of Image Processing '91, Birmingham*, 131-152.

Austin, M.P. & Margules, C.R. 1984. *The concept of representativeness in conservation evaluation with particular reference to Australia.* (Technical memorandum 84/11.) Canberra: CSIRO Institute of Biological Resources.

Barr, C.J. 1990. Mapping the changing face of Britain. *Geographical Magazine*, **62**, 44-47.

Barr, C.J., Ball, D.F., Bunce, R.G.H. & Whittaker, H.A. 1985. Rural land use and landscape change. *Annual Report of the Institute of Terrestrial Ecology 1984*, 133-135.

Barr, C.J., Benefield, C.B., Bunce, R.G.H., Ridsdale, H.A. & Whittaker, M. 1986. *Landscape changes in Britain.* Abbots Ripton: Institute of Terrestrial Ecology.

Bignall, E.M., Curtis, D.J. & Matthews, J. 1988. *Islay: land types, bird habitats and nature conservation. Part I, Land types and birds on Islay.* Peterborough: Nature Conservancy Council.

Brandon, O., Voyle, A., Dias, W., Bissett, T., Short, C., Bunce, R.G.H., Barr, C.J., Howard, D.C., Jones, M., Evans, S. & Buckland, S. 1989. *Environmental issues and agricultural land use options.* (Report to Department of the Environment, Ministry of Agriculture, Fisheries and Food, Nature Conservancy Council and Natural Environment Research Council.) Aberdeen: Aberdeen Centre for Land Use.

Budd, J.T.C. 1989. National Countryside Monitoring Scheme. In: *Rural information for forward planning,* edited by R.G.H. Bunce & C.J. Barr. (ITE symposium no. 21.) Grange-over-Sands: Institute of Terrestrial Ecology.

Bunce, R.G.H. 1979. Ecological survey of Britain. *Annual Report of the Institute of Terrestrial Ecology 1978*, 74-75.

Bunce, R.G.H., ed. 1989. *Heather in England and Wales.* (ITE research publication no. 3.) London: HMSO.

Bunce, R.G.H. & Claridge, C.J. 1985. The development of a rural land use information system – an example of co-operation between ecologists and planners. *Annual Report of the Institute of Terrestrial Ecology 1984*, 137-141.

Bunce, R.G.H. & Heal, O.W. 1984. Landscape evaluation and the impact of changing land-use on the rural environment: the problem and an approach. In: *Planning and ecology,* edited by R.D. Roberts & T.M. Roberts, 164-188. London: Chapman and Hall.

Bunce, R.G.H. & Heal, O.W. 1990. Ecological consequences of land use change (ECOLUC). *Annual Report of the Institute of Terrestrial Ecology 1989–90*, 19-24

Bunce, R.G.H., Pearce, L.H. & Mitchell, C.P. 1981. The allocation of land for energy crops in Britain. In: *Energy from biomass,* edited by W. Palz, P. Chartier & D.O. Hall, 103-109. London: Applied Science.

Bunce, R.G.H., Tranter, R.B., Thompson, A.M.M., Mitchell, C.P. & Barr, C.J. 1984. Models for predicting changes in rural land use in Great Britain. In: *Agriculture and the environment,* edited by D. Jenkins, 37-44. (ITE symposium no.13.) Cambridge: Institute of Terrestrial Ecology.

Bunce, R.G.H., Lane, A.M.J., Howard, D.C. & Clarke, R.T. 1991. *ITE land classification: classification of all 1 km squares in GB.* (Contract report to the Department of the Environment.) Grange-over-Sands: Institute of Terrestrial Ecology.

Coleman, A. 1961. The second land use survey: progress and prospect. *Geographical Journal,* **127**, 168-86.

Coppock, J.T. & Gebbett, L.F. 1978. *Land use and town and country planning.* (Reviews of UK statistical sources 8.) London: Pergamon.

Countryside Commission. 1991. *Landscape change in the National Parks: summary report of a research project carried out by Silsoe College.* Cheltenham: Countryside Commission.

Dane, C.W., Meadow, N.C. & White, J.B. 1977. Goal programming in land use planning. *Journal of Forestry,* **75**, 325-329.

de Veer, A.A. & de Waal, R.W. 1988. Landscape-ecological mapping of the Randstad area, The Netherlands. In: *Connectivity in landscape ecology,* edited by K.F. Schreiber, 169-172. (Proceedings of the 2nd International Seminar of the International Association for Landscape Ecology.) Paderborn: Ferdinand Schöningh.

Department of the Environment. 1992. *Land use change in England.* (Statistical bulletin (92)3.) London: DoE.

Fuller, R.M. 1987. The changing extent and conservation interest of lowland grasslands in England and Wales: a review of grassland surveys 1930–84. *Biological Conservation,* **40**, 281-300.

Fuller, R.M., Barr, C.J. & Marais, M. 1986. *Historical changes in lowland grassland. Final report.* Peterborough: Nature Conservancy Council.

Fuller, R.M., Jones, A.R. & Wyatt, B.K. 1989. Remote sensing for ecological research: problems and possible solutions. In: *Remote sensing for operational applications: technical contents of the 15th Annual Conference of the Remote Sensing Society, 1989,* compiled by E.C. Barrett & K.A. Brown, 155-164. Reading: Remote Sensing Society.

Fuller, R.M. & Parsell, R.J. 1990. Classification of TM imagery in the study of land use in lowland Britain: practical considerations for operational use. *International Journal of Remote Sensing,* **11**, 1901-1917.

Fuller, R.M., Parsell, R.J., Oliver, M. & Wyatt, G. 1989. Visual and computer classifications of remotely-sensed images. A case study of grasslands in Cambridgeshire. *International Journal of Remote Sensing,* **10**, 193-210.

Griffiths, G.H. & Wooding, M.G. 1989a. Pattern analysis and the ecological interpretation of satellite imagery. *Proceedings of the IGARSS 1988 Symposium, Edinburgh,* 917-921.

Griffiths, G.H. & Wooding, M.G. 1989b. *Use of satellite data for the preparation of land cover maps and statistics.* Farnborough: National Remote Sensing Society.

Haines-Young, R.H. 1992. The use of remotely sensed satellite imagery for land classification in Wales. *Landscape Ecology.* In press.

Harvey, D.R., Barr, C.J., Bell, M., Bunce, R.G.H., Edwards, D., Errington, A.J., Jollans, J.L., McClintock, J.H., Thompson, A.M.M. & Tranter, R.B. 1986. *Countryside implications for England and Wales of possible changes in the Common Agricultural Policy. Executive summary.* (Report to the Department of the Environment and the Development Commission.) Reading: Centre for Agricultural Strategy, University of Reading.

Highland Regional Council. 1984. *HRC/ITE land classification system.* (Planning Department information paper no. 5.) Inverness: Highland Regional Council.

Hooper, M.D. 1968. The rates of hedgerow removal. In: *Hedges and hedgerow trees,* edited by M.D. Hooper & M.W. Holdgate, 9-11. (Monks Wood symposium no. 4.) Abbots Ripton: Monks Wood Experimental Station.

Howard, D.C. & Barr, C.J. 1991. Sampling the countryside of Great Britain: GIS for the detection and prediction of rural change. In: *Applications in a changing world,* 171-176. (FRDA report 153.) Ottawa: Forestry Canada.

Hunting Surveys and Consultants Ltd. 1986. *Monitoring landscape change.* Borehamwood: Hunting Surveys and Consultants Ltd.

Lancashire County Council. 1991. *Lancashire – a green audit: summary.* Preston: Lancashire County Council.

Lopoukhine, N., Prout, N.A. & Hirvonen, H.E. 1978. *Ecological land classification of Labrador.* (Ecological land classification series no. 4.) Halifax, Nova Scotia: Lands Directorate (Atlantic Region), Fisheries and Environment Canada.

Lowe, P., Ward, N. & Munton, R.J.C. 1992. Social analysis of land use change: the role of the farmer. In: *Land use change: the causes and consequences,* edited by M.C. Whitby, 42-51. (ITE symposium no. 27.) London: HMSO.

Luff, M.L., Eyre, M.D., Cherrill, A.J., Foster, G.N. & Pilkington, J.G. 1992. Use of assemblages of invertebrate animals in a land use change model. In: *Land use change: the causes and consequences,* edited by M.C. Whitby, 102-110. (ITE symposium no. 27.) London: HMSO.

Maxwell, J.J., Sibbald, A.R. & Eadie, J. 1979. Integration of forestry and agriculture – a model. *Agricultural Systems,* **4**, 161-188.

Miron, J.R. 1976. *Regional development and land use models and overview of optimisation methodology.* (Research memorandum RM-76-20.) Laxenburg: International Institute for Applied Systems Analysis.

Molineux, A. 1978. Data bank at work. *Geographical Magazine,* **50**, 754-755.

Moreau, M. 1990. *The phase I habitat survey in Bedfordshire.* Letchworth: Nature Conservancy Council.

Moss, D., Wyatt, B.K., Cornaert, M.H. & Roekarts, M. 1991. *CORINE biotopes: the design, compilation and use of an inventory of sites of major importance for nature conservation in the European Community.* (EUR 13231.) Luxembourg: Commission of the European Communities.

Peters, J.C. 1992. Ecological survey of land and water in Britain. *Proceedings of the 4th Ecological Quality Assurance Workshop, Cincinnati.* In press.

Pollard, E., Hooper, M.D. & Moore, N.W. 1974. *Hedges.* (New naturalist series no. 58.) London: Collins.

Potter, C.A. & Gasson, R. 1988. Conservation through land diversion: results from a survey. *Journal of Agricultural Economics,* **39**, 340-351.

Rodwell, J.S., ed. 1991. *British plant communities. Vol. 1: woodlands and scrub.* Cambridge: Cambridge University Press.

Schaller, J. & Haber, W. 1988. Ecological balancing of network structures and land use patterns for land consolidation by using GIS technology. In: *Connectivity in landscape ecology,* edited by K.F. Schreiber, 181-187. (Proceedings of the 2nd International Seminar of the International Association for Landscape Ecology.) Paderborn: Ferdinand Schöningh.

Smith, R.S. & Budd, R.E. 1982. *Land use in upland Cumbria: a model for forestry/farming strategies in the Sedbergh area.* (Research monograph in technological economics no. 4.) Stirling: Technological Economics Research Unit, University of Stirling.

Stamp, L.D. 1937–47. *The land of Britain: the final report of the Land Utilisation Survey of Britain.* London: Geographical Publications.

Warnock, S. & Bell, M. 1987. Likely farmer response in the hills and uplands: results of a survey based on the ITE sample framework. In: *Farm extensification: implications of EC regulation 1760/87,* edited by N.R. Jenkins & M. Bell. (Merlewood research and development paper no. 112.) Grange-over-Sands: Institute of Terrestrial Ecology.

Whitbread, A. 1985. *Cumbria inventory of ancient woodlands (provisional).* Peterborough: Nature Conservance Council.

Wright, J.F., Armitage, P.D., Furse, M.T. & Moss, D. 1989. Prediction of invertebrate communites using stream measurements. *Regulated Rivers: Research & Management,* **4**, 147-155.

NERC/ESRC Land Use Programme (NELUP)

Decision-making in land use

J R O'Callaghan
Centre for Land Use and Water Resources Research, Dept of Agricultural and Environmental Science, University of Newcastle upon Tyne, Newcastle upon Tyne NE1 7RU

INTRODUCTION

The objective of the NERC/ESRC Land Use Programme (NELUP) is to bring together the results of research in the fields of agricultural economics, hydrology, and ecology that are relevant to decisions about land use, and to make them accessible to decision-makers in a form that would allow them to examine, at the planning stage, the likely long-term consequences of their proposals. It is assumed that the majority of decisions about land use are market-driven, but that the results of those decisions have implications for the environment through their impacts either on the quantity and quality of water flowing through the system, or on the diversity and rarity of assemblages of organisms and habitats.

Agriculture and forestry are practised on nearly nine-tenths of the land in Britain, but the activities of industry and of people in towns and cities in the other one-tenth also make demands on land for buildings, roads, water, waste disposal and recreation. An estimate by the Institute of Terrestrial Ecology (ITE) (Bunce & Heal 1984) of the allocation of the land surface of Britain in 1978 to various major land cover types is shown in Table 1. The patterns of agricultural land use which have evolved during the past 50 years have been the result of policies to increase food production and to keep farm incomes in step with those of the economy generally. The main instruments of agricultural policy have been price-setting, subsidies and grants aimed at increasing the production of particular commodities. We have now reached the stage where the disadvantages of such

Table 1. Allocation of the land surface of Britain to various major land cover types. The table is based on estimates derived from field survey in eight sample squares in each of the 32 land classes (Bunce & Heal 1984). Conversion into a Great Britain basis is made by estimating the proportion of the kilometre squares belonging to each land class. Areas are in hectares (figures in brackets = % of total)

Group	Subcategory	Area	(%)	Detail	Area	(%)
All crops 4 428 207 (19.6)	Cereals	3 426 148	(14.9)	Ploughed/fallow	107 389	(0.7)
	Other crops	709 013	(3.4)	Sugar beet	146 959	(0.6)
	Horticulture	293 046	(1.3)	Animal fodder	190 955	(0.9)
				Mixed crops	263 701	(1.2)
All grass 6 385 070 (27.8)	Leys	3 483 270	(15.2)	Short-term leys	2 357 204	(10.4)
				Other leys	1 098 820	(4.8)
	Permanent grass	2 901 800	(12.7)	Generally reseeded	1 447 997	(6.4)
				Older grassland	1 453 806	(6.3)
All wood 2 207 300 (9.6)	Broadleaved wood	561 010	(2.4)	Copses	781 433	(0.3)
				Shelterbelts	34 552	(0.2)
	Conifer	1 404 737	(6.1)	Scrub	241 556	(1.1)
	Scrub	241 556	(1.1)	Woodland	1 853 050	(8.1)
Semi-natural 5 514 553 (24.0)	Rough grassland	2 177 424	(9.5)	Rough grass	505 270	(2.2)
				Mixed rough grass	513 960	(1.4)
				Bracken dominant	360 530	(1.6)
				Rush dominant	374 358	(1.6)
				Mountain grass	612 306	(2.7)
	Moorland	3 337 129	(14.5)	Moor-grass dominant	761 907	(3.3)
				Cotton-grass	669 994	(2.9)
				Heather dominant	1 260 201	(5.5)
				General moorland	645 027	(2.8)
Unavailable 4 334 471 (18.9)	Aquatic	726 394	(3.2)	Buildings, etc	2 227 890	(9.9)
	Human	2 992 440	(13.0)	Communications	719 550	(3.1)
	Unavailable	615 637	(26)	Inland rock	169 403	(0.7)
				Maritime	446 234	(1.9)

single-minded, price-driven policies are apparent in their impact on the landscape and on both terrestrial and freshwater ecosystems.

Land use is not a simple matter of matching supply and demand for the delivery of food and fibre: there are a host of other activities which may be based on the same land. Land in multiple use meets such needs as water gathering and recreation, as well as providing habitats. As stated in *This common inheritance,* 'land is the common thread. It is a finite resource and we have to find enough for all our needs – homes, jobs, shops, food, transport, fuel, building materials and recreation – while protecting what we value most in our surroundings' (Department of the Environment 1990).

Conservation of habitats is seen as necessary for maintaining biodiversity and preventing the extinction on an unprecedented scale of species that are under great pressure because of the environmental changes imposed upon them, mainly by the new practices adopted in agriculture and forestry (Nature Conservancy Council 1982). While there is general acceptance of the urgency of the problem, there is less agreement about how to solve it. Conservation raises scientific issues about the designation of sites, their critical area in order to be effective, their management in perpetuity, and the number the country needs.

Access to the countryside and its enjoyment by all citizens have a long tradition which was captured in 1945 by the report of the Committee on National Parks in England and Wales:

> 'A National Park is an extensive area of beautiful and relatively wild country in which for the nation's benefit and by appropriate national decision and action,
>
> a) the characteristic landscape beauty is strictly preserved,
>
> b) access and facilities for public open air enjoyment are amply provided,
>
> c) wildlife and buildings and places of architectural and historic interest are suitably protected, while
>
> d) established farming use is effectively maintained'.

These demands on the land may be viewed as a conflicting set of property rights, where the rights of private ownership and private production co-exist with less well-defined public rights to access, environmental quality, and water gathering. The aim of the NELUP project is to construct a decision support framework which explicitly recognises the externalities generated by land-based production, and traces their effects through ecological and hydrological processes. The complexity of land use and its implications suggest that an optimum allocation of land for society as a whole is neither definable nor attainable within the present statutory framework. Thus, the decision support system is viewed as a means of providing information to assist the resolution of land planning problems within a comprehensive interdisciplinary framework.

THE LAND USE PROGRAMME

NELUP attempts to portray, in a quantitative way and at a river basin scale, the interactions between the different processes involved in land use activities. From an understanding of the processes that go to make up the system, it should be possible to track how a change at one place affects the other parts of the system. A river basin was chosen as the unit of study because it is a convenient geographical entity, and it was perceived essential to integrate the effects of land use with water gathering and ecological stability. The quality of the water flowing in a river reflects the agricultural husbandry in the rural areas and the waste treatment processes in the urban and industrial areas of its catchment. The Tyne was chosen as the river basin for which to develop the model, with a prototype version for the Rede, a tributary of the Tyne.

'Land cover' (Figure 1) is the common theme in NELUP that unites the three disciplines of agricultural economics, hydrology, and ecology, on which an understanding of the processes of land use is developed. A proposal about how to use an area of land, made in response to market or policy forces, manifests itself as a decision about land cover in the form of an agricultural crop, a forest or, possibly, concrete. As the crop canopy develops, it influences the hydrology on the site by the way it intercepts rainfall and influences evapotranspiration. The type, density, persistence and architecture of the crop canopy are major determinants of the assemblages of plants and animals which are likely to be found in the area.

The main source of land cover data for NELUP is the ITE land classification system of Great Britain. Although the classification system is based on physical attributes, it is a rich source of information on land cover through the data collected in three national ecological field surveys carried out in 1978, 1984 and 1990. The one kilometre grid square of the classification has been adopted as the basic spatial unit for NELUP. It is planned to augment the information in the ITE land classification with remote-sensed data on land cover.

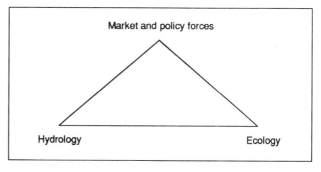

Figure 1. The land cover triangle

The June census of the Ministry of Agriculture, Fisheries and Food provides a long-run record of agricultural production on a parish basis. By disaggregating the census data from a parish to a one km grid square basis, and correcting for forestry and other uses not included in the census, another estimate of land cover is obtained, which can be used as a check on the survey estimates. By combining information from the Farm Business Survey with the census data, it is possible to calculate input/output relationships for a range of production activities in the different land classes. For example, by this means, a spatial distribution of nitrogen fertilizer usage over time may be estimated. The long time series of data from a combined census/survey offers an insight into how farmers change their production in response to price signals from the market.

Land cover has a major influence on how precipitation is partitioned and on the quantity of water that can be gathered in a river basin. Calculations of the water fluxes to the atmosphere, root zone, and deep percolation are carried out on a grid square basis using physical data from a large number of sources regarding topography, meteorology, crop cover, soil and subsurface geology. With additional information on land use and with a chemical/biological component added to the hydrological model, estimates are available of the quality as well as the quantity of the water flowing through the different pathways.

The ecology of an area is dependent on both the vegetation cover and hydrology at the site. While the range of plants and animals that might be included is very large, it has been decided to concentrate on the principal species assemblages of plants and animals in each land cover type, and to gauge the environmental factors and likely effects of land use which most influence them. The distribution of higher plants is accorded the greatest importance because of its influence on the micro-habitat of other groups of organisms. Beetles and spiders are regarded as good environmental indicators of soil and land management, while water beetles are considered to be indicators for static water bodies. Information on the distribution of breeding birds and butterflies will be included, and we hope to draw on the research of the Institute of Freshwater Ecology's River Laboratory for information on the fauna of running water. While the distribution of species assemblages within the land classes is in itself valuable information, a prediction of how species and species assemblages react to changes in land use is needed. The matrix model, developed as part of the Programme, is a promising method for predicting the direction and probable rates of change.

NELUP is a very big exercise in data gathering, and the Programme relies almost entirely on existing data sets. It aims to bring together, from a large number of sources, survey data in agricultural economics, ecology and soils, measured data in meteorology and land topography, and process models and relationships derived from experiments. Much of the information is at different scales, with a range of associated errors, and is, in some cases, incomplete. All of these data must be stored, transformed, retrieved and presented in a reliable and rapid fashion. Within NELUP, this is done by means of a geographical information system (geographic resource analysis support system – GRASS). Pre-processing algorithms for the transformation of data, from their original format to those required by the process models, are being built into GRASS in order to automate the production of model data. For the hydrology model, in particular, such automation is necessary, because the requisite data sets are so large and complex. Automation of data transformation has the added advantages of replicability and consistence, both within and between catchments.

NELUP has three main objectives.

1. To bring together from various sources the data that are relevant to the major processes involved in agricultural land use, water gathering and ecology, and to use the data to develop quantitative models that provide an understanding of how the processes are interlinked. This objective is within reach, and a framework exists which could accept models from other researchers to explain the processes in the land use/hydrology/ecology system.

2. To use the methodology as a means of examining the likely impact of a change in land use on the system as a whole. The economic time series has obvious possibilities for examining how farmers have reacted to changes in prices in the past, and for forecasting their likely response in the short/medium term to changes in the prices of what they produce. The 'knock-on' effects of new farm production plans on hydrology and ecology could be estimated. A complete change of land use, such as from grass to forestry, could be analysed, as well as the effect of new policies, such as a move towards adopting low-input systems.

3. To use the data base and simulation capability as a framework for a decision support system, which would allow planners from many disciplines to examine the likely results of different proposals for land use, especially with respect to long-term consequences, so that, by understanding better the problems which are to be faced now and in the future, improved decisions can be made now.

THE DECISION SUPPORT SYSTEM

Categories of decision-making

Decision-making may be placed into two broad categories. In the first category lie decisions about routine recurring problems that may be handled with a high degree of certainty. The management of most day-to-day operations is concerned with questions about which there is a store of historical experience,

and for which there are accepted rules for making a decision on appropriate courses of action. While the method of reaching a decision may range from a set of rules based on precedents to sophisticated computational techniques, a characteristic property of such problems is that the person making the decision is assumed to have fairly full knowledge about the factors influencing the decision, and about the various probable outcomes of the decision that is finally made.

A second category of decision-making is concerned with strategic decisions, which are characterised by uncertain cause/effect relationships and incomplete information about the preferred outcomes which are to be sought. Usually, the problems requiring a decision are of the 'one-off', non-recurring type, for which the decision-maker lacks complete information about the performance of the system and the preferences of the 'customer'. There is no single preferred method of reaching a decision about problems which are characterised by a high degree of uncertainty. However, there is broad agreement that the general problem-solving process should generate alternatives, use quantitative techniques, if possible, to reduce uncertainty, and recognise that 'satisficing' of locally maximising solutions is a more likely outcome than a 'globally maximising' one.

Decisions explored by NELUP will be mainly of the non-recurring, strategic kind, and in situations where it is impossible to state with certainty that the decision-maker is aware of all the options available to him. 'Satisficing' is a more appropriate method of choosing between alternatives than 'maximising'. However, in choosing between alternatives, there is scope for using quantitative techniques, where it is possible to associate measures of utility with different options, to estimate expected values, or to assign probabilities, either measured or subjective.

A decision-making cycle may be summarised under six headings.

1. *Setting managerial objectives.* The decision-making process starts with objectives, some of which may be conflicting. A particular cycle of decision-making terminates on reaching the objectives that gave rise to it, and the next complete cycle begins with the setting of a new set of objectives.

2. *Searching for alternatives.* Sets of alternative policies are the raw material of a decision-making process. Some alternative strategies can be generated internally, through the experiences of the managers working in the organisation. External inputs are likely to come from consultants and a search of the relevant literature. Clearly, the relevant information should be formulated into alternatives that seem likely to meet the objectives set out in 1. A limitation of quantitative techniques is their inability to generate alternatives.

3. *Comparing and evaluating alternatives.* The likely outcome of the alternatives put forward in 2 in meeting the objectives of 1 is evaluated in terms of cause and effect relationships. The major contribution of quantitative techniques is largely in this appraisal process. Ideas of probability, utility theory and expected value may be used to sharpen comparison.

4. *Choice.* By choosing a particular course of action, from among a set of alternatives, the decision-maker is proposing a solution to meet the managerial objectives that started the decision-making cycle in the first place.

5. *Implementation.* Implementing the chosen course of action to be carried out within the organisation is the point in the total decision-making cycle when the choice is transformed from an abstraction into an operational reality.

6. *Monitoring and control.* It is essential to ensure that the implemented decision results in an outcome that is in keeping with the objectives which were set at the commencement of the decision-making cycle.

Decision-making models

The extensive literature on models of the decision-making process emphasises the apparent superiority of closed decision models. The appeal of such models lies in their formal structure and normative solutions for a range of prototype problems. The models assume that decision-makers operate in a 'closed system', in which they are aware of all the options that are available to them, and from which they can isolate a single objective. It is also assumed that both the objective and the constraints can be expressed in quantitative terms.

There are, in fact, recurring routine problems, in the first category of decision-making, which involve the optimal allocation of scarce resources, and where the quality of the decisions can be improved through the use of mathematical programming. In such cases, the restrictive assumptions of the model can be met, such as that the decision-maker has complete quantitative knowledge about the alternative courses of action, and that the objective consists of simply choosing the most profitable course of action.

Empirical studies of decision-making within organisations have drawn attention to how little maximising models are used in practice in making strategic choices. The applications of the globally maximising approach are limited by the assumption that the decision-maker has perfect knowledge about all the options available to him, and that the objective of the decision-making cycle can be reduced to the maximisation of a single objective function. Empirical studies have emphasised the behavioural aspects of decision-making within the firm (Simon 1957; Cyert & March 1963; Harrison 1987). Simon noted five characteristics that reflect the behavioural approach to the decision-making cycle.

1. The problems faced in real organisations, which

have to deal with interest groups both within the organisation and outside it, are so complex that managers tend to divide the problems into roughly independent parts, and to deal with the parts on a piecemeal basis.

2. 'Satisficing' replaces 'maximising' as a way of evaluating alternatives because the decision-makers cannot be sure that they have all the alternatives available to them and, in any case, they are prepared to settle for the 'good enough'. In their book *A behavioural theory of the firm*, Cyert and March (1963) described the decision-making process within firms as an incremental one that focused on attainable objectives acceptable to the participants in the short/medium term. Alternative policies were considered until a satisfactory option emerged in a situation where evaluation and choice was by 'committee'. Uncertainty was avoided by following what was perceived to be the broad policy of the firm, and by reacting to feedback following implementation, rather than by attempting to predict the consequences of the decision.

3. Searching for alternatives within organisations is a relatively stable sequential process. The discovery of an alternative that meets the current managerial objective is usually the signal to end the search for further alternatives during the current decision-making cycle.

4. Uncertainty is reduced by making choices that put a premium on short-run feedback, so that further changes can be made if the outcome is found to be diverging too far from the managerial objectives set at the beginning of the decision-making process.

5. Organisations tend to hold in reserve second and third alternatives that may be offered for implementation, if feedback indicates that the satisfising choice is not yielding the desired outcome.

A decision support system is being developed for NELUP which utilises the information contained in the data base via the process models in order to make them available in a form that can assist decision-makers in reaching strategic choices about land use. The system should support rather than replace expert judgement. Decision support systems are defined as:

> Computer-based information systems that combine models and data in an attempt to solve poorly structured problems with extensive user involvement.

The NELUP decision support system (DSS)

The NELUP information environment is shown diagrammatically in Figure 2. At the centre of the system is the customer or decision-maker. It will usually be an individual wishing to analyse a decision or strategy about land use. In most cases, it is envisaged that the individual is acting on behalf of an

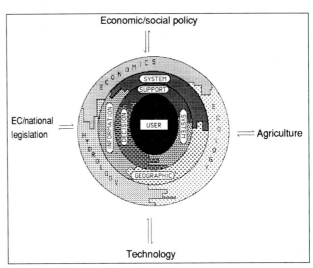

Figure 2. The NELUP decision support system

organisation, whose interests are at a regional level, rather than in his private capacity as a farmer or householder. Almost every decision about land use will be influenced by the policy environment within which the decision must fit. The decision must conform with existing and proposed legislation. It must be economically viable and socially acceptable. It will most likely be influenced by technological trends and, as agriculture is such a predominant user of land, the decision is likely to be dependent on what takes place in agriculture.

The decision support system is the main interface between the decision-maker and the general policy environment, which contains so much information, in such a wide variety of forms, that an attempt has to be made to select and interpret those parts of the information most relevant to the problem in hand. Three pathways have been chosen for organising the flows of information.

An economic unit interprets economic and social trends in order to predict changes in land use policy and evaluate the likely economic outcomes of a proposed decision. A hydrological unit can simulate quantitatively the surface water and groundwater flows that result from a particular use of land, as well as the quality of the water that is likely to result from chemical inputs at the land surface. An ecological unit predicts the assemblages of plant, vertebrate and invertebrate species that result from a particular land use, together with an indication of the long-term consequences.

The geographical information system (GIS) is a software technology for the management of data in space and time. It envisages space as being covered by a cartesian co-ordinate system, in which each separate attribute of the space is described by a separate overlay. So, for each point on the surface, the column vector of overlay values defines the values of all the properties at that point. Each location on each overlay is represented by a single pixel, and the value contained in the memory location for that pixel is the value of the property contained in that overlay. GIS provides a management tool for the large amounts of information that are relevant to

reaching decisions about land use, and to modelling the consequences of a range of impacts. GIS also links the storage and management of data with the various models that are used to predict the input/output relationships, which, in turn, provide the building blocks for the decision support system.

In designing a decision support system for a region such as a river basin, we should note that not only are there several demands competing for land, but that those demands are being exerted by a number of persons with property rights in respect of specific parcels of land. Property rights in land are discussed by Denman and Prodano (1972). They emphasise that authority for taking decisions about the use of land operates at two levels: a higher level where plans are made for regional and national purposes, drawing on general principles and criteria of social and economic studies; and a lower level by those who hold property rights over the land and who in consequence take positive decisions about its use.

Denman and Prodano make the point that national and regional planning of the use of land and natural resources has been mainly undertaken through the imposition of public controls on the use of land, and has in this sense been negative. In their opinion, planning by prohibition has culminated in a universal sense of ineffectiveness where neither the planners nor the planned are content. The planner is denied the power of positive planning, and the holders of property rights are discouraged from thinking proactively. They see the remedy in bringing together the holders of the property rights and the planners. In their words:

> 'By identifying and studying the proprietary land unit, planners will come to know and perhaps appreciate the motives and powers of the holders of the units and hence what lies behind the decision-making which issues in positive action for the use of land. Working with the planners, the holders of proprietary land units will see their own problems and the significance of the decisions they take within the social and economic framework of an entire planning district or region and even against the background of the national economy'.

In a paper on multiple land use, Whitby (1990) points out that a fully functional system of property rights must recognise the multiple nature of most of the demands placed on land; he identifies four sets of property rights, attributable to owners, occupiers, users, and the general public.

One of the challenges facing the designer of a decision support system is to propose a broad framework within which the overall pattern of land and water use in the river basin should operate in the long term, which should satisfy the various demands for land within the region, and should fulfil the reasonable expectations of the holders of the property rights.

The decision support system is summarised diagrammatically in Figure 3. At the centre are the mathematical models which are used to simulate how a system of land use functions, especially with respect to income, ecology, and hydrology. Inputs to the model are in the form of variables such as area and type of land cover, together with their spatial distribution, which the decision-maker can hope to influence, together with uncontrolled variables, such as weather and soil type, which have to be treated as exogeneous to the system. A considerable challenge for the agricultural economist is to translate the broad instruments of policy-making into a representative set of controlled variables. The output from the model is the outcome of the different policy options as they affect, for example, the income of the landholders, the ecology, and the hydrology. The modelling capability of NELUP allows the policy options to be analysed to different levels of detail, as required by the user. If the outcomes of a policy are deemed unsatisfactory, the decision-maker can react by 'feeding back' a modified policy into the system for further analysis.

In effect, the decision support system will concern itself with steps 1–4 of the decision-making cycle, discussed above.

1. Setting the managerial objectives

The managerial objectives will be set externally by the users of the system. However, they will be constrained by the capability of NELUP and the kinds of problems that it is programmed to tackle.

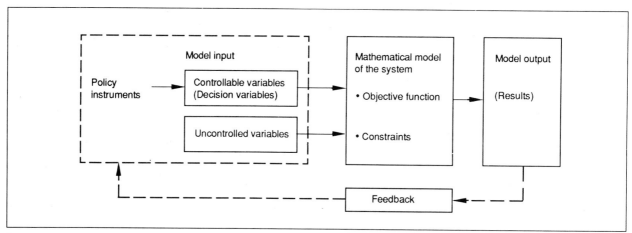

Figure 3. The NELUP decision support system

Feedback from potential users is the principal way of bridging the gap between the expectations of the users and the potential capability of the data base and computational algorithms. The more closely expectations can be identified with capability, the more user-friendly will be the system.

NELUP will contain a large data base on the river basins it has studied, as well as algorithms for calculating the outcomes of different scenarios for the use of land and water. One first use of the data is to present, in a series of overlays, background information of the kind listed in Table 2, relating to the catchment, which is relevant to setting objectives.

Table 2. Background information available from data base

General	Ordnance Survey map data
	Topography
	ITE land classes
	Sites of Special Scientific Interest, Areas of Outstanding Natural Beauty, Nature Reserves
	Population density
Agriculture	Farm structure
	Production potential
	Nitrogen use
Forestry	Location
	Type
	Maturity
Water	Drainage pattern
Ecology	Location of major terrestrial and aquatic assemblages

2. *Searching for alternatives*

As one of the principal aims of the decision support system is to involve the user actively in the search for solutions to meet the objectives of a decision-making cycle, it seems natural that he/she should have an active role in proposing policies for the way the land

is to be used. The data base and modelling capability can help by showing on screen, as background information, the existing uses; but the planner is likely to want to explore new options for the catchment and to assess their likely impacts. It is also possible to use the DSS to prompt the user in certain directions; the existence of a Nature Reserve, forest, or a particular level of nitrogen use on the background overlays may encourage further action in those areas. It is also possible to develop the data base/modelling facility of the system to produce a land capability classification that would rank spatially the potential of the catchment for growing selected crops. Judgement about the capacity of the plant/soil/water continuum to function in a way that does not contravene standards of good husbandry should influence the choice of alternative uses for a particular catchment, and is complementary to the hydrology/ecology evaluations that will be made by the data base/modelling facilities of the DSS.

In the first version of the DSS, it is proposed to use a matrix of the kind shown in Table 3 as one of the ways of interacting with the user. In the first column of Table 3, headed 'policy options', the DSS would probably select the first entry, which would be 'existing use', and the user would put in other options that are to be evaluated. It is proposed to divide the potential changes in land use into two categories: changes in type of land use, where the change results in a complete change in cover, converting permanent pasture to arable; and changes in intensity of land use, where the change results from an alteration in management of the same type of use, eg a change in fertilizer regime on a ley/pasture. While production options in agriculture will remain the only alternatives for the majority of land, the DSS will function just as well in evaluating options in water gathering, forestry, waste disposal, or conservation.

3. *Comparing and evaluating alternatives*

The underlying requirement of NELUP is that, in evaluating proposed patterns of land use, long-term ecological trends would moderate short-term

Table 3. Decision support table

Policy options	Economics			Ecology			Hydrology		
	Gross margin	Profit	Returns to land	Rarity Assemblages	Species	Diversity of habitats	Quantity Peak	Minimum	Quality
P_1									
P_2									
P_3									
P_n									

economic evaluations. The system of evaluation should provide an acceptably rigorous comparison of the alternatives proposed in 2 so that the decision-maker could be 'satisfied' in selecting an option to meet the objectives set in 1, and, if not, should have the possibility of feeding other options into the system for analysis, on the understanding that further development of the data base and algorithms might be required to make it capable of evaluating them.

Decision theory can be used to guide the decision-maker in situations where he has several policy options available to him. The 'satisficing' assumption is implicit in selecting a range of options in order to take account of the fact that the decision-maker lacks perfect knowledge about the whole range of possibilities available to him. Quantitative techniques are then used to choose from among those options. A pay-off table is a convenient framework for presenting the decision-making situation, because it uses the three concepts of probability, utility and expected value. The entry at the intersection of a row and column is the pay-off, or measure of utility, to the decision-maker through the selection of that option under one of the possible policies. With a probability weighting to take account of risk, the expected value for each option may be calculated. When a decision is not amenable to simple quantification, a 'flagging' procedure may be used to alert the decision-maker to the fact than an option fails to meet certain pre-set conditions and that further investigation is required.

Three sets of criteria based on considerations of income, ecological quality, and water quality are proposed for evaluating the alternatives. Income for those who exercise the property rights on land is proposed as the first measure by which a proposal for using the land should be judged. Income in itself is not necessarily the whole story, and it cannot be divorced from land values, but, unless those who own and work the land can expect a level of income broadly in line with those in employment in the rest of the economy, they are not likely to remain in farming.

On the basis of the land classes, and the options put forward for using each of them, it is possible to calculate an average gross margin per hectare, which is representative of a particular land class in the catchment, but could not be expected to have the accuracy of a farm plan, with its own individual set of opportunities and constraints. Reflecting the present pessimism about agricultural prices, it is prudent to look at what would happen to the gross margins in conditions of lower prices.

Each option should, in time, produce a land cover, which can be related to its land class. For the more likely options, probable species assemblages may be predicted from the models developed as a description of the relationships of species and communities to land classification, together with the influences of environmental factors on them. The consequences of land use change will be assessed by reference to a range of criteria, such as diversity and rarity, calculated for both organisms and habitats.

These criteria will be used for quantifying the effects of change and, where a large change would be produced as a result of implementing one of the options, that fact will be flagged against that option on the decision support matrix as a warning to the user that the situation should be analysed further.

Given the land cover and location of the grid squares, the hydrology component of the DSS can predict the water flows, surface and subsurface. These flows define the water gathering potential of the area, and, when aggregated over the whole region, the likely discharges in the river. From the proposed land use, it is possible to deduce information for the chemical subroutine of the hydrological model, which can then make a prediction of some aspects of the water quality.

It is conceivable that some of the options for using the land may not meet the ecological and/or hydrological constraints deemed to be desirable for the catchment. The DSS allows the planners to rerun the analysis, using the same option at a different intensity of production, or trying another policy.

4. *Choice*

The final choice of how to meet the managerial objectives that started the decision-making cycle in the first instance is at the discretion of the user, who can draw on the information in the decision support tables in a number of ways:

- as a representation of the catchment as a whole under present land use;

- as a representation of the contributions of the different land classes to the catchment as a whole under present land use;

- as a way of answering 'what if' questions about the likely impacts of introducing changes in the patterns of land use in the whole or parts of the catchment on farmers' incomes, ecological patterns, and the quantity and quality of water;

- for completing an INEQUALITY checklist as a management aid to land use in the whole or parts of the catchment, where the tables supply the results of simulations in income, and ecology, and the quantity and quality of water, and which could show at a glance if minimum criteria are being met. While the decision support table provides an easy link with the user for proposing options, the output need not be in tabular form, but could be represented in an overlay map on the screen or as hard copy.

DISCUSSION

Land use is a complex subject, in which there are a large number of players with many interests, some of which may be conflicting. The challenge for NELUP is to provide a framework in which the economic aspirations of the holders of property rights are brought face to face with the biological/physical limits of the plant/soil/water system under study. A very large amount of research results exists by way of

surveys, experiments, and process models, admittedly at different scales, which are relevant to an understanding of how such systems function. Three major components of the system have been selected for study in NELUP – the way the market influences agricultural production, and how production interacts with hydrology and with ecology.

Land cover is the key feature linking the three activities in a physical way. Geographical information systems tie the three parts together in spatial and quantitative models.

The objective of the decision support system is to make available to practitioners, in the field of land use, a methodology of quantitative analysis which draws on the large body of data incorporated in the models. Making due allowance for simplifying assumptions, and for what, at this stage, is a steady state approach, the models provide an understanding of the principal processes set in motion by land use, how they are interlinked, and the way they impinge on one another. As the capacities of the plant/soil/water system are very large relative to the disturbances imposed upon them, the assumption that the performance of the system can be captured in a series of steady state representations may not be important. To make the decision support system both relevant and user-friendly, it should be developed in working partnership with practitioners.

The prototype model of the Rede demonstrates that the representation of the land use system has been made operational. Other papers by my colleagues at this Conference report on the detailed research which is the foundation of the total model. It is hoped to have a fully operational model of the Tyne catchment by the end of this year, and to extend the methodology by considering a lowland river, the Cam, during 1993.

REFERENCES

Bunce, R.G.H. & Heal, O.W. 1984. Landscape evaluation and the impact of changing land use on the rural environment: the problem and an approach. In: *Planning and ecology,* edited by R.D. Roberts & T.M. Roberts, 164-188. London: Chapman and Hall.

Committee on Land Utilisation in Rural Areas. 1942. *Report.* London: HMSO.

Committee on National Parks in England and Wales. 1945. *Report.* London: HMSO.

Cyert, R.M. & March, J.G. 1963. *A behavioural theory of the firm.* New York: Prentice-Hall.

Denham, D.R. & Prodano, S. 1972. *Land use.* London: Allen and Unwin.

Department of the Environment. 1987. *Development involving agricultural land.* (Circular 16/87.) London: DoE.

Department of the Environment. 1990. *This common inheritance: Britain's environmental strategy.* (Cm 1200.) London: HMSO.

Harrison, E.F. 1987. *The managerial decision making process.* 3rd ed. Boston: Houghton Mifflin.

Nature Conservancy Council. 1982. *Seventh report.* London: HMSO.

Simon, H.A. 1957. *Models of man.* New York: Wiley.

Whitby, M. 1990. Multiple land use and the market for countryside goods. *Journal of the Royal Agricultural Society of England,* **151**, 32-43.

Software implementation of a decision support system for land use planning

R A Wadsworth

Centre for Land Use and Water Resources Research, University of Newcastle upon Tyne, Newcastle upon Tyne NE1 7RU

INTRODUCTION

The decision support system (DSS) which is being implemented as part of NELUP is aimed at decision-makers who are interested in aspects of land use at the river basin scale, eg National Rivers Authority, conservation bodies, agricultural planners. The system should be able to help and support such decision-makers – not to propose actions or policies.

Information systems, decision support systems and expert systems

The dividing lines between the three computer-based systems, DSS, information systems (IS) and expert systems (ES), are unfortunately blurred, and a certain amount of overlap and confusion occurs. There is a wide range of systems which have the title 'decision support systems', ranging from complex programmes using fourth generation computer languages down to 'off-the-shelf' spreadsheets. Their functions vary from little more than presentations of data, through modelling, to heuristic rule systems.

A workable definition of an IS is a collection of data stored in a computer in a convenient form; they are analogous with traditional filing systems but often include software to aid the interrogation of the data. The Institute of Terrestrial Ecology (ITE) at Merlewood has experimented with a hybrid ES/IS for the display of observed and predicted attributes of its land classification system. A single square (one kilometre grid), or collection of squares can be selected from a map of the UK and various statistics of those squares can be displayed in a series of tables, figures or maps. The system acts as an extensive, and to a certain extent intelligent, index to a set of pages.

An ES implies that all the links within a data set are known and may be expressed as a series of heuristic or process-based 'rules' which can recreate the human decision-making process for all aspects of problem solving in some area of knowledge. Successful ES seem to be restricted to small, well-defined, tightly structured problems, where there is a single solution which does not

have social or political implications. Examples of successful ES include such systems as the one for fault finding in an engine which will not start (Turban 1988). Experience by ITE at Merlewood would seem to suggest that a pure ES approach would be unsuitable for considering changes in land use. The main difficulty seems to be the extraction of the 'rules' used by human experts to solve a given problem, in a topic such as land use for which there is no well-established methodology for solving problems.

DSS lies somewhere between these two approaches. A DSS accesses the data and contains facilities to assist in their analysis and in solving problems, but it has no implications for what problems should/could be investigated or what the optimal solution should be. A definition of DSS which seems appropriate to our area of interest is:

> ' computer-based system that helps decision-makers confront poorly structured problems through direct interactions with data and analysis models' (Sprague & Watson 1986).

THE DESIGN PROCESS

Standard texts on DSS advocate an iterative design process between the decision-maker (the putative user), and the designer/developer. The cycle of discussion – build/modify – display – demonstration might be a short as two weeks (Sprague 1986). This is a council of perfection for DSS with a single end user, and by implication implies that the problems to be solved are or can be reasonably well defined as the system is being designed.

The first difference from the 'normal' case (for a DSS) is that we have a multi-user multi-purpose system, with the added disadvantage (in common with many other software projects) that none of our potential users has any financial or other commitment to our success. The decision-makers for whom we are designing are busy people with whom we can arrange one or two interviews. If we go too early, we run the risk of wasting their time, of being unable to demonstrate the potential to help them. If we go too late, making radical changes will

be difficult. This makes the timing of the approach to potential users critical. Some indication of the potential questions posed by some users can be gained from outside sources, eg ITE's Ecological Consequences of Land Use Change (ECOLUC) project, discussion with the Countryside Commission for Scotland, Nature Conservancy Council for Scotland, Department of Agriculture and Fisheries for Scotland, and the Scottish Development Department (Jeffers 1990), and from informal discussions with representatives from different organisations.

The second difference is that we have not been asked to produce a DSS to help deal with a specific problem. We have to produce a system which can be used for a variety of problems. Considerable discussion has gone on about what sort of case studies we might use to form the basis of selecting problems to be considered.

Despite the differences from the standard set of conditions, we have adopted an iterative design process, which consists of many cycles.

The construction of the DSS takes place on two fronts. An early version tests ideas, acting as a focus for discussion, to be quickly torn down and built up as required. This test version runs for two small catchments to test model output, transferability, ranges, ways of displaying and manipulating data, etc. The complementary version is built up as consensus on the inclusion of features is reached. It is the direct interface with the full geographical information system (GIS) and contains the complete data bases, data manipulation and analysis algorithms, and agreed graphical displays. It will interface directly with the different models.

The design cycles which are used are given below; the earlier in the sequence, the more rapidly each step is repeated.

1. Each group (hydrology, ecology, and economics) proposes new features relevant to its own concerns which should be included. These are discussed, implemented and refined until the group is satisfied.

2. The other groups comment on the new feature, to determine the following: if it makes sense to non-experts, if they think it might be useful, how it could interact with other work.

3. Visitors, 'friends', etc, not within NELUP, are shown the entire system from time to time. Their comments on different features are carefully noted, and modifications made if necessary.

4. 'Friendly' decision-makers and visiting dignitaries are shown the system, and their reactions noted.

5. Students are given tasks to do using the system. Where they go wrong or where the system fails is noted, as well as their direct comments.

6. Outside decision-makers are asked to test and comment on the system.

The first cycle has already been repeated several dozen of times, the fifth and sixth cycles are just starting.

DESIGN SPECIFICATIONS

What we are trying to produce is a system that not only could be useful to many different people, but is capable of showing them very quickly that it will be of use to them. None of our 'design customers' are going to have three or four weeks to understand the system, or to learn a new language, neither are they likely to be willing to wade through manuals to find out what it is going to do. They want something from which to get results quickly; as they get more used to it, they can find out the more subtle things that can be done and the sophisticated analyses which are possible.

Considerable work has been done on the psychology of software design, especially about how easy it is to use. The following guidelines are culled from a number of sources (Carroll & Rossen 1985; Bennett 1983; Wasserman & Shewmaker 1985).

- Users should be allowed to learn by being productive, not by having to carry out a series of lessons, learning commands and instructions.

- The restrictions caused by the limits of short-term memory and the requirements of psychological 'closure' need to be considered.

- The use of menus allows the user to recognise commands rather than remember them; they also help structure a session (Bennett 1983).

- The use of standard placements, operations and explicit codings gives the user confidence in the integrity of the underlying and coherent structure of the system.

- The use of 'survival forms' is useful.

- Logging errors during the design period allows the designer to see where improvements can be made.

- It is easy to introduce ambiguities, eg 'read file', but the use of special vocabularies can be unwittingly confusing.

- Mutually exclusive choices should use congruences, eg open and close.

- When selections are not appropriate, they should be 'protected' rather than hidden.

- Messages should be informative without being verbose, should be polite but not servile or anthromorphic, should not require special knowledge to be understandable, or make reference to manuals or other documents (if avoidable).

- A single picture is worth a thousand words.

The first step is to encourage the potential users to be confident that the system will work and produce sensible output, and that it has potential to help them. By being clear that the system can give assistance at different levels – presenting information, predicting changes, and comparing options – users can be led into the system gently.

Data base function

The DSS is usable as an 'information system', acting as the front end of the GIS. The data base contains a lot of published data which have been cleaned, transformed (where necessary), and transferred into the GIS for display, analysis and manipulation. The effort that has been expended in making some of these data useful should not be underestimated; even Government statistics like the Ministry of Agriculture, Fisheries and Food parish statistics require considerable work before any analysis is possible. The system also contains specialised data which have been derived from other data, eg the distribution of particular plant species (from survey data, national vegetation classification (NVC), Nature Conservancy Council (NCC) 'phase 1' habitat surveys, etc). The data include historical observations, as well as the current conditions, and are easy to access and manipulate. The system must be designed so that data on, say, water quality can be combined with data on farm types, and the position of forestry plantations with a soils map. The users can, therefore, construct their own thematic maps and associated statistics as required. There is no need for the user to start searching the library, abstracting data, cleaning data, transforming co-ordinate systems, etc.

Predictive function

The DSS is linked to a number of models which can predict the consequences of different changes. Some future states are pre-calculated and the results stored. The consequences can be described in terms of their economic and environmental effects, and therefore will give the decision-maker some idea of how a continuation of current policies, proposed legislation, or policy changes will affect their 'clients'. The DSS has been used to justify or support a particular choice or decisions that have been made on intuitive grounds or by using 'engineering judgement'. The predictive capability must also be capable of allowing an explanation of a chain of cause and effect.

Decision-making

The system can be used to help make choices between different decisions. The process of making choices can be systemised in many ways, but, given our description of how organisations deal with the real world in practice, many of them can be neglected as impactical. A simple but effective way to compare choices is the pay-off table. The body of the table constructed by the DS

contains economic measures and environmental 'flags', which warn of potentially unsatisfactory options requiring more investigation.

There are three aspects to every proposed action or change in land use planning – the economic, environmental, and technical implications or limitations. These three aspects should be considered explicitly.

Technical considerations will mainly act as constraints on land use; the type and condition of the soil, the climate and topography limit what can be done. Certain changes have an in-built inertia; for example, pollutants already in some groundwater systems will not be flushed out for several decades. Other land is more or less protected or reserved for or from certain uses, eg National Parks, Green Belts, Sites of Special Scientific Interest, etc.

Ecological or environmental considerations are often difficult for a non-expert to appreciate; there needs to be some way to summarise ecological change into a small enough number of generally understandable indicators or attributes to be easily comparable. The feasibility of incorporating an environmental impact assessment into the DSS is being investigated. This would allow the economic and environmental effects of a decision to be separated explicitly, while allowing the environmental effects to be summarised efficiently.

Economic considerations concentrate on the financial aspects of different uses of land, generally the gross margins.

Design specifications

To achieve these objectives, the following general design principles have been adopted:

- robust – it shouldn't crash,
- simple – familiarity with computers should not be needed,
- self-explanatory – no manuals needed,
- consistent – in design and execution,
- uncluttered – non-intimidatory and clear,
- fast – users become impatient.

SELECTION OF OPTIONS

The selection of options can be made without typing; everything is done by pointing a 'mouse' at a picture, map or a word and pressing one button. The selection of options takes place in a series of panels which are hidden until required. The primary options are presented in the form of a 'tree', in order to emphasise the linkages between the data and options but without constraining the order in which things are examined.

Within the panels different devices are used to indicate different types of choice. Where values

can take any one of a continuous range, 'sliders' are used; where discrete but not exclusive options or values are possible, 'toggles' are used; for exclusive options, 'choice' or 'cycles' are used. Where options should be executed immediately, 'buttons' are used. When an option has been selected, subsidiary panels may appear requesting additional choices before some process is performed. At the bottom of each panel there will be three constant choices – one closes the panel, the other two supply help and information.

There seem to be two opposing views of planning: either there is some optimum pattern of land use which can be discovered and implemented, or that land use results from the resolution of conflict between different groups. The design of the DSS reflects the second paradigm by presenting different subsets of options and data to try to reflect different 'world views', and laying emphasis on different features.

Although the description of the different groups in 'conflict' over land use planning is stereotypical, we see them as having value in three ways.

1. An individual can locate him/herself in the spectrum of 'world views' and be presented with the information that he/she holds to be important.

2. An individual can try and gain some understanding of what the other players are interested in.

3. A decision-maker can use it to see how his/her 'clients' might react to policy decisions or actions.

The different players whom we are attempting to help are:

- the general public – which represents the interests of society as a whole;

- farmers and landowners – the few individuals who hold great power as to what actually happens on the ground;

- concerned individuals – members of the public who have taken an interest in what goes on in the countryside, but who do not expect to benefit economically from changes;

- developers – those wishing for radical change in land use for economic considerations, and those whose actions are strongly constrained (economically) by patterns of land use;

- academics – who wish to look in detail at how these processes function.

It must be emphasised that this is not an attempt to restrict the knowledge to which different groups have access. It is an attempt to provide some structure to the system. As time goes on, other 'players' may be introduced.

Help and information functions have been separated. The help facility gives advice as to

what to do next or what the option means. Both the help and information panels consist entirely of text at present, and are specific to the options being chosen (at the expense of some duplication of data). The messages are designed to be explicit and informative, and do not require specific knowledge in order to be understood. They try to avoid being accusatory or verbose.

PRESENTATION OF RESULTS

Presentation of results needs to go beyond showing the data. There needs to be some way that a user can, after seeing a particular result, ask 'why did that happen?' Although this is an important feature, exactly how it should be implemented is still under discussion.

Additional information is provided above the direct presentation of the results. Such information includes the intention of the project, the reason for including different features, and suggestions as to how it could be used, as well as any limitations to the data, the assumptions made, and other caveats. The help and information (which are separate) are specific to the option being considered.

Results are presented primarily as a series of maps, graphs and tables. Additionally, a limited number of 'landscapes' will be produced, but textual information output is limited. Use is made of the concept of 'survival forms' (the idea that new technologies are adopted more rapidly if they can be seen in some way to resemble familiar features: the word processor – typewriter analogy). The main output of information from the DSS is in the form of maps, partly because these are familiar to virtually everyone, partly because many of the problems of how maps are perceived and used, such as the use of colours and symbols, have a long tradition. Other graphical output includes graphs and landscape sketches.

REFERENCES

Bennett, J.L. 1983. *Building decision support systems.* Reading, Ma: Addison-Wesley.

Carroll, J.M. & Rossen, M.B. 1985. *Advances in human-computer interactions,* edited by H.R. Hartson, 1-28. Norwood NJ: Ablex.

Jeffers, J.N.R. 1990. *The ECOLUC knowledge-based system.* (Report to the Institute of Terrestrial Ecology.) Grange-over-Sands: J.N.R. Jeffers.

Turban, E. 1988. *Decision support systems.* London: Macmillan.

Sprague, R. 1986. A framework for the development of DSS. In: *Decision support systems,* edited by R. Sprague & H.J. Watson. Englewood-Cliffs, NJ: Prentice-Hall.

Sprague, R. & Watson, H.J. 1986. Introduction to DSS. In: *Decision support systems,* edited by R. Sprague & H.J. Watson. Englewood-Cliffs, NJ: Prentice-Hall.

Wasserman, A.I. & Shewmaker, D.T. 1985. The role of prototypes in software engineering methodology. In: *Advances in human-computer interactions,* edited by H.R. Hartson, 191-210. Norwood, NJ: Ablex.

Areal interpolation of parish agricultural census data

P Allanson[1], D Savage[2] & B White[2]

[1]Countryside Change Unit, Dept of Agricultural Economics and Food Marketing,
University of Newcastle upon Tyne, Newcastle upon Tyne NE1 7RU
[2]Dept of Agricultural and Environmental Science, University of Newcastle upon Tyne, Newcastle upon Tyne
NE1 7RU

INTRODUCTION

The fundamental proposition which underlies the interdisciplinary approach adopted by the NERC/ESRC Land Use Programme (NELUP) is that changes in land use[1] are driven by interactions between the socio-economic system and the physical environment. The particular motivation for the study is an appreciation of the value society places upon certain aspects of the rural environment, including wildlife abundance and diversity, landscape, and water quality and supply. These concerns are also reflected in recent policy initiatives which have sought to satisfy the broader aspirations of society with regard to the rural environment[2]. The design of such policies must take account of a range of complex and uncertain issues concerning the interactions between land use decisions and ecological and hydrological systems. The resolution of these issues calls for interdisciplinary work, drawing on various aspects of geography, economics, ecology, and hydrology to create an integrated land use model. The reconciliation of different spatial units of measurement poses a particular problem in the development of this integrated approach.

The primary use of most land in rural areas is for agriculture. The main source of data on this form of land use is the annual June agricultural census, which employs what may be termed the 'farm parish' as the basic reporting unit. The farm parish does not form a suitable spatial unit for modelling and reporting purposes because of certain inherent limitations of the data which have long been recognised (Coppock 1955, 1960). First, the statistics do not relate to the entire agricultural area within the boundaries of a civil parish, but to a changeable set of unidentifiable holdings assigned to that parish. The land to which the data on these holdings relate is not known and may include land in other civil parishes. Second, agricultural land use patterns within any single farm parish may not be uniform because of variations in land capability. Thus, local variations in land use which may be of ecological or hydrological importance are not identifiable.

The simplest means of interpolating agricultural land use statistics to spatial units other than the farm parish is by areal weighting, on the assumption that land uses are uniformly distributed within each civil parish (Flowerdew & Green 1990). This interpolation is likely to be relatively inaccurate. Improved estimates of the spatial distribution of agricultural land use may be generated using information on land use from the Ordnance Survey (OS) and on land capability from the Institute of Terrestrial Ecology (ITE) land classification[3]. Even so, the spatial indeterminacy of agricultural statistics presents an intractable problem which will limit the predictive accuracy of any interpolation procedure.

The following section outlines an areal interpolation procedure for generating improved estimates of the spatial distribution of agricultural crops by ITE land class and kilometre grid square. The following section presents the results from the application of this procedure to the Tyne catchment. The final section summarises the main conclusions.

AREAL INTERPOLATION METHODOLOGY

The general nature of the areal interpolation procedure is introduced with reference to Table 1. This two-way frequency Table gives the joint

Table 1. Distribution of farm parish area by crop type and land class

$\alpha_{11p}L_{1p}$	$\alpha_{1jp}L_{1p}$	$\alpha_{1Np}L_{1p}$	L_{1p}
$\alpha_{i1p}L_{ip}$	$\alpha_{ijp}L_{ip}$	$\alpha_{iNp}L_{ip}$	L_{ip}
$\alpha_{M1p}L_{Mp}$	$\alpha_{Mjp}L_{Mp}$	$\alpha_{MNp}L_{Mp}$	L_{Mp}
C_{1p}	C_{1p}	C_{1p}	A_p

distribution by land class L_{ip} (i=1,...,M) and crop type C_{jp} (j=1,...,N) of the total area A_p of farm parish p (p=1,...,P). The area of land class i devoted to crop j (ie C_{ijp}) is not observed, but is assumed to be some proportion α_{ijp} of the land class area L_{ip}. Thus, the basic problem is to estimate a set of parameters, $\hat{\alpha}_{ijp}$, which ensure that each row and column of the main body of the Table sum to the given marginal totals.

Hotson (1988) provides one possible solution to this type of problem for the 2 x 2 case. All one km grid squares in identifiable non-agricultural uses are initially excluded, and the remaining grid squares divided between those deemed suitable for general agricultural use and those considered suitable for rough grazing only. The areas of all arable crops and grassland in a farm parish are then assumed to be evenly distributed across the grid squares within the associated civil parish which are suitable for general agricultural use, and the farm parish area of rough grazing is similarly allocated between the grid squares deemed suitable for rough grazing only. Hotson asserts that this procedure provides accurate predictions of agricultural land use at a 10 km x 10 km grid scale, though his claim is not substantiated by any statistical measures of goodness-of-fit. In any case, the procedure is not capable of generalisation to the M x N case, except on the basis that each 'land class' is exclusively devoted to a single 'crop'.

The following subsections present a more sophisticated approach which addresses the problem in three sequential stages. The first stage employs geographical information system (GIS) mapping techniques to identify land which is potentially in agricultural use, and to estimate the land class composition of each farm parish in the Tyne catchment. The second generates estimates of crop proportions by ITE land class for the Tyne catchment from the cross-sectional data on crop and estimated land class areas by farm parish. The resultant parameter set, $\hat{\alpha}_{ij}$, may be used to predict crop areas in each farm parish, but these predictions will not in general equal the observed crop areas, C_{jp}. Thus, the final stage is to calibrate the Tyne catchment model so as to reproduce exactly the known cropping pattern within any given farm parish or grouping of farm parishes. Estimates of the spatial distribution of crops by either land class or individual grid square may then be obtained using the calibrated parameter estimates, $\hat{\alpha}_{ijp}$, to predict the cropping on that land within each civil parish identified as potentially in agricultural use.

The GIS mapping procedure

The purpose of the first stage of the analysis is to identify land which is potentially in agricultural use, and to estimate the land class composition of each farm parish. The nature of this problem is illustrated in Figure 1, which shows the civil parish P_1, of which part is in non-agricultural use, and the associated farm parish consisting of the set of farms F_1 to F_5. The location of the farm parish will, in fact, be unknown,

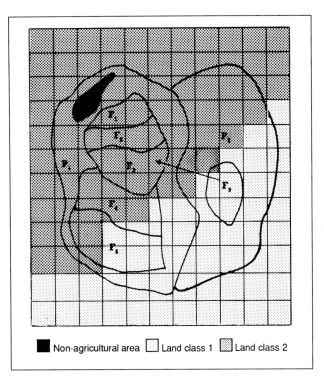

Figure 1. Schematic representation of the problem of estimating the land class composition of a farm parish (source: Coppock 1960)

but is depicted so as to include land within another civil parish, P_2, and to exclude some of the agricultural land in P_1. In effect, the farm parish constitutes an unidentifiable sample of agricultural land drawn from the vicinity of the civil parish. In the absence of additional information, the best feasible estimate of the land class composition of the farm parish will be given by the land class composition of that part of the civil parish P_1 which is potentially in agricultural use.

The problem is addressed using GIS mapping techniques. The GIS map of the Tyne catchment may be thought of as a series of overlays superimposed on the national Ordnance Survey one km square grid. These overlays map the boundaries of civil parishes, of land in non-agricultural uses, and of ITE land classes. Thus, the area of any region may be defined and computed as the area of the set of whole and part grid squares enclosed by its boundary.

The locations of civil parishes and of land in non-agricultural uses are derived from 1:50 000 OS maps. These maps record various land use features, including woods, forests, quarries, open water, and built-up areas. Subtraction of these areas of land in identifiable non-agricultural uses from the total area of a civil parish leaves an area which is deemed to be potentially in agricultural use. This area will tend to overstate the actual agricultural area of the civil parish as it is not feasible to identify or exclude all land not employed in agriculture.

The land classification of each grid square in the Tyne catchment has been provided by ITE. This information is used to determine the land class areas of the land within each civil parish which is potentially

in agricultural use. Estimates of the land class areas in each farm parish for use in the second stage of the interpolation procedure are obtained by scaling the land class areas for the 'agricultural' part of the civil parish so that they sum to the total agricultural area of the associated farm parish.

Estimation of crop proportions by land class for the Tyne catchment

The second stage of the analysis generates estimates of crop proportions by ITE land class for the Tyne catchment from the cross-sectional data on crop and estimated land class areas by farm parish. The use of a maximum likelihood (ML) estimator for this purpose would be statistically desirable. In a series of papers (Flowerdew & Green 1989, 1990; Green 1989), the North West Regional Research Laboratory has developed a set of ML estimators for the areal interpolation of count variables, such as population, based on the expected–missing (EM) algorithm (Dempster, Laird & Rubin 1977). However, similar techniques have not yet been developed for interval extensive variables[4], such as crop areas, which are non-negative, continuous variables that sum to a given total. Of necessity, a less-sophisticated approach based on an inequality–restricted least squares (IRLS) estimator is therefore adopted.

The IRLS estimates are obtained as the solution of a quadratic programming problem. This problem is defined using the notation employed in Table 1 as:

$$\underset{\hat{\alpha}_{ij}}{\text{Minimise}} \quad \sum_{p=1}^{P} \sum_{j=1}^{N} e_{jp}^{2} \qquad (1)$$

subject to:

$$e_{jp} = C_{jp} - \sum_{i=1}^{M} \hat{\alpha}_{ij} L_{ip} \qquad \text{for all j and all p} \quad (1a)$$

$$0 \leq \alpha_{ij} \qquad \text{for all i and all j} \quad (1b)$$

$$1 = \sum_{j=1}^{N} \alpha_{ij} \text{ for all i} \qquad (1c)$$

where the errors terms e_{jp} are defined in (1a) as the differences between the observed and predicted crop areas, and the non-negativity constraints (1b) and adding up constraints (1c) ensure that predicted crop areas are non-negative and sum to the total agricultural area in each farm parish. The errors e_{jp} may also be written as:

$$\begin{cases} e_{jp} = u_{jp} - \sum_{i=1}^{M} \hat{\alpha}_{ij}\, \lambda_{ip} \qquad \text{for all j and all p} \\[2ex] 0 = \sum_{j=1}^{N} e_{jp} = \sum_{j=1}^{N} u_{jp} = \sum_{j=1}^{N} \sum_{i=1}^{M} \hat{\alpha}_{ij}\, \lambda_{ip} \qquad (2) \\[2ex] 0 = \sum_{i=1}^{M} \lambda_{ip} \end{cases}$$

where u_{jp} arises from the random variation in crop proportions by land class across farm parishes, and λ_{ip} is the discrepancy between the actual and estimated area of land class i in farm parish p. The compound error term e_{jp}, and both error components, sum to zero over the full set of crop equations. However, the presence of measurement errors in the explanatory land class variables may give rise to biased parameter estimates in the individual crop equations.

The sampling properties of the IRLS estimator have not been developed analytically, so exact hypothesis tests cannot be employed for model verification. However, the standard errors of least squares regression (OLS) estimates of (1a)[5] will generally provide upper-bound estimates of the standard errors of the IRLS estimates, and therefore yield a conservative basis for testing the significance of parameters (Judge et al. 1980).

The goodness-of-fit of the model will depend inevitably on the strength of the relationship between agricultural cropping patterns and ITE land classes. The ITE land classification was not specifically designed as an indicator of the agricultural capability of land, and it is possible that other land classification schemes, such as that employed by the Ministry of Agriculture, Fisheries and Food (MAFF 1988), would provide a more appropriate proxy for this variable. Even so, whatever land classification is adopted, the model will not generate an exact fit of the data on crop areas in each farm parish.

Calibration of the Tyne catchment model

The third stage of the analysis is to calibrate the parameter estimates for the Tyne catchment so as to generate exact 'predictions' of the crop areas within any farm parish or grouping of farm parishes. This is technically known as a constrained matrix problem, and, with reference to Table 1, consists of choosing a set of parameters $\hat{\alpha}_{ijp}$, based on the initial estimates $\hat{\alpha}_{ij}$, that are consistent with the given crop and land class area totals. It should be noted that errors in these area totals will give rise to biased estimates of the distribution of crops by land class within the parish.

The general approach to this type of problem is to choose the $\hat{\alpha}_{ijp}$ so as to minimise some measure of distance between the predictions of the distribution of crops by land class generated by the initial and calibrated parameter estimates[6]. The choice in this study between alternative calibration techniques based on particular measures of distance is statistically arbitrary, as the nature of the distribution underlying the data generation process is unknown. Accordingly, both the RAS technique (see Bacharach 1970) and the weighted least squares procedure described by Stephan (1942) were tested in order to give some idea of the potential sensitivity of the estimates to the choice of calibration technique.

The RAS or biproportional matrix technique[7] is based on an iterative solution procedure, in which the starting values are adjusted so as to satisfy alternatively the row and column constraints. The

procedure converges on a set of calibrated values, $\hat{\alpha}_{ijp}$, equal to $r_i \, \hat{\alpha}_{ij} \, s_j$, where r_i and s_j are row and column multipliers, respectively. It follows that the calibrated parameters $\hat{\alpha}_{ijp}$ will satisfy the non-negativity condition (1b) and that zero elements in the initial parameter set will be preserved.

Stephan's method is equivalent to maximising a normal likelihood function defined over a set of independent variables[8]. The weighted least squares minimand is given by:

$$\text{Minimise}_{\hat{\alpha}_{ijp}} \quad \sum_{i=1}^{M} \sum_{j=1}^{N} (\hat{\alpha}_{ijp} \, L_{ip} - \hat{\alpha}_{ij} \, L_{ip})^2 \, / \, L_{ip}^2 \, \text{var} \, (\alpha_{ij}) \qquad (3)$$

where var (α_{ij}) is the population variance of the proportion of crop j on land class i. Equation (3) implies that the greater the variance of the area of crop j on land class i, $L_{ip}^2 \, \text{var} \, (\alpha_{ij})$, then the lower the weight placed on finding a solution close to the initial prediction. The solution to (3) subject to the non-negativity and adding up constraints, (1b) and (1c), is found by quadratic programming.

The main advantage of the RAS technique, which has been extensively used in both economics and demography[9], is computational ease. The weighted least squares method may be preferable, however, if reliable information on the variances of crop proportions by land class is available. In the current study, the only available information on these variances was from the 1978 ITE nationwide sample survey of land use by land class, based on eight grid squares within each land class.

EMPIRICAL RESULTS

The Tyne catchment covers land within 83 civil parishes, of which 12 were excluded from the analysis as being largely or wholly urban. Agricultural census records for the remaining 71 parishes are currently available on magnetic tape for the years 1975–87. The reported output from the application of the areal interpolation procedure to this sample has been selected, both to illustrate the changing pattern of land use in the Tyne catchment and to enable a fair assessment of the methodology. Limited results from each of the three sequential stages of the interpolation procedure are presented in turn.

The GIS mapping procedure

The total area of the 71 sample parishes is approximately 292 750 ha, of which the June agricultural census, together with the registered agricultural commons, accounted for 218 400 ha in 1975 and 210 550 ha in 1987[10]. Thus, the recorded agricultural area is roughly 73% of the total area, compared to 76% in England and Wales as a whole, with the remainder accounted for by forestry, woodland, quarries, inland water, urban, and other uses. From the most recent edition of the Ordnance

Survey, the location of nearly 61 500 ha of land in non-agricultural uses was identified and thereby excluded from the analysis. The remaining or adjusted sample area of roughly 231 250 ha was assumed to have been potentially available for agricultural use throughout the sample period[12].

Table 2 reports the ITE land class composition of the total and adjusted sample areas. The recorded agricultural area fell from 94.4% to 91.0% of the adjusted sample area between 1975 and 1987, with the residual discrepancies due to non-agricultural uses not identifiable from the Ordnance Survey, boundary problems due to the spatial indeterminacy of the agricultural statistics, and other measurement errors. On balance, the adjusted sample land class composition may reasonably be assumed to provide a reliable measure of the land class composition of agricultural land in the Tyne catchment. However, the adjusted parish land class mix may provide only a rough approximation to the true land class composition of the associated farm parish, because boundary problems will be more acute for individual parishes than for contiguous groupings of parishes; the ratio of the agricultural area to the adjusted civil parish area for individual parishes varies between 10% and 250%.

The Tyne catchment model of crop proportions by ITE land class

The Tyne catchment model was defined over four crop types: arable, temporary grass, permanent grass, and rough grazing[12]. ITE land classes 10 and 14, and 23 and 24 were aggregated due to the limited number of non-zero observations on land classes 14 and 24 (see Table 2). The IRLS estimates of the model for each year from 1975 to 1987, together with various associated regression statistics, are presented in Tables A1 to A4 of Appendix 1.

The goodness-of-fit of each crop equation to the farm parish data is indicated by the R_π^2 and root weighted mean square percentage error (RWMSPE) measures[13]. R_π^2 measures the relative improvement in the fit of an equation by allowing crop proportions to vary by land class, while RWMSPE is an indicator of the overall predictive accuracy of an equation, where the weights are given as the ratio of the farm parish crop area to the total area of the crop in the Tyne catchment. For example, the 1975 arable equation explains 77.2% of that part of the variation in arable areas which is due to the variation in farm parish arable shares about the average share in the Tyne catchment as a whole, though the overall predictive accuracy of the equation is poor with a RWMSPE value of 118.9%. In general, the degree of variability in the farm parish shares of a crop is positively correlated with the explanatory power, and negatively correlated with the predictive accuracy of the equation for that crop.

Aggregation of parishes to the subcatchment and Tyne catchment levels leads to a progressive

Table 2. Land class composition of sample area (source: Benefield & Bunce 1982)

ITE land class	Total sample area Hectares	%	Adjusted sample area Hectares	%	No. of parishes	General description and land use
10	11 913	4 06	10 617	4.63	25	Flat plains with intensive farming; mainly arable but with good grassland and pasture also widespread
14	102	0.03	102	0.04	2	Level coastal plains; mainly arable but also good grassland
19	2 719	0.93	2 268	0.98	11	Smooth hills; mainly rough grazing or forest, but some pasture
20	182 623	62.26	137 909	59.63	63	Mid-valley slopes; much pasture but some good grassland and occasional crops
22	59 577	20.32	46 877	20.27	24	Margins of high mountains, moorlands; mainly rough grazing, but also woodland and occasional crops
23	15 936	5.43	15 470	6.68	10	High mountain summits; limited open-range grazing
24	359	0.12	359	0.16	2	Upper steep mountain slopes; limited open-range grazing
25	7 066	2.41	6 458	2.79	17	Lowlands with variable land use; mainly barley, but with some good grassland
26	3 956	1.35	3 760	1.63	5	Fertile lowlands with intensive agriculture; mainly good grassland, but also much barley and pasture
27	6 731	2.30	6 261	2.71	12	Fertile lowland margins with mixed agriculture; arable, particularly barley, but also much pasture and good grassland
28	2 225	0.72	1 197	0.52	8	Varied lowland margins with heterogeneous land use; pasture or rough grazing predominate, but some good grassland also
Total	292 746	100	231 277	100	71	

improvement in predictive accuracy, as is suggested by the small percentage prediction errors for the Tyne catchment crop shares. There are two likely reasons for this improvement. First, boundary problems caused by the spatial indeterminacy of the agricultural statistics will be less severe for contiguous groupings of parishes. Second, the land within any land class in any contiguous group of parishes will tend to be more typical of the average land capability of that land class in the Tyne catchment as a whole. The latter problem of variable land quality within individual land classes is likely to be particularly acute in respect of ITE land class 20, which covers nearly 60% of the potential agricultural area in the Tyne catchment.

The IRLS estimates of crop proportions by ITE land

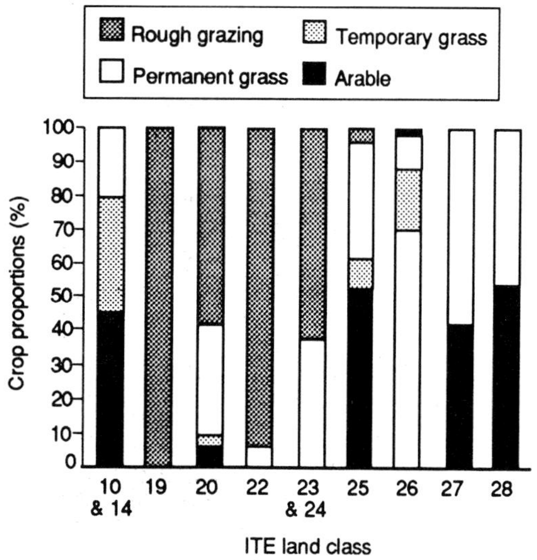

Figure 2. Mean estimates of crop proportions by ITE land class for Tyne catchment

Table 3. ITE survey estimates of percentage crop proportions by land class (source: ITE Merlewood)

Land class	Year	Arable	Temporary grass	Permanent grass	Rough grazing
10 & 14*	1978	44.2	23.3	23.6	8.9
	1984	52.3	17.5	26.2	4.0
19	1978	2.5	10.5	18.9	68.2
	1984	1.7	12.9	11.3	74.1
20	1978	4.8	15.6	31.4	48.2
	1984	4.5	8.8	34.2	52.5
22	1978	3.9	1.0	7.4	87.7
	1984	3.7	2.7	8.7	84.9
23 & 24*	1978	0	0	0.9	99.1
	1984	0	0	0	100.0
25	1978	48.3	36.4	6.8	8.5
	1984	52.8	14.0	23.3	9.9
26	1978	25.4	34.4	27.8	12.3
	1984	48.5	13.1	23.2	15.1
27	1978	35.5	22.9	33.3	8.3
	1984	48.4	17.9	30.7	3.0
28	1978	4.8	12.3	32.4	50.5
	1984	1.6	11.2	31.4	55.8

* Weighted in proportion to the areas in the adjusted sample (see Table 2)

class exhibit a fair degree of stability over time. These results may be usefully summarised, therefore, in terms of the mean estimated parameter values shown in Figure 2. The plausibility of these mean values may be assessed by comparison with the descriptions of the land classes given in Table 2 and with the estimates in Table 3, which were derived from the 1978 and 1984 ITE sample surveys of land use on individual land classes[14]. A clear progression is apparent: on the lowland and plains (land classes 10 & 14, 25, 26, 27 and 28), there are significant proportions of both arable and temporary grass; on the mid-valley slopes (land class 20), the cropping pattern is mixed; and on the upland and hills (land classes 19, 22 and 23 and 24), rough grazing and permanent grass predominate.

However, some of the parameter estimates do appear anomalous: in particular, the aberrant distribution of permanent grass in 1979; the transformation of land class 28 from mostly permanent grass in 1975 to almost entirely arable in 1987; and the designation of land class 19 entirely to rough grazing. One possible reason for these various anomalies is estimation bias due to measurement errors in the land class area variables. The magnitude of these errors may be large, if the scale of the discrepancies between the agricultural census and the adjusted parish areas provides a reliable indicator of the potential size of the problem.

The specific nature of the anomalies may be linked to the sampling properties of the estimator. The upper-bound standard errors of the parameter estimates are negatively correlated with both the explanatory power of an equation, as measured by R_π^2 and the observed sample proportion of a land class. It may be noted that the explanatory power of the permanent grass equation is much lower than those for the other crops, while neither land class 19 nor 28 account for more than 1% of the potential agricultural area in the Tyne catchment.

Figure 3 shows the predicted distribution of each crop in each year as a percentage of the total agricultural area in the Tyne catchment. These predictions were calculated on the basis of the fixed land class composition given in Table 2, and thus only allow for changes in crop areas due to changes in cropping mix by land class[15]. It should be noted that the net change in the total agricultural area between

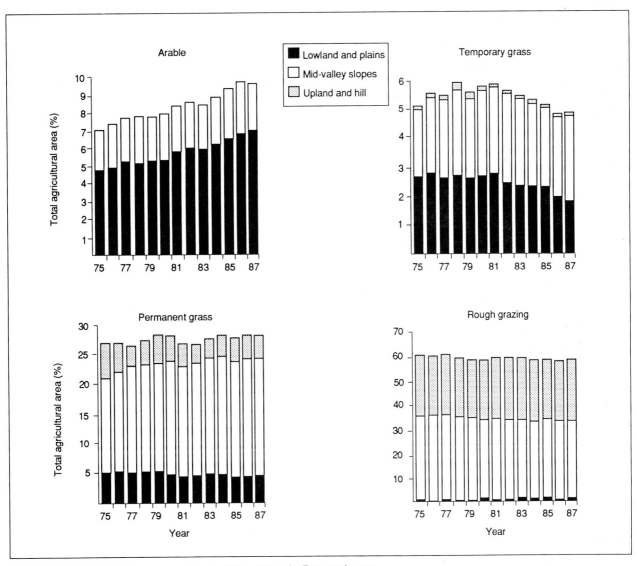

Figure 3. Mean estimates of crop proportions by ITE land class for Tyne catchment

1975 and 1987 is of the same order of magnitude as the changes in the areas of the individual crops.

Overall, there has been a slight increase in the proportion of arable, with a compensating decline in the share of the total area devoted to rough grazing. However, the changes underlying these trends have been more complex, with the substitution of arable for temporary grass and permanent grass on the lowland and plains; of arable, temporary grass and permanent grass for rough grazing on the mid-valley slopes; and of permanent grass for rough grazing on the upland and hills. The net effect of these changes is that the distribution of crops has become more polarised, with arable increasingly concentrated on the lowland and plains, temporary grass and permanent grass on the mid-valley slopes, and rough grazing on the upland and hills.

In conclusion, the ITE land classification does appear to provide a valid indicator of cropping pattern, though of uncertain predictive power given the spatial indeterminacy of parish agricultural statistics. Even if this relationship is rather tenuous, the model may still be expected to generate better estimates of the spatial distribution of agricultural crops than those derived from an areal weighting procedure (see Flowerdew & Green 1990). Indeed, the estimated cropping patterns by land class are generally plausible, and this fact provides reasonable grounds for confidence in the model.

Calibration of the 1987 Tyne catchment model for the Rede subcatchment

The Tyne catchment model may be calibrated so as to reproduce exactly the known cropping pattern in any particular farm parish or grouping of farm parishes. However, this procedure will not necessarily generate accurate predictions of the distribution of crops by land class within the chosen subregion. Thus, independent information on such distributions from field surveys, aerial photography, or remote sensing is required in order to verify the results of the procedure. Unfortunately, such information was not available at the time of writing, and the results presented in this subsection are merely intended to illustrate the potential degree of sensitivity of the calibrated estimates to the choice of adjustment technique. For this purpose, the RAS and weighted least squares methods were used to calibrate the 1987 Tyne catchment model for the Rede subcatchment.

The Rede subcatchment[16] is in the upper reaches of the Tyne catchment, and farming in the area is exclusively upland and hill livestock rearing. The crop cover is predominantly rough grazing, with a significant area of permanent grass, and relatively small areas of arable and temporary grass and arable crops. Table 4(i) shows that the actual cropping pattern in 1987 had a much higher proportion of rough grazing than predicted by the Tyne catchment

Table 4. Predictions of the 1987 distribution of crops by land class in the Rede subcatchment as a percentage of the total agricultural area

i. Based on the Tyne catchment model

| | | Crop | | | |
Land class	Arable	Temporary grass	Permanent grass	Rough grazing	Totals
19	0	0	0	3.679	3.679
20	3.461	3.923	26.844	42.688	76.916
22	0	0	0.732	13.347	14.079
23	0.000	0.009	0.511	0.908	1.427
25	2.680	0.008	0.927	0.280	3.895
27	0.001	0.000	0.001	0	0.002
Predicted totals	6.142	3.939	29.015	60.903	100
Actual crop totals	1.287	2.353	18.732	77.628	100
Differences	-4.856	-1.587	-10.283	16.726	0

ii. Based on the RAS calibrated model

| | | Crop | | | |
Land class	Arable	Temporary grass	Permanent grass	Rough grazing	Totals
19	0	0	0	3.679	3.679
20	3.474	2.333	16.334	57.875	76.916
22	0	0	0.340	13.740	14.079
23	0	0.004	0.287	1.136	1.427
25	0.912	0.015	1.770	1.199	3.895
27	0.000	0.000	0.002	0	0.002
Calibrated totals	1.287	2.353	18.732	77.628	100

iii. Based on the weighted least squares calibrated model

| | | Crop | | | |
Land class	Arable	Temporary grass	Permanent grass	Rough grazing	Totals
19	0	0	0	3.679	3.679
20	0	1.630	16.653	58.633	76.916
22	0	0	0.479	13.600	14.079
23	0	0.008	0.512	0.908	1.427
25	1.286	0.715	1.087	0.808	3.895
27	0.001	0.000	0.001	0.000	0.002
Calibrated totals	1.287	2.353	18.732	77.628	100

iv. Differences between the RAS and weighted least squares calibrated model distributions

| | | Crop | | | |
Land class	Arable	Temporary grass	Permanent grass	Rough grazing	Totals
19	0	0	0	0	0
20	0.374	0.703	-0.319	-0.758	0
22	0	0	-0.139	0.140	0
23	0	-0.004	-0.225	0.228	0
25	-0.374	-0.700	0.683	0.391	0
27	-0.001	0.000	0.001	0.000	0
Totals	0	0	0	0	0

model, and correspondingly lower proportions of the other crops.

The failure of the Tyne catchment model to predict accurately the actual cropping pattern may, in part, be due to the relatively unfavourable climatic conditions in the Rede: the agricultural capability of land in each class may be expected to be lower than the average for the Tyne because of the relatively high altitude of the Rede subcatchment. A second possible reason is that the estimates of the land class area variables are inaccurate, though this is unlikely to be a major cause of prediction error for the Rede given that the area of land identified as potentially in agricultural use is virtually identical to the actual agricultural area. However, it should be noted that the application of both calibration techniques is based on the assumption that the land class composition is known exactly.

Tables 4(ii) and 4(iii) show the predicted distributions of crops by land class, generated by the RAS and weighted least squares[17] methods. The most striking feature of the results is the similarity between the two sets of predictions. Table 4(iv) shows that the differences between the two calibrated distributions, expressed as percentages of the total agricultural area, are inconsequential. Both the calibration techniques inevitably accommodate most of the required increase in the area of rough grazing on land class 20, which accounts for over 75% of the total agricultural area. However, it may also be observed that the percentage increases in the area of rough grazing by land class are greatest for those land classes on which rough grazing is the least important crop.

On the basis of these results, it would appear that the choice of calibration technique does not lead to significant differences in the final estimates of the distribution of crops by land class. This impression has yet to be confirmed by applying the techniques to other parts of the Tyne catchment. Moreover, neither technique has been verified by comparing the calibrated distributions with independent information obtained by direct observation of the actual distribution of crops in the Rede.

CONCLUSIONS

The parish summaries of the agricultural census provide a rich source of information on agricultural land use, though certain features of the statistics impose limitations on their use for descriptive and analytical purposes. These limitations concern the comparability of the statistics over time; the identification of the land to which the statistics relate; and the level of spatial resolution of the statistics, given the heterogeneity of land as a productive resource and the geographic specificity of certain environmental impacts of land use activities.

The results of the Tyne catchment model demonstrate that cropping patterns are systematically related to

land capability: both arable and temporary grass are present in significant proportions on the lowland and plains; the cropping pattern is mixed on the mid-valley slopes; and rough grazing and permanent grass predominate on the upland and hills. Overall, the proportion of agricultural land in the Tyne catchment devoted to arable has increased slightly between 1975 and 1987, at the expense of rough grazing. However, the changes underlying these trends are more complex, with the distribution of individual crops increasingly concentrated on particular land classes.

The calibration of the Tyne catchment model generates estimates of cropping patterns differentiated by land class and district, which may be used to map the spatial distribution of crops on that land identified by the GIS analysis as potentially in agricultural use. The stability of this mapping over time will depend on the level of noise in the calibrated estimates, resulting from changes in the land to which the census data on individual farm parishes relate. Thus, it may be preferable to forego some degree of spatial resolution, by defining the calibration districts as agglomerations of parishes rather than as individual parishes, in order to obtain a clear portrayal of the main trends in land cover patterns.

The areal interpolation methodology developed in this paper is also applicable to a wide class of problems which require the conversion of areal data between inconsistent or incompatible spatial units. However, the particular application to agricultural census data raises a number of specific difficulties with regard to the spatial indeterminacy of the farm parish, and the lack of comparable independent information on the distribution of crops by land class for model validation. These difficulties prevent a comprehensive evaluation of the methodology, though further validation procedures should become possible once the results of the Nature Conservancy Council 'Phase 1' vegetation survey of the Tyne catchment are made available in late 1991. The results of the study to date do appear to warrant further development and application of the basic approach.

Footnotes

[1] The term 'land use' refers throughout this paper to both land cover (eg grass) and the set of practices associated with the management of that land cover (eg fertilizer applications, stocking etc).

[2] For example, the Wildlife and Countryside Act of 1981; the EC Environmental Impact Assessment Directive of 1985; Article 19 of the EC Structures Directive of 1985 concerning Environmentally Sensitive Areas; the EC Drinking Water Directive of 1980 and the subsequent provisions in the Water Act of 1989 for the designation of Nitrate Sensitive Areas; and the current Environmental Protection Bill.

[3] Bunce, Barr and Whittaker (1981a) outline the ITE system which classifies land in Great Britain into 32 classes, primarily on the basis of physical, vegetative and climatic features. Descriptions of the land classes are given in Bunce, Barr and Whittaker (1981b) and Benefield and Bunce (1982) – see also Table 2.

[4] This terminology is based on Goodchild and Lam (1980).

[5] OLS estimates may not satisfy the non-negativity constraint, though the estimated crop proportions by land class do sum to unity across crops.

[6] See Lecomber (1975) for a review of constrained matrix techniques.

[7] The RAS minimand is given by:

$$\text{Minimise} \sum_{i=1}^{M} \sum_{j=1}^{N} \hat{\alpha}_{ijp} \, L_{ip} \, \ln\{\hat{\alpha}_{ijp}/\hat{\alpha}_{ij}\}$$
$$\hat{\alpha}_{ijp}$$

[8] It is evident that the unobserved crop area by land class variables, $C_{ijp} \equiv \alpha_{ijp} L_{ip}$, are not normally and independently distributed as the α_{ijp} must be non-negative and sum to unity across crops.

[9] See Lecomber (1975) for references.

[10] Information on the location of and rights associated with commons is available from the County Registers of Commons. Given that their location is known, the agricultural commons could, if so desired, be excluded from the analysis by categorising them with the land in identifiable non-agricultural uses rather than with the potential agricultural area.

[11] The information on land use represented on the latest edition of the Ordnance Survey maps is collated from surveys conducted over a period of up to 20 years. It is not possible accurately to date individual items of this information set and there are no independent data on the location and timing of conversions of land between agricultural and non-agricultural uses. Thus, the area of land identified as potentially available for agricultural use must be assumed to be constant over the entire sample period.

[12] These categories correspond to the following agricultural census categories: total crops and bare fallow; grass leys reseeded within the last five years; other grass; and grassland unimproved by reseeding or drainage. The rough grazing category also includes the area of agricultural commons which are not covered by the agricultural census.

[13] These measures are defined for each crop equation in the following manner:

$$R_\pi^2 = (SSE_R - SSE_U) / SSE_R$$

where SSE_U and SSE_R are the sums of squared prediction errors generated respectively by the crop equation and by a restricted crop equation in which the proportion of the crop is constrained to be identical across all land classes. The conventional R^2 measure is inappropriate because the model lacks an intercept term.

$$RWMSPE = \sqrt{\sum_{p=1}^{P} S_{ip} \left[100 \, (\hat{C}_{ip} - C_{ip}) / C_{ip} \right]^2}$$

where C_{ip} and $\hat{C}_{ip}$ denote the actual and predicted crop area in parish p, and S_{ip} is the ratio of C_{ip} to the total area of the crop in the Tyne catchment. This measure is preferred to the standard RMSPE measure because the arbitrary definition of parish boundaries leads to large variation in crop areas between parishes

[14] The reliability and comparability of the ITE survey estimates are questionable (strictly speaking, the estimates should be compared with the model estimates for 1978 and 1984 respectively rather than the mean estimates). First, the estimates for each land class are based on a random sample of only eight one km grid squares in 1978 and 12 grid squares in 1984. The estimates do not appear to be uniformly robust, and the faith which can be placed in them is correspondingly limited. Second, the ITE surveys covered the whole of Great Britain and the estimates may not be typical of those which would be obtained from a similar survey of the Tyne catchment. Finally, the surveys record vegetative cover, and the interpretation of this information in terms of the crop classification employed by MAFF may be subject to error. This is likely to be a particular problem with regard to the assignment of grassland to either temporary or permanent grass, as the distinction between these two categories is based on the age rather than the species composition of the sward.

[15] An alternative approach would be to calculate the land class composition for the Tyne catchment in each year as the sum over parishes of the scaled land class area variables employed for model estimation. This calculation would allow for some variation in land class composition over time, but is likely to be less accurate than the preferred option.

[16] The Rede subcatchment is defined as the area covered by the following six Northumbrian parishes: Bavington, Corsenside, Elsdon, Kirkwhelpington, Otterburn, and Rochester. The area of land identified as potentially in agricultural use in the Rede is 34 863 hectares, compared to the total agricultural area of 34 935 hectares in 1987.

[17] The derivation of the weights employed in Stephan's method is given in his Appendix 2.

REFERENCES

Bacharach, M. 1970. *Biproportional matrices and input–output change.* Cambridge: Cambridge University Press.

Benefield, C.B. & Bunce, R.G.H. 1982. *A preliminary visual presentation of land classes in Britain.* (Merlewood research and development paper no. 91.) Grange-over-Sands: Institute of Terrestrial Ecology.

Bunce, R.G.H., Barr, C.J. & Whittaker, H.A. 1981a. An integrated system of land classification. *Annual Report of the Institute of Terrestrial Ecology 1980,* 28-33.

Bunce, R.G.H., Barr, C.J. & Whittaker, H.A. 1981b. *Land classes in Great Britain: preliminary description for users of the Merlewood method of land classification.* (Merlewood research and development paper no. 86.) Grange-over-Sands: Institute of Terrestrial Ecology.

Coppock, J.T. 1955. The relationship of farm and parish boundaries – a study in the use of agricultural statistics. *Geographical Studies,* **2,** 12-26.

Coppock, J.T. 1960. The parish as a geographical statistical unit. *Tijdschrift voor Economische en Sociale Geografie,* **51,** 317-326.

Dempster, A.P., Laird, N.M. & Rubin, D.B. 1977. Maximum likelihood from incomplete data via the EM algorithm. *Journal of the Royal Statistical Society Series B,* **134,** 1-38.

Flowerdew, R. & Green, M. 1989. *Statistical methods for inference between incompatible zonal systems.* (Research report 1.) Lancaster: North West Regional Research Laboratory, University of Lancaster.

Flowerdew, R. & Green, M. 1990. *Inference between incompatible zonal systems using the EM algorithm.* (Research report 6.) Lancaster: North West Regional Research Laboratory, University of Lancaster.

Green, M. 1989. *Statistical methods for areal interpolation: the EM algorithm for count data.* (Research report 3.) Lancaster: North West Regional Research Laboratory, University of Lancaster.

Goodchild, M.F. & Lam, N.S.N. 1980. Areal interpolation: a variant of the traditional spatial problem. *Geo-Processing,* **1,** 297-312.

Hotson, J.M. 1988. *Land use and agricultural activity: an areal approach for harnessing the agricultural census of Scotland.* (Working paper 11.) Edinburgh: Regional Research Laboratory for Scotland, University of Edinburgh.

Judge, G.G., Griffiths, E.G., Hill, R.C. & Lee, T.C. 1980. *The theory and practice of econometrics.* New York: Wiley.

Lecomber, J.R.C. 1975. A critique of methods of adjusting, updating and projecting matrices. In: *Estimating and projecting input–output coefficients,* edited by R.I.G. Allen & F.W. Gosling. London: Input-Output Publishing Co.

Ministry of Agriculture, Fisheries and Food. 1988. *Agricultural land classification for England and Wales.* London: HMSO.

Stephan, F.F. 1942. An iterative method of adjusting sample frequency tables when marginal totals are known. *Annals of Mathematical Statistics,* **13**, 166-178.

Use of assemblages of invertebrate animals in a land use change model

M C Luff[1], M D Eyre[1], A J Cherrill[1], G N Foster[2] and J G Pilkington[1]

[1]Centre for Land Use and Water Resources Research, Dept of Agricultural and Environmental Science, University of Newcastle upon Tyne, Newcastle upon Tyne NE1 7RU

[2]Scottish Agricultural College, Auchincruive, Ayr KA6 5HW

INTRODUCTION

Ecological models and land use change

Land use changes, documented extensively elsewhere in this volume, can affect any or all of the various organisms existing in the ecological system subjected to such changes. Ideally, models of the impact of land use change on biological organisms should be based on simulating the dynamics of the populations or assemblages of the species present. Such an approach takes into account the actual factors, processes and mechanisms acting on the species being modelled. It also enables underlying principles and theories to be incorporated into the model, such as the feedback effects of increasing population densities, and the established hypotheses of interactions between competing species.

The disadvantage of this approach is the resulting complexity and size of the models thus produced. Even within a single vegetation type, individual dynamic models of the major invertebrate species become difficult to link into a whole, and a truly realistic model of a single insect species can be awesomely complex (eg Cheng & Holt 1990). Attempts to simulate part or all of the ecosystem have to resort to simplification, such as treating whole complexes of species, or trophic levels, as single entities.

The problem is in some ways analogous to that faced by the système hydrologique Européen (SHE) model of water distribution and movement, considered elsewhere in this volume (Dunn, Savage & Mackay 1992), but, in place of the single dependent variable, an ecological model has potentially as many predicted outputs as there are species in the ecosystem.

An alternative to the dynamic modelling approach is that based on the known spatial and temporal distributions of organisms, and the statistical associations between them, and with other environmental factors. This method neither implies nor requires causal mechanisms between species, assemblages and their environment: it simply calculates probabilities of occurrence of organisms at any place or time, without the need to build the underlying processes into the model. It has the advantage that many species of assemblages can be considered economically. Extrapolation to consider the effects of new factors, however, may be unrealistic, as no causal mechanisms have been built into the model.

The ecological models being developed within NELUP at Newcastle use the latter, 'statistical' approach for pragmatic rather than theoretical reasons; Rushton (1992) outlines the mathematical basis of the model being used. During the last 20 years there has been much fundamental research on the ecology of systems with intrinsic wildlife interest, such as moorland (eg Coulson & Butterfield 1985), and several large ecological data bases have been collected which are significant for assessing the consequences of land use change. The national vegetation classification and the biological recording schemes run by the Institute of Terrestrial Ecology (ITE) Environmental Information Centre at Monks Wood, for instance, hold information on the structure and distribution of plant communities (Malloch 1985) and distributional data for many groups of plants and animals. Concurrent with the accumulation of these biological data, there have been advances in the description of the land base on which changes take place. Remote sensing information derived from satellite imagery and aerial photography can provide information on the changes in cover of different types of habitat, such as heather (*Calluna vulgaris*) moorland (Rushton & Byrne 1990), and changes in land use (Fuller *et al.* 1989). Such data bases enable the type of statistical models described above to be developed so as to attempt to predict the consequences of any given land use change. Smith, Rushton and Wadsworth (1992) and Eyre *et al.* (1992) consider using plant and bird species respectively; the purpose of the present paper is to outline an approach using invertebrate animals, within the framework of the ITE land classification in the Rede catchment in Northumberland.

Invertebrate animals

The invertebrates are the most diverse and

numerous of all multicellular organisms. They are found in all terrestrial and aquatic environments, and fill all ecological niches from herbivores to top carnivores, as well as being a vital component of the organic decomposition process. It is not surprising, therefore, that several invertebrate groups are used as indicators of conservation value (see papers in Luff 1987b) or of pollution levels (Furse *et al.* 1987). There is also ample evidence of the impact intensive agricultural practices can have on invertebrate assemblages that affect pest damage, eg in cereals (Greig-Smith 1989) and top fruit (Solomon 1987). Although many taxa contain only small (and to the layman insignificant) species, some insects, notably the butterflies (Lepidoptera) and dragonflies (Odonata), are more widely appreciated as contributing to the aesthetic appeal of the countryside; such groups may already have been the subject of population monitoring (eg Pollard 1977). There have also been extensive studies on the dispersal of economically important groups, such as aphids and moths (Taylor 1986).

The choice of invertebrate groups to use in the development of the NELUP model has, like the model itself, been based on pragmatic rather than strategic considerations. Whilst, ideally, choice should be based on a pre-knowledge of the groups that might best reflect land use change, or those about which most questions might be asked, in practice it has been convenient to use those types of animals for which data and expertise were readily available. Foster (1987) has outlined some criteria for the selection of invertebrate groups that might be useful in conservation assessments; the same principles apply when using invertebrates to assess the likely impacts of land use change. The most important of Foster's criteria are: (i) a reasonable number of readily identifiable, taxonomically stable, species; and (ii) data availability, preferably from a standardised sampling technique. In all the taxa listed below, we have used extensive data from our own sampling surveys, rather than pre-existing national or regional data bases, so as to be sure of the quality of the inputs to the model.

Selected taxa

In the land use context, it is evident that as wide a range as possible of land use types and habitats should be considered. For the purposes of developing applications of the NELUP ecological model outlined in Rushton (1992), we have selected four taxa for consideration in this paper: ground beetles (Coleoptera, Carabidae) and plant bugs (Homoptera, Auchenorrhyncha) of terrestrial habitats; water beetles (Coleoptera, mainly Dytiscidae and Hydrophilidae) of static water bodies; and selected invertebrates (Insecta except Diptera, Crustacea) of streams.

Carabidae are a major component of the soil surface and within-soil ecosystem, and have been the subject of a wide range of ecological studies (eg Stork 1990).

They are primarily predatory or scavenging (Luff 1987a). There are detailed distributional data from north-east England (Eyre, Luff & Ball 1986), and their assemblages reflect both habitat type (Luff, Eyre & Rushton 1989), agricultural practices (Rushton, Eyre & Luff 1990), and physical environmental parameters such as soil moisture (Rushton, Luff & Eyre 1991). They can also be readily collected using soil surface trapping in 'pitfall traps' (Luff 1975).

The plant bugs (Auchenorrhyncha), in contrast, are exclusively phytophagous, although they occur on nearly all vegetation types. The plant bug assemblage is known to alter with the stage of vegetation succession (Southwood, Brown & Reader 1979) and with management practices (eg Morris 1981), and to be indicative of the status of derelict land (Sanderson 1992). Either mechanised suction sampling (Duffey 1980) or sweep net sampling, complemented by pitfalling, can be used as a standard collection method.

Water beetles, including the predatory Dytiscidae and the phytophagous Hydrophilidae, are widespread in both static and running freshwater. They have been used for conservation assessments of both standing water bodies (Eyre & Foster 1989) and drainage channels (Eyre, Foster & Foster 1990), and the assemblages present reflect environmental features such as pH and substrate. As with the Carabidae, there are extensive distributional data from the geographical region within which the NELUP model is initially being developed (Eyre, Ball & Foster 1986). The wider community of invertebrates present in running water has been sampled extensively (Moss *et al.* 1987) and selected invertebrates in rivers have been used to develop a system to monitor and assess water quality (Furse *et al.* 1987). Within the Rede catchment, comparable data were therefore obtained from streams and other moving water bodies.

METHODS

The NELUP ecological model

The model is described in detail in Rushton (1992); only a necessary outline will be given here. The model attempts to predict the outcome of changes in both type and intensity of land use. The type of land use is reflected by the land cover type; the model calculates the probability of encountering a species or assemblage of species in a particular one kilometre square, based on knowledge (eg from the ITE land survey or remote sensing) of the land cover in that square, and (from our field survey or other data) of the probabilities of occurrence of the species in each land cover type represented. Modelling changes in intensity of land use involves recognising species assemblages characteristic of particular intensities; probabilities of occurrence of individual species are then calculated as for changes in land cover type. A matrix notation is used, and error terms can be calculated for the predicted probabilities of occurrence.

Sampling methods and data used

Ground beetles

A standardised pitfall protocol has been used since 1985 to sample Carabidae from sites throughout the Tyne catchment. Nine plastic cups, 8.5 cm diameter, were installed at each site, either in a 3 x 3 grid at 5 m spacing, or in a line at 2 m spacing. Traps were filled to a depth of one cm with ethylene glycol as a preservative, and emptied at monthly intervals from May to November. The catches from each date were pooled to give a simple presence/absence species list from each site. The land cover type at each site was assigned to groups of the categories as used by Bunce, Barr and Whittaker 1981. Soil moisture, pH and bulk density were measured at each site, as outlined in Rushton *et al.* (1991). These data were used to model the effects of change in type of land use.

Plant bugs

The relationships between plant bug assemblages and vegetation were assessed using data from 74 upland sites in the original ITE land class 20 within the Ministry of Agriculture, Fisheries and Food Redesdale Experimental Husbandry Farm. Sampling sites were at 75 m intervals along four parallel transects, 150 m apart, running up a hillside from 250 m above Ordnance Datum (OD) to the summit at 350 m OD. The plant cover at each site was sampled using a one metre square quadrat with 100 points and vegetation height was measured by dropping a 30 cm x 30 cm plate, weight 430 g, down a vertical pole from 10 cm above the maximum height of the vegetation. Soil moisture content was also recorded from each site. Bugs were sampled from five pitfall traps (as used above for Carabidae) in a line at one m spacing adjacent to each quadrat, emptied on three dates between 12 June and 25 September 1990, and by sweep net using 100 sweeps on each of three occasions (mid-July, early and late August) when the vegetation was dry. Both plant species data (% cover within each quadrat) and Auchenorrhyncha (presence/absence) at each site were analysed using DECORANA and TWINSPAN (Hill 1979a, b). The degree of association between the plant and bug assemblages was assessed subjectively from the classifications of each, and by correlation between DECORANA axis scores from each data set.

Water beetles from static water

A total of 302 static water sites have been sampled in the Tyne catchment between 1967 and 1989. Each site was worked, using standard collecting techniques (net or strainer), until all available species appeared to have been caught. Most sites were sampled only once, but this is usually sufficient for an adequate classification (Eyre *et al.* 1986) which is unaffected by the season of sampling. Species lists from each site were classified using TWINSPAN, and related to known environmental features of each site and to habitat requirements of individual species.

Invertebrates from running water

Between May and July 1990, 165 running water sites in the Rede catchment were sampled using nets and strainers as appropriate. At each site, both the centre and edge of the water course was sampled, as this aspect of invertebrate sampling in running water has been under-represented. Each region was sampled until a representative sample appeared to have been obtained. Sites with large boulders were more difficult to sample than those with a soft, clayey substrate; this factor was taken into account in the effort expended at each site.

Invertebrates of the insect orders Plecoptera, Ephemeroptera, Trichoptera, Megaloptera, Heteroptera and Coleoptera, together with Crustacea, were identified to species. Site species lists were analysed using TWINSPAN and a substratum index was determined using DECORANA. Estimates (in %) of the amount of silt (<0.2 mm), sand (0.2–2 mm), shingle (2–5 mm), pebbles (5–50 mm), cobbles (50–100 mm), boulders (>100 mm) and bedrock were made for each site. 'Species' of each substratum type were erected at 10% divisions, and a substratum 'species' list was assembled for each site. This was ordinated using DECORANA and the first axis of the ordination was used as a substratum index, to which the distribution of assemblages was related using logistic regression (Ter Braak & Looman 1986). Assemblages were also related to to water pH and to the estimated percentage of arboreal shade for each site.

RESULTS

Ground beetles

A total of 127 species were recorded from the sample sites. Rather than classify the fauna into assemblages, selected species were analysed, based on prior knowledge of their likely use as indicators of change between land cover types occurring in the Rede catchment. Their probabilities of occurrence in each land cover type (as listed in Table 1) are shown in

Table 1. Land cover types used in analysis of Carabidae

Number	Land cover type
1	Arable
2	Improved grass (upland and lowland)
3	Permanent grass
4	Rough pasture and rushes
5	Moorland and mountain grass
6	Peatland (mire)
7	Bracken
8	Marsh
9	Lake
10	Riverside
11	Deciduous woodland (including gillside woods)
12	Coniferous woodland
13	Mixed woodland
14	Scrub
15	Maritime
16	Urban and industrial

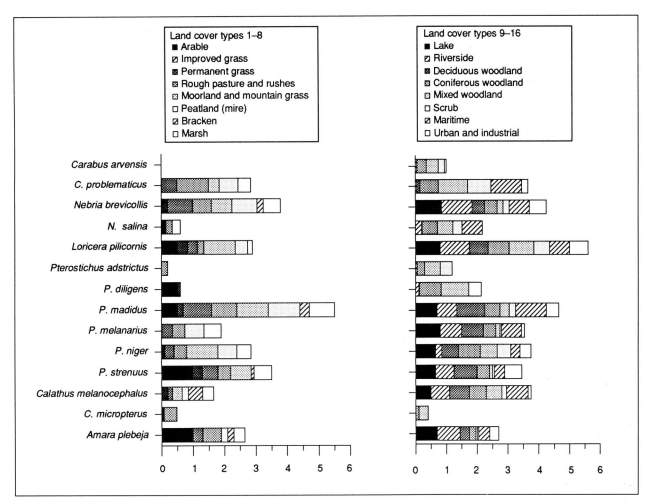

Land cover types 1–8
■ Arable
▨ Improved grass
▩ Permanent grass
▨ Rough pasture and rushes
▨ Moorland and mountain grass
□ Peatland (mire)
▨ Bracken
□ Marsh

Land cover types 9–16
■ Lake
▨ Riverside
▩ Deciduous woodland
▨ Coniferous woodland
▨ Mixed woodland
□ Scrub
▨ Maritime
□ Urban and industrial

Figure 1. Probabilities of occurrence of 14 species of ground beetle in the 16 land cover types

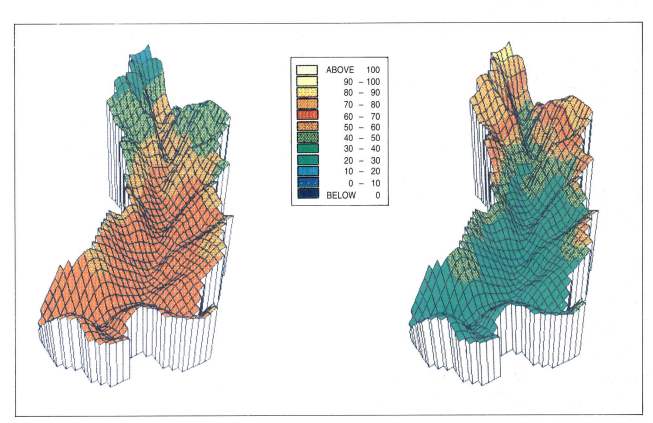

	ABOVE 100
	90 – 100
	80 – 90
	70 – 80
	60 – 70
	50 – 60
	40 – 50
	30 – 40
	20 – 30
	10 – 20
	0 – 10
	BELOW 0

Figure 2. Maps showing the calculated probabilities of occurrence of two ground beetle species in the Rede catchment: *Nebria brevicollis* (left) and *Carabus problematicus* (right)

Table 2. Predicted change in probabilities of occurrence of each selected carabid species over a 30-year period

Species	Land class 19	20	21	22	23	Overall
Carabus arvensis	-2.8	-2.8	-7.6	-1.8	-11.3	-5.3
C. problematicus	-14.0	-2.3	-26.0	-15.8	-25.0	-16.6
Nebria brevicollis	-3.1	-5.1	-0.6	-1.9	+0.7	-2.0
N. salina	-6.0	-3.8	-12.3	-4.9	-14.9	-8.4
Loricera pilicornis	-5.5	-8.9	-11.4	-2.2	-18.6	-9.3
Pterostichus adstrictus	-5.7	-2.0	-13.1	-5.8	-15.1	-8.3
P. diligens	-6.1	-5.2	-19.7	-4.3	-26.6	-12.4
P. madidus	-4.7	-4.1	-4.1	-4.7	-2.3	-4.0
P. melanarius	-2.9	-4.7	0.0	-1.7	+1.1	-1.6
P. niger	-4.0	-3.7	-10.6	-3.5	-13.5	-7.1
P. strenuus	-0.8	-2.0	+0.8	-1.6	+0.7	-0.6
Calathus melanocephalus	-2.3	-7.9	-4.2	+0.9	-9.5	-4.6
C. micropterus	-8.1	+1.0	-13.6	-10.5	-9.8	-8.2
Amara plebeja	-5.1	-2.2	-1.8	-5.8	+1.6	-2.7
Mean/land class	-5.1	-3.8	-8.9	-4.5	-10.2	-6.5

Table 3. Descriptions of the 15 water beetle assemblages interpreted from the TWINSPAN of 302 static water sites in the Tyne catchment

Assemblage	Description
1	Open lakes and quarry ponds with bare and stony substratum and basic water
2	Open, large, clay- and sand-based ponds with basic water and well-vegetated edges
3	Open, large clay-based basic ponds with poorly vegetated edges
4	Large, permanent, well-vegetated ponds with clay substratum and little open water
5	Medium-sized well-vegetated, clay-based and generally permanent marshes
6	Medium-sized well-vegetated ponds, clay-based and temporary to some degree
7	Small, well-vegetated pools with very temporary water
8	Small. well-vegetated, flush or spring-fed permanent pools
9	Small, well-vegetated pools, not as temporary as assemblage 7
10	Well-vegetated, clay-based, stream-fed permanent pools
11	Open, acidic loughs with a clay substratum and little vegetation
12	Open acidic loughs, clay-based with well-vegetated edges
13	Acidic shallow pools, some in woods and shaded, and spring- and stream-fed
14	Acidic mires with slow-moving water flowing through *Sphagnum* moss
15	Upland acid mires with static water, detritus and *Sphagnum*

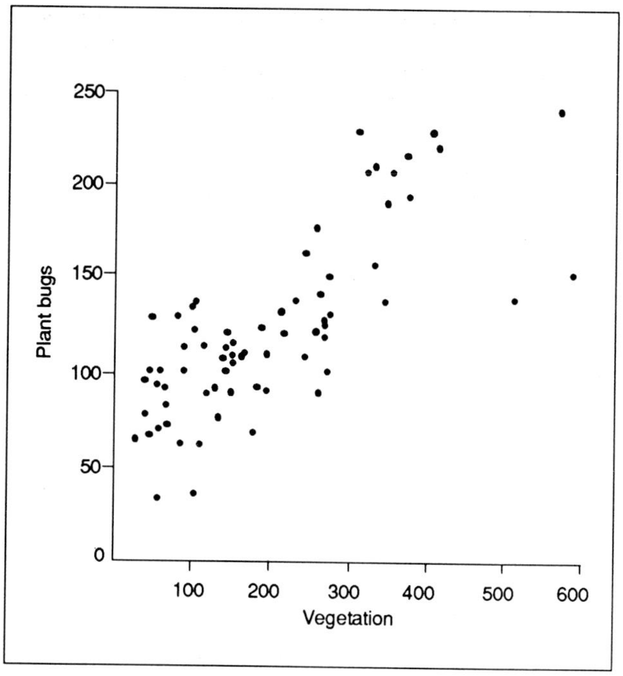

Figure 3. Scatterplot of first axis ordination scores for plant bugs and vegetation

Figure 1. The species selected included those thought characteristic of moorland *(Carabus arvensis, Nebria salina, Pterostichus adstrictus)*, of damp sites *(P. diligens)*, of upland and forest *(Carabus problematicus, Calathus micropterus, P. niger)*, of improved grassland *(Loricera pilicornis, Amara plebeja)*, as well as relatively ubiquitous species occurring in most land cover types (such as *Nebria brevicollis, P. madidus* and *P. melanarius*). The calculated probabilities of occurrence in the Rede catchment of two contrasting species, *C. problematicus* and *N. brevicollis,* are shown in Figure 2. The two are almost mutually exclusive, the first occurring mostly in the unimproved and higher squares, the latter in the lower, mostly improved, regions. The calculated overall change in probabilities of occurrence between now and in the year 2000 (based on documented changes in land cover types in Cumbria (Nature Conservancy Council 1987) showed a decrease in the case of all species (Table 2). *Amara plebeja,* a highly dispersive species found in most cover types, showed a slight increase in four cover types in land class 23, but this was offset by big decreases in its occurrence in most other cover types. Clearly, the model predicts a general decline in ground beetle occurrence, if present trends in land use change continue.

Plant bugs

A TWINSPAN classification of the sample sites by their bugs resulted in many similarities, with classification fused on the plant species present. A scatterplot of DECORANA first axis ordination scores (Figure 3) shows a high correlation ($r = 0.742$, $P<0.001$) between the major variation in vegetation and bug assemblages. The bug scores were also significantly ($P<0.05$) correlated with vegetation height ($r = -0.303$), soil moisture ($r = -0.354$) and

Table 4. The percentage occurrence of the 15 water beetle assemblages interpreted from TWINSPAN of 302 static water sites in the Tyne catchment in the ten cover types

Assemblage	Cover type									
	1	2	3	4	5	6	7	8	9	10
1 (9)	-	-	11	-	-	-	89	-	-	-
2 (31)	3	32	19	-	-	6	13	-	-	26
3 (30)	-	27	20	3	-	3	13	7	-	27
4 (43)	7	40	16	2	-	16	9	5	-	5
5 (17)	35	18	24	-	-	12	12	-	-	-
6 (20)	30	10	30	-	-	15	5	5	-	-
7 (24)	17	17	21	-	-	13	-	17	17	-
8 (9)	-	33	11	-	-	33	-	-	11	11
9 (17)	18	35	6	-	6	12	6	12	-	6
10 (5)	-	40	20	-	-	20	-	-	-	20
11 (20)	10	10	25	10	-	-	15	20	-	10
12 (12)	-	25	17	17	8	-	25	-	-	8
13 (17)	-	-	18	12	29	6	-	6	29	-
14 (24)	-	-	-	25	71	-	4	-	-	-
15 (24)	-	-	25	67	-	8	-	-	-	-

Key to land cover types
1 = arable
2 = agricultural grassland
3 = non-agricultural grassland
4 = moorland
5 = peatland
6 = marshes
7 = lakes
8 = deciduous woodland
9 = coniferous woodland
10 = urban

Numbers in brackets indicate the number of sites in each assemblage

Table 5. Descriptions of the eight invertebrate assemblages interpreted from the TWINSPAN of 165 running water sites in the Rede catchment

Assemblage	Description
1	Wide, open, fast-flowing streams and rivers with bare substratum of mainly large cobbles and boulders. Little edge vegetation
2	Large and medium-sized fast-flowing streams with bare riffles containing many pebbles and cobbles and with little vegetation
3	Small- to medium-sized fairly fast-flowing streams with riffles of shingle and pebbles and clay edges with grassy vegetation.
4	Small- to medium-sized fairly fast-flowing, clay-based streams with well-vegetated edges
5	Slow-flowing acidic, clay-based streams with very well-vegetated edges and some vegetation in mid-stream
6	Slow-flowing basic, clay-based streams with considerable vegetation in the edge and mid-stream
7	Acidic, slow-flowing streams with little vegetation, usually in coniferous forests
8	Small, usually fast-flowing streams on moorland with silty substrata and grass and moss edges

with the percentage cover of the main taxonomic/life history groupings of the plant species present (eg % cover of non-woody dicots r = 0.617). It can be concluded that, at least in upland grass and moor, the assemblages of Auchenorrhyncha could be predicted from knowledge of soil moisture and vegetation assemblages. Effects of land use change on the bugs should, therefore, be modelled via changes in plant communities.

Water beetles from static water

Fifteen species assemblages were interpreted from TWINSPAN analysis of data from the 302 sites. Descriptions of each are given in Table 3. The relationship between land cover and the distribution of assemblages is shown in Table 4. The only assemblages that had consistent distributional relationships with land cover were 1, 14 and 15. Assemblage 1 was found in lakes, and corresponded to that cover type, whilst assemblages 14 and 15 came from acidic water and were generally associated with moor and peatland. The environmental factors influencing the remaining assemblages were substratum, pH, permanence, and shade from vegetation.

Invertebrates from running water

Eight assemblages were interpreted from the TWINSPAN analysis and are described in Table 5. The cover types through which the sites of each assemblage run are given in Table 6. There was, again, little consistency between assemblage and cover type, and most of the sites ran through agricultural grassland, which is by far the major land cover in the Rede catchment area. However, assemblage 7 was generally associated with coniferous forest.

The relationships between assemblages and

Table 6. The percentage occurrence of the eight invertebrate assemblages interpreted from TWINSPAN of 165 running water sites in the Rede catchment in the ten cover types

Assemblage	Cover type									
	1	2	3	4	5	6	7	8	9	10
1 (29)	-	69	14	7	-	-	-	3	7	-
2 (26)	-	65	8	4	-	-	-	12	12	-
3 (37)	-	49	5	19	3	-	-	5	19	-
4 (14)	-	79	14	7	-	-	-	-	-	-
5 (18)	-	44	-	17	28	-	-	-	11	-
6 (15)	-	60	7	13	13	-	-	-	7	-
7 (17)	-	6	-	18	12	-	-	-	65	-
8 (9)	-	11	11	33	33	-	-	-	11	-

1 = arable
2 = agricultural grassland
3 = non-agricultural grassland
4 = moorland
5 = peatland
6 = marshes
7 = lakes
8 = deciduous woodland
9 = coniferous woodland
10 = urban

Numbers in brackets indicate the number of sites in each assemblage

substrata, pH and arboreal shade are shown in Figure 4. All eight assemblages were significantly correlated with the composition of the stream bed. The substratum index ranged from a large proportion of boulders and cobbles at the origin to total silt at the other end. Five of the assemblages were significantly related to pH, but assemblages 3, 4 and 8 showed no apparent preference. Only assemblage 7 gave a significant response to arboreal shade; the logistic response indicated that the more shade produced by afforestation, the more likely the presence of assemblage 7.

DISCUSSION

The first objective, when using any biological

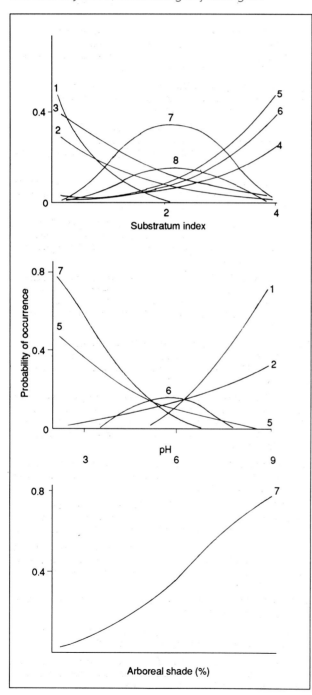

Figure 4. Fitted logistic regression curves, showing the calculated probabilities of occurrence of eight assemblages of freshwater invertebrates, in relation to: substratum index; pH; arboreal shade. Assemblages with non-significant regressions are not shown

organisms as indicators of land use change, is to obtain data which are as far as possible accurately identified to the species level, and obtained by standardised sampling techniques. These criteria are satisfied for all the groups considered in this paper, which should therefore give a realistic indication of the use of invertebrates in this context. Predicting changes in species' occurrence with time has so far only been attempted using the ground beetle data, because adequate knowledge is already available as to the assemblages present (Luff *et al.* 1989) and about the factors influencing their distribution in the cover types found in the Rede catchment (Rushton, Luff & Eyre 1989). The model predicted a future decline of almost all species, although this prediction is based on estimated changes in land cover in Cumbria (NCC 1987) which may not apply to the Rede catchment. In future, information on land use change to drive such ecological modelling should come from the economic component within NELUP (Allanson, Savage & White 1992).

Ground-dwelling groups such as Carabidae can be predicted from the land cover, rather than the actual vegetation composition, but the results given here show that plant-living species such as the Homoptera are more dependent on the composition of the vegetation present. In order to model such a group, it will be necessary to incorporate a vegetation classification into the model's hierarchy, as done by Smith *et al.* (1992). It remains to be decided whether modelling the phytophagous insects themselves has any further benefit, if modelling plant distributions is sufficient to predict their occurrence. This aspect will be tested further, following application of the national vegetation classification throughout the Rede catchment in 1991.

There was a poor relationship between land cover and the assemblages of both static water beetles and running water invertebrates; simply incorporating land cover into the matrix model to predict distributions of these aquatic invertebrates will therefore not be of great use. Work is at present being carried out within NELUP on the effects of pH, water permanence, and substratum exposure on the distribution of water beetle species and assemblages. Preliminary results indicate that it will be possible to model water beetle distributions relative to these factors. It will then be necessary to estimate the influence on these major factors of any likely land use change, if their future distributions are to be predicted. Thus, an extra 'intermediate' level will need to be incorporated into the model.

The assemblages of running water invertebrates were related mainly to stream bed composition, with pH and arboreal shade having a smaller effect. Any effects of land use change on these factors will affect the assemblage present. The current policy of the Forestry Commission is to replant afforested areas away from streamsides, which will provide more light and therefore more vegetation on the streamsides. Increased vegetation provides more habitats for

invertebrates, but the effect of afforestation on water acidity, soil erosion and silt deposition may still be paramount in determining the assemblage present. Any land change use which would increase water flow could also change stream bed composition by removing silt and exposing the underlying bedrock. In the Rede catchment, the underlying rock is a basic sandstone and the pH of most sites flowing over rock was above 6. Thus, pH only tends to be important where flow is slow and the substratum is silt.

In order to develop work on these invertebrates to the point where they can be used as ecological indicators in the land use decision support process (O'Callaghan 1992), we require not only information on how land cover relates to the key environmental factors for each group (see above), but also the appropriate transition matrices predicting change between and within cover types. We have not, as yet, modelled within-cover type changes for any of the invertebrate groups studied; data on changing agrochemical usage, or stocking intensities, would make this practicable.

It will also be necessary to validate the predicted distributions of species or assemblages. This validation requires new data, either from a different study area or, as used by Smith et al. (1992), an independent data set from the modelled study region. We propose to validate the ground beetle results using comparable data from Yorkshire.

Sources of error in the model also need to be considered. Rushton (1992) outlines these in some detail, and shows their mathematical inclusion into the hierarchical model structure. The most serious source of error, when applying the model to invertebrate communities, is the estimation of proportions of each cover type in each land class. Although the estimated cover types have been shown to give reasonably accurate estimates of national totals of particular crops (Bunce et al. 1981), on the regional scale there may be considerable local variation in the characteristics of any particular land class. Error in the predictions of plant distributions (Smith et al. 1992) arises largely from the inability to predict accurately the occurrence of small, patchy habitats which occur with low probability on an 'all or nothing' basis, such as small woods and marshes. As an alternative to relying on the average probability of such habitats, it would be preferable to map them explicitly within the study area. This is now being done for woodland within the Rede study catchment as part of the geographical information system (GIS) component of the NELUP project. The further extension of this approach is to determine the actual extent, in any study area, of all cover types. The ability to do this using remote sensing data is, therefore, being actively investigated.

REFERENCES

Allanson, P., Savage, D. & White, B. 1992. Areal interpolation of parish agricultural census data. In: *Land use change: the causes and consequences,* edited by M.C. Whitby, 92-100.(ITE symposium no. 27.) London: HMSO.

Bunce, R.G.H., Barr, C.J. & Whittaker, H.A. 1981. *Land classes in Great Britain: preliminary descriptions for users of the Merlewood method of land classification.* (Merlewood research and development paper no. 86.) Grange-over-Sands: Institute of Terrestrial Ecology.

Cheng, J.A. & Holt, J. 1990. A systems analysis approach to brown planthopper control on rice in Zhejiang Province, China. I. Simulation of outbreaks. *Journal of Applied Ecology,* **27,** 85-99.

Coulson, J.C. & Butterfield, J. 1985. The invertebrate communities of peat and upland grasslands in the north of England, and some conservation implications. *Biological Conservation,* **34,** 197-225.

Dunn, S., Savage, D. & Mackay, R. 1992. Hydrological simulation of the Rede catchment using the système hydrologique Européen. In: *Land use change: the causes and consequences,* edited by M.C. Whitby,137-146. (ITE symposium no. 27.) London: HMSO.

Duffey, E. 1980. The efficiency of the Dietrick vacuum sampler (D-VAC) for invertebrate population studies in different types of grassland. *Bulletin d'Ecologie,* **11,** 421-431.

Eyre, M.D. & Foster, G.N. 1989. A comparison of aquatic Heteroptera and Coleoptera communities as a basis for environmental and conservation assessments in static water sites. *Journal of Applied Entomology,* **108,** 355-362.

Eyre, M.D., Ball, S.G. & Foster, G.N. 1986. *An atlas of the water beetles of north-east England.* (Special publication no. 4.) Newcastle upon Tyne: Hancock Museum.

Eyre, M.D., Foster, G.M. & Foster, A.P. 1990. Factors affecting the distributions of water beetle species assemblages in the drains of eastern England. *Journal of Applied Entomology,* **109,** 217-225.

Eyre, M.D., Luff, M.L. & Ball, S.G. 1986. *An atlas of the ground beetles (Carabidae) of north-east England.* (Special publication no. 6.) Newcastle upon Tyne: Hancock Museum.

Eyre, M.D., Rushton, S.P., Young, A.G. & Hill, D. 1992. Land cover and breeding birds. In: *Land use change: the causes and consequences,* edited by M.C. Whitby, 131-136. (ITE symposium no. 27.) London: HMSO.

Foster, G.N. 1987. The use of Coleoptera records in assessing the conservation status of wetlands. In: *The use of invertebrates in site assessment for conservation,* edited by M.L. Luff, 8-18. Newcastle upon Tyne: Environmental Research Group, University of Newcastle upon Tyne.

Fuller, R.M., Parsell, R.J., Oliver, M. & Wyatt, G. 1989. Visual and computer classifications of remotely-sensed images: a case study in Cambridgeshire. *International Journal of Remote Sensing,* **10,** 193-210.

Furse, M.T., Moss, D., Wright, J.F. & Armitage, P.D. 1987. Fresh water site assessment using multi-variable techniques. In: *The use of invertebrates in site assessment for conservation,* edited by M.L. Luff, 45-61 Newcastle upon Tyne: Environmental Research Group, University of Newcastle upon Tyne.

Greig-Smith, P.W. 1989. The Boxworth project: environmental effects of cereal pesticides. *Journal of the Royal Agricultural Society of England,* **150,** 171-187.

Hill, M.O. 1979a. *DECORANA - a FORTRAN program for detrended correspondence analysis and reciprocal averaging.* Ithaca, NY: Section of Ecology and Systematics, Cornell University.

Hill, M.O. 1979b. *TWINSPAN - a FORTRAN program for arranging multivariate data in an ordered two-way table by classification of the individuals and attributes.* Ithaca, NY: Section of Ecology and Systematics, Cornell University.

Luff, M.L. 1975. Some features influencing the efficiency of pitfall traps. *Oecologia,* **19,** 345-357.

Luff, M.L. 1987a. Biology of polyphagous ground beetles in agriculture. *Agricultural Zoology Reviews,* **2,** 209-250.

Luff, M.L., ed. 1987b. *The use of invertebrates in site assessment for conservation.* Newcastle upon Tyne: Environmental Research Group, University of Newcastle upon Tyne.

Luff, M.L., Eyre, M.D. & Rushton, S.P. 1989. Classification and ordination of the habitats of ground beetles (Coleoptera, Carabidae) in the north-east England. *Journal of Biogeography,* **16,** 121-139.

Malloch, A.J.C. 1985. *VESPAN: FORTRAN programs for handling and analysis of vegetation and species distribution.* Lancaster: University of Lancaster.

Morris, M.G. 1981. Responses of grassland invertebrates to management by cutting. III. Adverse effects on Auchenorrhyncha. *Journal of Applied Ecology,* **18,** 107-123.

Moss, D., Furse, M.T., Wright, M.F. & Armitage, P.D. 1987. The prediction of the macro-invertebrate fauna of unpolluted running-water sites in Great Britain using environmental data. *Freshwater Biology,* **17,** 41-52.

Nature Conservancy Council. 1987. *Changes in the Cumbrian countryside.* (Research and survey in nature conservation no. 6.) Peterborough: Nature Conservancy Council.

O'Callaghan, J.R. 1992. Decision-making in land use. In: *Land use change: the causes and consequences,* edited by M.C. Whitby, 79-87. (ITE symposium no. 27.) London: HMSO.

Pollard, E. 1977. A method for assessing changes in the abundance of butterflies. *Biological Conservation,* **12,** 115-134.

Rushton, S.P. 1992. A preliminary model for investigating the ecological consequences of land use change within the framework of the ITE land classification. In: *Land use change: the causes and consequences,* edited by M.C. Whitby, 111-117.(ITE symposium no. 27.) London: HMSO.

Rushton, S.P. & Byrne, J.P. 1990. The dynamics of vegetation change and flock output of hill land. In: *British Grassland Society, second research conference.* Hurley: British Grassland Society.

Rushton, S.P., Eyre, M.D. & Luff, M.L. 1990. The effects of management on the occurrence of some carabid species in grassland. In: *The role of ground beetles in ecological and environmental studies,* edited by N.E. Stork, 209-216. Andover: Intercept.

Rushton, S.P., Luff, M.L. & Eyre, M.D. 1989. Effects of pasture improvement and management on the ground beetle and spider communities of upland grasslands. *Journal of Applied Ecology,* **26,** 489-503.

Rushton, S.P., Luff, M.L. & Eyre M.D. 1991. Habitat characteristics of grassland *Pterostichus* species (Coleoptera, Carabidae). *Ecological Entomology,* **16,** 91-104.

Sanderson, R. 1992. Diversity and evenness of Hemiptera communities on naturally vegetated derelict land in north west England. *Holarctic Ecology.* In press.

Smith, R.S., Rushton, S.P. & Wadsworth, R.A. 1992. Predicting vegetation change in an upland environment. In: *Land use change: the causes and consequences,* edited by M.C. Whitby, 118-130. (ITE symposium no. 27.) London: HMSO.

Solomon, M.G. 1987. Fruit and hops. In: *Integrated pest management,* edited by A.J. Burn, T.H. Coaker & P.C. Jepson, 329-360. London: Academic Press.

Southwood, T.R.E., Brown, V.K. & Reader, P.M. 1979. The relationships of plant and insect diversities in succession. *Biological Journal of the Linnean Society,* **12,** 327-348.

Stork, N.E., ed. 1990. *The role of ground beetles in ecological and environmental studies.* Andover: Intercept.

Taylor, L.R., 1986. Synoptic dynamics, migration and the Rothamsted insect survey. *Journal of Animal Ecology,* **55,** 1-38.

Ter Braak, C.J.F. & Looman, C.W.N. 1986. Weighted averaging, logistic regression and the Gaussian response model. *Vegetatio,* **65,** 3-11.

A preliminary model for investigating the ecological consequences of land use change within the framework of the ITE land classification

S P Rushton

Centre for Land Use and Water Resources Research, Dept of Agricultural and Environmental Science, University of Newcastle upon Tyne, Newcastle upon Tyne NE1 7RU

INTRODUCTION

Land use change over the last 50 years has accelerated as a result of political pressures to produce cheap food and changes in agricultural technology. These trends have been well documented (Raymond 1984; Eadie 1984) but, until comparatively recently, their implications for wildlife and the environment as a whole have been poorly known and unquantifiable. The land classification developed by the Institute of Terrestrial Ecology (ITE) (Bunce, Barr & Whittaker 1981) provides an objective stratification for land, within which these changes can be described, and land use change generally can be modelled (Bunce *et al.* 1984).

Whilst it has been possible to develop both descriptive and, to a lesser extent, predictive models of land use change using the ITE classification (Mitchell *et al.* 1983; Bunce *et al.* 1984), there have been fewer attempts to develop similar ecological models, even though the potential for linking land classification systems with ecological data has been recognised (Ball *et al.* 1982). Macdonald, Bunce and Bacon (1981), for instance, modelled the distribution of red fox *(Vulpes vulpes)* throughout the UK by linking the land classification with known habitat preference data for foxes. The purpose of this paper is to outline a simple procedure for linking large ecological data bases to the ITE land classification for the purpose of describing present and predicting future ecological consequences of land use change.

Changes in land use can be classified as either of 'type' or 'intensity'. Changes in type arise where whole cover types change from one sort to another. Changes in intensity result in more subtle changes in the ecology or species composition within individual cover types. A good example of a change in type would be a land use change from permanent pasture to arable, or a reversion of improved upland pasture to moorland. A similar example of a change in intensity would be a reduction in sheep stocking rates on moorland, resulting in an increase in dwarf shrubby species like heather *(Calluna vulgaris)*, or an increase in pesticide usage on a temporary ley. Clearly, these divisions are somewhat arbitrary because they are dependent on the scale of resolution of land cover types; they have been adopted here as a preliminary step in the development of a fully integrated model where the separation will not be apparent.

Modelling changes in type of land use

The essence of the problem is to extend our knowledge of species assemblages in particular habitats to predicting the likelihood of encountering species or species assemblages in each one kilometre square. The first stage is to link each species-by-site data base (derived from field sampling or the literature) to field-measured land cover attributes. These data could be derived from field survey, such as those used to describe the ITE land classification, or from remote sensing sources such as satellite imagery (eg Wyatt 1984; Fuller *et al.* 1989). In the former case, this link can be achieved by classifying the sites for which we have plant or animal data in terms of the land cover categories recorded in the ITE field surveys in 1978 and 1984. Given this classification, the most frequently encountered species in each group of sites comprising one cover type then constitute the assemblage typical of that land cover category. Clearly, the probability of encountering that assemblage at any point is then the proportional contribution of that land cover type to the total area of the one km grid square of that land class. Extending this, the probability of encountering an individual species at any point within a square is simply the sum of the probabilities of encountering it in each of the land cover categories, weighted by their contribution to the total area of the one km grid square.

In order to model the consequences of land use change within a land class, the change in the area of each cover type resulting from the land use change is first calculated. Next, new probabilities of encountering species or species assemblages are determined from the new proportional contribution of each cover type to the total area of the grid square. The probability data for individual species or

assemblages can then be mapped (or contoured), according to the distribution of squares of each land class within the study catchment.

Modelling changes in intensity of land use

It is clear that the approach outlined will be practical for modelling changes in area of 'land cover' categories, but it will not be useful for modelling changes in intensity of land use, where changes are more subtle. In these circumstances, the model needs to be extended to include within-cover type variation. This extension is quite simple, provided that the within-cover type variation can be quantified, distinct assemblages can be recognised, and the relative proportions that each contributes to the unit area of the relevant land cover types can be calculated. This, in effect, adds another hierarchical level to the model in the form of matrices relating the contribution of different assemblage types to each cover type. The consequences of changes in land use at the within-cover type level can then be modelled by considering changes in the proportional contribution of each assemblage type to the unit area of relevant cover types.

Matrix summary

The approach outlined is essentially a data base handling problem, but it can be summarised most simply in matrix form as follows.

Matrix composition

S = species-by-sites holding incidence data (presence=1, absence=0)

C = sites-by-assemblage type holding classification of sites in each assemblage type (membership-1, non-membership=0)

N = diagonal matrix holding total number of sites in each assemblage type

u = cover vector holding proportional contribution of each assemblage type to ITE cover types

U = assemblage-by-cover type matrix holding proportional contribution of each assemblage type to a unit area of each cover type (comprises all u vectors)

k = cover vector holding proportional contribution of each cover type to the different ITE land classes

K = cover-by-land class matrix holding proportional contribution of each cover type to a one km square of that land class (comprises all k vectors)

Pw = transition matrices holding probability of each assemblage changing to all others following change in intensity of land use. One matrix for each cover type for each specific change in intensity of land use, eg grazing pressure or pesticide use

Pb = transition matrices holding probability of each cover type changing to all others following land use change. One matrix for each land class

Model matrices

For each cover type

$Pw'.u = pw$ = change in assemblage cover vector for one cover type following a specific change in intensity of land use. One vector for each cover type

Pw = cover type change matrix comprising all pw vectors. Matrix made conformable by including zeros where assemblages are not present in individual cover types

For each land class

$Pb'.k = pb$ = change in cover vector for one land class following land use change. One vector for each land class

Pb = land class change matrix comprising all pb vectors

For all land classes

$S.C.N^{-1} =$ the species assemblage matrix, holding probability of encountering each species in each assemblage type

$S.C.N^{-1}.U =$ the species probability matrix for each cover type, holding probability of encountering each species in the unit area of each cover type

$S.C.N^{-1}.UK =$ the species probability matrix for each land class holding probability of encountering each species in one km square of each land class

$S.C.N^{-1}.Pw.K =$ the species probability matrix for each land class following changes in intensity of land use

$S.C.N^{-1}.U.Pb =$ the species probability matrix for each land class following changes in type of land use

$S.C.N^{-1}.Pw.Pb =$ both types of land use change considered together

The use of transition matrices in the model suggests that there may be some potential for modelling land use change of either type or intensity as a Markovian process.

In the special circumstances where the transition matrices derived from either sort of change can be shown to be stationary (see Usher 1979) and ergodic (see Isaacson & Madsen 1976), then it becomes possible, for instance, to estimate a limiting probability distribution of assemblages and cover types to which the model would converge, given time. Whilst it is clear that such transition matrices for land use change are unlikely to stay constant through time, the ability to estimate a final state in ecological terms may be a desirable feature of a predictive model, however unrealistic. In terms of the matrix summary outlined above, this would mean a different method of calculating Pw and Pb, the land cover and

land class transition matrices, whereby the transition matrices, P, for each land cover or class are subjected to eigen analysis and the first eigenvectors of each substituted for the respective vectors, pw and pb. If the transition matrices are stationary but non-ergodic, on the other hand, then analyses of absorption times and absorption probabilities from assemblage-to-assemblage and from cover type-to-cover type, may also be useful tools in investigating land use change.

ERRORS IN PREDICTING SPECIES OCCURRENCE IN COVER TYPES AND LAND CLASSES

Sources of error

The preliminary model is based on a series of matrix multiplications, which take data stored in a site/species data base and produce predictions of probability of species occurrence in one km squares.

$$\text{Probability for species} = S.C.N^{-1}.UK \qquad (1)$$

where S = species-by-site data base; C = site-by-assemblage classification; N = number of assemblages of each type in data base; U = assemblage-by-cover type matrix; and K = cover type-by-land class matrix.

Each of these matrices will have associated errors of varying size, which arise from different sources. These errors are of four types:

1. natural variation, such as the variation in area of different cover types within each land class (matrix k);

2. measurement errors arising from inaccuracies in measuring areas of land cover and assemblage type (matrices U and K);

3. assignment errors arising from mis-identification of species (matrix S) and mis-assignment of site species data to specific assemblage types (matrices C and N);

4. pre-determined errors arising from poor classification in the original definition of assemblage and cover types. These errors arise, in part, from attempts to make discrete partitions in continuous data.

There is no simple way of assessing the magnitude of the mis-identification errors associated with the S matrix and the pre-determined classification errors associated with defining cover and assemblage types. It is assumed that these will be comparatively small compared to the mis-assignment errors in 2, and are hence ignored from this point on.

Estimating the variance of probabilities of encountering species in each assemblage

If the probability of encountering each species is the P matrix, then the variance for an estimate of any probability is derived from:

$$\text{Variance} = \text{probability} \ (1 - \text{probability})/(\text{number of samples} - 1) \qquad (2)$$

Thus, the variance for estimates of the probabilities of encountering species in each assemblage will be held in the V matrix:

$$V = (Po \ (J - P)).(N - I)^{-1} \qquad (3)$$

where o refers to Schur product (see Barnett 1990), and J is a matrix of 1's.

Estimating the variance of probabilities of encountering species in each cover type

The probability of encountering individual species within cover types is obtained from the matrix:

$$P.U$$

Clearly, if there are n assemblages recognised within each cover type, estimating the variance for each component of the species probability matrix involves n multiplications of two variance estimates, and n additions of one combined variance estimate arising from each of the preceding multiplications.

Let E hold the variances of the estimates of the mean proportions of each assemblage occurring in each cover type (matrix U), and let:

$$L = (PoP).E \qquad (4)$$
$$\text{and } M^T = V.(UoU) \qquad (5)$$

or, for comparison with (4);

$$M = (UoU)^T.V^T$$

where o again refers to Schur product, and the matrices (UoU) and V in equation (5) are transposed to illustrate the similarity of the two equations.

If we can assume that data in the $S.C.N^{-1}$ matrix are independent of those in the U matrix, then, following Burrough (1986), the variance of the mean estimate for the probability of encountering species in each cover type is:

$$F = L + M^T \qquad (6)$$

If we can assume that the data in the U matrix and the K matrix are independent, and that Z holds the variances of the estimates of the mean proportions of each cover type present in each land class, then:

$$R = ((P.U) \ o \ (P.U)).Z \qquad (7)$$
$$Q = (KoK)^T.F^T \qquad (8)$$

If k is the number of land classes represented in the K matrix, then the variance of the estimate of the probability of encountering each species in each land class is held in matrix W:

$$W = R + Q^T \qquad (8)$$

Correlation between proportions of assemblages within cover types and cover types within land classes

It is possible that the estimates of the proportional contribution of each assemblage to a cover type (matrix U) and the equivalent data for cover type to land class (matrix K) are not independent. The trivial example that certain cover types, like 'inbye pasture', are almost certainly going to be found together with others, like 'improved pasture', in squares of the

same land class does not need elaborating on. Where such correlations are expected or known, the covariance structure of the different cover or assemblage types should be included in the determination of the F and W matrices. If the proportional contributions of particular assemblages to cover types (or cover types within land classes) are positively correlated, then there should be no overall increase in variance in these two matrices. If negative correlations are known or expected, however, then this would increase the variance estimates, the increase depending on the strength of the correlation between the cover or assemblage types being considered.

Test data set: the occurrence of spiders of the genus *Walckenaeria* in Redesdale

As a simple test of the model, results are presented for a genus of small spiders, *Walckenaeria* (Linyphiidae, Araneae), which have different environmental optima (Rushton 1991), are known to occur in a wide variety of habitats (Roberts 1987), and which hence might be expected to show responses to changes in land use. In this example, the assemblage data have been grouped for each cover type for simplicity, and within-cover type variation in spider assemblages has not been considered. The spider data base comprises published species lists from 183 sites in the Tyne catchment sampled by Rushton, Eyre and Luff between 1985 and 1989 (Rushton, Topping & Eyre 1987; Rushton, Luff & Eyre 1989). Currently there are limited arachnological records for woodland in the Tyne catchment, so spider records for 63 woods in Yorkshire and Cleveland, kindly provided by C J Smith, National Organiser of the Spider Recording Scheme, were used to provide data on this land cover type.

All of the 330 one km grid squares in the Redesdale catchment fall into four land classes (19, 20, 22 and 23); land cover data for these four land class types are taken from Bunce *et al.* (1981). Changes in land use between 1976 and 1990 were recorded for land in nine one km squares on the Redesdale Experimental Husbandry Farm (EHF) by the Ministry of Agriculture, Fisheries and Food. These data have been collated and kindly made available by J P Byrne of Redesdale EHF. All but one of the squares are classified as land class 20, and data from the latter only were used to calculate a transition matrix, listing the probability of land use changes between each of seven land cover types.

RESULTS

Matrices listing the probability of encountering eleven species of *Walckenaeria* in seven different land cover types and the four land class types in the Rede catchment are shown in Tables 1 and 2. The variances of the estimates of the probability of encountering each species in each land class are given in Table 3.

Table 1. The probability of finding 11 species of *Walckenaeria* in each of six land cover types – Matrix S.C.N^{-1}

Species	Ley	Perm pasture	Rough pasture	Rushes	Moor-land	Peat-land	Woods
W. acuminata	0.06	0.00	0.82	0.50	0.95	0.83	0.20
W. antica	0.03	0.00	0.44	0.17	0.46	0.48	0.03
W. antrotibialis	0.00	0.00	0.06	0.00	0.05	0.39	0.00
W. clavicornis	0.00	0.00	0.00	0.00	0.00	0.04	0.00
W. cucullata	0.00	0.00	0.00	0.01	0.00	0.00	0.09
W. cuspidata	0.06	0.07	0.00	0.17	0.00	0.09	0.17
W. incisa	0.00	0.00	0.00	0.00	0.00	0.02	0.01
W. kochi	0.00	0.00	0.00	0.00	0.16	0.65	0.01
W. nudipalpis	0.13	0.13	0.31	0.33	0.73	0.83	0.06
W. unicornis	0.00	0.07	0.00	0.00	0.00	0.00	0.06
W. vigilax	0.26	0.27	0.94	0.67	0.81	0.30	0.01

Table 2. The probability of finding 11 species of *Walckenaeria* at any point in a one km square of four land classes – Matrix S.C.N^{-1}.U

Species	Land class 19	20	22	23
W. acuminata	0.48	0.37	0.45	0.68
W. antica	0.23	0.19	0.20	0.37
W. antrotibialis	0.04	0.06	0.06	0.20
W. clavicornis	0.00	0.00	0.00	0.02
W. cucullata	0.02	0.00	0.03	0.01
W. cuspidata	0.06	0.05	0.08	0.06
W. incisa	0.00	0.00	0.00	0.00
W. kochi	0.08	0.05	0.12	0.31
W. nudipalpis	0.51	0.28	0.57	0.59
W. unicornis	0.00	0.02	0.00	0.00
W. vigilax	0.43	0.45	0.31	0.44

The most obvious feature is the considerable variation in probability of occurrence between species in different land cover types. *W. acuminata* and *W. nudipalpis* had an order of magnitude and greater ranges in probability of occurrence over the seven habitat types considered, but were present in all.

Table 3. The variance of the probability of finding eleven species of *Walkenaeria* in one km square of four land classes

Species	Land class 19	20	22	23
W. acuminata	0.854	0.431	0.852	3.855
W. antica	0.199	0.109	0.195	0.937
W. antrotibialis	0.007	0.003	0.009	0.066
W. clavicornis	0.000	0.000	0.000	0.002
W. cucullata	0.005	0.000	0.009	0.000
W. cuspidata	0.021	0.005	0.033	0.006
W. incisa	0.000	0.000	0.000	0.000
W. kochi	0.036	0.010	0.040	0.237
W. nudipalpis	0.840	0.229	1.082	2.339
W. unicornis	0.000	0.002	0.000	0.000
W. vigilax	0.620	0.452	0.575	2.719

Table 4. Transition matrix derived from measured changes in land use for nine one km grid squares of land class 20 at Redesdale EHF – Matrix P

Cover	Ley	Perm pasture	Rough pasture	Rushes	Moor-land	Peat-land	Woods
Ley	0.00	1.00	0.00	0.00	0.00	0.00	0.00
Perm pasture	0.16	0.84	0.00	0.00	0.00	0.00	0.00
Rough pasture	0.00	0.50	0.44	0.06	0.00	0.00	0.00
Rushes	0.00	1.00	0.00	0.00	0.00	0.00	0.00
Moorland	0.00	0.03	0.00	0.01	0.96	0.00	0.00
Peatland	0.00	0.00	0.00	0.00	0.00	1.00	0.00
Woods	0.00	0.00	0.00	0.00	0.00	0.00	1.00

Species like *W. cucullata, W. kochi* and *W. clavicornis,* on the other hand, were present in only one or two cover types. These differences reflect the restricted range of habitats preferred by these species (woods, bogs and mountainous regions, respectively). There was also obvious variation in the likelihood of finding each species in the different land classes; for instance, species like *W. antrotibialis* and *W. kochi,* species associated with upland habitats, had higher probabilities of occurrence in the more upland land class 23 than in lowland land classes. The variances of all the probability estimates were very large, however, reflecting the rather small data set used to calculate the proportional contribution of each land cover type for each land class.

The land cover change transition matrix is shown in Table 4. There were insufficient data to assess either the extent to which the transition matrix for land cover change at Redesdale was stationary, or to produce a complementary error matrix for each transition.

Consideration of the matrix shows that the change in cover types during this period was not ergodic, because the peatland and woodland cover types were effectively non-interactive with any of the other cover types. Consequently, a long-run probability vector for each of the land cover types was not estimated. Further analysis of the non-ergodic matrix indicated that three of the cover types were transient: rough pasture, rush-invaded (*Juncus* spp.) pasture,

Table 5. The predicted probability of encountering 11 *Walckenaeria* species in a one km square of land class 20, following land use change predicted from changes observed at Redesdale EHF 1975–90 – Matrix S.C.N⁻¹.pb

Species	1990	Year 2005	2020
W. acuminata	0.39	0.27	0.21
W. antica	0.19	0.11	0.09
W. antrotibialis	0.04	0.03	0.03
W. clavicornis	0.00	0.00	0.00
W. cucullata	0.00	0.00	0.00
W. cuspidata	0.05	0.06	0.08
W. incisa	0.00	0.00	0.00
W. kochi	0.05	0.05	0.05
W. nudipalpis	0.25	0.20	0.18
W. unicornis	0.02	0.04	0.04
W. vigilax	0.46	0.33	0.28

and moorland. Assuming stationarity and a simple first-order Markov process in cover type changes, then the mean absorption times for these states into the permanent pasture persistent state were 28, 15 and 378 years, respectively. The predicted changes in the probability of encountering the 11 *Walckenaeria* species in one km grid squares of land class 20 in the years 2005 and 2020 are shown in Table 5. In general, the probability of encountering most of the species in a one km grid square declined with the predicted land use change. The only exception was *W. cuspidata,* for which there was a slight increase in probability of occurrence. This decline reflects the progressive increase in permanent pasture at the expense of the well-vegetated habitats favoured by most species of this genus.

DISCUSSION

Fundamental research has given ecologists considerable understanding of the underlying mechanisms which determine the structure and functioning of managed ecosystems, but much of this research has been undertaken at the small plot or quadrat scale. The planner, faced with assessing the consequences of land use change, is not usually interested in the plot scale, but rather in areas of four or five orders of magnitude greater, at the catchment or regional level. Clearly, the applied ecologist has to generalise from the results of his small-scale research to provide the planner with the information he requires. The matrix approach outlined above is essentially an objective procedure that allows extrapolation from the small to the large scale in a series of steps. The hierarchical nature of the approach means that the consequences of land use change can be assessed at either the individual species or assemblage level, and at the cover type or land class scale. Analysing land use change in this way means that data from ecological survey undertaken at different scales could be utilised as data bases for the modelling process, provided that the scale of measurement on which the data were collected is known. Data from the national vegetation classification and the various biological recording schemes currently run by the ITE Environmental Information Centre at Monks Wood, for instance, could be used to provide species assemblage matrices (S.C.N⁻¹) for plants and animals in different cover types.

Whilst virtually any survey data could potentially be incorporated into this model, the adoption of a matrix approach necessitates that plant and animal assemblages are classified into discrete groups at some level below that of the land class. Both the degree of hierarchical division and the number of states in each division will depend on the group considered. In the spider example considered above, individual assemblages within each cover type were not modelled, and only eight cover types were considered for simplicity, but there is evidence

to suggest that, even within simple habitats such as intensively managed leys, several distinct spider assemblages exist (Rushton & Eyre 1989). Clearly, there has to be a rationale for deciding on the number of hierarchical divisions and the states considered at each division. Usher (1979) suggested that multivariate procedures could be used to define the states in successional models, and this definition could be used to identify the plant and animal assemblages within specific cover types. One possible approach would be to analyse the site-by-species data matrices for individual cover types, for each group of organisms, individually. A simple two-stage procedure for making these decisions could involve assessing the extent to which each site-by-species data matrix for each cover type was heterogeneous. This assessment could be undertaken by creating a between-sites similarity or distance matrix, and subjecting this to eigen analysis. The size (or possibly the relative ratios) of the first two eigenvalues could then be used as a measure of the heterogeneity of the site-by-species data matrices. If these measures exceeded some critical level, then the model could be extended to incorporate a collection of assemblages for that plant or animal group. Having identified cover types that fail the homogeneity criterion, a classification algorithm such as TWINSPAN (Hill 1979) could be used to identify assemblages within the site-by-species data matrices. The resulting classification would then be used to create u vectors, and hence the U matrix. In this case, stopping criteria for the classification process would need to be developed to ensure that habitat types or assemblages could be identified objectively.

Predicting the short-term consequences of 'one-off' changes in intensity and type of land use is comparatively simple, provided that there are sufficient data available to create the transition matrices for within-cover type and between-cover type changes. It is envisaged that the economic models being developed in the NELUP project will provide information to derive transition matrices for land use changes at this level. Creating transition matrices for changes in intensity of land use within individual cover types will be more difficult. Much past research has concentrated on specific land use practices, such as altered grazing or fertilizer regimes, but these have generally been investigated under rather specific conditions. Whilst there is much information in the literature, it is unlikely that data are available to estimate transition probabilities between all of the states in any one cover type. These data will have to be collected from a variety of sources, one possible approach being to use 'chronosequences' (Facelli & Pickett 1990) in an analogous way to past studies of ecological succession.

Predicting the long-term consequences of land use change using Markov modelling approaches is problematical, and will depend on the extent to which changes in intensity and changes in type of land use

can be considered Markovian. In the first instance, it would appear unlikely that changes in land use arising from short-term changes in policy will be Markovian; nonetheless, there have been several applications of Markov modelling to land use change at the cover type level (eg Krenz 1964; Debusche et al. 1977).

With the exception of Leps, Soldan and Landa (1989), who analysed the long-term deterioration in water quality in rivers, there have been few past applications of Markov modelling to changes in intensity of land use. Most applications in ecology have been concerned with successional changes (eg Waggoner & Stephens 1970; Horn 1975; Usher & Parr 1977; Usher 1979). Usher (1979) concluded that widespread use of Markov modelling in ecology is restricted because of the large data requirements for the transition matrices. Predicting the long-term consequences of land use change using single transition matrices is also severely restricted by the extent to which the transition probabilities are stationary through time. It is unlikely that either changes in type or intensity of land use will have ecological consequences that are so simple. Whilst it is possible to assess stationarity and the extent to which change is Markovian, it is unlikely that there is sufficient information available to do so for either type of land use change. Whether this restricts the usefulness of this model depends on the modelling objectives and the frequency of land use change. If the end user is interested in the ecological consequences of year-on-year changes in land use, as predicted by economic models responding to short-term market factors such as fertilizer price, then the Markovian approach is not required. If the long-term consequences of such changes are required, then the constraints of using the Markovian approach need to be considered more closely.

The approach to modelling the ecological consequences of land use change outlined here is by no means the definitive model. This paper outlines a simple framework which is being modified and extended, where necessary, to suit different plant and animal groups and different types of land use change. Eyre et al. (1992), for instance, detail two different approaches to modelling bird distributions. Furthermore, much more research is required on error propagation arising from the raw data and subsequent matrix manipulations to provide limits for the output predictions. The data presented here suggest that error propagation in this model may be quite large. The magnitude of these errors arose largely from the small number of replicates used to calculate the mean cover of each land cover type in a land class. Research by ITE has indicated that the number of squares that should be sampled to provide cover data should exceed 30 (Griffiths & Wooding 1989); the data used in this study were derived from eight squares only. These problems have been recognised: having the simple modelling framework as a reference point from which to tackle

them is the first step to solving them, and is desirable in any type of modelling.

ACKNOWLEDGEMENTS

I would like to thank Drs M Lane, D C Howard and R G H Bunce for providing me with details of the land classes for the Rede catchment; J P Byrne and C Smith for land use change data and spider records for woodlands, respectively; and Dr M L Luff and Professor J R O'Callaghan for comments on the manuscript.

REFERENCES

Ball, D.F., Dale, J., Sheail, J. & Heal, O.W. 1982. *Vegetation change in upland landscapes.* Grange-over-Sands: Institute of Terrestrial Ecology.

Barnett, S. 1990. *Matrices, methods and applications.* (Oxford applied mathematics and computing science series.) Oxford: Oxford University Press.

Bunce, R.G.H., Barr, C.J. & Whittaker, H.A. 1981. *Land classes in Great Britain: preliminary descriptions for users of the Merlewood method of land classification.* (Merlewood research and development paper no. 86.) Grange-over-Sands: Institute of Terrestrial Ecology.

Bunce, R.G.H., Tranter, R.B., Thompson, A.M.M., Mitchell, C.P. & Barr, C.J. 1984. Models for predicting changes in rural land use in Britain. In: *Agriculture and the environment,* edited by D. Jenkins, 37-44. (ITE symposium no. 13.) Cambridge: Institute of Terrestrial Ecology.

Burrough, P.A. 1986. *Principles of geographical information systems for land resources assessment.* Oxford: Clarendon.

Debusche, M., Godron, M., Lepart, J. & Romane, F. 1977. An account of the use of a transition matrix. *Agro-ecosystems,* **3**, 81-92.

Eadie, J. 1984. Trends in agricultural land use: the hills and uplands. In: *Agriculture and the environment,* edited by D. Jenkins, 13-20. (ITE symposium no.13.) Cambridge: Institute of Terrestrial Ecology.

Eyre, M.D., Rushton, S.P., Young, A.G. & Hill, D. 1992. *Land cover and breeding birds.* In: Land use change: the causes and consequences, edited by M.C. Whitby, 131-136. (ITE symposium no. 27.) London: HMSO.

Facelli, J.M. & Pickett, S.T.A. 1990. Markovian chains and the role of history in succession. *Trends in Ecology and Evolution,* **5**, 27-30.

Fuller, R.M., Parsell, R.J., Oliver, M. & Wyatt, G. 1989. Visual and computer classifications of remotely-sensed images: a case study in Cambridgeshire. *International Journal of Remote Sensing,* **10**, 193-210.

Griffiths, G.H. & Wooding, M.G. 1989. *Use of satellite data for the preparation of land cover maps and statistics.* Farnborough: National Remote Sensing Centre.

Hill, M.O. 1979. *TWINSPAN – a FORTRAN program for arranging multivariate data in an ordered two-way table by classification of the individuals and attributes.* Ithaca, NY: Section of Ecology and Systematics, Cornell University.

Horn, H.S. 1975. Markovian properties of forest succession. In: *Ecology and evolution of communities,* edited by M.L. Cody & J.M. Diamond, 196-211. Cambridge: Ma: Harvard University Press.

Isaacson, D.L. & Madsen, R.W. 1976. *Markov chains, theory and applications.* New York: Wiley.

Krenz, R.D. 1964. Projection of farm numbers for north Dakota with Markov chains. *Agricultural Economics Research,* **16**, 77.

Leps, J., Soldan, T. & Landa, V. 1989. Prediction of changes in ephemeropteran communities – a transition matrix approach. In: *Mayflies and stoneflies,* edited by I.C. Campbell, 281-287. Dordrecht: Kluwer.

Macdonald, D.W., Bunce, R.G.H. & Bacon, P.J. 1981. Fox populations, habitat characterisation and rabies control. *Journal of Biogeography,* **8**, 145-151.

Mitchell, C.P., Brandon, O.H., Bunce, R.G.H., Barr, C.J., Tranter, R.B., Downing, P., Pearce, M.L. & Whittaker, H.A. 1983. Land availability for production of wood energy in Great Britain. In: *Energy from Biomass,* edited by A. Strub, P. Chartier & G. Schleser, 159-163. (2nd EC Conference, Berlin, 1982.) London: Applied Science.

Raymond, W.F. 1984. Trends in agricultural land use: the lowlands. In: *Agriculture and the environment,* edited by D. Jenkins, 7-13. (ITE symposium no. 13.) Cambridge: Institute of Terrestrial Ecology.

Roberts, M.J. 1987. *The spiders of Great Britain and Ireland. Vol. 1. Linyphiidae.* Colchester: Harley.

Rushton, S.P. 1991. A discriminant analysis and logistic regression approach to the analysis of *Walckenaeria* habitat characteristics in grassland (Araneae: Linyphiidae). *Bulletin of the British Arachnological Society,* **8**, 201-208.

Rushton, S.P. & Eyre, M.D. 1989. The spider fauna of intensively managed agricultural grasslands. *Journal of Applied Entomology,* **108**, 291-297.

Rushton, S.P., Luff, M.L. & Eyre, M.D. 1989. The effects of pasture improvement on the ground beetle and spider fauna of upland grasslands. *Journal of Applied Ecology,* **26**, 489-503.

Rushton, S.P., Topping, C.J. & Eyre, M.D. 1987. The habitat preferences of grassland spiders as identified using detrended correspondence analysis (DECORANA). *Bulletin of the British Arachnological Society,* **7**, 165-170.

Usher, M.B. 1979. Markovian approaches to ecological succession. *Journal of Animal Ecology,* **48**, 413-427.

Usher, M.B. & Parr, T.W. 1977. Are there successional changes in arthropod decomposer communities? *Journal of Environmental Management,* **5**, 151-160.

Waggoner, P.E. & Stephens, G.R. 1970. Transition probabilities for a forest. *Nature, London,* **255**, 1160-1161.

Wyatt, B.K. 1984. The use of remote sensing for monitoring change in agriculture in the uplands and lowlands. In: *Agriculture and the environment,* edited by D. Jenkins, 162-168. (ITE symposium no. 13.) Cambridge: Institute of Terrestrial Environment.

Predicting vegetation change in an upland environment

R S Smith[1], S P Rushton[2], R A Wadesworth[3]

Dept of Agricultural and Environmental Science, University of Newcastle upon Tyne, Newcastle upon Tyne NE1 7RU

Centre for Land Use and Water Resources Research, Dept of Agricultural and Environmental Science University of Newcastle upon Tyne, Newcastle upon Tyne NE1 7RU

Centre for Land Use and Water Resources Research, University of Newcastle upon Tyne, Newcastle upon Tyne NE1 7RU

INTRODUCTION

Mapping the current and future distribution of plant communities in landscapes is of considerable concern to conservationists and land managers. The distribution patterns are an integral component of wildlife and amenity values attributed to landscapes, and are a consequence of the interaction between basic natural environmental factors, such as geology, geomorphology, topography, soil, altitude and climate, and management factors imposed by different land use practices. These natural environmental and management factors interact to produce the well-defined distribution patterns characteristic of different regions.

Definition of the current pattern in a region is a surveying problem. For vegetation, the two basic approaches are exemplified by the Nature Conservancy Council's (NCC) 'phase 1' habitat surveys (Nature Conservancy Council 1990) and the Institute of Terrestrial Ecology's surveys (Bunce & Heal 1984). In the first case, the survey objectives are to cover the whole of the region and to allocate all the vegetation to a series of pre-determined categories. Survey is rapid and reliant upon the ability of surveyors to identify homogeneous vegetation types by eye, with the minimum of quantitative effort. Such effort is restricted to a later date when more detailed quadrat survey is restricted to areas thought to contain some conservation interest. A picture of the vegetation in a region is then built up over a long period of time from a knowledge of the component parts, with particular emphasis on those elements of interest to conservationists because they are, for instance, rare or species-rich vegetation types. More recently, the national vegetation classification (NVC) has defined the range of plant communities in Britain and described their species composition in detail. The alternative approach adopted by Bunce and

Smith (1978) is to sample vegetation in detail within pre-determined sampling strata. Quadrat-based surveys are then feasible to provide details of the species composition of the vegetation within the strata. Large (200 metre square) quadrats are positioned at random within each of the four quarters of a kilometre grid square. Their detailed species composition is assessed and changes over time are noted (Barr et al. 1986). The regional picture is then built up from the characteristics and distribution of each stratum. The strata are land classes defined by multivariate classification techniques, and their utility is dependent upon their predictive ability. This, in turn, is dependent upon how well they summarise the variation in natural environmental and related land management factors.

The one km square land class approach has been used as the basis for modelling land use at a regional level (Smith 1982; Smith & Budd 1982), and is the approach adopted for modelling the Tyne catchment in the NERC/ESRC Land Use Programme. A land classification of the catchment aims to provide information on the distribution pattern of flora and fauna in one km grid squares. Direct information from other sources is not available as the catchment has not been surveyed extensively, although there is detailed information on the vegetation of upland mires (Smith & Charman 1988), alluvial deposits on the rivers Tyne and South Tyne (Macklin & Smith 1990), and on spider and beetle assemblages of upland grassland (Rushton, Luff & Eyre 1989; Luff, Eyre & Rushton 1989) and freshwaters (Eyre, Foster & Foster 1990). The limited available ecological data for the catchment as a whole mean that field survey will be necessary to characterise the ecological variation in the land classes. However, there is little information on the accuracy of the current regional vegetation distribution predicted from such

sample surveys. Most of such classifications to date have been successful in characterising the main vegetation features of a region (Smith 1982). However, it is to be expected that the sampling methods used would not pick up variation in the more infrequent vegetation types as the land classes predict the distribution of plant communities from characteristics measured in a few randomly chosen quadrats from a few sample grid squares in each land class.

Some assessment of current methodology is needed, particularly the effectiveness of the survey methods of Bunce and Smith (1978) in comparison with the Nature Conservancy Council's 'phase 1' habitat survey methods. At the same time, methods need to be developed for predicting the consequences for vegetation of changes in land use and other environmental factors. This may involve the translation of predicted species distributions into functional characteristics relevant to the ecological processes at work under different management regimes, and external environmental factors such as the influence of a changing climate. The use of functional characteristics, such as Grime's (1979) plant strategies, will simplify the prediction of change in the *status quo* of current vegetation, and may facilitate the prediction of the probability of any one vegetation type changing into another. Regardless of how these probabilities are assessed, a land classification model offers the possibility of adding a landscape dimension to predictions of vegetation change.

These concerns have led to this analysis of vegetation pattern in the Sedbergh area of the Yorkshire Dales National Park. The area consists of the three parishes of Sedbergh, Dent and Garsdale, and contains Dentdale, Garsdale, the Rathey and Lune valleys, all converging at Sedbergh at the foot of the Howgill Fells. The Rawthey valley runs north/south and separates the Howgill Fells to the west from the eastern limestone uplands more typical of the rest of the Yorkshire Dales. Agriculture is predominantly pastoral, with dairy farming on the better, low-lying land around Sedbergh, beef cattle further up the valleys, and sheep farming at the dale heads and on the fells. There are some larger conifer plantations at the head of Dentdale and Garsdale.

In 1980, Cumbria County Council published a statutory local plan for the area. The preparation of this plan had entailed the collection of a considerable amount of vegetation data, using the methods of Bunce and Smith (1978). The Nature Conservancy Council carried out a 'phase 1' habitat survey for the whole area. The distribution of plant species had also been separately mapped on a tetrad (4 km²) basis, as part of the *Flora of Cumbria*. Records of vegetation change in the period 1940–80 were available for the whole of Cumbria (Nature Conservancy Council 1987). A large part of the Sedbergh area had been fortuitously included

in this latter assessment, making its conclusions particularly relevant. These data provide the basis for predicting the vegetation pattern in 1978 and in the 1940s, and for evaluating the usefulness of the land classification method for modelling vegetation change in the Tyne catchment.

METHODS

The predictive model presented here is based entirely on the manipulation of various types of matrices. It is essentially a data base handling solution to the prediction problem. It aims to extend knowledge of plant communities in particular habitats and land cover types to predict the likelihood of encountering individual plant species or communities in each land class. The first stage is to create a species-by-quadrat data base and, from this, and with data on plant communities within cover types, to calculate the probability of encountering an individual species within a land class. This is simply the sum of the probabilities of encountering a species in each of a number of land cover categories, weighted by the cover's proportional area in a land class. Modelling the consequences of land use change within a land class requires the calculation of the change in the area of each cover type. The new probabilities of encountering species or communities can then be determined, and these can be mapped or contoured according to the distribution of each land class within the study catchment. The assumption here is that major changes in land use will be reflected in a shift from one cover type to another, eg from upland rough grazing to forest.

This approach is practical for modelling changes in the area of the land cover categories. However, it will not be useful for modelling changes in the intensity of land use, where changes are more subtle. Here it is assumed that changes in the intensity of a land use will be reflected in a shift from one plant community to another. Three matrices make up the model (Rushton 1992):

$S.C.N^{-1} =$ the matrix which holds the probability of encountering each species in each plant community – this is equivalent to the constancy table that describes the species composition of a plant community, defined by an appropriate classification or by Rodwell (1991)

$S.C.N^{-1}.U =$ the species probability matrix for each cover type, holding the probability of encountering each species in a unit area of each cover type

$S.C.N^{-1}.UK =$ the species probability matrix for each land class, holding the probability of encountering each species in each class

119

There are three matrices for predicting the landscape consequences of ecological change:

$S.C.N^{-1}.Pw.K$ = the species probability matrix for each land class following changes in the intensity of a land use, resulting in a change in the balance of plant communities

$S.C.N^{-1}.U.Pb$ = the species probability matrix for each land class following changes in type of land use, resulting in a change in the balance of cover types;

$S.C.N^{-1}.Pw.Pb$ = both types of land use change considered together. Pw and Pb are transition matrices.

The contents of these and the other matrices are defined in Table 1.

The land classification for the K matrix was based on data from 288 0.25 km squares, nested within the National Grid (Smith 1982); 1:50 000 First Series (metric conversion) Ordnance Survey maps and geological maps provided 28 continuous variables and 15 presence/absence variables that were measured from these squares (Table 2). The range of values for each continuous variable was

Table 1. The composition of the model matrices

Matrix	Composition
S	Species-by-quadrats data base in which the data are stored in Cornell condensed form, ie plant species recorded by the presence of their national vegetation classification (NVC) code number (Malloch 1990), plus a measure of their abundance
C	Quadrats-by-community type, holding the classification of quadrats in each community defined by, for example, a separate TWINSPAN analysis (Hill 1979a)
N	Diagonal matrix holding the total number of quadrats in each community type
u	Cover vector holding the proportional contribution of each plant community to a cover type. The cover types are generally recognised landscape units, eg deciduous woodland, rough grassland, and improved inbye pastures and meadows
U	Community-by-cover type matrix holding the proportional contribution of each plant community to a unit area of each cover type (comprises all vectors u)
k	Cover vector holding the proportional contribution of each cover type in a given land class
K	Cover type-by-land class matrix holding the proportional contribution of each cover type in a square of each land class (comprises all vectors k)
Pw	Transition matrices holding the probability of each plant community changing to all others following a change in the intensity of land use. There is one matrix for each cover type for each specific change in intensity of land use, eg grazing pressure or fertilizer usage
Pb	Transition matrices holding the probability of each cover type changing to all others following a land use change. there is one matrix for each land class

Table 2. Map characteristics used to generate the land classification (modified from the original report of the Sedbergh Rural Land Use Study Steering Group (1980)

Continuous variables

1. Main road (km)
2. Secondary road (km)
3. Metalled road < 4 m wide (km)
4. Metalled road > 4 m wide (km)
5. Minor road (km)
6. Unfenced minor road (km)
7. Area of settlement (ha)
8. Number of settlements
9. Highest contour (m)
10. Gradient (degrees)
11. Length of slope (m)
12. Land between 76–198 m altitude (ha)
13. Land between 198–448 m altitude (ha)
14. Land between 488–1189 m altitude (ha)
15. Distance to hill (km)
16. Height of hill (m)
17. Distance to valley bottom (km)
18. Railways in use (km)
19. Disused railways (km)
20. Stream (km)
21. River (km)
22. Stream forks (no.)
23. Woodland area (ha)
24. Number of woods
25. Distance to A-road (km)
26. Distance to other metalled road (km)
27. Degrees from north
28. Degrees from east

Presence/absence variables

29. Land below 76 m altitude (ha)
30. Lakes
31. Paths
32. Cliffs
33. Quarry
34. Marsh
35. Rough grass
36. Motorway
37. Silurian strata
38. Basement beds
39. Coniston limestone
40. Carboniferous limestone
41. Millstone grit
42. Basaltic strata
43. Ordovician

divided into four to enable conversion to a presence/absence format for analysis by indicator species analysis (Hill, Bunce & Shaw 1975). This not only grouped the grid squares into land classes, but also produced a dichotomous key that enabled the remaining 616 grid squares to be allocated to a land class.

The S matrix (species-by-quadrat) was defined using plant species data collected in 1978 from large (20 m² quadrats and 30 m² linear quadrats.

The survey method was that used by Bunce and Shaw (1973) for a survey of woodlands in the UK, modified for use in 0.25 km squares. Sixty-three grid squares were selected at random for the vegetation survey, with at least three squares from each land class. Each surveyed grid square was divided into four quarters, and one large quadrat was positioned

at random within each quarter. Within each quadrat all vascular plants and the larger mosses and lichens were recorded, together with a visual estimate of their relative cover. At least one additional linear quadrat was positioned on one side of the nearest linear feature (hedgerow, wall, stream or roadside verge), and the same vegetation data were gathered. All vascular plant species recorded in 1978 were renamed where necessary from Clapham, Tutin and Moore (1987).

The communities in the C matrix (quadrat-by-community type) were defined in a number of ways. The 200 m² quadrats had originally been classifed by indicator species analysis (Hill, Bunce & Shaw 1975) into 16 types (Sedbergh Rural Land Use Study Steering Group 1980), which were retained as the main plant communities in the area. Additional linear community types were defined by two-way indicator species analysis (Hill 1979b) and detrended correspondence analysis (Hill 1979a) of the linear quadrat data. Inspection of these data showed that the limestone grassland cover types in the U matrix (community-by-cover type) were not represented by any real data. Dummy quadrats were, therefore, added to the S matrix to compensate for this omission. These quadrats were based on the constancy tables for two calcareous grassland communities, presented by Rodwell (1987) as the blue sesleria/Sterner's bedstraw (*Sesleria albicans/Galium sterneri*) grassland, typical subcommunity (type CG9b), and the sheep's fescue/common bent-grass/wild thyme (*Festuca ovina/Agrostis capillaris/Thymus praecox*) grassland, white clover/field woodrush (*Trifolium repens/Luzula campestris*) subcommunity (type CG10a). The species in these dummy quadrats were assigned cover values at random within the range given by the national vegetation classification for each species.

The cover types in the U matrix were defined from the NCC 'phase 1' habitat survey. The relative abundance for each community type in each cover type was obtained by locating the square and linear quadrats on the habitat maps supplied by the NCC: 30% of the limestone grassland was allocated to the CG9b NVC type, and 70% to the CG10a NVC type.

Conversion of the 1978 species distributions to those of the 1940s (transition matrix Pb) was based on data from aerial photographs of Cumbria by the Nature Conservancy Council (1987). These data enabled an assessment to be made of the probability that each land cover type present in the 1940s would have changed into any of the other cover types by the 1970s. Separate assessments were made for lowland (valley bottoms), intermediate (foothills), and upland zones within Cumbria, thereby allowing measurement of rates of change within these zones over that time period.

The predicted distribution of plant species in 1978, based on the manipulation of the above matrices, was calculated and presented for the most frequent and the most characteristic species in each cover type. The latter was defined from the relative cover of each species in the quadrats, and identifies those species with a large proportion of their population in each land cover type. The distribution maps for these species show the relative cover of each species or the probability of finding a species at any particular point, in any amount, in a land class, ie the presence/absence distribution. The distribution of all species was converted to a tetrad distribution to allow comparison with the *Flora of Cumbria*. A species was assumed to be present in a tetrad if it was predicted to occur, even at a low probability, in a land class that occurred in the tetrad. The predicted and the *Flora of Cumbria* dot distribution maps were compared for the 41 tetrads that were wholly within the Sedbergh area. The comparisons were made noting for each tetrad whether or not a species had been found by the *Flora of Cumbria* (observed), or had been predicted by the model (predicted), or whether or not it had been predicted and observed (both). Five types of matches were recognised and, within these, the fit between the observed and the predicted distribution was assessed from $(P - O)^2/O$, where P was the predicted and O was the observed number of tetrads. This 'chi-square' contingency index should be low when there is a good fit between the distributions, although this is not the case in all situations.

Plant strategies were assigned to as many species as possible, using data from Grime, Hodgson and Hunt (1988). For each strategy the sum of the weighted species frequencies was calculated from the species abundances, to give the probability of finding each strategy in each land class. Biodiversity was measured as the inverse of Simpson's Index based on the species probability matrix for each land class.

RESULTS
Land cover type-by-land class matrix K

Sixteen land classes in four topographical groups were recognised (Sedbergh Rural Land Use Study Steering Group 1980). The grid squares were apportioned in similar amounts between the four topographical groups, 21.3% being from the upper slopes and fell tops (land classes 5–8), 20.6% being from the upper middle slopes (land classes 1–4), 34.7% being from the lower middle slopes (land classes 9–12), and 23.0% being from the lowland valley bottoms (land classes 13–16) (Figure 1). These main groups were distinguished from one another primarily by the area of land between various contour intervals.

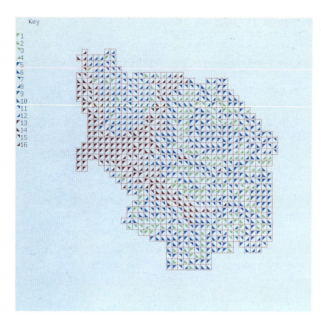

Key
1
2
3
4
5
6
7
8
9
10
11
12
13
14
15
16

Figure 1. The distribution of land classes in the Sedbergh area

Twelve cover types were defined from the NCC 'phase 1' habit survey. These were:

1. acid, unimproved grassland
3. upland calcareous grassland
4. semi-improved grassland
5. improved and reseeded grassland
6. marshy grassland
7. broadleaved woodland
8. conifer plantation
9. scrub
10. bracken
12. dwarf shrub heath
13. a mosaic of grassland and heath
14. blanket and flush mire.

Three linear cover types were added to these, ie:

15. river and stream
16. roadside verge
17. hedgerow

The distribution of these cover types within the land classes comprises the K matrix (Table 3).

Plant species in the species-by-quadrats matrix S

Altogether, 276 species were recorded from 252 square quadrats, and 251 species from 63 linear quadrats. The constancy tables for the CG9b and CG10a calcareous grassland types from the national vegetation classification contained 53 and 116 species respectively.

Plant communities in the quadrats-by-community type matrix C

The characteristics of 16 plant communities originally defined from the large (200 m²) quadrat

data were given in detail by the Sedbergh Rural Land Use Study Steering Group (1980). In summary, they consisted of eight groups comprising:

1. high-level blanket peat, predominantly covered with mat-grass *(Nardus stricta)* grassland and *Sphagnum*/cotton-grass *(Eriophorum)* bog (plant communities 5 and 6)

2. upland moorland, ditch-drained conifer plantations on moorland and mineral flushed grassland (plant communities 7 and 8)

3. upland moorland on well-drained slopes, plus screes and crags (plant communities 3 and 4)

4. wet, high-altitude moorland, plus *Sphagnum* and rush *(Juncus)* bogs (plant communities 1 and 2)

5. upland grassland and some mineral flushes, often enclosed, plus some badly drained permanent pasture (plant communities 9 and 11)

6. permanent pasture plus neglected and overgrown leys (plant communities 10 and 12)

Table 3. The K matrix

Land class	Land cover types and the proportion (%) of each land class that they occupy
1	1 (38), 3 (6), 7 (1), 8 (25), 10 (12), 12 (11), 14 (1)
2	1 (47), 4 (26), 6 (22), 14 (5)
3	1 (84), 4 (4), 5 (4), 12 (4), 14 (4)
4	1 (92), 8 (2), 13 (1), 14 (4)
5	1 (67), 10 (5), 13 (19), 14 (7)
6	1 (79), 14 (20)
7	1 (45), 6 (11), 12 (43), 14 (1)
8	1 (38), 6 (38), 12 (19), 14 (6)
9	1 (14), 4 (27), 5 (51), 6 (6), 10 (3)
10	1 (19), 5 (76), 6 (1)
11	1 (43), 3 (3), 4 (20), 5 (14), 6 (1), 7 (1), 8 (4) 12 (3), 13 (2), 14 (6)
12	1 (37), 4 (3), 5 (10), 6 (21), 8 (24), 14 (1), 15 (4)
13	5 (77), 7 (3), 12 (5), 16 (2), 17 (1)
14	5 (91), 7 (1), 12 (1), 16 (3), 17 (1)
15	4 (11), 5 (56), 7 (4), 10 (3), 13 (23)
16	1 (37), 4 (10), 5 (22), 6 (27), 7 (1), 14 (3)

Key to land cover types

1	= *Acid, unimproved grassland*	9	= *Scrub*
2	–	10	= *Bracken*
3	= *Calcareous grassland*	11	–
4	= *Semi-improved grassland*	12	= *Dwarf shrub heath*
5	= *Improved and reseeded grassland*	13	= *Grass/heath mosaic*
6	= *Marshy grassland*	14	= *Bog and flush*
7	= *Broadleaved woodland*	15	= *River and streamside*
8	= *Conifer plantation*	16	= *Road verge*
		17	= *Hedgerow*

Table 4. A summary of the constancy tables for the linear plant communities 17–22
Con = constancy class: V (frequency 80–100%); IV (frequency 60–79%); III (frequency 40–59%)
Cov = cover/abundance values on a five-point scale: 1 = <2%; 2 = 2–4%; 3 = 5–9%; 4 = 10–19%; 5 = >19%

Community	17 Con.Cov		18 Con.Cov		19 Con.Cov		20 Con.Cov		21 Con.Cov		22 Con.Cov	
Nardus stricta	V	1-5	IV	1-5	-	-	-	-	-	-	-	-
Rhytidiadelphus squarrosus	V	1	-	-	-	-	-	-	-	-	-	-
Anthoxanthum odoratum	V	1-3	IV	1-3	IV	1-5	-	-	III	1-3	-	-
Trifolium repens	V	1-3	III	1-4	IV	1-4	-	-	IV	1	III	1
Galium saxatile	-	-	V	1-4	-	-	-	-	-	-	-	-
Agrostis capillaris	-	-	IV	3-5	III	1-4	-	-	-	-	-	-
Polytrichum commune	IV	1-3	IV	1-5	-	-	-	-	-	-	-	-
Festuca rubra	IV	4-5	IV	3-4	III	1-4	-	-	-	-	-	-
Sphagnum palustre	IV	1-4	-	-	-	-	-	-	-	-	-	-
Ranunculus repens	IV	1	III	1-4	V	1-4	-	-	III	1-3	-	-
Potentilla erecta	IV	1-3	III	1-3	IV	1	-	-	-	-	-	-
Agrostis stolonifera	IV	1-4	III	1-4	III	1-4	-	-	III	1-3	IV	1-3
Sagina procumbens	IV	1	-	-	-	-	-	-	-	-	-	-
Juncus effusus	IV	1-4	V	1-5	IV	1-4	-	-	-	-	-	-
Prunella vulgaris	IV	1	-	-	IV	1-3	-	-	-	-	-	-
Cardamine pratensis	IV	1	-	-	-	-	-	-	-	-	-	-
Juncus squarrosus	III	1-3	-	-	-	-	-	-	-	-	-	-
Thuidium tamariscinum	III	1	-	-	-	-	-	-	-	-	-	-
Bryum pseudotriquetrum	III	1	-	-	-	-	-	-	-	-	-	-
Potentilla sterilis	III	1	-	-	-	-	-	-	-	-	-	-
Philonotis fontana	III	1-5	-	-	-	-	-	-	-	-	-	-
Sphagnum recurvum	III	1	-	-	-	-	-	-	-	-	-	-
Ranunculus acris	III	3	-	-	III	1-3	-	-	-	-	-	-
Drepanocladus revolutens	III	1	-	-	-	-	-	-	-	-	-	-
Holcus lanatus	III	1-3	III	1-3	IV	1-5	IV	1-4	-	-	III	1-4
Deschampsia flexuosa	III	1-4	III	1-4	-	-	-	-	-	-	-	-
Taraxacum officinale	III	1	-	-	III	1	IV	1-3	V	1-4	-	-
Carex nigra	III	1-5	-	-	III	1-5	-	-	-	-	-	-
Ranunculus flammula	III	1	-	-	-	-	-	-	-	-	-	-
Juncus articulatus	III	1-4	-	-	IV	1-3	-	-	-	-	-	-
Rumex acetosa	-	-	III	1-3	III	1-3	-	-	-	-	-	-
Polytrichum juniperinum	-	-	III	1-4	-	-	-	-	-	-	-	-
Luzula campestre/multiflora	-	-	III	1	-	-	-	-	-	-	-	-
Cynosurus cristatus	-	-	-	-	IV	1-4	-	-	-	-	-	-
Stellaria alsine	-	-	-	-	III	1-3	-	-	-	-	-	-
Cerastium fontanum	-	-	-	-	III	1-3	III	1	-	-	IV	1
Caltha palustris	-	-	-	-	III	1-3	-	-	-	-	-	-
Plantago lanceolata	-	-	-	-	III	1-4	-	-	III	1	III	1
Dactylis glomerata	-	-	-	-	-	-	IV	1-5	V	1-5	III	1-3
Poa annua	-	-	-	-	-	-	IV	1-5	-	-	-	-
Urtica dioica	-	-	-	-	-	-	IV	1-5	III	1-5	IV	1-3
Rumex obtusifolius	-	-	-	-	-	-	III	1	-	-	-	-
Plantago major	-	-	-	-	-	-	III	1	III	1	-	-
Lolium perenne	-	-	-	-	-	-	III	1-4	V	1-4	III	1-3
Poa pratensis	-	-	-	-	-	-	III	1-5	-	-	-	-
Poa trivialis	-	-	-	-	-	-	III	1-5	-	-	-	-
Galium aparine	-	-	-	-	-	-	III	1	-	-	-	-
Veronica chamaedrys	-	-	-	-	-	-	-	-	IV	1	-	-
Fraxinus excelsior	-	-	-	-	-	-	-	-	IV	1-5	-	-
Achillea millefolium	-	-	-	-	-	-	-	-	III	1-4	-	-
Centaurea nigra	-	-	-	-	-	-	-	-	III	1-4	-	-
Arrhenatherum elatius	-	-	-	-	-	-	-	-	III	3-4	-	-
Anthriscus sylvestris	-	-	-	-	-	-	-	-	III	1-3	-	-
Eurhynchium praelongum	-	-	-	-	-	-	-	-	III	1	-	-
Crataegus monogyna	-	-	-	-	-	-	-	-	-	-	IV	3-5
Cruciata laevipes	-	-	-	-	-	-	-	-	-	-	III	1-3
Lotus uliginosus	-	-	-	-	-	-	-	-	-	-	III	1
Corylus avellana	-	-	-	-	-	-	-	-	-	-	III	3-4
Digitalis purpurea	-	-	-	-	-	-	-	-	-	-	III	1
Calluna vulgaris	-	-	-	-	-	-	-	-	-	-	III	1-3
Salix capraea	-	-	-	-	-	-	-	-	-	-	III	5
Filipendula ulmaria	-	-	-	-	-	-	-	-	-	-	III	1-3

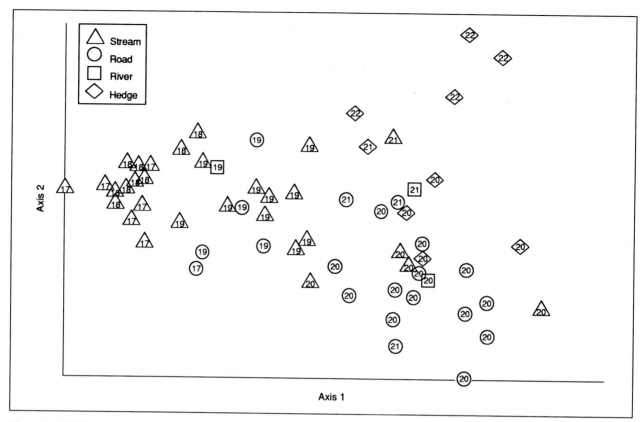

Figure 2. DECORANA ordination of the linear vegetation quadrats

7. deciduous woodland plus overgrown leys and recreational land in and around settlements (plant communities 15 and 16)

8. improved pastures and short-term leys (plant communities 13 and 14)

Ordination of the linear quadrats and a comparison with the stream, roadside, riverside and hedge locations from whence they came enabled six types of linear vegetation to be defined (Table 4; Figure 2). These were wet, flushed edges to upland streams in acid pastures (community 17); drier vegetation on mineral soils adjacent to these same streams (community 18); lowland roadside verges and streams in permanent pastures (community 19); lowland roadside verges and streamsides in meadows that were either disturbed (cut or grazed) (community 20) or undisturbed (community 21); lowland hawthorn *(Crataegus)* hedgerows (community 22).

The calcareous grassland communities assumed to be present in the area are described by Rodwell (1987), and were referred to as communities 23 (CG10a) and 24 (CG9b) in the C matrix. The distribution of all the plant communities within cover types comprises the U matrix (Table 5).

The prediction of species distributions in 1978

The *Flora of Cumbria* lists 563 vascular plant species from the 41 tetrads that are wholly within the Sedbergh area. However, predicted distributions were calculated for 589 species from the S matrix. Comparison of the predicted and observed dot distribution maps, together with the chi-squared type statistic, showed that frequent (>60%) matches occurred for 154 species (Figure 3). Less frequent

Table 5. The U matrix: plant communities-by-land cover type. Land cover types are defined in Table 3; plant communities are defined in the text

Plant community	Land cover types and the proportion (%) of each type occupied by the plant community
1	1 (18), 4 (9), 6 (25), 8 (7), 12 (8)
2	1 (9), 4 (9), 6 (50), 8 (7), 9 (100), 10 (100), 13 (6), 14 (29)
3	1 (26), 6 (13), 12 (33), 13 (31)
4	1 (1), 12 (33), 13 (19)
5	1 (15), 12 (8), 13 (6), 14 (21)
6	1 (8), 8 (14), 13 (31), 14 (29)
7	1 (11), 12 (17), 13 (6), 14 (7)
8	1 (2), 8 (36)
9	1 (5), 4 (36), 5 (2), 8 (14), 14 (7)
10	4 (9), 5 (8)
11	1 (3), 4 (9), 5 (2), 8 (7), 14 (7)
12	4 (9), 5 (5), 6 (13)
13	5 (22)
14	4 (5), 5 (33)
15	1 (1), 4 (14), 5 (28), 7 (33), 8 (14)
16	7 (67)
17	15 (18), 16 (5)
18	15 (27)
19	15 (33), 16 (19)
20	15 (15), 16 (62), 17 (44)
21	15 (7), 16 (14), 17 (12)
22	17 (44)
23	3 (70)
24	3 (30)

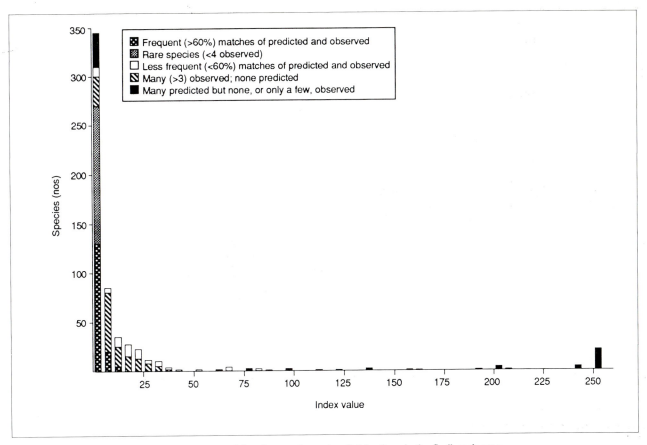

Figure 3. The match between the predicted and the observed species distributions in the Sedbergh area

(<60%) matches occurred for 67 species; 137 species were rarely observed (<4 tetrads) from the *Flora of Cumbria* and were not found at all in the sample survey; 145 species were more frequently observed (>3 tetrads) but were never predicted by the sample survey; 71 species were frequently predicted, but were either never observed or only occurred in a few tetrads (>5).

There was a well-defined distribution for species that were particularly associated with fertile, improved lowland agricultural land, eg rye-grass *(Lolium perenne)* (Figure 4) and with acid, overgrazed rough grassland, eg mat-grass *(Nardus stricta)*. The distributions were more widespread for species with a wider ecological range, eg white clover *(Trifolium repens)* and common tormentil *(Potentilla erecta)*.

Taxonomic problems occurred in a minority of cases (15). There was scope for possible misidentification by the surveyors in 1978. In some cases, taxa had been referred only to the genus, eg sedge *(Carex)* and hawkweed *(Hieracium)* species. In other cases, the taxa were mixed; for example, many-headed woodrush *(Luzula multiflora)* and field woodrush *(L. campestris)* were not separated in the vegetative state.

Predicted distributions of plant strategies and biodiversity

The probability of finding a species of each of the seven primary and secondary plant strategies varied considerably with each strategy and each land class. Stress tolerators and C–S strategists showed a limited distribution, with their highest probabilities (P<0.44 and P<0.12 respectively) on the fell tops and upper middle slopes. C–S–R strategists showed the opposite distribution, being most likely to be found (P<0.52) in the valley bottoms. The remaining strategies were all concentrated in the valleys, with relatively low maximum probabilities of being found: P<0.06 for competitors and ruderals, P<0.18 for C–R strategists, P<0.04 for S–R strategists.

Biodiversity showed a distinct regional pattern. The

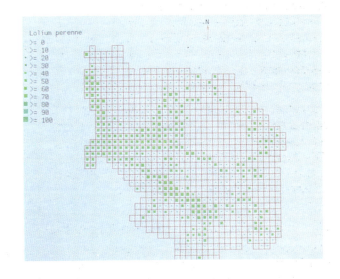

Figure 4. The predicted 1978 distribution of perennial rye-grass *(Lolium perenne)*

fell tops were the least diverse areas, followed by the middle slopes of the Howgill Fells. The valley bottom around Sedbergh was the next most diverse, followed by the middle slopes on limestone, to the west of the Dent Fault, then the upper dales on limestone. Land class 15 showed a pattern of isolated, very diverse grid squares, scattered across the region.

The vegetation of the 1940s

The main changes in the lowland zone of Cumbria, from the 1940s to the 1970s, have been the losses of unimproved grassland (84.5 km²), dwarf shrub heath (21.3 km²), and broadleaved woodland (25.0 km²); the gains have been in urban areas (58.7 km²), arable land (54.7 km²), and coniferous and mixed woodland (49.1 km²) (Nature Conservancy Council 1987) (Table 6). In the intermediate (foothills) zone, the losses have been of lowland raised mire (17.5 km²), unimproved grassland (56.9 km²), and

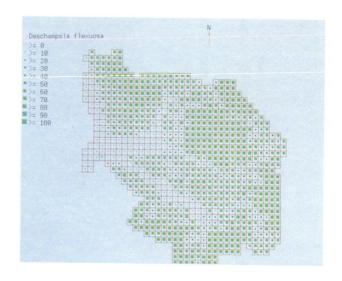

Figure 5. The predicted 1940 distribution of wavy hair-grass (Deschampsia flexuosa)

dwarf shrub heath (76.2 km²); the main gains have been in bracken (Pteridium aquilinum) (17.4 km²) and conifer plantation (55.0 km²). In the upland zone, the losses have mainly been of dwarf shrub heath (194.0 km²), with gains in unimproved grassland (178.2 km²) and semi-improved grassland (50.0 km²). The most dramatic loss of wildlife habitat in the whole of Cumbria has involved a 70% loss of all heathland from the uplands and lowlands. The transition matrix based upon these changes predicted very compatible shifts in species, biodiversity and plant strategies in the Sedbergh area. Differences from the overall Cumbria pattern are explainable in terms of the particular range of habitats around Sedbergh. The most significant changes can be interpreted in terms of the agricultural improvement of the inbye land in the valley bottoms and the great increase in sheep numbers on the fells.

Changes in the probability of finding various plant species and strategies in the Sedbergh area were predicted from the model, with the predicted 1940s distribution being used as the baseline for mapping relative changes. Wavy hair-grass (Deschampsia flexuosa) (Figure 5), mat-grass, bilberry (Vaccinium myrtillus) and heath rush (Juncus squarrosus) showed major decreases in the lowlands and small increases in the uplands. Heather (Calluna vulgaris) generally declines, but with an increase on parts of the Howgills and some of the lower middle slopes elsewhere. Self-heal (Prunella vulgaris) increased throughout the area, although this increase is very small as it occurs in the upland areas where it was only present in very small amounts in 1940. Sweet vernal-grass (Anthoxanthum odoratum) (Figure 6) decreased slightly in the valley bottoms and increased in the uplands, particularly on the flat fell tops east of the Dent Fault where there was the lowest probability of finding it in 1940.

Table 6. Transition matrices for land cover change in Cumbria, 1940s to 1970s. The rows of these matrices contain the probability that the cover type in 1978 would have changed to another in 1940. Land cover types are defined in Table 3. Types are only shown when there is a probability that there will be some change over the time period

Probability matrix for lowland land classes 13–16

Land cover types 1978	Land cover types 1940								
	1	4	5	7	8	9	10	12	13
1	.88	.09	0	0	0	0	.02	.01	.01
4	.15	.37	.43	0	0	0	0	.02	.02
5	.02	.04	.93	.01	0	0	0	0	0
7	0	0	.05	.08	0	.13	0	.02	.02
8	.25	.01	0	0	.44	0	0	.15	.15
9	.16	0	.11	.12	0	.61	0	0	0
10	.46	0	0	0	0	0	.54	0	0

Matrix for intermediate land classes 1–4 and 9–12

Land cover types 1978	Land cover types 1940								
	1	4	5	7	8	9	10	12	13
1	.97	.01	0	0	0	0	0	.01	.01
4	.13	.72	.09	0	0	0	0	.03	.03
5	.01	.03	.96	0	0	0	0	0	0
7	0	0	.02	.89	0	.03	0	.03	.03
8	.33	.22	0	0	.07	0	0	.19	.19
9	.05	0	.03	.04	0	.88	0	0	0
10	.16	0	0	0	0	0	.84	0	0

Matrix for upland land classes 5–8

Land cover types 1978	Land cover types 1940									
	1	3	4	5	7	8	9	10	12	13	14
1	.49	.01	0	0	0	0	0	0	.21	.21	.08
4	.71	0	.18	.10	0	0	0	0	.01	.01	0
5	.07	0	.15	.77	.01	0	0	0	0	0	0
7	0	0	0	.03	.92	0	.03	0	0	0	0
8	.02	0	0	0	0	.97	0	0	.01	.01	0
9	.46	0	0	.06	.13	0	.35	0	0	0	0
10	.47	0	0	0	0	0	0	.53	0	0	0

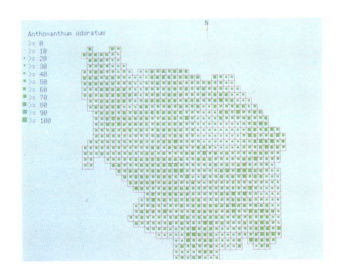

Figure 6. The predicted 1940 distribution of sweet vernal-grass (*Anthoxanthum odoratum*)

The probability of finding stress tolerators showed the greatest declines in those areas where these species were only present in small amounts (Figures 7 and 8). There was a 30% decline in the lowland valley bottoms in Dentdale, the Rawthey and Lune valleys, and around Sedbergh. There was a 13% decline on the middle slopes, with a 4% increase on the fell tops, where they were already the dominant strategy. Ruderals showed a slight increase (3%) in the valleys, especially around Sedbergh; their greatest increases (9%) were on the fell tops, where there was very little likelihood of finding them in 1940. Competitive species showed a 4–10% decrease in the marginal uplands, and very slight increases in the valley bottoms, where they were most likely to be found in the 1940s. The greatest increases (9%) were on the fell tops, where they were least likely to be found in the 1940s.

C–S strategists showed a 24–33% decline in the valley bottoms and marginal uplands, with a 12% increase in the steeper upland areas. C–R strategists showed 16–25% increases on the fell tops, where they were uncommon (1%) in 1940, a 6% increase around Sedbergh, and slightly smaller increases in the valley bottom areas in general; there was a slight decline in some marginal areas. S–R strategists did not generally show any changes greater than 6% either way. C–S–R strategists showed only very slight changes throughout.

The biodiversity of the area showed the same main patterns in both decades. However, there were important differences in detail. There was a 7–10% decrease in the lowlands around Sedbergh and in Dentdale, a 5% decrease on the fell tops, and a 13–16% increase in the dale heads and lower middle slopes (Figures 9 and 10).

DISCUSSION

The classification into five types of matches between observed and predicted species distributions was much more informative than the contingency values calculated for each match. The latter were high for the poorer matches but, conversely, they could also be extremely low for poor matches. When a species was not predicted to occur, its contingency value was the number of observed occurrences.

Matches between predicted and observed species distributions for 1978 were considered to be acceptable for the 154 species that occurred with >60% matches. Many species were rare (137), and no regional sample survey could be expected to predict their distributions. The absence of any predicted distributions for these species was, therefore, considered to be

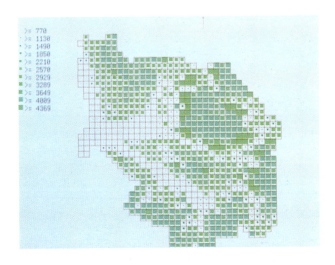

Figure 7. The predicted 1940 distribution of stress-tolerant plant species

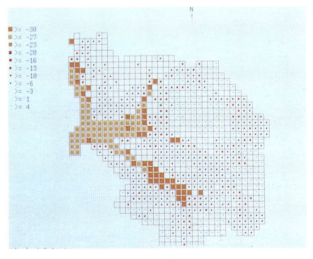

Figure 8. The relative change (1940–78) in the distribution of stress-tolerant plant species

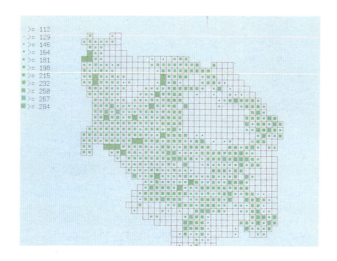

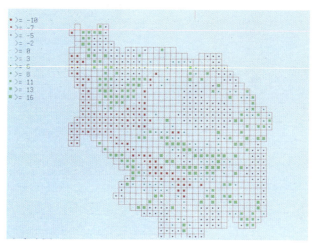

Figure 9. The predicted 1940 distribution of biodiversity

Figure 10. The relative change (1940–78) in the distribution of biodiversity

acceptable. Most of the first 154 species were common, with distributions in the Sedbergh area that fitted their known ecological range. Species such as common bent-grass (*Agrostis capillaris*), sweet vernal-grass, yarrow (*Achillea millefolium*), heather, lesser knapweed (*Centaurea nigra*), cock's-foot (*Dactylis glomerata*), wavy hair-grass, heath bedstraw (*Galium saxatile*), mat-grass, heath rush, rough-stalked meadow-grass (*Poa trivialis*), common tormentil, self-heal, creeping buttercup (*Ranunculus repens*) and white clover were all associated with their normal permanent pasture or rough grassland habitats.

The less acceptable matches were those for which the coincidence of the occurrence of predicted and observed matches in tetrads was less than 60%. These 67 species included many that were typical (often common) of the more infrequent habitats, eg broadleaved woodland and hedgerow [lords-and-ladies (*Arum maculatum*), figwort (*Scrophularia nodosa*), common St John's wort (*Hypericum perforatum*), slender false-brome (*Brachypodium sylvaticum*), enchanter's nightshade (*Circaea lutetiana*), crosswort (*Cruciata laevipes*), large campanula (*Campanula latifolia*)], mire [sundew (*Drosera rotundifolia*), cross-leaved heath (*Erica tetralix*), bog asphodel (*Narthecium ossifragum*)], fen [flote-grass (*Glyceria fluitans*), reed-grass (*Phalaris arundinacea*), marsh horsetail (*Equisetum palustre*)], arable land [common hemp-nettle (*Galeopsis tetrahit*)], limestone grassland [hoary plantain (*Plantago media*)], rock ledges and screes [dovedale moss (*Saxifraga hypnoides*)] and roadside verges [herb Robert (*Geranium robertianum*)].

The species which had bad matches between observed and predicted distributions included the 145 that were frequently observed but never predicted, and the 71 that were frequently predicted but never occurred. The first group of

145 included many species that had a limited habitat distribution and probably occur at a low frequency in that habitat. It included moschatel (*Adoxa moschatellina*), hybrid enchanter's nightshade (*Circaea intermedia*), sweet woodruff (*Galium odoratum*) and hairy woodrush (*Luzula pilosa*) (woods and hedgebanks); wall-rue (*Asplenium ruta-muraria*) and ivy-leaved toadflax (*Cymbalaria muralis*) (walls and rocks); star-wort (*Callitriche stagnalis*) (freshwaters); chickweed willow-herb (*Epilobium alsinifolium*) and forget-me-not (*Myosotis stolonifera*) (upland springs and streams); all-good (*Chenopodium bonus-henricus*) (arable); hairy oat (*Avenula pubescens*) (old meadows); few-flowered spike-rush (*Eleocharis quinqueflora*) (fens), and fragrant orchid (*Gymnadenia conopsea*) (limestone grassland). It also included snowdrop (*Galanthus nivalis*) and spring whitlow grass (*Erophila verna*), vernal species that were likely to have been missed by the surveyors in mid- to late-summer.

Species that were frequently predicted, but which were never recorded in the *Flora of Cumbria*, could only have had this pattern if they only occurred in the S matrix. This could have arisen through miscodings in the S matrix and through genuine first records found by the 1978 surveyors, as the records from the 1978 survey were not available to the authors of the *Flora of Cumbria*. However, 29 species had this pattern by virtue of their presence in the constancy tables for the NVC calcareous grasslands, eg squinancy wort (*Asperula cyanchica*), common rockrose (*Helianthemum nummularium*), hairy violet (*Viola hirta*) and salad burnet (*Sanguisorba minor*). Many of these species have a high fidelity but low frequency in the calcareous grassland types, a reflection of the large number of samples used by Rodwell (1987) to create them. Whilst it was possible that some of these species may have been missed by the

surveyors of the *Flora of Cumbria*, it is also possible that their absence reflects a genuine local deviation from the norms defined by the national vegetation classification.

These results were not unexpected, given the different survey methods employed in both cases. The 1978 land class-based survey used random quadrats from randomly chosen grid squares, whereas the surveyors for the *Flora of Cumbria* actively sought out the uncommon habitats where extra species were likely to find suitable niches. However, it was unfortunate that the unacceptable matches included so many species from local, specialised habitats of limited occurrence in the Sedbergh area. Such species comprised 37% of the Sedbergh flora. The distribution of their habitats was likely to be very unevenly spread between the grid squares of a land class. Their observed distribution will, therefore, be more clumped than their predicted distribution as the latter was often based on very low probabilities of occurrence in a land class. This was a consequence of using mean values for land cover types in the K matrix. Predicting the distributions of species that show a high fidelity to particular discontinuous habitats will, therefore, always be prone to errors of this sort.

These omissions must cause considerable concern for the prediction of the wildlife conservation interest of the general landscape, as so much of this interest resides in these small habitats of limited extent. The difficulties encountered in predicting the distribution of such species probably stems from the survey methods used to identify vegetation in the grid squares. Random sampling tends to pick up the common land cover types. If more detail is required, then the surveys need to be more intensive. More grid squares can be sampled from each land class and/or all the land in a sample grid square needs to be surveyed, rather than sampling random points. The Nature Conservancy Council's 'phase 1' habitat survey has been shown to be useful for defining land cover types. It is a well-used and well-documented national system used for complete surveys (Nature Conservancy Council 1990). However, it does not provide any information on the detailed species composition of the vegetation. Detailed quadrat-based survey would still be needed for this information. An alternative would be to use the national vegetation classification, which allocates visually homogeneous vegetation to nationally defined plant communities. It is particularly attractive as it offers the possibility of rapid survey after initial definition of the range of possible communities within land cover types (NCC 'phase 1' survey categories). It provides an accepted national framework and its community descriptions offer a wealth of detail in the constancy tables. This detail could provide the basic data for predicting individual species distributions at the catchment

level, based on their relationship with the land cover types.

This would then reduce the survey problem to one of characterising the 'phase 1' survey cover types in terms of the NVC communities within them. The lack of quadrat data for the infrequent land cover types was the most likely cause of the errors in predicting many species. The mismatches between the predicted and the observed distributions of species characteristic of such habitats were mainly a consequence of inadequate sampling. Such sampling is likely to take less effort, especially as sample surveys of cover types would be possible for data on the more frequent NVC plant communities within them. Whilst this would mean that some communities would be missed by the survey, the errors are likely to be less if all cover types are surveyed. Estimates of the probability of finding various NVC plant communities in a cover type might be obtained from the literature (Rodwell 1987, 1991) and unpublished local sources, and could be verified by survey.

This approach shows how it is possible to work with three different survey methods, all currently used within national frameworks, but so far used in isolation from each other. The methods should complement each other. The grid square land classification provides the modelling framework; the 'phase 1' survey provides the rapid definition of land cover types; the NVC plant communities provide the detailed data needed for predicting the distribution of individual species and functional characteristics.

The matrices show that the quantity of data required to predict the 1978 vegetation pattern is considerable, but feasible to acquire. However, while the prediction of future vegetation patterns is feasible for a limited number of cases, there are many possible combinations of environmental and land use factors differentially influencing individual species. Several transition matrices will be needed to investigate any particular change, if they proceed at different rates at different times in the different land classes. The description of the influence of these many factors on individual species must remain a goal for future ecological research. However, the achievement of current modelling objectives requires some reduction of the number of species to a few common features. Simplification is probably best achieved by characterising plant communities in terms of their functional characteristics, such as those described by Grime *et al.* (1988) and used as the basis for predicting vegetation change under changing environmental conditions. Prediction of the changes in the relative abundance of plant strategies and regeneration strategies is followed by an assessment of the available species capable of finding a niche under the changed circumstances. The probability of finding different species in a region is a basic output from land

classification, which we suggest is capable of adding a landscape dimension to the changes in vegetation predicted by such 'process' models.

ACKNOWLEDGEMENTS

We are indebted to R Pilling, R Gibson, E Chipperfield and A Watts for the original 1978 vegetation surveys and land classification; to M Eyre for help with the classification of the 1978 vegetation data; to A Malloch for access to the data from the *Flora of Cumbria;* and to the Nature Conservancy Council (North West Regional Office) for access to their 'phase 1' habitat survey maps of the Sedbergh area.

REFERENCES

Barr, C.J., Benefield, C., Bunce, R.G.H., Ridsdale, H.A. & Whittaker, M. 1986. *Landscape changes in Britain.* Abbots Ripton: Institute of Terrestrial Ecology.

Bunce, R.G.H. & Heal, O.W. 1984. Landscape evaluation and the impact of changing land use on the rural environment: the problems and an approach. In: *Planning ecology,* edited by R.D. Roberts & T.M. Roberts, 164-188. Oxford: Blackwell Scientific.

Bunce, R.G.H. & Shaw, M.W. 1973. A standardised procedure for ecological survey. *Journal of Environmental Management,* **1**, 239-258.

Bunce, R.G.H. & Smith, R.S. 1978. *An ecological survey of Cumbria.* (Structure Plan working paper 4.) Kendal: County Planning Department, Cumbria County Council.

Clapham, A.R., Tutin, T.G. & Moore, D.M. 1987. *Flora of the British Isles.* 3rd ed. Cambridge: Cambridge University Press.

Eyre, M.D., Foster, G.N. & Foster, A.P. 1990. Factors affecting the distribution of water beetle species assemblages in drains in eastern England. *Journal of Applied Entomology,* **109**, 207-225.

Grime, J.P. 1979. *Plant strategies and vegetation processes.* Chichester: Wiley.

Grime, J.P., Hodgson, J.G. & Hunt, R. 1988. *Comparative plant ecology: a functional approach to common British species.* London: Unwin Hyman.

Hill, M.O. 1979a. *DECORANA – a FORTRAN program for detrended correspondence analysis and reciprocal averaging.* Ithaca, NY: Section of Ecology and Systematics, Cornell University.

Hill, M.O. 1979b. *TWINSPAN – a FORTRAN program for arranging multivariate data in an ordered two-way table by classification of the individuals and attributes.* Ithaca, NY: Section of Ecology and Systematics, Cornell University.

Hill, M.O., Bunce, R.G.H. & Shaw, M.W. 1975. Indicator species analysis: a divisive polythetic method of classification and its application to a survey of native pinewoods in Scotland. *Journal of Ecology,* **63**, 597-613.

Luff, M.L., Eyre, M.D. & Rushton, S.P. 1989. Classification and ordination of habitats of ground beetles (Coleoptera, Carabidae) in north-east England. *Journal of Biogeography,* **16**, 121-130.

Macklin, M.G. & Smith, R.S. 1990. Historic riparian vegetation development and alluvial metallophyte plant communities in the Tyne Basin, north-east England. In: *Vegetation and erosion: processes and environments,* edited by J.B. Thornes, 239-256. Chichester: Wiley.

Malloch, A. 1990. *VESPAN.* Lancaster: Institute of Biological and Environmental Sciences, University of Lancaster.

Nature Conservancy Council. 1987. *Changes in the Cumbrian countryside.* (Research and survey in nature conservation no. 6.) Peterborough: Nature Conservancy Council.

Nature Conservancy Council. 1990. *Handbook for phase 1 habitat survey – a technique for environmental audit.* Peterborough: Nature Conservancy Council.

Rodwell, J.S. 1987. *National vegetation classification: calcicolous grasslands.* Pre-publication manuscript.

Rodwell, J.S., ed. 1991. *British plant communities: woodlands and scrub.* Cambridge: Cambridge University Press.

Rushton, S.P. 1992. A preliminary model for investigating the ecological consequences of land use change within the framework of the ITE land classification. In: *Land use change: the causes and consequences,* edited by M.C. Whitby, 111-117. (ITE symposium no. 27.) London: HMSO.

Rushton, S.P., Luff, M.L. & Eyre, M.D. 1989. Effects of pasture improvement and management on the ground beetle and spider communities of upland grasslands. *Journal of Applied Ecology,* **26**, 489-503.

Sedbergh Rural Land Use Study Steering Group. 1980. *Sedbergh rural land use study.* Kendal: County Planning Department Cumbria County Council.

Smith R.S. 1982. *The use of land classification in resource assessment and rural planning.* Cambridge: Institute of Terrestrial Ecology.

Smith, R.S. & Budd, R.E. 1982. *Land use in upland Cumbria: a model for forestry/farming strategies in the Sedbergh area.* (Research monograph in technological economics no. 4.) Stirling: Technological Economics Research Unit, University of Stirling.

Smith, R.S. & Charman, D.J. 1988. The vegetation of upland mires within conifer plantations in Northumberland, northern England. *Journal of Applied Ecology,* **25**, 259-594.

Land cover and breeding birds

M D Eyre[1], S P Rushton[1], A G Young[1] and D Hill[2]

[1]Centre for Land Use and Water Resources Research, Dept of Agricultural and Environmental Science, University of Newcastle upon Tyne, Newcastle upon Tyne NE1 7RU
[2]British Trust for Ornithology, National Centre for Ornithology, Nunnery Place, Thetford, Norfolk IP24 2PU

INTRODUCTION

Research on the relationship between the distribution of birds and land use and cover has generally been confined to localised areas or specific habitat types. Sykes, Lowe and Briggs (1989) and Avery (1989) looked at the effects of afforestation on the birds of both forest and moorland, whilst Beintema and Muskens (1987) studied breeding birds on agricultural grasslands. The individual landscape factors affecting the breeding distribution of eight upland bird species were investigated by Haworth and Thompson (1990). There have been few studies at the large scale, although Blondel and Farre (1988) considered the distribution of birds in different European forests. Multivariate analyses were carried out by these workers, and by Lebreton and Yoccoz (1987) using bird counts, to interpret the factors affecting distribution. This approach is appropriate for investigating the effects of differing land and sea cover types on breeding bird distribution, and for assessing and predicting change when land use alters as a consequence of changes to land use policy.

In the present paper, breeding bird records from northern England and southern Scotland are related to land and sea cover data using the multivariate techniques DECORANA and TWINSPAN (Hill 1979a, b) and logistic regression (Ter Braak & Looman 1986). These methods can focus on species assemblages, in particular, which is of especial interest in view of the fact that previous work has generally taken a species approach, and that avian community ecology has particular scientific merit (Wiens 1989). The aim of this work is to enable prediction of changes in bird distribution following changes in land use as part of the NERC/ESRC Land Use Programme. It will also demonstrate the application of this methodology to a fuller analysis covering the rest of Great Britain.

MATERIALS AND METHODS

Bird data

Data from 495 10 km squares in the north of England and the south of Scotland (National Grid 100 km squares NR, NS, NT, NU, NW, NX, NY and NZ) were used. Lists of confirmed breeding species were assembled for each square from the British Trust for Ornithology and Irish Wildbird Conservancy atlas (Sharrock 1976). Presence and absence data lists were compiled for each of the species occurring within the squares.

Cover data

The percentage covers of sea, cultivated land, improved grassland, rough grassland and moor, woodland, lakes and urban land were obtained for each 10 km square from the land characteristics data base supplied by the ESRC Data Archive and described in Ball, Radford and Williams (1983). The dominant trend in the cover was determined as the first axis of a detrended correspondence analysis (DECORANA – Hill 1979a), using data on covers for each 10 km square. Each of the cover types was divided into 10% bands and the presence of a band in a square was used as a 'pseudospecies' (sensu Hill 1979a) in the analysis. In order to convert the 10 km data to a one km resolution, the land cover data given by Bunce, Barr and Whittaker (1981) for each land class of the Institute of Terrestrial Ecology (ITE) land classification were used. The individual land cover attributes (80 in all) were grouped so that the seven cover types given by the land characteristics data base were estimated for each land class. For example, 25 grassland and moor cover types were combined to produce the percentage figure for rough grassland and moor, and 11 woodland and scrub types for woodland cover.

Analysis

Bird species assemblages were identified using a two-way indicator species analysis (TWINSPAN – Hill 1979b) of the lists of breeding birds from each of the 10 km squares. A constrained ordination (CANOCO – Ter Braak 1987) was used with the percentage sea, cultivated land, improved grassland, and rough grassland and moor data to relate assemblages to cover. Both the bird assemblages and the individual bird species were related to the cover axis using logistic regression (Ter Braak & Looman 1986).

Presence and absence of data of either the assemblage or the species were used as the response variable, and the grid square scores on the cover axis as the predictive variable. Logistic approximations to the Gaussian and sigmoid response curves were fitted to the data by the method outlined by Jongman, Ter Braak and Van Tongeren (1987), using the generalised linear interactive modelling (GLIM) package (Baker & Nelder 1978).

The Gaussian logistic model is:

$$\log_e[p(x)/(1 - p(x))] = b_0 + b_1x + b_2x^2$$

which can be related to the Gaussian response curve:

$$= a - (x - u)^2/2t^2$$

where u is the optimum (the value of the environmental variable, x, with the highest probability of occurrence), t is the tolerance (a measure of ecological amplitude), and a is related to the maximum probability of occurrence. These can be determined from the coefficients of the first equation by simple algebra (Ter Braak & Looman 1986). When the parameter b_2 is zero, the model reduces to the linear logistic which produces a sigmoidal increase (or decrease) in the probability of occurrence with the variable considered. A one-tailed t-test was used to test whether the highest-order individual regression coefficients in each model were significantly different from zero (Jongman et al. 1987). For further information, see Rushton, Luff and Eyre (1991).

The above method allows the probability of occurrence of either an assemblage or a species to be calculated if its position along the cover axis is known. DECORANA square (site) scores are means of attribute (species) scores, and the position of each of the 32 land classes along the cover axis was calculated from the cover data for each of the classes. The seven cover types estimated from the 80 cover attributes given by Bunce et al. (1981) were divided into the 10% bands used to generate the land characteristics cover axis, and the 'species' scores of each band were summed and averaged. This gave the position along the cover axis from which the probability of occurrence of an assemblage or a species was calculated using the predicted regression equation.

The probability of occurrence of each assemblage in each land class was calculated. Each species had a probability of occurrence within the assemblages derived from a TWINSPAN frequency table. The product of this probability and that of the occurrence of the assemblage in the land class gave a total of eight species probabilities for each land class (one for each assemblage). The sum of these probabilities gives the probability of occurrence of a species in a land class.

The probability of occurrence of an individual species in a land class was also calculated directly from where the land class occurs on the cover axis, using the regression equation relating probability of occurrence of each species to the DECORANA cover axis.

RESULTS

Bird assemblages

Descriptions of the covers found in the squares of the assemblages interpreted from the TWINSPAN of 495 breeding bird lists are given in Table 1. Assemblage 1 contained approximately 50% land and sea, with the terrestrial areas being lowland. This group contained none of the upland bird species. Nearly all the coastal bird species occurred, with only black guillemot (Cepphus grylle) and red-throated diver (Gavia stellata) missing. The small amount of coast in the squares of assemblage 2 led to the presence of shelduck (Tadorna tadorna). Most of the species recorded have a lowland distribution, eg willow tit (Parus montanus) and garden warbler (Sylvia borin), which were not found in assemblage 1. Assemblage 3 had very little coast, and no associated seabirds, and differed from assemblage 2 in the presence of birds of open habitats, such as yellowhammer (Emberiza citrinella), and such woodland species as the marsh tit (Parus palustris) and jay (Garrulus glandarius).

Red grouse (Lagopus lagopus) also occurred in assemblages 2 and 3, but it was much more frequent in assemblages 4 and 5. Assemblage 4 contained other moorland species, like black grouse (Lyrurus tetrix) and short-eared owl (Asio flammeus), together with ring ouzel (Turdus torquatus) and green woodpecker (Picus viridis). The squares in assemblage 5 contained larger areas of woodland than those in assemblage 4, but had fewer woodland

Table 1. Descriptions of the squares in the eight breeding bird 'assemblages' interpreted from TWINSPAN of 495 10 km squares in northern England and southern Scotland. Numbers in brackets give the number of squares in an assemblage

Assemblage	Description
1 (39)	Squares with up to half the area sea and a low coastline of mainly improved grassland and arable areas
2 (109)	Lowland squares of a mixture of improved grassland arable, rough grassland and urban areas and up to 10% sea
3 (89)	Lowland squares with more improved grassland and arable than assemblage 2 and only very little sea
4 (51)	Upland squares of mainly rough grassland and moor, with some improved grass and woodland and little arable and urban
5 (102)	Upland squares on mainly rough grassland and moor, with more woodland than assemblage 4
6 (34)	Coastal squares of up to 25% sea and a considerable amount of rough grassland, moor and woodland
7 (73)	Coastal squares of up to 66% sea, with the rest mainly rough grassland
8 (6)	Coastal squares with over 90% sea and little else

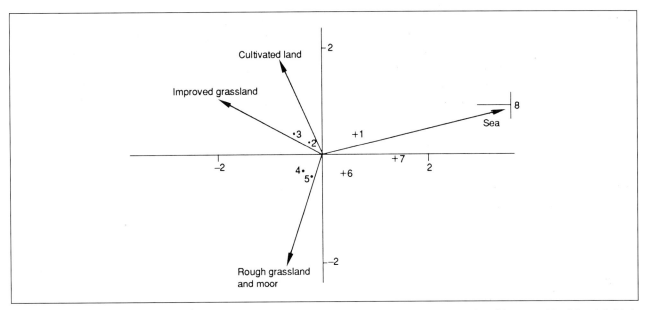

Figure 1. CANOCO biplot showing the relationship between four cover variables (shown by the arrows) and the centroids of the eight bird groups derived from TWINSPAN. Spokes indicate standard errors and where there are none they were too small to show

species. It is probable that these areas were coniferous forest and therefore did not contain deciduous woodland breeding species. Thus, assemblage 5 did not have the woodland species occurring in assemblage 4 and had mainly moorland species. Assemblage 6 also contained the upland moor species, such as the eider *(Somateria mollissima)* and herring gull *(Larus argentatus)*. This assemblage only occurred in the west of the region studied, where the land rises rapidly inland from the coast. Most of the area in the squares of assemblage 7 was sea, leading to a greater proportion of coastal breeding species and a lower incidence of inland species than in assemblage 1. Assemblage 8 contained only six squares with very little land and only a small list of coastal breeding species, such as shag *(Phalacrocorax aristotelis)* and herring gull, and limited incidence of such ubiquitous species as house sparrow *(Passer domesticus)*, starling *(Sturnus vulgaris)*, and jackdaw *(Corvus monedula)*. All except the house sparrow are species of rocky outcrops. There was over 90% incidence of common species, such as song thrush *(Turdus philomelos)*, swallow

(Hirundo rustica), and robin *(Erithacus rubecula)*, in assemblages 1 to 6, a lower incidence in assemblage 7, and they did not occur in assemblage 8.

The CANOCO biplot relating the assemblage centroids to a number of cover types is shown in Figure 1. Axis 1 was related to the presence of sea in the squares and the centroid of assemblage 8 was a considerable distance from the origin of the axis. The other assemblages with sea in their squares were also spread along axis 1, the distance being relative to the amount of sea in the squares. Axis 2 showed differences in the amount of cultivated land and improved grassland in assemblages 2 and 3 and the amount of rough grassland and moor in assemblages 4 and 5, and showed a basic lowland/upland trend.

Bird assemblage and species logistic regressions

The relationships of the assemblages to the DECORANA cover axis are shown by the logistic regression curves in Figure 2. The cover axis also had sea furthest along it, as in the CANOCO analysis. The origin of the cover axis was related to the woodland and rough grassland attributes, with the lakes, cultivated, improved grass, and urban attributes lying between the two extremes. All assemblages were significantly related to the index of cover produced by DECORANA (P<0.05). Assemblages 7 and 8 gave logistic curves favouring the sea end of the axis, whilst assemblage 5 showed the opposite logistic response. There were Gaussian responses with optima near the middle of the axis in the cases of assemblages 2 and 6, whilst the Gaussian responses of assemblages 1 and 4 had optima nearer the sea end and the woodland and moor end, respectively.

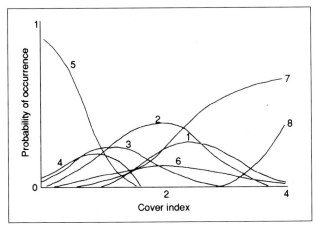

Figure 2. Curves showing the predicted probability of occurrence of the eight bird groups derived from TWINSPAN in relation to the cover index derived from DECORANA

There were 136 significant individual species responses along the cover axis, out of a total of 157 species analysed. The 21 that did not give significant responses were species which were rare within the

Table 2. Regression coefficients from logistic regressions of probability of occurrence of 16 bird species against the cover index. Where only two coefficients are given, the Gaussian model did not improve significantly on the sigmoidal model, which was therefore used

Species	b_0	b_1	b_2
Teal	0.977	−0.00820	−
Shoveler	−5.969	0.05098	−0.0001454
Eider	−7.186	0.05665	−0.0001045
Mute swan	−2.894	0.04030	−0.0001078
Buzzard	−1.369	0.00919	−0.0000303
Sparrowhawk	0.222	0.00258	−0.0000325
Merlin	−0.467	−0.01126	−
Kestrel	2.817	−0.00894	−
Red grouse	2.018	−0.01255	−
Black grouse	0.857	−0.01502	−
Grey partridge	0.872	−0.00699	−0.0000377
Pheasant	2.067	0.00489	−0.0000354
Lapwing	5.258	−0.01463	−
Golden plover	1.630	−0.02170	−
Snipe	0.968	−0.00267	−0.0000289
Woodcock	−0.107	−0.00906	−0.0000515

area studied. Of the significant responses, three were positively logistic, 36 were negatively logistic, and 97 were Gaussian.

The results of 16 analyses are given here. The regression equations for these 16 species are shown in Table 2. The responses of four duck and swan species and of four raptor species are shown in Figure 3. The eider, shoveler *(Anas clypeata)* and mute swan *(Cygnus olor)* all showed Gaussian

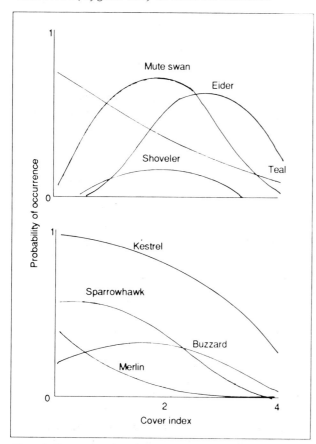

Figure 3. Curves showing the predicted probability of occurrence of four duck and swan species and four raptor species in relation to the cover index derived from DECORANA

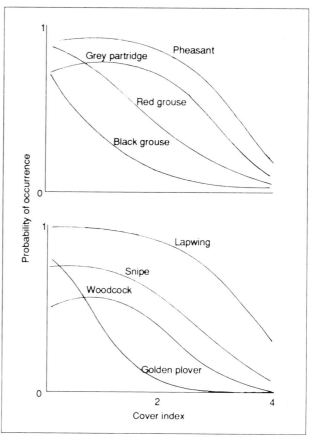

Figure 4. Curves showing the predicted probability of occurrence of four game bird species and four wader species in relation to the cover index derived from DECORANA

responses. The optimum for the eider was near the sea end of the axis, whilst that of the shoveler was near the middle of the axis. There was a logistic response with the teal *(Anas crecca)*, with less probability of occurrence as sea cover increased. The kestrel *(Falco tinnunculus)*, sparrowhawk *(Accipter nisus)* and merlin *(Falco columbarius)* all showed a preference for rough grassland and moor, but the buzzard *(Buteo buteo)* gave a Gaussian response with an optimum near the middle of the cover axis. Four game bird and four wader species responses are shown in Figure 4. Although the pheasant *(Phasianus colchicus)* and the grey partridge *(Perdix perdix)* gave Gaussian responses and the red grouse and the black grouse gave logistic curves, all four species preferred rough grassland and the probability of occurrence reduced quickly as the area of sea increased. A similar pattern was seen with the waders, with the probability of occurrence of finding the golden plover *(Pluvialis apricaria)* becoming zero well before the end of the cover axis.

Species probabilities

The probabilities of occurrence of each of the species in Figures 3 and 4 in the 1991 ITE land classes in the Rede catchment (19, 20, 22, 23, 25, 27 and 28), calculated using either the assemblage data or the individual species' responses, are given in Table 3. The two methods of calculating probabilities gave similar results, the largest difference being the

Table 3. The probability of finding 16 bird species in land classes 19, 20, 22, 23, 25, 27 and 28 using assemblage (A) and individual species (I) data

Land class	Teal	Shoveler	Eider	Mute swan	Land class	Buzzard	Sparrowhawk	Merlin	Kestrel
19A	0.53	0.01	0.06	0.51	19A	0.25	0.52	0.16	0.88
19I	0.56	0.07	0.05	0.47	19I	0.31	0.55	0.18	0.88
20A	0.52	0.01	0.07	0.52	20A	0.25	0.52	0.15	0.87
20I	0.55	0.08	0.06	0.49	20I	0.32	0.54	0.18	0.88
22A	0.56	0.01	0.05	0.46	22A	0.27	0.53	0.18	0.88
22I	0.58	0.06	0.04	0.42	22I	0.31	0.55	0.20	0.90
23A	0.61	0.00	0.02	0.30	23A	0.31	0.54	0.26	0.89
23I	0.65	0.02	0.01	0.19	23I	0.26	0.57	0.28	0.92
25A	0.52	0.01	0.07	0.54	25A	0.24	0.52	0.14	0.87
25I	0.55	0.08	0.06	0.50	25I	0.32	0.54	0.17	0.88
27A	0.54	0.01	0.06	0.51	27A	0.25	0.53	0.16	0.88
27I	0.56	0.07	0.05	0.47	27I	0.31	0.55	0.18	0.88
28A	0.50	0.01	0.09	0.58	28A	0.22	0.51	0.12	0.86
28I	0.53	0.10	0.09	0.54	28I	0.32	0.53	0.16	0.87

Land class	Red grouse	Black grouse	Partridge	Pheasant	Land class	Lapwing	Golden plover	Snipe	Woodcock
19A	0.67	0.35	0.78	0.89	19A	0.97	0.37	0.72	0.55
19I	0.71	0.38	0.77	0.90	19I	0.98	0.41	0.73	0.57
20A	0.66	0.33	0.78	0.89	20A	0.97	0.35	0.72	0.55
20I	0.70	0.36	0.77	0.90	20I	0.98	0.40	0.72	0.57
22A	0.72	0.40	0.78	0.89	22A	0.97	0.43	0.73	0.55
22I	0.73	0.41	0.77	0.90	22I	0.98	0.46	0.73	0.57
23A	0.86	0.53	0.76	0.89	23A	0.98	0.62	0.73	0.53
23I	0.82	0.56	0.75	0.90	23I	0.99	0.68	0.74	0.54
25A	0.64	0.32	0.78	0.89	25A	0.96	0.33	0.72	0.55
25I	0.69	0.35	0.77	0.90	25I	0.97	0.38	0.72	0.57
27A	0.68	0.35	0.79	0.90	27A	0.97	0.37	0.73	0.55
27I	0.71	0.38	0.77	0.90	27I	0.98	0.41	0.73	0.57
28A	0.60	0.27	0.77	0.88	28A	0.96	0.27	0.71	0.54
28I	0.67	0.32	0.77	0.90	28I	0.98	0.34	0.72	0.57

mute swan and buzzard in land classes 23 and 28, respectively. There were some slight differences (eg golden plover, buzzard), but the other interesting observation is that there is generally little difference between the probabilities in each of the land classes.

DISCUSSION

There can be little doubt that there is a considerable relationship between land cover and the distribution of breeding birds. This relationship has been seen previously in relation to particular habitat types (eg Sykes et al. 1989; Avery 1989). The approach outlined in this paper has shown that the distributions of most breeding bird species in the north of England and south of Scotland are affected by land cover. However, there are several refinements required for the calculated probabilities to be accurate enough for use in predicting land use change.

The major problem is one of scale; 10 km resolution is probably too large for accurate estimations of bird distributions even at the river catchment level. On the other hand, the one km scale used in the ITE land classification may be too small for some bird species, like the raptors, which range over large areas. One possible compromise would be to use breeding bird records from tetrads (2 km x 2 km).

It is obvious that the cover data are too crude. Furthermore, it is likely that the resolution of individual habitats is too coarse, and certain covers such as rough grassland and moor and woodland need to be differentiated into more meaningful components. One alternative would be to estimate land covers using remote sensing, and this is at present being carried out for various areas of the United Kingdom (see Fuller et al. 1990). This methodology might provide an accurate assessment of cover throughout the whole of a catchment, but some additional measurement of linear features might be needed, as well as an analysis of effects of habitat pattern.

In order that the effects of land use change on breeding bird distribution be more accurately assessed, the sea data should be removed. The ordination axis of cover used as the basis of the analysis above was greatly affected by the coastal 10 km squares. When this variable was removed, a better definition of land cover was produced. The purely land cover analysis approximates to the second axis of the CANOCO plot presented here, with an upland/lowland, cultivated/rough grassland axis produced. DECORANA provides a method for recalculating sample scores, in this case the square

scores, because these scores are means of the species scores. Thus, if the cover attributes (pseudospecies) change because of a land use change, the new score can be used to predict the probability of occurrence of particular species using the logistic regression equations.

The methodology outlined in this paper should enable the accurate prediction of changes in the distribution of breeding birds brought about by the economic factors affecting land use (see Allanson, Savage & White 1992). These economic changes produce land use transition matrices which can be used within the modelling framework outlined by Rushton (1992) to predict cover change, leading to the prediction of bird distributions.

REFERENCES

Allanson, P., Savage, D. & White, B. 1992. Areal interpolation of parish agricultural census data. In: *Land use change: the causes and consequences,* edited by M. C. Whitby, 92-101. (ITE symposium no. 27.) London: HMSO.

Avery, M. I. 1989. Effects of upland afforestation on some birds of the adjacent moorlands. *Journal of Applied Ecology,* **26,** 957-966.

Baker, R.J. & Nelder, J.A. 1978. *The generalised linear interactive modelling system.* Oxford: Numerical Algorithms Group.

Ball, D. F., Radford, G.L. & Williams, W. M. 1983. *A land characteristic data bank for Great Britain.* (Bangor occasional paper no.13.) Bangor: Institute of Terrestrial Ecology.

Beintema, A. J. & Muskens, G. J. D. M. 1987. Nesting success of birds breeding in Dutch agricultural grasslands. *Journal of Applied Ecology,* **24,** 743-758.

Blondel, J. & Farre, H. 1988. The convergent trajectories of bird communities along ecological successions in European forests. *Oecologia,* **75,** 83-93.

Bunce, R. G. H., Barr, C. J. & Whittaker, H. A. 1981. *Land classes in Great Britain: preliminary descriptions for users of the Merlewood method of land classification.* (Merlewood research and development paper no. 86.) Grange-over-Sands: Institute of Terrestrial Ecology.

Fuller, R.M., Parsell, R.J., Oliver, M. & Wyatt, G. 1990. Visual and computer classifications of remotely-sensed images. A case study in Cambridgeshire. *International Journal of Remote Sensing,* **10,** 193-210.

Haworth, P.F. & Thompson, D.B.A. 1990. Factors associated with the breeding distribution of upland birds in the south Pennines, England. *Journal of Applied Ecology,* **27,** 562-577.

Hill, M.O. 1979a. *DECORANA - a FORTRAN program for detrended correspondence analysis and reciprocal averaging.* Ithaca, NY: Section of Ecology and Systematics, Cornell University.

Hill, M.O. 1979b. *TWINSPAN - a FORTRAN program for arranging multivariate data in an ordered two-way table by classification of the individuals and attributes.* Ithaca, NY: Section of Ecology and Systematics, Cornell University.

Jongman, R.H., Ter Braak, C.J.F. & Van Tongeren, O.F.R. 1987. *Data analysis in community and landscape ecology.* Wageningen: Pudoc.

Lebreton, J.D. & Yoccoz, N. 1987. Multivariate analysis of bird count data. *Acta Oecologica Generalis,* **8,** 125-144.

Rushton, S.P. 1992. A preliminary model for investigating the ecological consequences of land use change within the framework of the ITE land classification. In: *Land use change: the causes and consequences,* edited by M.C. Whitby, 111-117. (ITE symposium no. 27.) London: HMSO.

Rushton, S.P., Luff, M.L. & Eyre, M.D. 1991. Habitat characteristics of grassland *Pterostichus* species (Coleoptera, Carabidae). *Ecological Entomology,* **16,** 91-104.

Sharrock, J.T.R. 1976. *The atlas of breeding birds in Britain and Ireland.* Calton: Poyser.

Sykes, J.M., Lowe, V.P.W. & Briggs, D.R. 1989. Some effects of afforestation on the flora and fauna of an upland sheepwalk during 12 years after planting. *Journal of Applied Ecology,* **26,** 299-320.

Ter Braak, C.J.F. 1987. *CANOCO - a FORTRAN program for canonical community ordination by partial detrended correspondence analysis, principal components and redundancy analysis (version 2.1).* Wageningen: TNO Institute of Applied Computer Science.

Ter Braak, C.J.F. & Looman, C.W.N. 1986. Weighted averaging, logistic regression and the Gaussian response model. *Vegetatio,* **65,** 3-11.

Wiens, J.A. 1989. *The ecology of bird communities. 1. Foundations and patterns.* Cambridge: Cambridge University Press.

Hydrological simulation of the Rede catchment using the système hydrologique Européen (SHE)

S Dunn, D Savage and R Mackay

Dept of Civil Engineering, University of Newcastle upon Tyne, Newcastle upon Tyne NE1 7RU

INTRODUCTION

The NERC/ESRC Land Use Programme (NELUP) has as its main objective the integration of those parts of the physical, ecological and economic sciences that underpin the allocative choices which are essential to land use planning. This objective is being realised through the development of a computer-based decision support system (DSS) (O'Callaghan 1992). The decision support system will provide a user-friendly environment within which planners or interest groups will be able to interrogate the consequences of policy decisions and/or economic factors resulting in large-scale land use change.

The methodology underpinning the DSS depends on the integration of a hierarchy of quantitative models covering hydrology, ecology and economics, through a geographical information system (GIS). The GIS, coupled with a proprietary data base, will provide the basic storage and manipulation facilities for handling the data input to and output from the component models. The information generated by the models will then be interrogated through the decision support system user interface via the GIS.

The river basin has been chosen as the basic regional unit over which prediction of the impacts of land use change will be made. Whilst the application of both the proposed ecological models (Rushton 1992) and the economic models (Allanson, Savage & White 1992) is not constrained regionally to this unit of area, the river basin is particularly convenient for assessing changes to both water discharges and water quality. To demonstrate the utility of the DSS, it is to be applied to the Tyne river basin in the first instance, with subsequent application to the Cam river basin, East Anglia.

The central theme of the hydrological modelling research programme within NELUP is the further development and application of the système hydrologique Européen (SHE) for predicting the hydrological consequences of land use change. The SHE is a physically based, spatially distributed modelling system and, as such, is well suited for this purpose. However, the computational and data requirements of the SHE are large. Consequently, significant developments must be made to permit its integration within the DSS framework. These developments will be focused on minimising the data handling and computational effort needed to resolve the hydrological consequences of land use change over the timescales (>20 years) and space scales (>3000 km^2) appropriate to land use planning for river basins within the United Kingdom.

The problem of data acquisition is being tackled within NELUP through the use of national data bases relevant to hydrology, which are already established in the UK. A methodology has been formulated which involves the implementation of a number of algorithms for transforming the various data held in these data bases into forms suitable for input to the SHE. Once each algorithm is tested, it will be established as an automatic routine within the framework of the GIS, facilitating the manipulation of the data bases for all subsequent studies. Moreover, automation of data entry to the SHE is intended to realise the potential for fully interactive model operation through the DSS.

The objectives of the first stage of the research programme comprise the identification of the relevant data bases, the development of the individual algorithms for data transformation, and the testing of each algorithm. Initially, the testing of the algorithms is being performed through a trial application of the SHE to the Rede catchment, a subcatchment of the Tyne river basin. As a first step in the testing programme, a preliminary set of uncalibrated simulations, describing the hydrological regime of the Rede and derived using very simple data transformations, has been prepared. This set of results provides the base scenario for future comparison with more sophisticated data transformation algorithms. As each new algorithm is prepared and tested, the changes to the simulations arising from implementation of the algorithm will be assessed. Refinements to the algorithms will be introduced progressively to improve the simulations. Once the complete suite of algorithms has been implemented without further significant improvement of the simulation results, the robustness of the combined algorithms will be examined through further applications to the remaining subcatchments of the Tyne basin.

At present, the work on the development of data transformation relates solely to the problems of simulating the flow components of the hydrological cycle using SHE. Ultimately, this work will be extended to include data transformations related to the simulation of water quality changes. This extension currently awaits the completion of the new components, being developed, for the simulation of sediment and contaminant transport.

The paper describes the uncalibrated results from the application of the SHE to the Rede catchment using a minimal data approach. The priorities for developing the above modelling methodology for the hydrology component of NELUP are also described.

THE TRIAL STUDY AREA

The Rede catchment (Redesdale) stretches from the border with Scotland at Carter Bar in the north to Redesmouth in the south, forming part of the Tyne river basin. The river Rede drains the catchment from the north-west to the south-east, joining the North Tyne river at Redesmouth. The catchment covers an area of 344 km² and is bounded by hills forming part of the Cheviots, with elevations rising to about 580 m. The outlet of the Rede is at a height of 105 m above Ordnance Datum. In the upper reaches of the catchment lies Catleugh reservoir, which provides water for the Gateshead Water Company. This reservoir effectively impounds runoff from the upper reaches of the catchment, allowing only sporadic excess water into the reaches downstream of the dam. The area of the catchment above the reservoir has been omitted from the present study as the

overland and channel flow component presently implemented in the SHE is not capable of simulating either the presence, or the hydrological impact, of reservoirs. A revised surface flow component is presently being developed.

Redesdale's climate is typical of upland areas in northern England. Rainfall is high, with an annual average in the order of 1200 mm, and occurs all year round. Variation between winter and summer rainfall is predominantly related to the temporal distribution of rainfall events rather than to total rainfall depths. Snow occurs in most winters. The mean minimum temperature for January is 0°C and mean maximum temperature for July is 19°C.

The catchment is covered by a dense network of small streams confirming the dominance of surface flow for the transport of water throughout the catchment. Drainage through the soils in the region is generally restricted by relatively low-permeability clay loam and sandy clay loam horizons, overlying relatively low-permeability geological units comprising sandstones, shales and limestones. Blanket peat is found on the hilltops around the head of Redesdale, where it forms an important subsurface water reserve maintaining stream flows during dry periods. Springs are observed at the base of the Fell Sandstone units in the upper regions of the dale, but these tend to exhibit short-duration responses to rainfall events. Similar short-term responses to rainfall through ephemeral spring discharges arise from some of the limestone sequences found in the southern region of the catchment. The region offers only very restricted

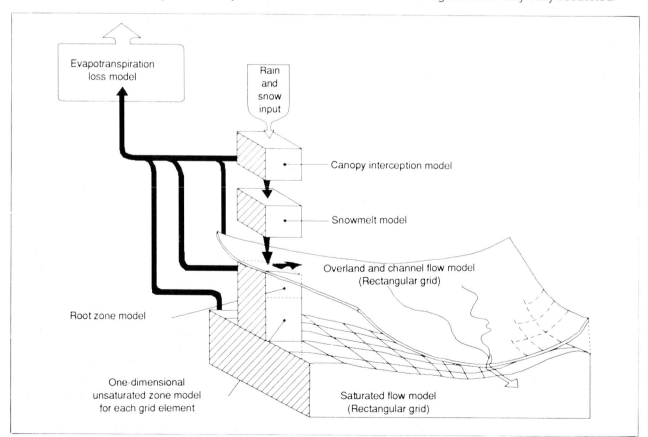

Figure 1. Schematic representation of the structure of SHE (source: Beven, Warren & Zaoui 1980)

potential for groundwater development.

Approximately 20% of the Rede catchment is forested. Most of the forested region lies in the upper reaches of the catchment. Of the remaining area, the majority is open fell and common. It is generally unsuitable for cultivation, and sheep farming predominates. A substantial proportion of the catchment is owned by the Ministry of Defence. This area is maintained in a semi-natural state.

THE SYSTÈME HYDROLOGIQUE EUROPÉEN (SHE)

Background

The SHE was developed through a joint venture by the British Institute of Hydrology, the Danish Hydraulic Institute, and Sogreah, France, with financial support provided by the Commission of the European Communities (Abbott *et al.* 1986a, b). The primary reason for establishing the SHE arose from the belief that conventional rainfall/runoff models were inappropriate for simulating the effects arising from changes to land use. As a result, the underlying aim, expressed during the development of the SHE, was to minimise the reliance of predictions on the availability of historical records of hydrological activity. For this reason, the modelling system is largely based on the integration of process equations that can be parameterised using data collected directly from the field. The SHE is specifically designed to simulate the spatial and temporal variations of water flows throughout the river basin.

The hydrological processes modelled in the SHE are illustrated in Figure 1. Representation of the spatial distribution of the catchment characteristics is provided through the discretisation of the catchment horizontally into an orthogonal network of grid squares. At each grid square, the catchment is further discretised into a vertical column of layers to represent the vertical pathways for flow from the atmosphere, through the vegetation canopy into the soil and unsaturated zones, and down to the saturated zone below. Parameter values are assigned to each layer within each grid square covering the model domain. Lateral flow is permitted as either overland flow, channel flow, or subsurface saturated zone flow.

Rivers and streams are assigned to the edges of the grid squares to form a continuous network of river links. The rivers can interact both with the surface and subsurface flow systems.

Data requirements for the SHE

Table 1 summarises the data needed for input to the SHE, the distributional requirements for the individual data types, and the potential sources of data bases from which the data may be derived. The data are categorised according to the hydrological component within which they are needed.

A brief inspection of this data list demonstrates the

Table 1. SHE model – data and parameter requirements (flow calculations only)

(x,y = continuous space; X,Y = specified location; t = time varying; crop = crop-specific; soil = soil-specific; OS = Ordnance Survey; MOD = Ministry of Defence; ITE = Institute of Terrestrial Ecology; BGS = British Geological Survey; IH = Institute of Hydrology; MO = Meteorological Office; RS = remote sensing; SS = Soil Survey; Lit = Literature; Geog, Ag = Depts of Geography & Agriculture; WA = Water Authority; NRA = National Rivers Authority Survey)

Frame component

Ground surface elevation	(x,y)	OS, MOD, ITE
Impermeable bed elevation	(x,y)	BGS
Meteorological station locations	(x,y)	NRA, IH, MO
Soil and vegetation distributions	(x,y)	Ag, ITE, SS, MAFF, RS

Interception component

Drainage parameters	(crop)	Lit
Canopy storage capacity	(crop,t)	Lit
Ground cover indices	(crop,t)	Lit, Ag
Rainfall rate	(t)	NRA, IH, MO

Evapotranspiration component

Canopy resistance	(crop,t)	Lit
Aerodynamic resistance	(crop,t)	Lit
Ground cover indices	(crop,t)	Lit
Potential evapotranspiration	(crop,t)	Lit, MO, NRA
Root profiles	(crop,t)	Lit, Ag
Meteorological data	(t)	NRA, IH, MO

Overland and channel flow component

Strickler roughness coefficients	(x,y)	Lit, NRA, WA
Weir discharge relationships	(X,Y)	NRA, WA
Boundary flow conditions	(X,Y,t)	NRA, WA
Control structures	(X,Y,t)	NRA, WA
Channel cross-sections	(x,y)	WA
Topography of overland flow plane	(x,y)	Geog

Unsaturated zone component

Soil moisture/tension relationships	(soil)	Lit, SS
Unsaturated hydraulic conductivity	(soil)	Lit, SS

Saturated zone component

Porosities/specific yields	(X,Y)	BGS
Saturated hydraulic conductivities	(X,Y)	Lit, NRA, WA
Impermeable bed elevations	(x,y)	BGS, NRA, WA
Specified flows or potentials	(X,Y,t)	NRA, WA
Pumping and recharge data	(X,Y,t)	NRA, WA

Snowmelt component

Degree day factor	(t)	Lit
Snow zone plane displacement	(-)	Lit
Snow roughness height	(-)	Lit
Meteorological and precipitation data	(t)	NRA, IH, MO

significant level of detail needed to undertake a comprehensive simulation of spatial and temporal flow patterns within a catchment. The approach to data acquisition employed for the SHE applications published to date (Bathurst 1986a, b) assumes that the input data are derived from a mixture of field data defining local parameter values, and descriptive data, such as soil distribution mapping, that permit the transfer of the local data to the surrounding region. Where local field data are non-existent, or of poor quality, it has been assumed that representative parameter values from similar media can be taken from studies made outside the catchment and used as input to the SHE. The generation of input data sets to the SHE has traditionally been constructed in a 'one-off' mode by an experienced hydrologist, with little attempt to automate the thought and data handling

processes employed in their construction.

The features of the development process of an input data set can be summarised as follows:

1. identification of lateral extent of catchment;
2. identification of grid pattern for the discretisation of the catchment;
3. identification of surface topography and subsurface structure (soils and geology), and definition of the vertical discretisation of the soil/rock profile;
4. identification of vegetation distributions and stream/river distributions;
5. identification of boundary conditions for lateral flow out of the catchment and initial conditions characterising the state of the system prior to simulation;
6. identification of meteorological record and the setting of maximum and minimum time-stepping rates;
7. identification of output data requirements;
8. identification of parametric of data for items 3–7 for each grid square over the domain.

Within NELUP, the grid structure was fixed at the outset to be consistent between the different model components of the DSS. The Ordnance Survey (OS) one km grid was chosen as the reference grid for simulations, all other data being superimposed on this basic grid structure.

For each of the features of the development process, algorithms are needed to provide, first, identification of the spatial variation of individual distributions and, second, the parameterisation of the distributions. In the following sections, the minimum data transformations used to construct the data sets for the first simulations of the trial catchment are described.

METEOROLOGICAL DATA

Data sources

Within Redesdale, observations are made at one standard meteorological station recording daily at 0900 hours, and at one automatic rain gauge recording precipitation totals every 15 minutes. The meteorological station is situated on the Redesdale Experimental Husbandry Farm (EHF) (GR 383595), whilst the rain gauge is located at Catcleugh reservoir (GR 374603) towards the head of the catchment. The data from the two sites have been distributed over the catchment using a Thiessen polygon approach. The boundary between the two polygons has been regularised to the Ordnance Survey grid.

SHE requires hourly data on:

- precipitation;
- net radiation;
- windspeed;
- net radiation;
- windspeed;

- air temperature;
- slope of saturation vapour pressure (SVP)/temperature (T) curve;
- vapour pressure deficit (VPD) of the air.

Hourly records are directly available for precipitation from the Catcleugh rain gauge (summing the 15 minute totals). All other hourly data have had to be approximated and interpolated from the data recorded daily at Redesdale or estimated from first principles.

The Redesdale station records daily precipitation totals, daily sunshine hours, wet and dry bulb temperatures (maximum and minimum), and daily wind run.

Data transformations

Precipitation

Catleugh precipitation data were directly converted from the 15 minute totals to hourly values for the simulation period. Hourly precipitation data could not be so readily determined for the Redesdale station. Disaggregation of the daily precipitation records by cross-correlation with the data from Catcleugh was found to be impracticable. No correlation between the values and distribution of precipitation at the two sites could be found. Moreover, trends in the daily patterns of precipitation in terms of intensity and duration could not be identified. However, for Catcleugh, the total precipitation did correspond closely with the number of 15 minute intervals in which it rained. Given this apparent lack of pattern in the data and the lack of any alternative physical basis for distributing the daily precipitation records, a distribution of rainfall was generated by allocating the rainfall (assuming constant intensity) to randomly assigned 15 minute slots in the day. The derived 15 minute rainfall distribution was then converted to hourly totals.

Sunshine hours

The daily distribution of sunshine hours is required for net radiation estimates used in the calculation of evapotranspiration. These data were obtained using the same techniques employed to assign the precipitation distribution, subject to the constraint that sunshine and precipitation events should not be coincident. Sunshine hours were assumed to be identical at the two stations, and the daily sunshine totals were distributed to the non-rain 15 minute slots within daylight hours.

Temperature

Daily mean temperature was calculated simply from the mean of the recorded maximum and minimum temperature. The daily maximum was assumed to occur at 1400 hours and the minimum at dawn. The timing of dawn was calculated for each day of the year, assuming a sinusoidal variation in daylight hours over the year. Hourly temperatures were

140

interpolated linearly from these data.

Windspeed

Wind run data for the 24 hours up to 0900 hours are recorded at Redesdale. These data were converted to an equivalent mean windspeed for the 24 hour period. A running mean of the windspeeds over successive two-day periods was then used to distribute the windspeed data over each day.

SVP/T and VPD

A number of polynomial expressions have been developed for calculating saturation vapour pressure at a particular temperature. For computational simplicity and accuracy, the following expression was employed (Richards 1971):

$$e^* = 1013.25exp$$
$$(13.318t_r - 1.976t_r^2 - 0.6445t_r^3 - 0.1299t_r^4)$$

where e^* = SVP, T = temperature in K, and $t_r = 1 - (373.15/T)$.

The derivative of this expression gives the gradient of the SVP/T curve at temperature T.

Vapour pressure deficit is calculated as the difference between vapour pressure at temperature T and the corresponding SVP. The vapour pressure of the air was derived from the corresponding wet bulb temperature and SVP, using the following expression:

$$VPT_a = SVP_{wb} - 0.66 (T - T_{wb})$$

where VPT_a = vapour pressure for air temperature, T, and SVP_{wb} = SVP at wet bulb temperature, T_{wb}. Given the lack of recorded dry and wet bulb temperatures during the day, single values of the gradient of SVP/T and VPD were calculated for each day and applied uniformly throughout the 24 hours.

Net radiation

In the absence of direct radiation measurements for Redesdale (a radiometer is not installed at the meteorological station), estimates of surface radiation receipt and outgoing radiation were made from general principles of radiation variation over the year. The derived net radiation was then distributed across the day according to the modelled distribution of sunshine hours.

The principles and formulae described in Wiesner (1970) were applied to the attenuation of outer atmospheric solar radiation. Radiation at the top of the earth's atmosphere was first approximated over the year by fitting a sine curve to known values corresponding to latitude 50°N. This yielded discrepancies of less than 1.5% between observed and predicted values. Radiation received at the earth's surface was modified by an estimated albedo and the ratio of sunshine hours/daylight hours (sun ratio). A constant value of albedo, typical of moorland vegetation, was used.

Net radiation is defined as the difference between incoming radiation and outgoing radiation. The latter was computed as if the earth is a black body, radiating at its mean temperature modified by the sun ratio (Wiesner 1970). Modelled daily totals of net radiation receipt were redistributed over 24 hours, using a first-order approximation of the diurnal distribution of net radiation given no cloud. This distribution was represented by a triangle peaking at mid-day and falling to zero at dawn and dusk. The area under the triangle equals the total daily incoming radiation and the peak value can be calculated knowing daylight hours. The sunshine hour distribution gives the proportion of each hour for which it was 'sunny', and for each non-zero record the corresponding value on the radiation triangle was calculated and adjusted by the proportion of that hour which had sunshine. This calculation yielded an approximate distribution of net radiation receipt under 'sunny' conditions, which was supplemented by evenly distributing the remaining radiation across all 'non-sunny' daylight hours. The resultant distribution of net radiation is rectilinear in shape, with spurs to meet the underlying triangular base during periods of sunshine.

OVERLAND & CHANNEL FLOW DATA

Channel network

The SHE requires an input of elevation for each grid square in a catchment and for each river link. Grid square elevations for the Rede were available directly from the Ministry of Defence digital terrain model. The elevations were calculated as the arithmetic average of the 100 m resolution spot heights for each square kilometre. In the absence of any automated channel data, the channel elevations were manually abstracted from OS 1:50 000 maps. Where these elevations were higher than the adjacent grid elevations, the channel elevations were adjusted appropriately. The grid square elevations were not changed.

The location of the river links was derived from Institute of Hydrology 1:250 000 river mapping. For the preliminary simulations, the positions were manually adjusted so that the river links coincided with the edges of grid squares. Figure 2 shows the Rede catchment divided into one km grid squares, with the river links superimposed. The hatched area represents the area of the catchment above Catcleugh reservoir.

Channel geometry and roughness

For each river link, the SHE requires data on the shape of the channel and the roughness of the channel bed controlling water movement. On the basis of no measured data, simple trapezoidal channels of varying sizes were allocated by inspection of the approximate catchment area commanded by the channel. Channel roughness values were taken from the literature.

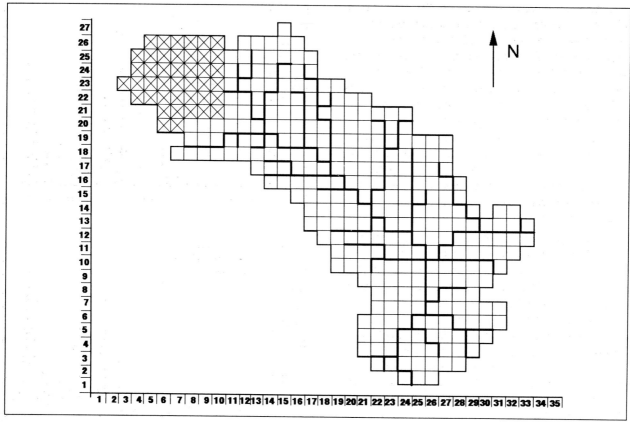

Figure 2. Rede catchment river network

VEGETATION, SOILS AND GEOLOGICAL DATA

Vegetation

Data describing the distribution of the different vegetation types over the catchment are required for input to the SHE. In addition, parametric data describing the impact of each vegetation type on the evapotranspiration of water from the soil/land surface to the atmosphere are required. The Institute of Terrestrial Ecology (ITE) land use classification (Bunce, Barr & Whittaker 1981) was used to assign the vegetation distribution over Redesdale. This classification assigns one of 32 land classes to each kilometre grid square over the country. Each land class represents the likely characteristics over all grid squares assigned to that class, and defined from a set of map attributes collected at each square. The map attributes are related statistically to more detailed descriptions of the character of particular land classes measured at a limited number of sample squares distributed throughout the United Kingdom. Thus, the representative data held for each grid square are essentially a probabilistic estimate of the characteristics of the square defined by the classification.

Numerous vegetation types are identified for each land class, each of which has a probability of occurrence within any particular grid square of that class. The identification of actual vegetation found in a particular grid square is, therefore, not relevant in this classification. As an initial estimate of vegetation

influences on the hydrological regime of Redesdale, an average of parameters for each vegetation type, weighted by their probability of occurrence, was used to assign vegetation data to each grid square. In this way, the land classes are assumed to represent single 'averaged' vegetation types. The parametric data for each of the underlying vegetation types used in the development of the 'averaged' vegetation characteristics were largely extracted from experimental data given in the literature.

Soils

Distribution of soil types and soil hydraulic properties for the preliminary simulations was also based on the ITE land classification. This classification does not describe soils in terms of their hydrological characteristics, but in terms of a set of 11 different soil descriptions. The conversion of this data set to parameter values describing the hydraulic characteristics of the soils was taken from Rijtema (1969). Rijtema develops very complete fluid flow and storage parameterisation for a range of different homogeneous soil types. A first-order attempt was made to link the ITE land classification descriptions to the Rijtema soil types, allowing a conversion of the ITE data into the required form for input to the SHE.

Geology

The solid geology of the region is complex, due to

the presence of rock masses from four different periods of geological development that have been substantially distorted through tectonic activity. Perched water tables are evident. Moreover, responses to surface water infiltration are rapid but are generally localised in effect and short-lived. These responses lead to the presence of ephemeral spring lines. Development of an equivalent two-dimensional, continuous representation of the geology of the catchment was, therefore, carried out through an assessment, over depth, of the potential for contributions from each formation to lateral transport of subsurface water. Both solid and drift deposits are capable of providing storage and transmission of water.

A simple approximation of the storage for each unit was estimated in terms of an equivalent depth, assuming a vertically homogeneous media profile of specified yield. The sum of equivalent depths for all formations at a point over the domain yields the depth to the effective impermeable bed for the two-dimensional representation required by the SHE. The hydraulic parameters of the vertical profiles were estimated from the relative flow contributions expected from each formation. Thus, areas adjacent to the stream are primarily influenced by the recent alluvium, whilst areas with substantial boulder clay deposits essentially restrict lateral transport to interflow in the soil horizons.

PRELIMINARY SIMULATION RESULTS
Background

The intention for the first SHE simulations of the Rede was to apply the simplest and most readily available data sets defined in the preceding sections. The modelling procedure was further simplified by selecting periods for simulation during which no snowfall was recorded. This meant that the SHE snowmelt component was not required. Moreover, in the summer and autumn, little water is released from Catcleugh reservoir. Therefore, simulation in these two seasons avoids the need to disaggregate the influences of reservoir releases.

Taking into account the above simplifications, two periods were chosen for the initial simulations. The first of these was a three-month period from the beginning of September to the end of November 1986. This was a relatively dry period, during which no snowfall was recorded.

The second period chosen was one of very high rainfall, between 20 and 30 July 1988. This simulation enabled the performance of the model under very wet conditions to be examined to give an indication of the peak surface runoff response of the catchment.

Results
1986 simulation

Some of the results from the 1986 simulation are illustrated in Figure 3. Figure 3(i) shows the daily rainfall for the period, as recorded at the Redesdale

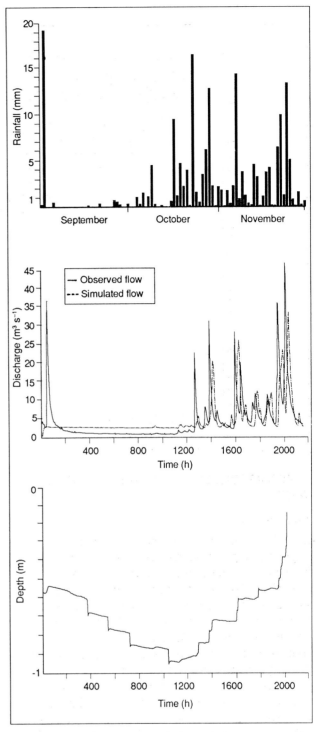

Figure 3. SHE simulation of Rede catchment for 1 September to 30 November 1986
i.   Daily rainfall at Redesdale
ii. Comparison of observed and simulated flows to river Rede at Redebridge
iii. Depth of phreatic surface below ground level for grid square (23, 15)

EHF rain gauge. Figure 3(ii) shows both the simulated and recorded discharge at Redebridge. It can be seen from this comparison that the simulated flow corresponds reasonably well with the observed flow. It is worth noting that all results presented herein were obtained without making any attempt to fit the model to the observations.

A few areas can be identified where improvement in the results would be desirable. It would appear that the predicted baseflow in the river is too high,

suggesting that the storage capacity of the saturated zone is too great. The peak flows in the simulation are all slightly delayed. This delay may be a result of estimating the elevation at the centre of each grid square from an average of the elevations across the grid square. In many cases, the slope of the ground, between the centre of a grid square and a river link, is then reduced, leading to a reduction in the rate of overland flow.

From Figure 3(ii), it is apparent that approximately two months were required for the model to settle and produce reasonable predictions. Prior to this time, the results were heavily influenced by the initial conditions input to the model. Figure 3(ii) also illustrates how sharply the river rises during rainfall events, because of the low permeability and infiltration rate of the soils which result in frequent overland flow in the catchment.

Figure 3(iii) shows how the depth of the phreatic surface varied during the simulation, at a particular point in the catchment. The initial depth of 0.5 m is probably slightly low, as a high discharge was observed at Redebridge just two days into the simulation period. Despite this, the predicted depth of the phreatic surface never falls below a depth of 0.95 m, during the very dry spell in September. After the rain in October, the phreatic surface rises again, until the soil becomes saturated towards the end of the simulation. These predictions suggest that the phreatic surface rarely falls below a depth of one m.

1988 simulation

Results from the simulation during the period of high rainfall are illustrated in Figure 4. Figure 4(i) shows the input of rainfall at Redesdale EHF with the estimated hourly distribution. The comparisons of simulated and recorded discharges at Redebridge are shown in Figure 4(ii).

After the first five days, the simulated flow corresponds well to the measured flow. This is a very short time to allow the model to settle, and suggests that the effects of initial conditions can be minimised if the simulation period begins with several days of heavy rainfall. The predicted peak flow of 87 m³ s⁻¹ compares very well with the measured peak flow of 80 m³ s⁻¹; the timing of the peak is also good.

Figure 4(iii) shows a grid distribution of overland flow depth at 200 hours from the start of the simulation. This distribution is shortly before the peak discharge was recorded, and therefore represents the maximum overland flow during the period. The figures indicate an average overland flow depth of around 5 mm. A time series plot of overland flow depth for a particular grid square showed that there was no surface runoff until a time of about 190 hours. This timing coincides with the start of the rise in river level, and indicates the time at which the catchment became saturated.

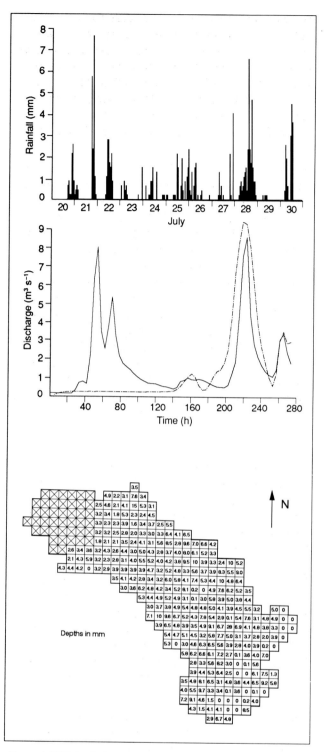

Figure 4. SHE simulation of Rede catchment for 20–30 July 1988
 i. Hourly rainfall at Redesdale
 ii. Comparison of observed and simulated flows to river Rede at Redebridge
 iii. Grid distribution of overland flow depths at 8am on 28 July 1988

Discussion of the modelling procedures

The main problems encountered in application of the SHE were associated with the channel geometries. The input data describing channel geometry proved to be insufficient to carry the water during periods of very high flow. Whilst the baseflow in the Rede is of the order of 2 m³ s⁻¹, peak flows are commonly of the order of 30 m³ s⁻¹. In practice, considerable flooding is likely to take place. However, this flooding is not

easily modelled by the current version of the SHE, and a deep channel is required, therefore, to carry the peak flows. These problems indicate the need for more accurate data to describe channel geometry. Also, the more realistic representation of flooding events within the SHE, already being implemented within the revised overland flow component, is essential for the future application of the model to such catchments.

The second major area of concern is that of the effect of initial conditions on the results. For the short three-month simulation, the model did not begin to respond until the second major period of rain, at the end of October. The heavy rainfall on the second day was insufficient to overcome the initial conditions. The primary controlling factor is the initial level of the phreatic surface. The 1986 simulation was repeated with an initial phreatic surface depth of 1.5 m below ground level. The effect of this change was that the predicted discharge at Redebridge never rose above 2.5 m^3 s^{-1}. A relatively small error in estimating the depth of the phreatic surface can give, therefore, very misleading results for early times. Longer simulation times exceeding one or more years will be required to avoid this problem.

FUTURE WORK

The use of national data sets and the results of the preliminary simulations have given confidence that algorithms can be developed that will permit successful application of the SHE in the framework established for the NELUP decision support system. Sources of data and outline methodologies have been identified which will enable automatic derivation of input data for the SHE. Consequently, the next phase of work will concentrate on the development of the appropriate numerical algorithms and their implementation within the GIS and data base. The first routines which must be developed are those aimed at establishing the frame data set for SHE input (Table 1) and the channel geometries.

The preliminary simulations have highlighted a number of areas where there are likely to be difficulties. The procedures for derivation of topographic elevation must be very robust. Indeed, the SHE's component models, describing each of the main hydrological processes, impose many constraints on the data needed for a successful simulation, each of which must be accounted for within the final algorithms.

Similarly, these are potentially many problems that must be tackled before a satisfactory routine for the automatic derivation of channel geometry can be completed. If the predicted geometry is too great, problems of stability of the numerical solution of streamflows are evident in the results of the SHE output. This situation arises where channel widths are large relative to the simulated depth of water. Conversely, if the predicted geometry is too small,

the channels cannot cope with peak flow volumes. It is anticipated that the new version of SHE, as previously noted, will overcome many of these problems. Nevertheless, estimates of channel geometry and topographic elevation combined will need to be sufficiently accurate not only to reflect the hydraulic potential for flooding, but also to define the likely future geometries of channels. Such geometries will influence the presence or absence of aquatic flora and fauna, and are required as input to the ecological models.

In addition to these areas of development, much further research is required to transfer the soils and geological data (Lunn, Younger & Mackay 1992), as well as the vegetation and meteorological data, for input to SHE.

ACKNOWLEDGEMENTS

The authors would like to thank all those members of the NELUP research team involved in the provision of data in this study. In particular, the authors would like to thank Ms S White for her major contribution during the early development of the data set for the Redesdale simulations.

REFERENCES

Abbott, M.B., Bathurst, J.C., Cunge, J.A., O'Connell, P.E. & Rasmussen, J. 1986a. An introduction to the European hydrological system – système hydrologique Européen, "SHE". 1: History and philosophy of a physically based distributed modelling system. *Journal of Hydrology*, **87**, 45-59.

Abbott, M.B., Bathurst, J.C., Cunge, J.A., O'Connell, P.E. & Rasmussen, J. 1986b. An introduction to the European hydrological system – système hydrologique Européen, "SHE". 2: History and philosophy of a physically based distributed modelling system. *Journal of Hydrology*, **87**, 61-77.

Allanson, P., Savage, D. & White, B. 1992. Areal interpolation of parish agricultural census data. In: *Land use change: the causes and consequences*, edited by M.C. Whitby, 92-101. (ITE symposium no. 27.) London: HMSO.

Bathurst, J.C. 1986a. Physically based distributed modelling of an upland catchment using the système hydrologique Européen. *Journal of Hydrology*, **87**, 79-102.

Bathurst, J.C. 1986b. Sensitivity analysis of the système hydrologique Européen for an upland catchment. *Journal of Hydrology*, **87**, 103-123.

Beven, K., Warren, R. & Zaoui, J. 1980. SHE: towards a methodology for physically-based distributed forecasting in hydrology. In: *Hydrological forecasting,* 133-137. (IAHS Publication no. 129.) Wallingford: International Association of Hydrological Sciences.

Bunce, R.G.H., Barr, C.J. & Whittaker, H.A. 1981. *The land classes of Great Britain: preliminary descriptions for users of the Merlewood method of land classification.* (Merlewood research and development paper no. 86.) Grange-over-Sands: Institute of Terrestrial Ecology.

Lunn, R., Younger, P.L. & Mackay, R. 1992. Development of a methodology for hydrological simulation at the basin scale using SHE. In: *Land use change: the causes and consequences,* edited by M.C. Whitby, 147-158. (ITE symposium no. 27.) London: HMSO.

O'Callaghan, J.R. 1992. Decision-making in land use. In: *Land use change: the causes and consequences,* edited by M.C. Whitby, 79-87. (ITE symposium no. 27.) London: HMSO.

Richards, J.M. 1971. Simple expression of the saturation vapour pressure of water in the range -50 to 140. *British Journal of Applied Physics,* **4**, L15-L18.

Rijtema, P.E. 1969. *Soil moisture forecasting.* (Nota 513.) Wageningen: Instituut voor Cultuurtechniek en Waterhuishouding.

Rushton, S.P. 1992. A preliminary model for investigating the ecological consequences of land use change within the framework of the ITE land classification. In: *Land use change: the causes and consequences,* edited by M.C. Whitby, 111-117. (ITE symposium no. 27.) London: HMSO.0

Wiesner, C.J. 1970. *Hydrometeorology.* London: Chapman and Hall.

Development of a methodology for hydrological simulation at the basin scale, using the système hydrologique Européen (SHE)

R Lunn, P L Younger and R Mackay

Dept of Civil Engineering, University of Newcastle upon Tyne, Newcastle upon Tyne NE1 7RU

INTRODUCTION

Within the framework of the NERC/ESRC Land Use Programme (NELUP), the central theme of the hydrological research is the further development and application of the système hydrologique Européen (SHE). The SHE, a physically based distributed modelling system, is to be used to make predictions of the hydrological consequences of land use change at the river basin scale. Two long-term hydrological factors that are considered important for river basin management are the change to the overall water balance (including change to the spatial and temporal distributions of the water), and the change to the presence and distribution of contaminants transported with the water across the basin. These factors may affect not only the control and usage of the water for irrigation and potable water supply but, equally, they may alter the terrestrial and aquatic habitats for flora and fauna. Consequently, predictions of hydrological change are required as input to both the agroeconomic models (Allanson, Savage & White 1992) and ecology models (Rushton 1992) being developed within NELUP.

At present, considerable computational effort and a substantial volume of physical data are needed to predict the flow of water and contaminants through the many pathways within the hydrological cycle using the SHE. Given the large spatial (>3000 km²) and temporal scales (>20 years) appropriate to land use planning at the river basin scale, significant developments are needed to minimise both of these requirements if the SHE is to be operated within the framework of a decision support system (O'Callaghan 1992). A methodology has been established to solve the data problem. National data bases relevant to hydrology are being investigated to assess their potential for providing the bulk of the data necessary for river basin hydrological characterisation using the SHE. In general, the data held in these data bases are not directly usable. Consequently, a large number of algorithms are under development to transform the various source data into the required forms. Once each algorithm has been tested, it will be established as an automatic routine within the framework of a geographical information system, thus greatly facilitating the manipulation of the chosen data bases for all subsequent studies.

The testing of the methodology for the simulation of water flow only is being addressed through a trial application of the SHE to the Rede catchment (Redesdale), a subcatchment of the Tyne river basin (Dunn, Savage & Mackay 1992). This work will eventually be extended to include the application of the SHE to the whole of the Tyne river basin and to the simulation of contaminant transport.

In this paper, the identification of the hydraulic properties of the soils and the underlying geological formations of the Rede catchment is addressed. Preliminary methods for automatically transforming the available data for both soils and geology of a catchment are discussed. These methods are the subject of ongoing investigation.

THE SYSTÈME HYDROLOGIQUE EUROPÉEN

Background

The SHE modelling system was developed through a joint venture by the British Institute of Hydrology, the Danish Hydraulic Institute, and Sogreah, France (Abbott *et al.* 1986a, b). The primary reason for establishing the SHE arose from the belief that conventional rainfall/runoff models were inappropriate for simulating the effects arising from changes to land use. As a result, the underlying aim expressed during the development of the SHE was to minimise the reliance of predictions on the availability of historical records of hydrological activity. For this reason, the modelling system is based largely on the integration of process equations, parameterised using data that can be collected directly from the field. The input data requirements for the whole of the SHE are described by Dunn *et al.* (1992). Of specific interest here is the development of the data sets for the unsaturated and saturated zone components of the modelling system.

Simulation of groundwater flow in the SHE

Figure 1 provides a schematic representation of the

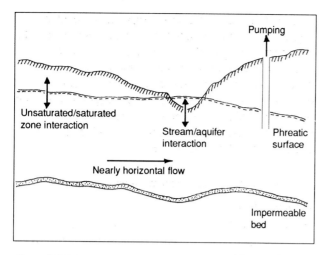

Figure 1. Schematic representation of the groundwater flow processes modelled in SHE

processes modelled in the saturated zone component of the SHE. In its present form, the SHE is capable of modelling only single-layer, unconfined aquifers under the assumption of essentially horizontal two-dimensional flow. Spatial variation of the properties of the groundwater zone is restricted to the magnitude of the vertically averaged horizontal hydraulic conductivity, Kx, Ky. The movement of groundwater under these conditions is described by the non-linear Boussinesq equation (Bear & Verruijt 1987):

$$S\frac{\partial h}{\partial t} = \frac{\partial}{\partial x}(K_x H\frac{\partial h}{\partial x}) + \frac{\partial}{\partial y}(K_y H\frac{\partial h}{\partial y}) + R \qquad (1)$$

where $S(x,y)$ = specific yield; $h(x,y,t)$ = phreatic surface level; $K_x(x,y)$ = saturated hydraulic conductivity in direction x; $K_y(x,y)$ = saturated hydraulic conductivity in direction y; $d(x,y)$ = elevation of impermeable bed; t = time; x,y = space co-ordinates; and $R(x,y,t)$ = vertical accretion of water into the saturated zone.

In addition to accretion from the vertical movement of water to or from the unsaturated zone, the groundwater flow component also provides representations of coupling with surface water activity through stream channel beds, through direct seepage at fully saturated ground surfaces, and through pumped abstraction points.

It is assumed that the hydrogeological characteristics of any catchment can be adequately summarised by a two-dimensional areal saturated zone component. This assumption is stringent. Whilst it has been found adequate in the past (Bathurst 1986a, b), the problems of simulating subsurface flows over large catchments, such as the Tyne, with this restrictive form of subsurface model are significant. Inspection of the geology of the Rede catchment illustrates the potential for substantial deviation from this idealised conceptualisation of a groundwater system.

Given this problem, two approaches to the use of the SHE have been considered:

1. to upgrade the SHE's saturated zone component

to allow the flow pathway through complex geological systems to be simulated directly;

2. to formulate procedures that permit adequate 'effective' representations of the major flow paths in complex geological systems, and that can employ the simplified single-layer representation already in place in the SHE.

Whilst the first option is the most attractive for the long-term development of the SHE, given the physically based description of the geological system implied in the development of the new model component, it was decided to address the possibility of employing the second approach in the first instance. The procedures being developed, based on this approach, are described later.

Simulation of unsaturated zone flow in the SHE

The unsaturated zone provides the primary link between the groundwater and the surface water systems. Simulation results have been shown to be sensitive to the parameterisation of hydraulic properties of this zone. For this reason, and because of the high degree of non-linearity of the basic equation governing unsaturated zone flow, a considerable proportion of the computational effort required by the SHE is used for defining flow through this zone. Lateral transport in this zone (ie through interflow pathways) is not modelled.

The governing equation for vertical flow through the unsaturated zone is Richard's equation:

$$C\frac{\partial \psi}{\partial t} = \frac{\partial}{\partial z}(K\frac{\partial \psi}{\partial z}) + \frac{\partial K}{\partial z} - S \qquad (2)$$

where ψ = soil moisture tension; t = time; z = vertical dimension; C = soil water capacity ($\approx \partial\theta/\partial\psi$); θ = volumetric water content; K = hydraulic conductivity; and S = source/sink flux rate.

Functional relationships are required to link moisture content, θ, to the hydraulic conductivity, K, and moisture tension, ψ, of the soil. These relationships are dependent on soil type, which may vary both areally and over depth in the soil profile. Provision is made in the SHE for up to four different soil layers within the soil profile.

Solution of Richard's equation is dependent on the provision of appropriate initial and boundary conditions. The upper and lower boundaries are, respectively, the ground surface and the phreatic surface. The phreatic surface functions as a moving boundary, and involves a complex linkage to the underlying groundwater flow component to maintain mass conservation. Figure 2 shows the various water movements that are simulated within the unsaturated zone. Defining appropriate initial conditions for this zone is generally impractical. Fortunately, errors in initial conditions will normally decay rapidly over the early simulation period.

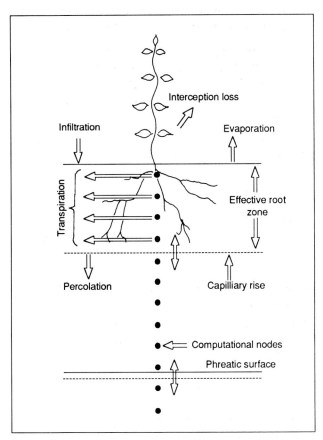

Figure 2. Schematic representation of the unsaturated zone flow processes modelled in SHE

GEOLOGY/HYDROGEOLOGY

Introduction

Hydrogeological data fall into three categories:

1. geological structure;
2. material hydraulic properties;
3. material hydrogeochemical properties.

The data base for defining geological structure is most readily derived from the borehole records held by the British Geological Survey (BGS), combined with the available mapping of both the solid and drift geology. Hydraulic and hydrogeochemical data for each of the primary geological units are generally sparse for areas such as Redesdale, where only limited groundwater exploitation has taken place. In general, it is anticipated that this information will be forthcoming from searches of the relevant literature and by reference to the data and knowledge held by hydrogeologists in the relevant water companies, the National Rivers Authority regional offices, and the British Geological Survey.

Given this situation, two problems need to be overcome. First, the available data must be transferred into the NELUP data base in a form that minimises the need for interpretation by a trained hydrogeologist. Second, an algorithm or algorithms must be established to manipulate the data into a form that can be employed within the existing SHE model. A two-tier study of the hydrogeology of the Rede catchment has been implemented to examine these problems. This study comprises a detailed appraisal of the hydrogeological characteristics of the catchment using all available data sources and without regard to automation of the approach. A second, less detailed, appraisal involving the development of a semi-automatic interpretation of the readily available geological data has also been conducted. The latter approach is specifically aimed at automating the data to SHE.

Geology of the Rede catchment

Introduction

Published works on the geology of the Rede catchment are few, and the treatise of Miller (1887) remains the main source of reference for the area. Marginal areas of the catchment are covered by Clough (1889) and Frost and Holliday (1980). Frost (1969) has published details of Lower Limestone group stratigraphy in the catchment.

Rocks of four geological time periods occur in the Rede catchment: namely, Silurian, Devonian, Carboniferous and Quaternary. All of the Carboniferous units in Redesdale are of Dinantian (Lower Carboniferous) age. The major lithostratigraphic subdivisions recognised in Redesdale are shown in Figure 3.

The pre-Carboniferous basement rocks

The oldest rocks exposed in Redesdale are Silurian greywackes and shales, which have been correlated with the extensive body of rocks of the same facies forming the southern uplands of Scotland (Johnson 1980). They are well exposed in the Lumsdon and Ramshope burns. The greywackes are poorly sorted lithic sandstones, up to 2 m thick, separated by laminated mudstones up to 20 m thick.

Overlying the Silurian sediments in Redesdale are andesite lavas of Devonian age. These lavas belong to the major igneous complex of the Cheviot Hills, which stretches for more than 30 miles along the Northumbrian/Scottish border. The lavas are dark purple, with primary flow foliations lacking visible apertures.

Dinantian rocks of the Northumberland basin

Crustal stretching in northern Britain commenced in the late Devonian as a consequence of the Hercynian orogeny (Leeder 1987). Hinged at the north by the stable Cheviot massif, the downwarping of the Northumberland basin was controlled to the south by the Stublick – Ninety Fathom fault system, which trends along the Tyne/Solway gap. This fault system was active throughout the Dinantian and is responsible for the marked contrast in rocks of the same age on either side of it. To the south of the fault system, on the Alston block, the Dinantian comprises a 600–700 m sequence of thick limestones with minor sandstones and shales, whereas up to 4500 m of predominantly clastic Dinantian sediments are recorded in the Northumberland basin (Fordham 1989).

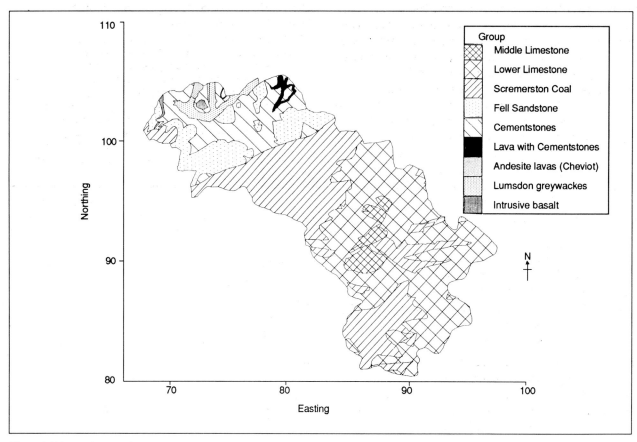

Figure 3. Lithostratigraphic map of the Rede catchment

Sedimentation in the Northumberland basin was cyclical, so that the preserved sediments occur in 'cyclothems'. The archetypal cyclothem is:

Coal
Sandstone
Shale
Limestone

Within the different lithostratigraphic groups in Redesdale, the cyclothems are consistently underdeveloped. Thus, in the Fell Sandstone group, coals and limestones are rare, and shales are subordinate to sandstones. In the Scremerston group, the coal in a given cyclothem is almost always present, while the limestone is usually absent. In the Lower and Middle Limestone groups, by contrast, the limestones in the cyclothems are always present, but the coals are restricted to only a few cyclothems (eg the Fourlaws Coal). It is on this basis that the distinction between groups is made. Even in the Limestone groups, however, limestones are generally thin (5–10 m) compared to the overlying sandstones (10–50 m).

Quaternary deposits

Unlike many Northumbrian tills, the tills of Redesdale are little more than reworked fragments of the underlying bedrock. This is because the uplands of Redesdale and the Cheviot Hills formed a local ice-spreading centre during the cold stages of the Quaternary.

Little is known of the valley-train sand and gravel bodies which line the axes of the major valleys, except that they comprise thin (up to 2.5 m) units of interbedded gravel, sands and laminated clay, with recorded total thicknesses up to 12.5 m.

Blanket peat occurs on the hilltops around the head of the Dale, and also in isolated patches on shale plateaux beneath sandstone scarps. These deposits are generally about 2 m thick, although they can locally attain a thickness of 4.5 m.

Hydrogeology of the Rede catchment

Data on the hydrogeology of the Rede catchment are sparse. Of the 39 known borehole records for the catchment, only four give yield–drawdown information, and these are all within the Lower Limestone group. Transmissivities estimated from these data vary from 16 to 160 m^2 day^{-1}. Most of the recorded boreholes in the Dale are 19th century coal exploration holes which are no longer extant. A few sizeable private borehole abstractions (up to 150 m^3 day^{-1}) occur from thick sandstones in the Lower Limestone group near Otterburn, but most groundwater supplies in the Dale are from springs.

Using primary geological field observations and thin-section studies, an appraisal of the relative hydrogeological importance of different lithological units within Redesdale has been made. Most of the catchment is underlain by shaley sequences, which typically include thin lenticular fine-grained sandstones. Petrographic analysis of one such sandstone found it to have a porosity of only 3%,

implying low hydraulic conductivity. The Silurian greywackes are similarly tight, and the Cheviot lavas are virtually impermeable. Groundwater circulates in the thicker sandstones and limestones in response to topographical factors, which are themselves a consequence of geological structure. For most aquifer units, flow is dominated by localised recharge and discharge in outcrop escarpments, where the aquifers are unconfined. Scarps are generally west-facing, and dips to the south-east of around 10–20° soon introduce confined conditions, where flow is sluggish and probably responds only to long-term changes in recharge–discharge dynamics in the adjacent outcrop area.

The limestones in Redesdale exhibit virtually no intergranular porosity, and thus flows are wholly restricted to solution-opened joints (unusually, bedding plane fractures are not important). The limestones never exceed 10 m in thickness, and only two of those studied showed any signs of active groundwater flow.

The sandstones vary from 25 m to 150 m thick, and they have appreciable intergranular porosity and permeability. Jointing is ubiquitous, though of low frequency, and a dual-porosity, dual-permeability structure controls all flow. Finite permeabilities exist in both the joint and matrix block systems.

High hydraulic conductivities (up to 200 m day^{-1}) are thought to characterise the fluvial sands and gravels, which act as an exchange zone between the bedrock aquifers and the rivers. 'Perched' groundwater systems in the peat deposits are a source of sustained flow in upland streams. Data for both of these Quaternary aquifer systems are lacking, but it is possible to infer the orders of magnitude of their hydraulic parameters by reference to deposits in nearby catchments in Northumberland and Scotland

Table 1. Hydrogeological data for Dinantian groups from boreholes outside Redesdale

(SC = Scremerston Coal group; ML = Middle Limestone group; LL = Lower Limestone group; FS = Fell Sandstone group; T = transmissivity; K = hydraulic conductivity. K values are calculated from T values using saturated thickness (b) data from borehole logs, and the formula K = T/b)

Site	Grid reference	Stratigraphic unit	T (m² day⁻¹)	K (m² day⁻¹)
Thornton Mains	NT961476	FS	96	0.88
Thornton Farm	NT950476	FS	100	1.67
Murton	NT971487	FS	88	1.07
Dock Rd, Berwick	NT995521	FS	34	0.46
Fowberry	NT027293	FS	135	2.20
Spadeadam	NY621739	FS	60	1.20
Holy Island	NU134428	ML	22	0.50
Stamford Links	NU210209	ML	14	0.20
Gallow Moor	NU218208	LL	57	0.90
Kyloe Woods	NU058388	SC	13	0.20
Stonehaugh, Shields	NY799765	SC	27	0.35

Table 2. Hydrogeologically significant units in the Carboniferous of Redesdale

(C = Cementstones; F = Fell Sandstones; S = Scremerston; L = Lower Limestones; U = Upper Limestones. K values: for sandstones estimated from petrographic data; for limestones calculated from fracture frequency and assumed one cm aperture using a cubic law (Freeze & Cherry 1979, p74). Specific yield for sandstones taken as 54% of effective porosity, following data on specific retention properties of sandstones(Pettyjohn 1985, p8). For limestones, set equal to calculated fracture porosity. Thicknesses approximate, calculated from boreholes where available, otherwise from map measurements. BPN = bedding plane normal)

Unit	Group	K (m day⁻¹)	Sy (%)	Thick-ness (m)	No. BPN joints m⁻²	Rank
Lower Sandstones	C	0.3	7	80	-	2
Fell Sandstones	F	0.2	9	150	<0.5	1
Bellshiel sandstone	S	1.3	·11	30	<0.5	6
Huel Crag sandstone	S	-?-	-?-	40	0.4	8
Callerhuel Crag sandstone	S	-?-	-?-	20	2.0	7
Redesdale limestone	L	1.0	2	6	1.9	9
Hepple Heugh sandstone	L	0.2	6	25	0.8	5
Wanney Crags sandstone	L	0.1	5	35	0.9	4
Lunga Crags sandstone	L	1.7	12	2	1.3	3
Oxford limestone	U	0.4	0.7	6	0.75	10

(see especially Ingram 1987; Ledger & Harper 1987; Brown & Ingram 1988).

Given the general lack of hydrogeological information available from the Rede catchment itself, data on hydraulic parameters have been obtained from other areas within the Dinantian Northumberland basin; data from Carboniferous rocks outside these areas are not applicable. Table 1 summarises the hydrogeological data from boreholes in the Northumberland basin beyond Redesdale. In addition to these data, laboratory-determined values for porosity and permeability in the Fell Sandstone group are available in a number of publications (Hodgson & Gardiner 1971; Bell 1978; Cradock-Hartopp & Holliday 1984; Fordham 1989).

Table 2 lists the ten most important aquifers in the Dinantian succession in Redesdale, with estimated hydraulic parameters. A subjective ranking system has been used to illustrate the relative importance of each unit (1 = most important). The ranks are meant to represent a synthesis of all relevant parameters (thickness, continuity, hydraulic conductivity).

An approach to automating hydrogeological data collection

Construction of a hydrogeological data set

As noted above, hydrogeological data fall into three main categories: geological, hydraulic and

hydrogeochemical. For the evaluation of regional groundwater flow, interest lies primarily in obtaining data in the first two categories. The available geological data provide the primary source of information on the geometry of the formations beneath the catchment. Hydraulic data yield information on the water transmission properties of the individual formations. The first step towards defining the hydrogeological characteristics of the groundwater system is to identify the three-dimensional structure of the formations. Where hydrogeological mapping has been carried out by BGS, the data on formation characteristics can be taken directly from the available maps. However, these maps do not yet cover all regions of the United Kingdom. The alternative is to use the basic geological mapping (both drift and solid) alongside available borehole data.

Generally, the borehole data provide high-resolution information about the structure of the geological formations over depth, but only at the point of measurement. For regions with limited groundwater usage (such as Redesdale), the number of such boreholes is few. Consequently, the borehole data alone are insufficient to yield the required data on formation geometries. Outcrop mapping has a lower resolution as it is already interpreted from point observation data. Unfortunately, data on formation thicknesses are not readily identifiable from the maps. However, the outcrop patterns and data on the maps can be used to define the geometry of the formations in two ways. First, the elevation of the formation contact surfaces can be readily defined at outcrop. Second, the orientation and magnitude of the dip of the formation contacts are often marked where measurements are available. By combining both sets of information, the position of the formation contacts over the region can be defined. By choosing selected marker horizons that are considered to be both continuous and regular, a reference set of surfaces is established. Discontinuities in the formation surfaces may arise from faulting. Faults thus define the limits for interpolation of the various data.

All remaining surfaces defining the geometry of the formations can be referenced to the chosen marker horizons. Thus, a basic geological structure model can be developed.

The second phase of the model development is to assign the hydraulic data to the individual formations. Data on the hydraulic properties of individual formations must be prescribed in the first instance using locally derived information. Where such information is difficult to obtain, then representative data from the literature are used. It is abundantly clear from the earlier discussions that the use of averaged values for specific media types (eg limestone) can be misleading and very inaccurate.

Whilst both steps in the development of the subsurface model appear relatively clear when undertaken by hand, the implementation of the steps through a robust algorithm is not trivial. The large

variation in the quality and form of the supporting data produces substantial automation problems. To avoid these problems, therefore, it is proposed that the data base of information should be hand-cleaned prior to implementation in support of the modelling studies. Such enhancements may include prior identification of marker horizons and adding point data to assist the implementation of the interpolation routines. It will also be necessary to regularise formation names between maps. Unfortunately, this is an area requiring considerable effort. However, the utility of the data will be much enhanced.

Automating data input to the SHE

The three-dimensional hydrogeological model proposed above will provide the reference data set for the final phase of automation. The primary requirements of this automation are:
- to establish the hydrological significance of the individual formations;
- to establish an equivalent two-dimensional representation of the groundwater flow system that can provide the input parameters to the SHE.

A methodology for achieving both of these requirements has been identified that yields results acceptable for flow simulation. However, refinements

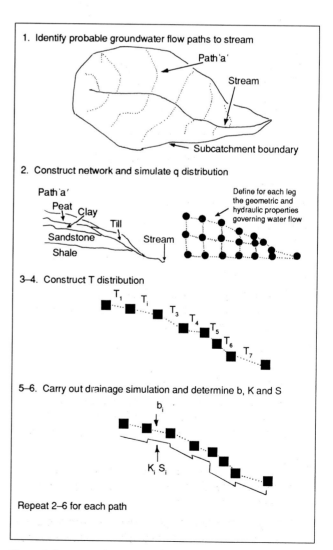

Figure 4. An approach to automatic geological data input to SHE

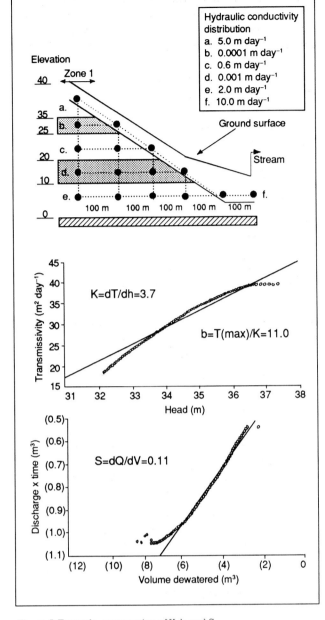

Figure 5. Example construction of K, b and S

will probably be needed to update the model for contaminant transport simulation. The general methodology is presented in Figure 4. The steps are described as follows.

- Using topographic data, identify a set of reverse flow path lines from the stream channels to the edge of the catchment.

- For each path, construct a vertical profile network model that describes the groundwater flow pathways to the stream.

- Carry out steady-state simulations using the network model, and identify the head distribution, h, and the flux distribution, q, along the profile.

- Construct a one-dimensional distribution of transmissivity, T, to recover the same potential and flux distributions.

- Carry out a drainage (ie transient) simulation with the network model, and identify the rate of decay of q and h over the profile.

- Decompose T into thickness, b, and hydraulic conductivity, K, components, and establish values of the storage coefficient, S.

- Using linear interpolation procedures, transfer the derived b, K and S values to the neighbouring SHE grid squares.

An example of the results of applying the technique to a single profile is shown in Figure 5.

Whilst refinements to the operation of the model are needed to optimise the decomposition of T and to establish S, the preliminary results are encouraging. However, work on improving the methodology is continuing.

SOILS

Introduction

Data describing the soils of the United Kingdom are available from the Soil Survey of Great Britain. TheSoil Survey provides two primary formats for its data: first, soil maps with accompanying books describing, in detail, the soil characteristics, and, second, digital data held in a spatial data archive on computer. The latter data form is more appropriate for the purposes of NELUP simply because of its accessibility. However, the data stored are based on a soil classification which groups soil units into soil associations. The basis of the classification into individual soil associations for each soil type, whilst having some relationship to soil hydrology, does not directly permit parameterisation of soil hydraulic properties. Thus, techniques are needed to perform this task.

The soils classification for England and Wales distinguishes 296 soil associations. The distributions of the soil associations are provided to users at either 100 m or one km resolutions. For each grid point, the data base provides the percentage of each soil association identified within the grid square defined around the grid point. Every soil association comprises a number of soil series which define more precisely the character of the soil profiles within the soil associations. Whilst soil series are potentially amenable to hydrological characterisation, they are not readily identified for each grid point given information only about the association. Because individual series within an association can be hydrologically dissimilar, the need to unravel the relationships between soil associations, series and hydrological properties becomes important.

In the following sections, a methodology is examined using soils data for the Rede catchment.

Soils of the Rede catchment

The Soil Survey classification of the Rede catchment at a resolution of one km is shown in Figure 6. The number given for each km square identifies the dominant soils association within the square. The Rede catchment soils are divided between 14 soil associations, of which only 12 are dominant at the one

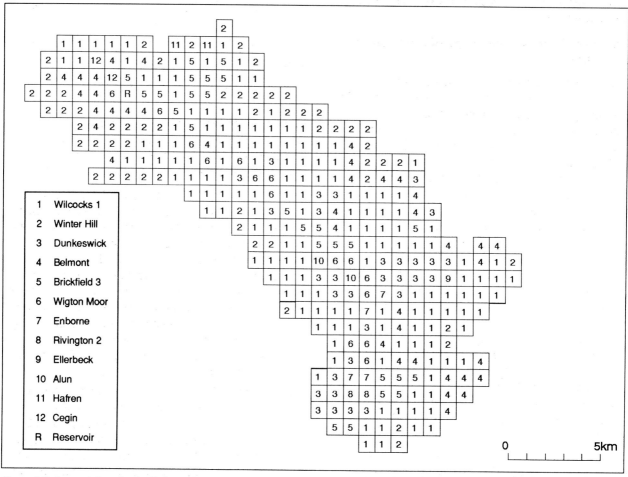

Figure 6. Soil associations for the Rede catchment

km scale. Of these 12 associations, five associations account for 91% of the total catchment area: Wilcocks 1, Winter Hill, Belmont, Dunkeswick, and Brickfield 3 associations. The basic characteristics of each are reproduced in Table 3.

Table 3. The dominant soil associations in the Rede catchment

Association	% of total catchment area	Description
Wilcocks 1	46.5	Slowly permeable, seasonally waterlogged, fine loamy and fine loamy over clayey upland soils with a peaty surface horizon. Very acidic where not limed. Strongly gleyed
Winter Hill	·16.5	Thick, very acidic, raw peat soils. Perennially wet
Belmont	11.8	Coarse, loamy, very acidic upland soils, with a wet, peaty surface horizon and thin ironpan
Dunkeswick	8.8	Slowly permeable, seasonally waterlogged, fine loamy and fine loamy over clayey soils
Brickfield 3	7.9	Slowly permeable, seasonally waterlogged, fine loamy, fine loamy over clayey and clayey soils

The Wilcocks 1 association is the most extensive, covering 46% of the total catchment area. It contains three major soil series: Wilcocks, Kielder and Fordham, and five minor soil series: Winter Hill, Brickfield, Roddlesworth, Ipstones, and Onecote. Of these, the Wilcocks series is dominant. The profile for this series is typified by an organic surface layer, 10–14 cm thick, underlain by clay loam or sandy clay loam horizons which are grey and strongly mottled. The occurrence of this soil is related to a geological sequence at the outcrop of alternating shales and thick sandstone beds. The Kielder series is similar to the Wilcocks series, but becomes clayey at depth. This series is often found in Northumbria. Unlike the Wilcocks and Kielder series, the Fordham series comprises sandy loam, with gleying caused not by lowly permeable subsoil, but by high groundwater levels. The Fordham series is common where the drift geology comprises thick head accumulated below sandstone exposures.

The other four common associations of Redesdale similarly contain a number of soil series. Data for these five common associations and three others, Enborne, Rivington 2 and Ellerbeck, have provided the basis for the development and preliminary testing of a methodology for defining hydrological parameters for input to SHE from the Soil Survey's data archive.

Hydrological classification of the soils of the Rede catchment

A methodology for assessing soil hydrological properties

Two general approaches to soil hydrological property identification can be envisaged for each km grid square over a catchment. The first is to cross-correlate soil association data with other features, such as topography and geology, to define the most likely soil series for the given association. For example, it is clear from the descriptions of the soil series in the preceding section that geology correlates, in many cases, with the presence of particular soil series within an association. However, reliance on this relationship to provide a strong indication of the dominant soil series within the grid square cannot be assumed. The second approach is to classify the soil series into a small number of hydrological categories. These categories may represent a particular form of response to drainage and infiltration. For each square, the mean characteristics of the most likely category for the given association are then adopted. In practice, the two approaches will not individually prove satisfactory for all situations. A hybrid approach has, therefore, been identified which includes both techniques within a single algorithm.

The first step in the development of this hybrid approach is to establish the hydrological significance of each individual soil series. For this purpose, a one-dimensional model for unsaturated zone flow in layered soils was employed. Data defining the hydraulic properties of each soil layer for each soil series potentially existing in the Rede were obtained from the Soil Survey. The data were combined within the flow model and a set of numerical experiments was performed to assess the major flow and storage characteristics of each soil series.

There are two features of particular interest relating to soil water flow:

1. the rate of storage of water in the soil profile during precipitation events; and

2. the rate of drainage of the soil water to the underlying groundwater system.

The numerical experiment was designed to elicit both these pieces of information.

The model developed for this study solves Richard's equation for a one-dimensional soil column with no sources and sinks, subject to a range of possible upper and lower boundary conditions and initial conditions. A finite difference numerical scheme was implemented to ensure conservation of mass. The soil hydraulic properties of the individual soil layers within each soil profile were characterised using the following constitutive relationships between soil moisture and hydraulic conductivity and pressure head:

$$\theta = \theta_r + \frac{(\theta_s - \theta_r)}{[1 + (\alpha \mid h \mid)^n]^m} \qquad (3)$$

$$K = K_s \Theta^{1/2}[1 - (1 - \Theta^{1/m})^m]^2 \qquad (4)$$

where

$$\Theta = \frac{\theta - \theta_r}{\theta_s - \theta_r} \qquad (m = 1 - \frac{1}{n}) \qquad (5)$$

and θ = soil moisture content; θ_r = residual moisture content; θ_s = saturated moisture content; K_s = saturated hydraulic conductivity; h = pressure head; K = hydraulic conductivity.

The Soil Survey data for soil hydraulic properties are in the form of field- and laboratory-measured values for residual and saturated moisture content, saturated hydraulic conductivity, and four values of soil moisture at different soil pressures. These data are provided at standard depths below ground surface and, in general, correspond to the major soil layers in the soil series profiles. Some of the soil series within Redesdale have alternative data sets, corresponding to two different possible land use regimes. These data were used to derive, for equations (3) and (4), estimates of the coefficients, α and m.

Fully drained initial conditions were established for each soil profile, assuming the presence of the groundwater table at the base of the soil profile, by applying a zero flux boundary condition to the top of the soil column and a zero pressure head boundary condition to the bottom. The model was then run until a negligible flow rate was obtained at the base of the column. The next step in the experiment was to replace the top boundary condition by a variable flux/head boundary condition simulating a daily rainfall rate of 4 cm. Simulations were then undertaken until the infiltration and drainage rates converged to a single steady state value.

The infiltration and drainage curves defined for each of the soil profiles yield simple representative data that can be used to compare the results from the different soil profiles. The time to reach 99% of the steady state drainage corresponds broadly to the diffusivity (ie storage/hydraulic conductivity) of the soil profile, and the steady state drainage rate corresponds to the leakage capacity of the soil profile.

Application to the soils of the Rede catchment

The results of applying the numerical experiment outlined in the previous section to the soil associations of the Rede catchment are shown in Figure 7. Four typical drainage response curves are identifiable. The main factor determining the shape of the response curves for each of the soil series is the hydraulic conductivity distribution over the representative profiles.

The Fordham A series (Figure 7(i)) displays no decrease in infiltration rate from the maximum daily rainfall rate of 5 cm and a drainage rate that increases steadily to this value. This series is characterised by those soils in which the minimum value of saturated

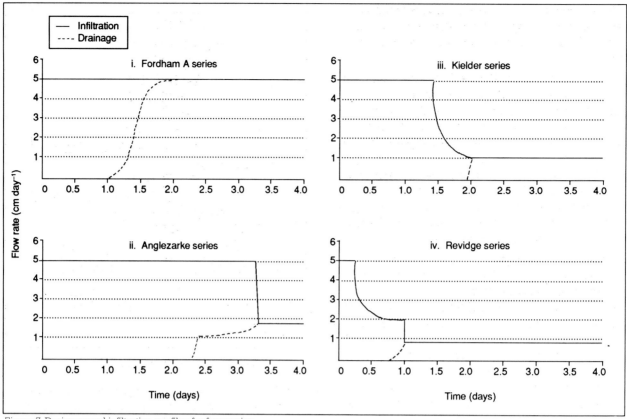

Figure 7. Drainage and infiltration profiles for four series

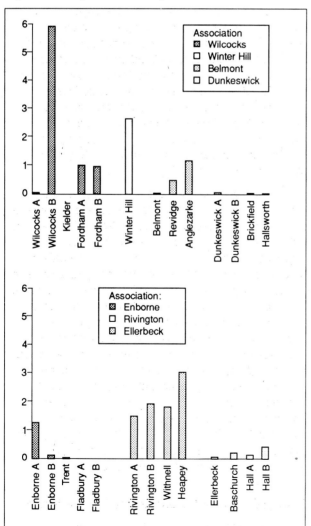

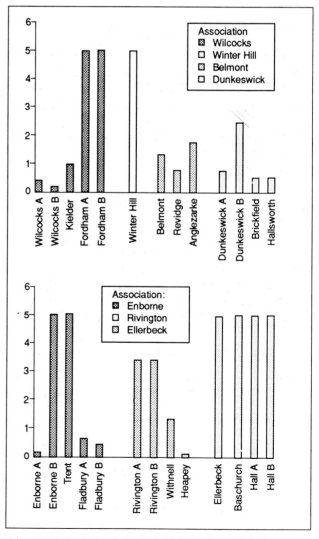

Figure 8. Time taken for the drainage rate to increase from 1% to 99% of its steady state value

Figure 9. Flow rate towards which the infiltration and drainage rates converge for an applied rainfall rate of 5 cm day⁻¹

hydraulic conductivity across the layers is greater than 5 cm day^{-1}. They correspond to the series in Figure 8 with steady state drainage rates of 5 cm day^{-1}.

The Anglezarke series (Figure 7(ii)) has a drainage rate that increases slowly, but the change in infiltration is almost instantaneous as the ground surface becomes saturated. Curves displaying this shape are obtained where the top soil layers have values of saturated hydraulic conductivity greater than 100 cm day^{-1}, with a value of saturated hydraulic conductivity in the bottom layer less than 10 cm day^{-1}. Soils of this type correspond to those series in Figure 8 with high values for the time taken for the drainage rate to reach 99% of steady state value.

The Kielder series (Figure 7(iii)) shows a slow change in infiltration, with a more rapid change in drainage rate. Curves of this type are obtained from soil series in which the upper layers have values of saturated hydraulic conductivity between 10 and 100 cm day^{-1}, and the bottom layer a value of saturated hydraulic conductivity less than 10 cm day^{-1}. The value for steady state drainage in Figure 9 from this soil type is determined by the value of saturated hydraulic conductivity in the bottom layer, and the time taken to reach 99% drainage in Figure 8 is negligible.

Finally, the Revidge series (Figure 7(iv)) displays a two-stage drop in infiltration, with a rapid drainage response. This is obtained for soils in which the upper layers have a value of saturated hydraulic conductivity between 10 and 100 cm day^{-1}, but the values in the bottom two layers are both less than 10 cm day^{-1}. These give steady state drainage rate values (Figure 9) determined by the smallest hydraulic conductivity measurement and negligible times to reach steady conditions in Figure 8.

Two associations in Figure 9, the Wilcocks 1 association and the Enborne association, display large variation in the steady state drainage rates of their component soil series. In the Wilcocks 1 soil association, the Fordham series has a much higher drainage capacity than the other two. This series, however, is only found in regions with a very high water table, suggesting probable geological control on infiltration to the subsurface environment. Thus, it

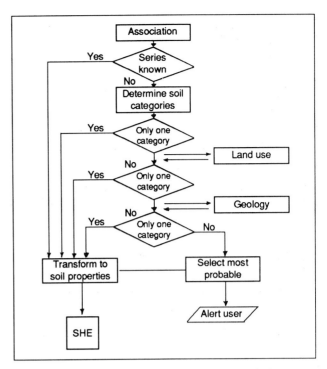

Figure 10. Automatic soil data input to SHE

should be expected that the impact of ignoring the Fordham series results will not be significant. In the Enborne association, the Enborne B series and the Trent series have a much higher drainage capacity than the other series in the association. In this association, the Fladbury series is not common and the others may be distinguished through land use. Enborne A is a series associated with arable farming, whilst Enborne B and Trent are associated with permanent grass. Thus, having distinguished the need to resolve the soil series more closely, additional information on geology, topography and land use can be used to distinguish finally between alternative soil systems.

As previously noted, the drainage response time shown in Figure 8 is generally indicative of storage in the soil profile. An exception is the Wilcocks B series of the Wilcocks 1 association. Here, the slow response is entirely related to the low permeability of the upper horizon. In terms of drainage, the response time is not significant as the drainage rate is very low. However, in terms of the infiltration response time, the implications for overland flow are significant. Under such circumstances, it would normally be important to determine the existence of the series on a square. Unfortunately, the information available on land use and geology is not sufficient to assist in the identification of the series. In consequence, the algorithm would assign the category containing the Wilcocks A and Kielder series, as these are the most common series of the association. A flag would be raised noting this problem at run time.

An approach to automating soil data collection

A summary of the findings of the simulation experiment discussed in the previous section is presented in Table 4. In this summary, the four

Table 4. General soil characteristic categories (UL = upper layer, LL = lower layer)

Category	K (cm day^{-1})	Drainage rate	Storage capacity	Saturation to ground surface
A	UL>10 LL>10	High	Low	None
B	UL>100 LL<10	Low	High	Rapid response
C	10<UL<100 LL<10	Low	Low	Rapid response
D	UL<100 LL1<10, LL2<10	Low	Low	Slow response

different response forms are identified as hydrological categories to which soil series can be assigned. If all series in one association are assigned to a single category, then the explicit identification of the series for the grid square is not required. The average properties for the category (comprising only data from the association) are used as representative input data to the SHE. Clearly, there are series within a single association that lie within different response categories. In this case, various checks can be undertaken on the geology of the grid square and its land use, which normally permit the identification of the appropriate category for the square. Figure 10 illustrates the algorithm in the form of a flow chart. The advantage of this approach lies in the simplifications inherent in the use of a limited number of soil categories. The process of constructing categories and assigning series to each category need only be performed once, and the data are stored for all subsequent calculations.

The extension of the results of this early work on the Rede to the entire soil series of the United Kingdom may alter the number of categories, but is unlikely to alter the general approach considered here.

REFERENCES

Abbott, M.B., Bathurst, J.C., Cunge, J.A., O'Connell, P.E. & Rasmussen, J. 1986a. An introduction to the European hydrological system – système hydrologique Européen, "SHE". 1: History and philosophy of a physically based distributed modelling system. *Journal of Hydrology*, **87**, 45-59.

Abbott, M.B., Bathurst, J.C., Cunge, J.A., O'Connell, P.E. & Rasmussen, J. 1986b. An introduction to the European hydrological system – système hydrologique Européen, "SHE". 2: History and philosophy of a physically based distributed modelling system. *Journal of Hydrology*, **87**, 61-77.

Allanson, P., Savage, D. & White, B. 1992. Areal interpolation of parish agricultural census data. In: *Land use change: the causes and consequences*, edited by M.C. Whitby, 92-101. (ITE symposium no. 27.) London: HMSO.

Bathurst, J.C. 1986a. Physically-based distributed modelling of an upland catchment using the système hydrologique Européen. *Journal of Hydrology*, **87**, 79-102.

Bathurst, J.C. 1986b. Sensitivity analysis of the système hydrologique Européen for an upland catchment. *Journal of Hydrology*, **87**, 103-123.

Bear, J. & Verruijt, A. 1987. *Modelling groundwater flow and pollution*. Dordrecht: Reidel.

Bell, F.G. 1978. Petrographical properties relating to porosity and permeability in the Fell Sandstone. *Quarterly Journal of Engineering Geology*, **11**, 13-126.

Brown, J.M.B. & Ingram, H.A.P. 1988. Changing storage beneath a stationary water table – an anomaly of certain humified peats. *Quarterly Journal of Engineering Geology*, **21**, 177-182.

Clough, C.T. 1989. *The geology of Plashetts and Kielder. Explanation of quarter sheet 108 SW. (New Series Sheet.)* London: HMSO.

Cradock-Hartopp, M.A. & Holliday, D.W. 1984. *The Fell Sandstone group of Northumberland.* (Investigation of the geothermal potential of the UK.) Keyworth: British Geological Survey.

Day, J.B.W. 1970. *Geology of the country around Bewcastle.* (Memoirs of the Geological Survey of Great Britain.) London: HMSO.

Dunn, S., Savage, D. & Mackay, R. 1992. Hydrological simulation of the Rede catchment using the système hydrologique Européen (SHE). In: *Land use change: the causes and consequences,* edited by M.C. Whitby, 137-146. (ITE symposium no. 27.) London: HMSO.

Fordham, C.E. 1989. *The influence of sedimentary structures and facies on the fluid flow (permeability) in the Fell Sandstone, Northumberland.* M Phil thesis, Department of Geology, University of Newcastle upon Tyne.

Freeman, B., Kemperer, S.L. & Hobbs, R.W. 1988. The deep structure of northern England and the Iapetus Suture Zone from BIRPS deep seismic reflection profiles. *Journal of the Geological Society*, **145**, 727-740.

Freeze, R.A. & Cherry, J.A. 1979 *Groundwater.* Englewood-Cliffs, NJ: Prentice-Hall.

Frost, D.V. 1969. The Lower Limestone group (Vise'an) of the Otterburn district, Northumberland. *Proceedings of the Yorkshire Geological Society*, **37**, 277-309.

Frost, D.V. & Holliday, D.W. 1980. *Geology of the country around Bellingham.* (Memoirs of the Geological Survey of Great Britain.) London: HMSO.

Hodgson, A.V. & Gardiner, M.D. 1971. An investigation of the aquifer potential of the Fell Sandstone of Northumberland. *Quarterly Journal of Engineering Geology*, **4**, 91-109.

Ingram, H.A.P. 1987. Ecohydrology of Scottish peatlands. *Transactions of the Royal Society of Edinburgh: Earth Sciences*, **78**, 287-296.

Johnson, G. A.L. 1980. Lower Palaeozoic rocks. In: *The geology of north east England*, edited by D.A. Robson, Newcastle upon Tyne: Natural History Society of Northumbria.

Ledger, D.C. & Harper, S.E. 1987. The hydrology of a drained, afforested peat bog in southern Scotland. 1977–1986. *Transactions of the Royal Society of Edinburgh: Earth Sciences*, **78**, 297-303.

Leeder, M.R. 1971. Initiation of the Northumberland basin. *Geological Magazine*, **108**, 511-516.

Leeder, M.R. 1987. Tectonic and palaeogeographic models for Lower Carboniferous Europe. In: *European Dinantian environments*, edited by J. Miller, A.E. Adams & V.P. Wright, 1-20. (Geological Journal special issue no. 12.) Chichester: Wiley.

Miller, H. 1887. *The geology of the country around Otterburn and Elsdon. Explanation of sheet 8.* (Memoirs of the Geological Survey of Great Britain.) London: HMSO.

O'Callaghan, J.R. 1992. Decision-making in land use. In: *Land use change: the causes and consequences*, edited by M.C. Whitby, 79-87. (ITE symposium no. 27.) London: HMSO.

Pettyjohn, W.A., ed. 1985. *Protection of public water supplies from groundwater contamination.* (EPA/625/4-85-016.) Washington, DC: US Environmental Protection Agency.

Rayner, D.H. 1981. *The stratigraphy of the British Isles.* 2nd ed. Cambridge: Cambridge University Press.

Rushton, S.P. 1992. A preliminary model for investigating the ecological consequences of land use change within the framework of the ITE land classification. In: *Land use change: the causes and consequences*, edited by M.C. Whitby, 111-117. (ITE symposium no. 27.) London: HMSO.

Case studies

Kielder Water, Kielder Forest and the North Tyne valley

M D Newson

Dept of Geography, University of Newcastle upon Tyne, Newcastle upon Tyne NE1 7RU

QUESTIONS RAISED BY THE VISIT

One of the most pressing constraints on the use of rural land in the next few decades is likely to be the off-site effects of each potential use and the management which accompanies that use. The principles of integrated pollution control demand that 'off-site' effects include those on neighbouring bodies of land, air and water; as more research emerges on the true nature of pollution pathways, each of these transport media requires re-evaluation. At present, however, only freshwater pathways are equipped, via the Control of Pollution Act, the Water Act, and the Environmental Assessment legislation, with the policy and agency structures to permit a new approach to rural land use planning. In short, conjunctive management of land and water resources is now feasible through the powers and duties of the National Rivers Authority; early examples include Nitrate Sensitive Areas and the new approaches to urban development on river floodplains. But how easy will it be to apply conjunctive management to remote rural areas such as the North Tyne? Here, there are no apparent problems of eutrophication or urbanisation brought on by development. The 'problem' is, rather, the reverse – centuries of isolation and marginality.

We, therefore, ask the following questions of those responsible for managing the land and water environment of the North Tyne.

1. Are there potential or actual conflicts between land use and water use? For example, does Kielder Forest have unacceptable effects on runoff quantity or quality?

2. Does Kielder Water (in the ownership of 'plc' share-holders) represent a great white hope for tourism and other new developments for the valley? If so, is a recreational use compatible with agriculture, forestry, and the regulation of the river North Tyne, an important freshwater fishery?

3. Are such remote areas best managed for conservation to the exclusion of other uses? If so, what steps are the landowning and environmental agencies taking towards this end?

4. What is the knowledge base for making decisions affecting land and water management in this area?

5. Is the agency structure and public consultation system adequate for bringing about sustainable patterns of land use and for conciliation between those with differing management targets?

6. What scenarios can we develop to enable us to anticipate the effects of climatic change during the longer-term planning period?

AN INTRODUCTION TO THE LAND USE OF THE NORTH TYNE VALLEY

'The North Tyne valley is stamped with the mark of modern human endeavour: vast stands of monotonous dark green conifers and a huge man-made lake'. So begins Charlton's description of the location of our case study visit (Charlton 1987, p9). To those who appreciate the wilderness of Britain's remote uplands, words like 'vast' and 'huge' are often used to describe those changes which seem to threaten the tranquillity and diversity of the traditional scene. In many ways, however, large-scale changes are inevitable, given the scale of the landscape and land tenure of the uplands. To local people, tranquillity and diversity may equate with neglect and disuse. One of the traditions of the uplands is change, particularly during periods of mineral exploitation; the challenge of modern upland management is the moderation and modulation of such inevitably rapid and extensive changes. The objective for this management is increasingly and broadly one of conservation, a fact often interpreted by rural people as being equivalent to mummification for the benefit of town-dwellers. Viewed more charitably and more realistically, one could equally see this new phase as underwriting the interdependence of town and country, as a guarantee of no more neglect and disuse.

Charlton reviews 6000 years of human occupation of the North Tyne valley; deforestation by Neolithic and subsequent developers represents the earliest land use change on record – its rate and extent are easier to appreciate given the Roman activity in the north, and it is quite possible that the population of the valley reached its maximum (ever) around 2000 years ago, in the Romano-British period. Agriculture, largely transhumance livestock with subsistence arable in sheltered, lower parts, came to dominate the landscape by the late 13th century, together with

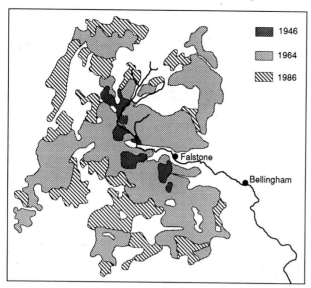

Figure 1. The growth in extent of Kielder Forest as revealed by Ordnance Survey maps (source: Porter 1989)

the network of settlements remaining to this day. For well over 500 years, the valley's seclusion in a border position then led to conditions of semi-independence underwritten, rather superficially, by special administrative structures and the domination of a few families: Charlton, Milburn, Dodd, Robson.

Enclosure Acts between 1770–1820 and 1845–1870, together with the widespread use of lime and the introduction of subsidised tile drainage in the Drainage Act of 1846, increased the productivity of agriculture, but stocking rates were low and 'there was a good deal of white land and peat moss' in 1863 (Charlton, p64). Iron, lead, and coal extraction provided economic diversions and extra income for the owners of estates; coal is still extracted on the north side of Kielder Water.

Charlton records the typical land use for one estate in 1839 (Hawkhope):

1764 acres fell land
44 acres arable

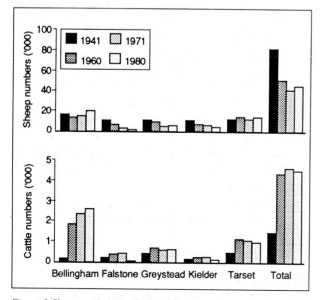

Figure 2. Sheep and cattle numbers for the parishes of the North Tyne valley, 1941–80 (source: Porter 1989)

87 acres enclosed meadow and pasture
7 acres woodland
5 acres roads, waste, etc.

The arrival of modern forestry occurred through a combination of vision ('The district . . . is recommended as one of the few in which a really extensive forest area can generally be established' (Forestry Commission) and opportunity (the need to sell parts of the Duke of Northumberland's estate in 1930 to raise death duties). The promise of State forestry to support rural communities appeared valid by 1951 when the expansion of Kielder Forest (Figure 1) meant that nearly 300 staff were employed, requiring housing and services; Kielder Village was built.

Porter (1989) has reviewed the more recent agricultural and population data for the North Tyne valley: Figure 2 indicates the continuing domination of livestock farming, whilst Table 1 indicates that there has been a steadying of the post-War rate of population decline.

Table 1. Post-War population by parish for the Upper North Tyne

Parish	1951	1961	1971	1981
Bellingham	1086	1224	1151	1146
Falstone	343	345	252	181
Greystead	134	105	94	85
Kielder	377	462	328	212
Tarset	335	236	181	319
Total	2275	2372	2006	1943

WATER TO TYNESIDE – AND BEYOND

The history of the supply of water to Tyneside (Rennison 1979) also provides an interesting historical backcloth to contemporary issues of pollution and land use. Rennison traces the expanding needs of the fast-growing Tyneside conurbation for pure water. Following the cholera epidemics of 1832 and 1853, it was clear that the Tyne was an unsuitable source, and more remote catchments were chosen (see Figure 3). The North Tyne was prospected as early as 1854, and a detailed plan was available from 1886; nevertheless, the first truly upland reservoir of the scale and type beloved of Victorian health reformers was constructed on the Rede.

As part of the centralised assessment of water resources instigated by the Water Resources Act (1963), a new policy of regulating reservoirs was considered for those parts of England and Wales for which population and economic growth projections predicted a shortfall of supplies. For a region such as the north-east, the very last thing desired by local politicians was any loss of potential to reverse the job losses in mining, ship-building – and other traditional heavy industry. The steel industry on Teeside was particularly demanding of water and, in a spirit of high anticipation (countered by a considerable environmental protection protest), a search was

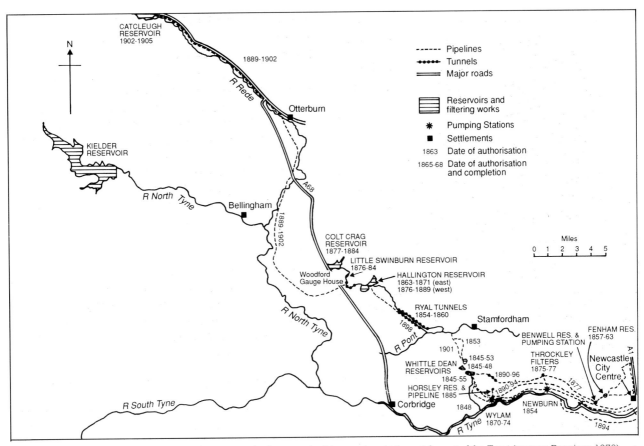

Figure 3. Water to Tyneside: the progressive 'capture' of remote, 'safe' resources in the catchment of the Tyne (source: Rennison 1979)

made, totalling 38 potential sites, for the site of a reservoir which would be capable of supplying the Tyne, Wear and Tees with adequate water supplies until 2001 AD. Despite the option of using a Private Bill to promote their choice of the Kielder site, the river authority yielded to an inquiry at which 188 objectors made representation. Charlton (1987) holds the view that environmental objections were weakened by the failure of the Countryside Commission, Nature Conservancy or Forestry Commission to support them. 'There was widespread hope that one artificial environment, a reservoir, would be situated in another, a commercial soft-wood forest' (p153). In view of the potential land use battles between forestry and water to come (see below – the basic argument over increased water losses was already well-rehearsed at the time of Kielder's promotion), it is surprising that no reference can be found to the effect of land use upon water yield or water quality at Kielder. Conciliation was hardly necessary in an atmosphere in which the foresters 'did not object to' the presence of the water development.

A considerable number of unforeseen points of friction, often tragic (Charlton 1982), were thrown up by the inquiry which was forced to reopen ten months after its apparent conclusion. The Order was signed in 1974 and coincided with the implementation of the Water Act 1973; the new Northumbrian Water Authority was, under that Act, a multi-functional organisation charged with management of the entire water cycle. The Authority could therefore take co-ordinated action on a number of public accountable topics such as environmental protection, and a North Tyne Valley Consultative Committee was established to co-ordinate remedial action in support of local people; nevertheless, 42 properties were 'drowned' beneath the Reservoir's water as it filled between December 1980 and its opening by the Queen in May 1982. The cost of Kielder Water, estimated as £23 million in 1969 and £85 million in 1973, eventually amounted to £167 million. There was considerable European investment in the scheme; more capital outlay was to follow as the dam's functions were altered to incorporate hydroelectric power generation. This profit-making activity was introduced during a period when it seemed that Kielder's main purpose would be recreational (New Scientist referred to 'the Kielder white elephant'); indeed, such was the turn-down in population and economic growth in the region that brochures for Kielder's water (as supply) were issued in Arabic with a view to export sales via the holds of empty oil tankers moored at Teesport. Other unplanned uses for Kielder's water were to dilute pollution from an incident in the upper reaches of the Tees in 1983 – this required operation of the pumped transfer scheme.

Kielder Water's vital statistics (from Brady, Davis & Douglas 1983; Johnson 1988) are given in Table 2.

IMPACTS OF KIELDER WATER ON THE RIVER NORTH TYNE

Thanks to the development of reservoir storage at Kielder, the north-east has had no restriction of public

Table 2. Kielder Water, physical and hydrological data

Reservoir and dam		Hydrology
Usable storage	188 Mm³	Average rainfall 1370 mm
Maximum depth	52 m	Average river flow 6.6 cumecs
Surface area	1 086 ha	Compensation flow 0.6–1.3 cumecs
Catchment area	24 150 ha	Hydropower flow 15.4 cumecs

supply during recent drought summers; an illuminated hoarding at Newcastle Airport greets visitors with 'Water: no problem', superimposed over an aerial view of Kielder Water.

However, river regulation by reservoir releases produces potentially costly damage to freshwater ecology. Care was taken to study the likely impact of the original operational design before, during and after construction (eg Carling 1979; Crisp 1984; Boon 1987), and £23,000 was forsaken in revenue from hydropower generation by using a compatible regime (Brady *et al.* 1983). Nevertheless, concern has often been expressed by the powerful fishing lobby on the North Tyne about the apparently detrimental effects of the pronounced diurnal rise and fall of river levels. The overall flow and temperature effects of the reservoir are shown in Figure 4. Floods are reduced but low flows are augmented; with the development of hydropower, a considerable increase has occurred in mid- to high-flows.

For the last five years, the University of Newcastle has been carrying out research on the impacts of river regulation on the North Tyne; such impacts may be relatively narrow in terms of freshwater habitats and ecology, but have wider implications through the commercial aspects of the use of the river by anglers: in 1988 rod licences raised nearly £0.25 million in revenue from the river.

The initiation of research by Northumbrian Water Authority in 1986 came after the revision of the operating rules for Kielder Reservoir, from an orientation to water supply to one of power generation (Johnson 1988). Between 1981 and 1983, 5.5 Mwatt of capacity was installed at the dam,

requiring a diurnal, 16-hour cycle of releases at a rate of 15 cumecs, ten times the compensation flow from the dam, and produced for maximum efficiency from the scour valve drawing 'bottom-water' from the reservoir. Because the reservoir thermally stratifies, such a release strategy could have a considerable effect on water quality.

Haile, James and Sear (1989) conclude from the first three years of monitoring that the upper 14 km of regulated river North Tyne have experienced the following impacts:

- dislocation of the reproductive cycle of fish, as a result of deposition of a fine sediment/algal mat on the bed;

- seasonal change of the thermal regime of river flow (annual amplitudes of variation have halved from 15°C to 7.5°C), which affects the feeding patterns of newly hatched fish;

- disruption of spawning through bed armouring (finer sediments are transported downstream leaving only coarse sediments).

As Tables 3 and 4 show, there is a measurable impact on both invertebrate and salmonid fish populations. Furthermore, most indications are that, whilst the impact is restricted at present, it may extend downstream, unless certain modifications are made to the operation of the generating sets at the dam. The use of scour valve flows means that water of the least well-matched quality (especially in terms of temperature) is released into the regulated reaches. The longer term may also see an extension of the effects of regulated flows on the sediment dynamics of the river: the diurnal peak flows are insufficient to remove sediments wholesale, but have the effect of strengthening the bed on riffles, making it more difficult for salmonids to spawn. At confluences with unregulated tributaries, the sediment load carried by floods in the latter become deposited in the lower-flowing North Tyne as bars, which then disrupts velocity patterns causing erosion and increased liability of flooding (Petts & Thoms 1987).

Finally, it must be stressed that the impacts of Kielder Water on the river Tyne as a whole are considered to be beneficial, especially in providing low-flow regulation and maintaining cool water during

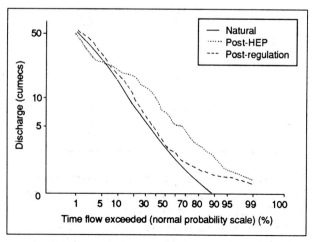

Figure 4. Changes in flow duration before and after the impoundment of the North Tyne in Kielder Reservoir and after redeployment of releases to generate power (source: Boon 1987)

Table 3. Invertebrate and fish numbers at sites on the North Tyne (Butteryhaugh is above Kielder Water and other sites at increasing distances downstream of the dam)

Site	Salmon/trout density 1988	Invertebrate abundance (observed/predicted**)
Butteryhaugh	0.044 m⁻²	43.7
Yarrow	0.003	35.5
Falstone	0.055	46.1
Ridley Stokoe	1.3	63.4
Newton	2.24	64.9

**Predictions based on the Institute of Freshwater Ecology's river invertebrate prediction and classification system (RIVPACS)

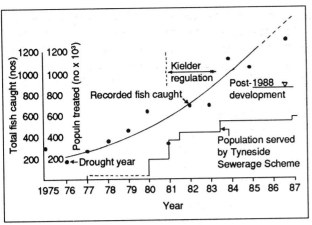

Figure 5. Salmon catch in the Tyne in relation to upstream river regulation and downstream sewerage improvements (source: Johnson 1988)

heatwaves; the operation of Kielder, coinciding as it has with the sewerage improvements on Tyneside, is thought to have helped promote the meteoric rise of the Tyne to the position of best salmon river in England (see also Figure 5).

IMPACTS OF CONIFEROUS AFFORESTATION ON STREAMS IN THE UPPER NORTH TYNE

At the time of Kielder Water's promotion and design, it was regarded as highly satisfactory that the majority of land in the valley was owned by a friendly public authority – the Forestry Commission. Any debate between the two land uses normally involved a certain hesitancy on the part of the water interest, in view of its need for the felling of those trees below the projected water level.

From the late 1970s onwards, however, a series of issues concerning the use and management of upland catchments for coniferous afforestation has surfaced, following the publication of research by hydrologists (Newson 1990 provides a summary).

The issues have been as follows.

- The interception and subsequent re-evaporation of rainfall by conifer canopies which, when added to transpiration by the trees, may more than double annual evaporation rates from a catchment.

- The acidification of surface waters in catchments draining plantations as a result of the impaction and capture of air pollutants, again on the canopy. This effect is thought to be exacerbated by aspects of forest management, such as drainage which denies runoff access to possibly neutralising subsoils.

- The widespread reports of sediment pollution during ground preparation for afforestation, and the lingering increase in gravel transport from drainage ditch networks in steeply sloping plantations.

More recently, these issues have been seen as having synergistic disadvantages for the freshwater ecology of forest streams (Maitland, Newson & Best

1990), and additional detrimental impacts have been published concerning timber harvesting, eg on nutrient loads.

The response of the forest industry has been to use 'good practice', and the Forest and Water Guidelines (Forestry Commission 1988) are now the accepted definition of good practice. Whilst designed for use by those proposing new plantations and an essential element of proposals for forest grants or environmental assessment, the Guidelines are being applied retrospectively in many aspects of the restructuring of Kielder Forest (Forestry Commission 1989). Stream margins are being targeted in a campaign to fell large areas of single-age monoculture forest; broadleaved trees and natural regeneration will be used to mark the channels out as positive landscape elements and wildlife corridors. In addition, the corridors may also act as buffer strips to reduce sedimentation and acidification to streams.

Haile (1990) has described a programme of stream monitoring in Kielder Forest designed to discover the effect of parent material and forest age/structure on streamwater chemistry; surveys of invertebrates and fish are also being extended to the minor forest streams, with moorland controls for comparison. The summary results for the first three years are listed in Table 4. A feature for concern is that certain of the forested streams show episodes of low pH and high aluminium contents, with a slight correlation between high aluminium and tree age. The overwhelming control on water chemistry patterns is, however, exercised by the distribution of drift deposits; boulder clay in the area appears to have good buffering capacity if acidified forest runoff contacts with it – blanket peat, by contrast, offers little buffering capacity (see Table 4: Yet Burn results).

Table 4. Chemical studies of streamflow in tributaries of the North Tyne within Kielder Forest

Determinand and statistic	Yet Burn (4.2 km²)	Lewis Burn (54.5 km²)
pH		
Mean	6.9	6.9
Maximum	8.1	8.6
Minimum	3.6	4.5
Al (soluble)		
Mean	0.0	0.16
Maximum	0.2	1.4
Minimum	0.0	0.0
Colour		
Mean	179	196
Maximum	300	400
Minimum	100	70

The programme of study continues, both in feeder streams to Kielder Water, where loss of water quality in small tributaries is unlikely to be of major consequence, and at the long-running catchment experiment west of Kielder at Coalburn. Robinson and Hind (1992) have summarised the effect of coniferous afforestation on the runoff behaviour at

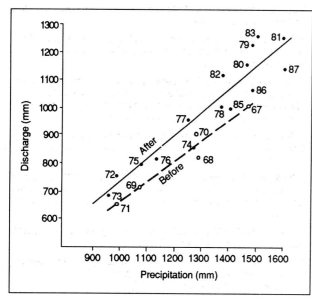

Figure 6. Rainfall and runoff at the Coalburn experimental catchment, prior to (o) and following (•) afforestation (source: Robinson & Hind 1992)

Coalburn, having gathered data both before and after cultivation and drainage of the catchment. Figure 6 shows that, after ground preparation, a larger proportion of rainfall was discharged from the catchment, both as flood peaks (a much 'flashier' response) and as increased low flows. Now that the forest canopy has closed at Coalburn, there are signs in the runoff data that interception is reducing runoff once again.

Using the simple equation proposed by Calder and Newson (1979), it is possible to calculate the effects of Kielder Forest on runoff from the catchment of Kielder Water. The outcome is a small but significant increase in loss, ie from 418 mm to 559 mm per annum. It remains to be seen whether the 'missing millimetres' will become critical to the water supply or energy-generating roles of Kielder Water.

CONSERVATION, WATER AND FORESTRY

Another piece of remedial land management recently carried out by the Forestry Commission in Kielder and neighbouring forests concerns the Border Mires, wetlands remaindered within the forest area simply because they were too dangerous for mechanised ground preparation. Controversial planting in Caithness and Sutherland has shown that mechanical methods can now triumph over such conditions to create the essential drainage network for forest crop establishment. However, at Kielder, the reverse (literally) has been the case; following recommendations from a multidisciplinary and multi-agency Management Committee, a programme of restoration has been implemented by the Forestry Commission, Nature Conservancy Council and the Northumbrian National Park to block drains, protect against erosion, and fell unpromising tree crops from large areas of the 39 mires. A programme of research has also been launched to evaluate the relative impacts of forestry, grazing and air pollution on the floristic composition of the mires, which is said

to have suffered a measurable decline in recent years (see Smith & Charman 1988).

Conservation issues were addressed during the design and construction of Kielder Water by the creation of a 'reservoir within a reservoir' – the 67 ha Bakethin conservation area at the north-west end of the lake. Surveys revealed over 200 plant and 60 bird species in the area, and the Bakethin dam ensures that water levels are maintained throughout the fluctuations caused by normal reservoir operation. Zoning of recreational activity also helps to ensure that this is the 'quiet end' of Kielder Water.

RECREATION AND TOURISM

The circumstances of physical environment which combine to make the upper North Tyne valley an ideal reservoir site do not produce a recreational area to suit mass markets; remoteness is a further problem. Charlton (1982) bemoans the financial outlay at Kielder Water 'in constructing a midge-infested lake 50 miles from the nearest centres of population'. The midge problem remains, but careful targeting of recreational developments and a mixture of very active and passive pursuits have proved to be successful policies.

Realising the importance of the recreational argument at Kielder, Northumbrian Water funded the construction of 13.5 km of new and realigned roads during the reservoir scheme; the Kielder Information Centre was already open in September 1977, interpreting the panoramic views of construction. Thanks to the good relationship with the Forestry Commission and because of the latter organisation's growing role in recreation, special forest management practices were introduced in the 'Kielder Working Circle' of 1900 ha, with the 44.25 km of lake shore treated especially sensitively.

As the visit will reveal, the water industry has turned over a new leaf in recreation compared to the days of mass trespass on 'gathering grounds' in the 1930s. The effects of human access on water quality are much less of a problem at regulating reservoirs than at direct-supply reservoirs. At Kielder, sailing, wind-surfing, power-boating and canoeing are offered on the lake, together with cycling, horse-riding and endurance courses around the margins. Viewpoints and picnic sites are also provided. To counter the problems with the weather, an all-weather sports centre has been constructed and there are specialist facilities to promote adventure holidays for the disabled.

Climate change could play a large part in the future development of tourism in the North Tyne valley, both directly as an influence on visits, and indirectly via the operation of the reservoir. Reservoirs are designed to be empty; in other words, their water supply role requires that their storage volume be deployed as a direct benefit to society rather than to create visual amenity. A regular deployment of the contents of the reservoir, exposing wide shores, would have a detrimental effect on amenity at Kielder.

Tourism in Northumberland depends heavily on the motor car; the oil crisis of the 1970s drastically reduced visitor numbers to 'England's best-kept secret'. There are signs now that numbers have rebuilt and that the North Tyne valley, through the Kielder Tourism Development Action Programme and other ventures, will become a well-known 'honey-pot' in the north-east. Confusion may, however, play its part; recent customers of the Pheasant Inn near Kielder Water asked the landlord where 'all the shops' were – they thought they had arrived at that other great north-east attraction, the Metro Centre!

REFERENCES

Boon, P.J. 1987. The influence of Kielder Water on Trichopteran (caddisfly) populations in the river North Tyne (northern England). *Regulated Rivers: Research and Management*, **1**, 95-109.

Brady, J.A., Davis, J.M. & Douglas, E.W. 1983. First filling of Kielder reservoir and future operational considerations. *Journal of the Institution of Water Engineers and Scientists*, **37**, 295-312.

Calder, I.R. & Newson, M.D. 197. Land use and upland water resources in Britain – a strategic look. *Water Resources Bulletin*, **15**, 1628-1639.

Carling, P. 1979. *Survey of physical characteristics of salmon spawning riffles in the river North Tyne.* Ambleside: Freshwater Biological Association.

Charlton, B. 1987. *Upper North Tynedale, a Northumbrian valley and its people.* Newcastle upon Tyne: Northumbrian Water.

Charlton, W. 1982. Spending money like water. *The Spectator*, 22nd May.

Crisp, D.T. 1984. *Water temperature studies in the river North Tyne after impoundment by Kielder dam.* Ambleside: Freshwater Biological Association.

Forestry Commission. 1988. *Forests and water guidelines.* Edinburgh: Forestry Commission.

Forestry Commission. 1989. Forest of the future. Re-structuring Kielder. *Forest Life*, **5**, 8-9.

Haile, S.M. 1990. *Stream ecology in Kielder Forest.* Newcastle upon Tyne: Department of Civil Engineering, University of Newcastle upon Tyne.

Haile, S.M., James, A. & Sear, D. 1989. *The effects of Kielder Reservoir on the ecology of the River North Tyne.* (Report to Northumbrian Water on completion of Phase One.) Newcastle upon Tyne: University of Newcastle upon Tyne.

Johnson, P. 1988. River regulation: a regional perspective – Northumbrian Water Authority. *Regulated Rivers: Research and Management*, **2**, 233-255.

Maitland, P.S., Newson, M.D. & Best, G.A. 1990. *The impact of afforestation and forestry practice on freshwater habitats.* (Focus on nature conservation no.23.) Peterborough: Nature Conservancy Council.

Newson, M.D. 1990. Forestry and water: 'good practice' and UK catchment policy. *Land Use Policy*, **7**, 53-58.

Newson, M.D. 1991. Catchment control and planning. Emerging patterns of definition, policy and legislation in UK water management. *Land Use Policy*, **8**, 9-15.

Petts, G.E. & Thoms, M.C. 1987. Morphology and sedimentology of a tributary confluence bar in a regulated river. *Earth Surface Processes and Landforms*, **12,** 433-440.

Porter, A. 1989. *The public policy framework for the integrated management of land and water resources within major river basins taking the North Tyne as an example.* BA dissertation, Huddersfield: Huddersfield Polytechnic.

Rennison, R.W. 1979. *Water to Tyneside. A history of the Newcastle and Gateshead Water Company.* Newcastle upon Tyne: Newcastle and Gateshead Water Company and Northumberland Press.

Robinson, M & Hind, P. 1992. The Coalburn catchment experiment, 1966 to present. *Proceedings of the North of England Soils Discussion Group*, no. 26. In press.

Smith, R.S. & Charman, D.J. 1988. The vegetation of upland mires within conifer plantations in Northumberland, northern England. *Journal of Applied Ecology*, **25,** 579-594.

Land use change in the Northumberland National Park

R S Smith[1] and T F Carroll[2]

[1]Dept of Agricultural and Environmental Science, University of Newcastle upon Tyne, Newcastle upon Tyne NE1 7RU

[2]National Park and Countryside Department, Northumberland County Council, Eastburn, South Park, Hexham, Northumberland NE46 1BS

NATIONAL PARK OBJECTIVES

The National Parks and Access to the Countryside Act of 1949 was the enabling legislation that resulted in the designation of the ten National Parks in England and Wales. The main function of these Parks is the conservation of their landscape and wildlife and the provision of recreation and public access to open land. Where recreation directly conflicts with conservation, the latter should have priority. In addition, National Park Authorities are obliged by the Countryside Act of 1968 to have 'due regard to the needs of agriculture and forestry and to the economic and social interests of rural areas'. The legislative framework, organisation and finance are described by the Countryside Commission (1987) and by MacEwen and MacEwen (1982, 1987).

The Northumberland National Park is the most northerly of the ten Parks, and covers 100 000 ha of upland Northumberland. It is administered as part of the system of local government, being managed by a committee of the county council, with district council and central Government nominees. As with the other Parks, 75% of the funding and advice is provided by the Department of the Environment; the Countryside Commission plays an advisory role. The priorities for conservation and recreation in the Northumberland National Park are defined in a National Park Plan (Macdonald 1977, 1984), currently undergoing its second review, as required by Section 17 of the Local Government Act of 1972.

The plan defines overall and specific objectives for conservation, recreation, and the local community, and underpins these with suites of policies which provide detailed guidance on a range of matters. These latter include liaison with other organisations, the protection of important sites and buildings, tree planting schemes, the protection of moorland from agricultural improvement, the control of afforestation and urban development, informal recreation in various parts of the Park, the promotion of tourism, the provision of holiday accommodation, the maintenance of public rights-of-way, site management, and services for the visitor.

The four overall conservation objectives are detailed here as they define the main priorities of Northumberland County Council's National Park and Countryside Committee.

1. The first is concerned with the conservation of the varied landscapes of the Park. Safeguarding the essential qualities of openness, remoteness, and the characteristic vegetation diversity of open hill and moorland is a priority. In the valley and moorland edge areas, priority is given to maintaining a varied landscape of improved farmland, rough grazings, woodlands, hedgerows, stone walls, and buildings. Finally, there is a perceived need to attain greater diversity in areas of commercial forest.

2. The second gives priority to wildlife conservation, particularly to increasing the level of protection afforded to the characteristic wildlife habitats of the Park.

3. The third gives priority to helping to protect sites of archaeological importance and to ensuring the preservation of significant buildings and groups of buildings of architectural or historic interest.

4. The fourth objective aims to encourage sound agricultural and sylvicultural practices, based on the principle of caring for and making wise use of natural resources.

THE ACHIEVEMENT OF NATIONAL PARK OBJECTIVES

The achievement of National Park objectives occurs through the implementation of detailed policies in a number of ways. These include the application of finance, controls, influence, education, guidance, persuasion and exhortation to individuals and organisations whose activities impinge on the

conservation, recreation, and other responsibilities of the National Park Committee. These practices have been particularly applied in the agricultural improvement of moorland and in developing proposals for the afforestation of 'open' land throughout much of the 1970s and 1980s. There is considerable concern for the protection of the moorland landscape identified by the map of moor and heath (required under Section 43 of the 1981 Wildlife and Countryside Act and later superseded by Section 3 of the 1985 Amendment Act), and detailed in the policies for moorland conservation. Some monitoring of agricultural change is possible for improvements that will be grant-aided by the Ministry of Agriculture, as these now require the prior approval of the National Park Authority. Control over the afforestation of 'open' land is achieved through a voluntary agreement reached with the Forestry Commission. In more recent years, grant aid for many agricultural improvements (drainage, moorland reclamation, buildings) has been withdrawn, removing the threat of agricultural intensification. The Government has also announced that no grant aid is to be available for afforestation in the English uplands.

The control of development and mineral extraction is achieved by the fact that the Northumberland National Park and Countryside Committee is the statutory planning authority for the Park, with powers equivalent to those of a district council. Whilst persuasion and guidance are important in modifying proposals to achieve higher standards of development, the Committee can refuse permission if it is thought to be against National Park objectives. However, such refusals can still be overturned by the Secretary of State for the Environment on appeal by the applicant.

Direct action to achieve National Park objectives is frequently taken, albeit within the limits of budgetary constraints. Management agreements can be negotiated between the National Park and Countryside Committee and landowners and tenants. Typical examples would include the conservation of semi-natural relict woodlands, mires, hay-meadows, areas of moorland, and archaeological sites. Provision can be made for public access where appropriate. Substantial grant aid is offered by the Committee to assist farmers and landowners with the upkeep of important landscape features and to create new landscape features or wildlife habitats, eg trees and woodlands, farm ponds, stone walls, traditional farm buildings, hedgerows, etc. Such practical work is implemented, in co-operation with farmers, using a combination of local contractors and Park field staff. A wide range of services are provided for visitors to the Park, including information centres, guided walks and events, interpretive publications, an educational service, and a warden service. A basic infrastructure of car parks is provided and a great deal of effort is invested in managing the extensive network of footpaths and bridleways.

CASE STUDIES TO ILLUSTRATE THE ACHIEVEMENT OF OBJECTIVES

Grasslees management agreement

This agreement was negotiated with the Ministry of Defence and its farm tenant. It controls the type of military training activity and makes provision for the management of moorland (burning and bracken (Pteridium aquilinum) control), management of woodland, creation of a small car park, and permissive walking route giving access to Bardon Lough.

The control of sporadic development in the valley of the river Coquet

The Park operates policies in which isolated development is strictly controlled. Planning applications for speculative development are received regularly, and judgements have to be made about the need for such development in satisfying the demand for housing, compared with the likely effect on National Park landscape values.

The conservation of hay-meadows and broadleaved woodland at Barrow Mill, Alwinton

Species-rich hay-meadows are now very rare in the Park. They can only be conserved through the maintenance of traditional farming practices. Farmers may only agree to follow these practices if adequate financial compensation is paid annually. Broadleaved woodlands are often neglected and grazed, so preventing the regeneration of tree species. Agreements can be negotiated whereby the National Park Committee takes on the management responsibilities for a specific period (25 years), undertaking any necessary fencing works and enrichment planting or other management action.

Lordenshaw management agreement

Overwintering of cattle has seriously affected the condition of this moorland site. The Committee and the Nature Conservancy Council have offered to pay two-thirds of the costs of erecting a building to house the cattle. The agreement also provides for public access to archaeological remains, reorganisation of rights-of-way (to minimise conflict with shooting interests), the development of two car parks (removing unsightly roadside parking), and other positive conservation action, such as bracken spraying and woodland management.

The relevance of land use models to National Park management

This Conference is much concerned with the use of models in land use planning. However, at this point in time, no use is made of such models in the definition and achievement of National Park

objectives. It would be very useful if suitable models could be developed to help decision-makers understand the conservation implications of changing land use practices and patterns. Benefits for the Northumberland National Park would accrue if models of ecosystem processes were sufficiently advanced to predict the ecological consequences of, for example, lowering sheep numbers on heather *(Calluna vulgaris)* and grass moorland, or to suggest suitable management regimes for the diversification of species-poor grassland. They should have a landscape dimension to show the geographical implications of the predictions from these 'process' models. Such models would be particularly valuable if they were developed to act as tools to predict the consequences of choosing various courses of action. Officers and Committee members would then have more refined information which would assist the decision-making process and provide greater confidence in applying public funds to the conservation of the National Park landscape. Control would be retained over the decision-making process, rather than losing it to the assumptions and priorities built into the model by its makers.

REFERENCES

Countryside Commission. 1987. *The National Park Authority, administration, policy and powers: a briefing note for members of National Park Authorities.* (CCP 230.) Cheltenham: Countryside Commission.

Macdonald, A.A. 1977. *Northumberland National Park plan.* Morpeth: National Park and Countryside Committee, Northumberland County Council.

Macdonald, A.A. 1984. *Northumberland National Park plan: first review.* Morpeth: National Park and Countryside Committee, Northumberland County Council.

MacEwen, A. & MacEwen, M. 1982. *National Parks: conservation or cosmetics?* (Resource management series no. 5.) London: Allen and Unwin.

MacEwen, A. & MacEwen, M. 1987. *Greenprints for the countryside? The story of Britain's National Parks.* London: Unwin Hyman.

Redesdale: a preliminary test catchment for the NERC/ESRC Land Use Programme

S P Rushton[1], J P Byrne[2] and A G Young[1]

[1]Centre for Land Use and Water Resources Research, Dept of Agricultural and
Environmental Science, University of Newcastle upon Tyne, Newcastle upon Tyne NE1 7RU

[2]MAFF/ADAS Redesdale Experimental Husbandry Farm, Rochester, Otterburn,
Northumberland NE19 1SB

TOPOGRAPHY AND GEOLOGY OF THE REDE CATCHMENT

The river Rede is a medium-sized, essentially
upland, river of some 43 km length that forms a
tributary of the North Tyne. The catchment of the
Rede is at the north-eastern extremity of the Tyne
system, rivers to the east draining into the Coquet,
those to the south-east into the Wansbeck. The
catchment is one of the largest in the Tyne system,
comprising some 330 km². Topographically,
the Rede is comparatively simple, following
a long narrow valley of some 35 km length by
10 km wide. This valley runs in an approximately
east/south-easterly direction from the source of the

river at the Scottish border at Carter Bar to its
junction with the North Tyne at Redesmouth. A
contour map showing the general trends in altitude
along the valley forms Figure 1. From its source at
Carter Bar, the river drops rapidly from 408 m
above Ordnance Datum to 250 m at Catcleugh
reservoir, some 7 km downstream. This upper part
of the catchment is typified by comparatively flat-
topped hills rising to 579 m, with steep-sided incised
valleys running off to either side. Below Catcleugh,
the river enters the Otterburn Basin, a low flat area
where the Elsdon Burn drains from the north-east,
before the river turns south-west and drains into the
Tyne. In this area of the catchment, the hills are less
obvious and the landscape is more undulating. This
change in landscape at Byrness reflects changes in
the underlying geology.

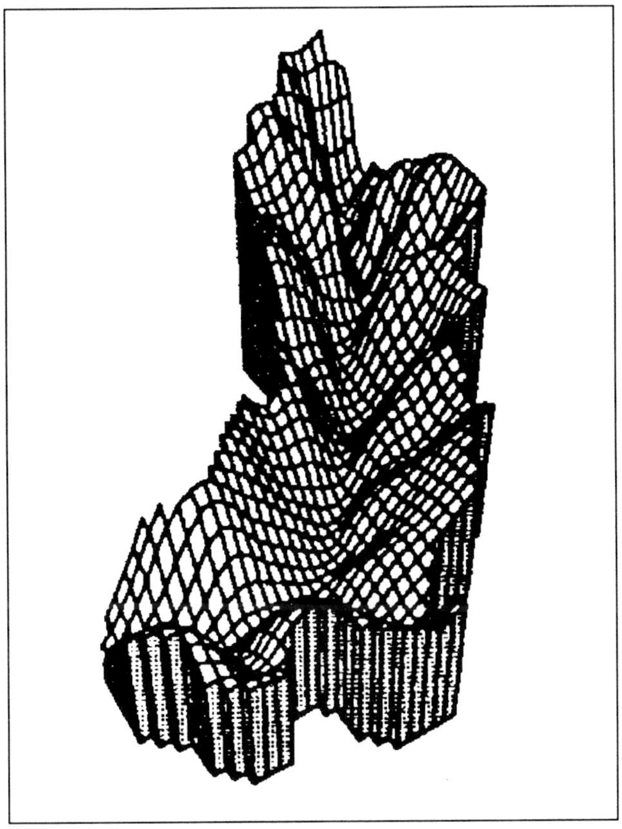

Geologically, the Rede catchment can be divided
into two broad regions. At the upper end of the
catchment, north of Byrness, the bedrock is of two
broad types: deposits of the Lower Carboniferous
and associated igneous intrusions. These latter at
Carter Bar mark the end of the southern uplands.
The Lower Carboniferous deposits are of two types:
the Fell Sandstones and the Cementstones. The
former overlay the latter and comprise the rounded
hilltops typical of the upper parts of the catchment.
Where the river has eroded the Fell Sandstones
away, the Cementstone deposits are prevalent. The
igneous intrusions are of basalt, specifically the
Lumsdon Law, and intrusive andesites of Lower Red
Sandstone age. Fault lines separate the Fell and
Cementstone deposits from the second region,
which is dominated by Scremerston sandstone and
Middle and Lower Limestones of the Lower
Carboniferous.

The overlying drift reflects the topography, in so far
as there are few alluvial deposits above Byrness
and considerable areas in the lower catchment,
where the Otterburn basin forms an alluvial plain of
approximately 3 km². North-west of Byrness, the hill
tops on the Fell Sandstones are covered with
blanket peat. In contrast, blanket peat is patchy

Figure 1. Topography of the Rede catchment (viewed from the
south-east)

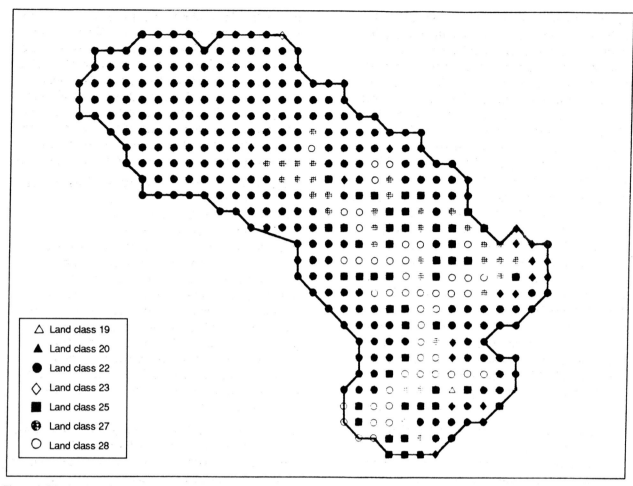

Figure 2. Distribution of ITE land classes in the Rede catchment

or sporadic below 350 m altitude and is infrequent south-east of Byrness. River terrace deposits are infrequent and only occur sporadically throughout the catchment.

THE INSTITUTE OF TERRESTRIAL ECOLOGY LAND CLASSES AND THE LAND COVER PRESENT IN THE REDE CATCHMENT

The 330 one km National Grid squares in the Rede catchment fall into seven of the 32 land classes recognised by the Institute of Terrestrial Ecology (ITE) (Figure 2). The most abundant land class is 22, which dominates the upper part of the catchment and the high land at the watersheds on either side of the valley. Typically the land form in this land class is slopes or plateaux of broad glacial valley type (Bunce, Barr & Whittaker 1981) – a good description of much of the upper region of the Rede valley. The majority of the lower catchment is a mixture of three land classes of broadly similar type, comprising land classes 25, 27 and 28, all valley floor or alluvial floodplain in type, and again a good description of this part of the catchment.

These data are derived from the most recent assignment of squares to land classes (March 1991) and are different to those used elsewhere in this volume.

LAND USE AND LAND COVER IN THE REDE CATCHMENT

Redesdale is a sparsely populated valley comprising land in nine parishes, of which Rochester, Otterburn and Bellingham are the largest. There are two large villages, Otterburn and Elsdon, which are situated in the lower region of the catchment. The former lies on the route of one of the two trunk roads running along the valley. These roads join south of Otterburn and form an important access from England to Scotland after the A1 and A74. The valley has three main land uses: forestry, military range and livestock farming. Much of the upper catchment, particularly on the Fell Sandstones is afforested. This is mainly coniferous plantation, forming part of the Kielder Forest which extends nearly 30 km in a south-westerly direction from Redesdale. Much of this Forest dates from plantings in the 1930s and areas are progressively being felled and cleared. The northern valley-side is given over to military use, from just below Carter Bar some 18 km south-eastwards to Elsdon. This military land and the remainder of the catchment are given over to pastoral agriculture.

The agricultural activity in both the upper and lower zones of the catchment is almost exclusively livestock based, with sheep rearing dominating beef production. Dairying is almost non-existent, following the restructuring of the dairy industry in

the late 1970s and early 1980s. The land use is reflected in the land cover, with the predominant land cover type at low altitudes being semi-improved pasture or rough grazing. Improved pasture is found on the better soils on the alluvial plain, but arable farming is virtually absent, apart from the occasional field of fodder turnips. Above 200–250 m, the land cover generally changes to grass moorland. On the peatier soils higher up the valley, cotton grass (*Eriophorum* spp.) and heather (*Calluna vulgaris*) are abundant.

The recent agricultural potential of the Rede valley has never been fully exploited, because of the extent and requirement of the military range, and forestry activity. Of the remainder, economics, human ability, inclination, and land use restriction (imposed by the Northumberland National Park Authority) act to restrain realisation of full agricultural potential.

Systems of production in the Rede and similar districts can no longer depend on an animal's ability to thrive and survive (McGreggor Cooper & Thomas 1982). Market developments and advantages of vertical integration mean that agricultural output now comes from four sources:

1. hefted hill flocks producing replacements, store and/or finished lambs;
2. retained draft ewes producing cross-bred breeding stock and finished lamb;
3. retained cross-bred ewes producing finished lamb;
4. hill cows producing replacements, store stock, fat stock and cross-bred stock for retention, etc.

The eventual sale of drafted animals, wool, and the hire of labour and machinery must not be forgotten and are also important sources of revenue. The more diverse activities include the production of heather honey, and ewes' milk cheese. Whilst production is relatively straightforward, meeting market specifications is much more difficult, as systems are based predominantly on hill stock that start with an inherent disadvantage for the characteristics that achieve the highest prices. Profitability is still marginal, despite grants and subsidies.

These changes in output have only been possible by technical development, and policies of self-sufficiency. Feeding of livestock is 90% dependent on forage, grazed and conserved on-farm.

Selection of grass and clover cultivars for yield, suitability for grazing or cutting, and other important characteristics have transformed the stock carrying capacity and output of the inbye. The adoption of silage conservation systems allows winter forage of higher quality to be made, and without the inherent risks attached to hay-making. The process is also faster and less labour-intensive.

Drier and more fertile areas on the hill have been improved to release the inbye to forage production for winter feeding and lamb finishing. As a result, ewe numbers on the hill have been increased. Whilst forage production systems use relatively high fertilizer nitrogen applications, the success of hill improvement depends almost entirely on clovers for this nutrient. Establishment and productivity of both these sward types have only been possible because of the understanding of the interaction between fertilizer requirement and timing of application, and stock requirements.

Flock prolifigacy has been increased, as well as stocking rate, as a result of the better understanding of the ewes' nutritional requirements. Grazing improved swards at strategic periods plays its part, but the ability to rely on grazed swards and less on expensive purchased feeds has been a more recent development. Together, the production and rearing of twin lambs can be both self-sufficient and profitable. Cattle, relatively non-selective graziers, can balance the negative grazing selectivity attribute of sheep when properly managed, and are essential in maintaining both inbye and improved hill swards in desirable agricultural heart.

Replacement of indigenous vegetation with sown swards does remove habitat for ground-nesting birds, such as lapwing (*Vanellus vanellus*) (Baines 1990), but compensates in part by providing improved feeding areas. In Redesdale, extensive afforestation has resulted in very large populations of corvid species. On the Ministry of Agriculture farm, unpublished research has shown that a decline in successful breeding of ground-nesting birds is attributable to nest robbing by corvids.

From the point of view of the future, the impetus for change is already occurring. The Nature Conservancy Council (Felton & Marsden 1990) has offered the view that a continued agricultural presence is necessary to achieve the aim of improvement of moorland. In this respect, the Ministry of Agriculture, Fisheries and Food has initiatives to integrate farming and conservation objectives (Rushton & Byrne 1990; Byrne, Wildig & Rushton 1992). In a wider context, the agricultural sector most affected by such changes has also recognised the need to be responsive to the new initiatives (Nitrate Sensitive Areas, 1991), also found during a 'straw poll' of hill farmers (Byrne 1991).

A consensus seems to have appeared, recognising the importance of agriculture in maintaining the semi-natural habitats of these areas. It will involve reductions in ewe numbers and changes in management of flocks. Further agricultural land improvement is unlikely, in the absence of grants. Maintenance and renewal will hopefully continue. Changes in practices may be compensated by a move to environmental grants (Curry 1991). Hill farmers, like those in the Rede valley, will still

have to rely on innumerable skills to meet the new requirements profitably. Clear objectives and stability would help them to do so.

ACKNOWLEDGEMENTS

We would like to thank Drs M Lane, R G H Bunce and D C Howard for providing us with details of the land classifications for the one km grid squares in the Rede catchment.

REFERENCES

Baines, D. 1990. The role of predation, food and agricultural practice for determining breeding success of lapwings (*Vanellus vanellus*) on upland grassland. *Journal of Animal Ecology*, **59**, 915-929.

Bunce, R.G.H., Barr, C.J. & Whittaker, H.A. 1981. *Preliminary descriptions for users of the Merlewood method of land classification.* (Merlewood research and development paper no. 86.) Grange-over-Sands: Institute of Terrestrial Ecology.

Byrne, J.P. 1991. *Meetings of the Redesdale Sheep Association.* February 1991 to March 1991. Unpublished.

Byrne, J.P., Wildig, J. & Rushton, S.P. 1992. Growth and utlisation of heather under contrasting managements. In: *Land use change: the causes and consequences,* edited by M.C. Whitby, 192. (ITE symposium no. 27.) London: HMSO.

Curry, D. 1991. Speech to the Oxford Farming Conference.

Felton, M. & Marsden, J. 1990. *Heather regeneration in England and Wales.* (Feasibility report for the Department of the Environment.) Huntingdon: Nature Conservancy Council.

McGreggor Cooper, M. & Thomas, R.J. 1982. Sheep farming in Britain. In: *Profitable sheep farming,* 24-38. Ipswich: Farming Press.

National Sheep Association. 1991. Conclusion. In: *Conservation and sheep farming. Report of the Conservation Committee.* (Environment and conservation report 20.) Malvern: Aldine Press.

Rushton, S.P. & Byrne, J.P. 1990. The dynamics of vegetation change and flock output of hill land. In: *British Grassland Society second research conference.* Hurley: British Grassland Society.

Policy

A policy perspective on land use research*

A A C Phillips

Director, Countryside Commission for England and Wales,
John Dower House, Crescent Place, Cheltenham, Gloucestershire GL50 3RA

LAND USE CHANGE

My brief is to provide you with 'a clear policy perspective' on land use research – this to be done in less than half-an-hour of 'substance and relaxed comment'.

In that I must disappoint you. The gloomy news I have to give you tonight is that there is, at present, no such thing as a clear policy perspective in the countryside, so the substance of policy may be hard to find and you have no grounds to relax. On the contrary, there is a policy vacuum and a great deal of confusion, especially in relation to the key question: what should be the future of Britain's agriculture? That does not mean that research has no point – far from it. In a confused situation, research can be exciting and throw up new policy options; but, if the policy context is uncertain, researchers will have to be fleet of foot to sieze the opportunities. Let me explain.

Land use is the product of interaction between humankind and land. For many centuries, the pattern of rural land use has been affected to an extreme by decisions which were taken centrally by the government of the day. Thus the Romans built roads by Imperial edict (at least, that is how I imagine their alignment got decided upon – a process only marginally more autocratic, some might say, than decisions taken these days by the Department of Transport). Norman kings imposed their castles on the land; and parliaments in the 18th century sanctioned the enclosures which gave shape to much of our familiar farmed countryside. It is only in the second half of the 20th century that the influence of public policies has such an all-pervading impact on rural land use.

To some extent, that impact has been achieved through planning policies – new and expanded towns, National Parks and Green Belts, etc – working in their way through the Town and Country Planning system. But the hand of central Government (individually or collectively with our European partners) has been no less evident in agriculture. Thus, while agricultural land use has

not been planned through the Town and Country Planning system, it has most certainly been planned. Not, of course, in the sense that a Commissar has identified each acre as suitable for this or that (or at least, not since the demise of the 'War-Ag Committees'), but through the equally effective means of price signals and specialised advice (free until recently), backed up by well-funded programmes of research in agronomy, veterinary sciences, and so on. Those price signals came in the form of price supports for the main agricultural products and subsidies to encourage improved farm practice and re-equipment. Together, they have led farmers to grow crops where their fathers would never have remotely considered: cereals on the heavy Midland clays, oil seed rape – it seems on an early summer's day – all over the countryside. While farmers have always argued the virtues of independence and have resisted all attempts to place them under the planner's yoke, they seem to have had few complaints about jumping to the dictates of a set of public policies which bore little resemblance to the workings of a truly free market.

Here, indeed, was a clear policy perspective: 'grow more food, be more efficient, follow the price signals'. Rural land use evolved according to fairly predictable patterns. Confidence was the order of the day for everyone involved in the business of agriculture – in Brussels, in Whitehall, in the laboratory, on the farm.

You will know well, of course, the blind alley into which such policies, pursued with single-minded determination, have led – to spiralling Common Agricultural Policy (CAP) expenditure and surplus foodstuffs on the one hand, to environmental destruction on the other. As a result, throughout the second half of the 1980s, agricultural policy and, as a consequence, the prospects for rural land use have been in turmoil. Let us consider some of the key developments, partly nationally led, partly driven from Brussels.

1984   Milk quotas, which with hindsight can be seen as marking the first major shift away from a single-minded pursuit of production

*This paper represents the 'after-dinner' speech at the Conference dinner

1984 The Halvergate grazing marshes experiment in the Broads – the first attempt, pioneered by the Countryside Commission and with Ministry of Agriculture support, to reward farmers for farming in the traditional manner

1986 Environmentally Sensitive Areas introduced – the application, in a number of key areas, of the Halvergate principles

1987 The Alternative Land Use and Rural Economy (ALURE) initiative – an attempt by Government to set forth a coherent policy for the countryside

1987 The Farm Woodland Scheme – a novel arrangement to encourage farmers to plant trees on the better farmland

1988 Set-Aside – an effort to cut agricultural output by taking land out of production altogether

1989 The Countryside Premium Scheme – another pioneer scheme by the Countryside Commission to show that Set-Aside land can be used to benefit the environment

1989 Nitrate Sensitive Areas – with regulations over nitrogen applications in particularly sensitive areas

1990 The Countryside Commission's Countryside Stewardship Scheme announced (of which more below).

What patterns can one detect here? A limited greening of agricultural policy – and a partial attempt to cut the costs of the CAP and reduce surpluses.

Thus far, so good, yet the current debate on the future of agriculture suggests that each group is pulling in a different direction. Not only the future of British agriculture, but also that of rural land use depends on the outcome of this debate.

What are each of the main parties asking for? The negotiators in the General Agreement in Tariffs and Trade (GATT) – and especially the Americans and other members of the Cairns group – want tariff barriers lowered so that world prices reign in Europe. They will tolerate a certain amount of 'decoupled' support for European farmers – that is support for things such as environmental care which do not distort trade – but they suspect the protectionist motives of some, at least, of the European Community (EC) governments. Those governments, in turn, declare a wish to see real cuts made in the still-rising CAP budget (up from £18 billion to £22 billion this year), but seem reluctant to will the means, especially where farmers have such influence over the political system of many European governments. Environmental groups want environmentally friendly farming, with stringent controls over pollution; some also want help for small farmers.

Consumer groups want cheap and safe food. And the farmers of Europe are themselves divided:

some claim to welcome greater exposure to market forces, some want to go the green route to organic farming, most probably yearn for the relative comfort of the past, with the near certainty of rising prices for their produce and a position of esteem in society.

No wonder, then, that there are so many policy options on the table, each with a different set of land use implications. At one extreme, some people advocate major cuts in guaranteed prices in the CAP, sharply lower tariff barriers, and allowing the world 'market' to regulate output. Others would go along with some 'renationalisation' of agricultural policy in the EC, whilst maintaining a free internal market for food products (how could it be otherwise with 1992 on its way?), within a general framework which outlaws unfair competition between EC countries. Some, as in the proposals put forward by the European Agricultural Commissioner MacSharry, would want to keep many of Europe's small farmers in business, whilst looking to the larger farmers (of which Britain has a disproportionate number) to bear the brunt of cutting back on output and taking land out of production. Some would want to use Set-Aside as the principal means to cut output (making it mandatory, rather than – as now – voluntary); others favour taking only marginal land out of production. While some favour across-the-board cuts in agricultural production through quotas on *inputs* such as nitrogen, others prefer that this be achieved by placing limits on *outputs*, eg quotas on cereal tonnage. Some see salvation in putting land under crops, not for consumption but for industrial use, such as ethanol from cereals or energy from short-rotation coppice.

What nearly everyone agrees on is that there must be far tighter controls over agricultural pollution and that some, at least, of the money currently given to production should go to encouraging greater environmental care by farmers; most people see a case for more forestry and woodlands, providing these bring environmental and leisure benefits, as well as income from timber production.

As a footnote to this commentary, I should add that the picture looks different from where you view it in Europe. The perspective of a peasant farmer in Sicily or Greece, a part-time farmer in Germany, a cereal-baron in the Paris basin or East Anglia, or a crofter in Scotland will be very different. Neither is it just the farmers' perceptions which vary: environmental and consumer interests differ country by country – and the 12 Ministers arguing their respective corners in Brussels must be alive to the full range of these domestic, political and economic pressures. It is this huge range of interests, all seeking to adjust to a rapidly changing economic climate (not to mention a possible long-term change in the physical climate), which makes many people feel the days of the CAP in its present form are numbered.

But, as we all know, the debate is not yet resolved. The clear policy framework has yet to be found. Where once there was certainty, now there is doubt; where once there was clarity, now there is confusion.

Despair not, though. Tough as the present situation may be for the farmers who have seen their incomes fall steeply in recent years and for whom the outlook is grim indeed, there will be potential winners too. Conservation interests certainly stand to gain if the right policy mix emerges from the maelstrom. And I suspect that those engaged in land use research should also be able to benefit, if they are ready to seize the new opportunities.

I suggest that there are four subject areas for land use research in the light of this analysis, and five methodological approaches. Let me take them in turn, briefly. First, everyone seems agreed that agricultural policy must in future encourage better care of the countryside, involving not only protection for the best of existing landscapes and wildlife habitats, but also the restoration, or recreation, of features – such as downland or heath – which have been destroyed. The Countryside Commission is just about to embark on a major pilot scheme involving the payment of incentives to farmers, to better care for, and restore, such features. It will be called Countryside Stewardship Scheme. The kind of research questions which suggest themselves are as follows. What kind of financial incentives will persuade farmers to join the Scheme? Do we have the practical knowledge to advise farmers on such work? What sort of technical back-up is needed to ensure that the advice is sound? What are the public expenditure and other implications of extending countryside stewardship to the countryside as a whole?

Next, in practically every policy package, there is an expectation that substantial areas of *lowland* England will go under trees. Again, the Countryside Commission is leading here, with its programme of 12 community forests near large cities (each of about 50 square miles), and a new national forest in the English Midlands (some 150 square miles or so in area). How can such ambitious and large land use changes be brought about? What kind of planting ought we to be encouraging? How should these forests be designed so as to make their full contribution to meeting the leisure needs of society? And what is to be the role of the occupying farmers and landowners in creating new lowland forests?

Third, if we, and others, embark upon bringing about large-scale changes in the countryside through countryside stewardship and new lowland forests, what is the right policy framework within which decisions should be taken? Do we need some kind of landscape strategy – or a series of such strategies at the national, regional, and local levels – to steer such change? How can the public express their interest in what the landscape of the future should look like?

Fourth, most policy options assume a greater diversity of rural land use in future. In particular, we expect to see greater access to the countryside for sport and recreation. Though in many ways the public enjoyment of the countryside reinforces the case for conservation, there are conflicts too, especially with nature conservation interests. We need better answers than we have now to the following questions. What is the effect on ground-nesting birds of free access to open country? What is the impact of public access on wildlife, on lakes, rivers and canals? And, most importantly, what management techniques are there for maximising both the public enjoyment and the nature conservation value of sensitive environments?

These four subject areas for land use research may be examined in more detail using the following five research methodologies.

1. Studies of past land use change. We need to know more about the effect of public policy in the recent past upon rural land use, in order to understand better the implications of alternative options available to us now.

2. Development of alternative scenarios. Policy-makers need to know more about the possible land use implications of alternative strategies for the countryside.

3. Experimental and monitoring work. In a climate of uncertainty, there is a premium upon testing new ideas. Such experiments need to be carefully monitored. Countryside Stewardship and the new lowland forestry initiatives of the Countryside Commission are good examples.

4. Environmental inventories. For example, in the recently published report by the National Parks Review Panel, set up by the Countryside Commission, the Panel has suggested that each National Park needs a comprehensive statement based on geographical information systems of the environmental resources within its area.

5. Interdisciplinary approaches. For example, there is a growing interest in establishing the value of the farmed countryside for environmental purposes, as opposed to its potential for food production: this means bringing together the skills of the economist, the ecologist, and others, so that we can identify the 'market' in terms of public demand for conservation and access to the countryside.

Possible land use changes in the European Community

H C van Latesteijn

Scientific Council for Government Policy, PO Box 20004, 2500 EA The Hague, The Netherlands

INTRODUCTION

The Netherlands Scientific Council for Government Policy (in Dutch: *Wetenschappelijke Raad voor het Regeringsbeleid* – WRR) is currently involved in research aimed at exploring long-term development possibilities for the rural areas in the European Community (EC). Two observations form the basis for this study.

First, the ever-increasing budgetary problems of the EC necessitate knowledge about the cost-effectiveness of investments for agricultural development in the rural areas of the Member States. Decisions on the deployment of EC funds (eg the European Agricultural Guidance and Guarantee Fund (EAGGF)) are taken in a knowledge vacuum. In view of the need to apply the limited resources from the funds as effectively as possible, a more informed assessment of the different alternatives for the use of resources is desirable. For The Netherlands, as one of the Member States of the EC-12, this type of information is needed to formulate a clear policy view.

Second, developments within the agriculture sector reveal an ongoing increase in productivity. This seems to be an autonomous process, constantly changing the conditions for policy-making. The developments in agriculture considered here relate in particular to the continued increase in production per unit of land area and per unit of livestock. Although the market and price policy pursued hitherto have led in recent years to production cutbacks for a number of products, the policy has had little influence on this unremitting increase in productivity. Factors which play a greater part in determining the speed of this process are the technical developments in cultivation methods and, increasingly, in the environmental field. If the present area of land under cultivation is maintained, without any change in land use, the structural overproduction which has developed over the past ten years in virtually all major agricultural products will take on even greater proportions.

Hence, agriculture is going through a phase of accelerating changes that call for major policy decisions. For adequate policy reactions, a clear understanding of the overall developments in agriculture is indispensable. Information must then be provided on the way in which different agricultural activities contribute to the achievement of other regional objectives, such as the creation of jobs, the generation of income, and conservation of nature and landscape.

One way to provide this sort of information is to assess the quantitative relationship between a number of self-contained technical development processes in agriculture, and objectives from other points of view, such as socio-economic aspects, environmental protection and nature conservation, and the consequences of these interactions for rural areas in Europe. In short, this is the purport of the research carried out by the WRR.

APPROACH

The aim of the study is to obtain consistent information about changes in agriculture that will have an impact on other goals throughout the EC. Thus, changes in agriculture must be measured as changes in regional income generation and employment (generally speaking, the socio-economic aspects), in the regional intensity and scale of agricultural production (generally speaking, the agrotechnical aspects), and in emissions of environmentally hazardous substances from farming and the disruption of nature and landscape (generally speaking, the environmental protection and nature conservation aspects). This is done by considering the more or less stable conditions over time, the *ceteris paribus* conditions. For agriculture, soil characteristics, climatic conditions, and crop properties are such stable conditions.

The development possibilities outlined above can be quantified if land use is chosen as the central theme. Through changes in land use, all other changes can be linked with each other. The limits to the development possibilities of agriculture are assessed using a combined qualitative and quantitative analysis of the long-term agricultural potential of the rural areas in the EC. The qualitative analysis is based on soil characteristics stored in a

geographical information system (GIS), and shows where certain forms of land use are possible. The quantitative analysis consists of a combination of the GIS information and simulation studies.

Using a crop growth simulation model, the agricultural production potential of the various European regions is assessed based on the properties of the soil and the climatological conditions.

Two different levels of levels of exploitation are discerned:

1. *potential yield*
   where optical, physiological, phenological and geometric characteristics of the crop, incident radiation and temperature alone determine the yield or production attainable per unit of land area for different product groups;

2. *water-limited yield*
   those production situations in which one of the growth factors – water – is lacking during part of, or the entire, growing season.

It must be clear that these levels of exploitation can differ considerably from the *actual yield* for which, in addition to growth-limiting factors such as the shortage of water and nutrients, and growth-reducing factors, such as diseases, pests, weeds and crop management techniques, play an important role.

The potential yield fixes the upper bounds of agricultural production. An implicit assumption is that agriculture in the EC will be performed only by using the best technical means, and moreover that no regional differences other than soil and climate are influencing the upper bounds. If one looks at the enormous and unexpected changes in agriculture over the last three decades, this assumption might not be too exaggerated.

Next, a linear programming model that contains several objective functions is constructed. With the model, regional allocation of land use activities can be calculated while optimising the objectives. The main emphasis is on probing the conflicts between different desiderata, or, in other words, exploring the trade-offs between the different objectives at stake. This optimisation model, GOAL (General Optimal

Allocation of Land use), contains eight objective functions formulated in terms of agrotechnical, socio-economic and environmental aspects of agricultural production, as given in Table 1.

The procedure that is followed using the GOAL model is shown in Figure 1. By first calculating an optimum for the various objectives separately, it is possible to determine what optimal values can be achieved for these objectives. Requirements can then be set for the minimum values to be attained for certain other objectives. A consequence is that the optimum values of other objectives have to be brought down to a suboptimal level. This demonstrates the interchanges between different objectives. If the requirements in respect of the various objectives are then intensified step by step (indicating the different desiderata), the consequences of the policy pursued can be illustrated in a number of scenarios. It should be borne in mind here that scenarios do not show what the most probable development will be. No forecast is produced. However, a description is given of what can happen when certain outline conditions have to be met. In this way, various scenarios do provide an advance indication of possible development orientations.

A requirement may, for example, be set that agricultural production should be achieved at minimum cost, so that production is allocated to the different regions in an optimum manner from the point of view of cost. If, however, the requirement is that agricultural production should provide more than a certain number of jobs, an entirely different distribution among the regions may be obtained. Prompted by differences of opinion on the objectives to be achieved, several scenarios can be devised in this way, built up from the values obtained for the various objectives and the associated allocation of land uses to the different regions.

Some requirements cannot be moulded into the rigid outlines of the model. Recreation and nature conservation contain strong spatially differentiated demands. These demands are hard to represent by a number that holds true for the EC as a whole. Therefore, these claims and demands are put on a map and are compared to the spatial results of the scenario calculations. In this way, it is possible to identify conflicts that may lead to the formulation of additional constraints. Finally, an indication is given of the ways in which the European system of regulatory provisions should be involved to bring the scenarios outlined to fruition. The existing European regulatory system is assessed for its effectiveness, and recommendations may be made with regard to new directions in which the system can be developed. This means not only the reorientation of the Common Agricultural Policy, but also the implementation of a selective regional economic policy. It may become apparent in this context that scenarios considered feasible in other

Table 1 Objectives relating to the use of rural areas in Europe, taken from EC publications, and their operationalisation in the GOAL model

Agrotechnical	Maximisation of soil productivity
	Minimisation of costs per unit product
Socio-economic	Minimisation of costs per output
	Maximisation of employment in agriculture
Landscape	Minimisation of land use changes
Environmental protection	Minimisation of pesticide use ha^{-1}
	Minimisation of nitrogen use ha^{-1}

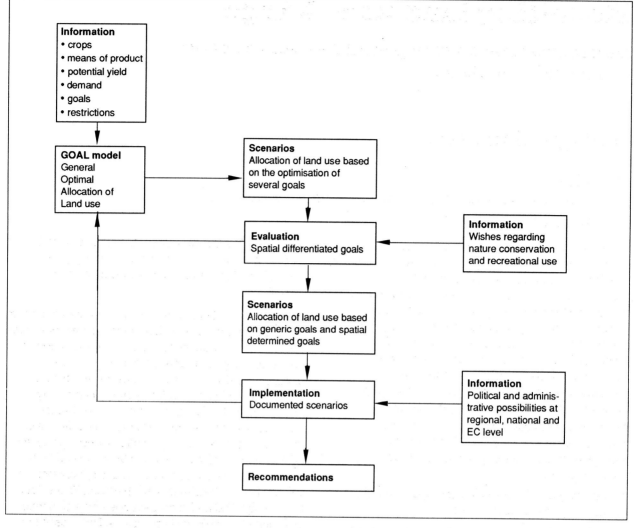

Figure 1. The framework of the GOAL model

respects have to be discarded for political or administrative reasons.

CONCLUSION

The study does not aim at a blueprint for rural policy to be pursued at European level. Neither is it the intention to present forecasts of rural developments for one or more regions, based on the developments outlined above. The ultimate purpose of the study will be to provide a number of pictures of possible consistent developments in rural areas in the EC. Agrotechnical, socio-economic, environmental protection and nature conservation objectives, and considerations for the EC as a whole are involved.

These pictures are achieved by constructing a number of scenarios in which conflicts arising from increasing productivity, market saturation, uneven distribution of production within the EC, and an increasing concern for the environment and landscape are made visible. These scenarios can act as a reference for the formulation of various policies at EC level, geared to the development of rural areas. In addition, the study provides a basis for a set of provisions at regional level through which the consequences of the various scenarios developed at European level can be included in the formulation of regional economic policy.

Modelling land use change

The following three papers represent the discussions at the three modelling workshops

Ecological factors

J P Grime

NERC Unit of Comparative Plant Ecology, Dept of Animal and Plant Sciences,

University of Sheffield, Sheffield S10 2TN

Until recently, many ecologists have conducted their work with a narrow focus upon particular habitats and populations, using methods of data collection which have varied enormously. This has severely limited their scope for integrating data from different sources, for 'scaling up', and for developing models of wide applicability and predictive value. The purpose of the discussion reported here was to assess how far the situation is changing as a consequence of new perspectives, new funding initiatives, and recent technical developments.

Before reviewing the main conclusions of this discussion group, it may be helpful to locate ecological modelling within a broader framework, which includes:

- the sources of information and inspiration drawn upon by the modellers; and

- the mechanisms whereby the models are tested and refined.

Figure 1 consists of a simple flow diagram in which two main sources (surveys and screening) are identified as foundations for ecological modelling. Surveys have a well-established pedigree in ecology, and involve documentation of the spatial distributions of organisms and of the associated variation in environmental factors and features of management. Screening which relies upon comparison of the basic characteristics and tolerances of organisms observed under controlled conditions has a smaller following, although there are now well-established botanical screening traditions in Britain (Grime 1965), Canada (Keddy 1990),

and Japan (Washitani & Masuda 1990), and work such as that of Clutton-Brock and Harvey (1979) shows how this approach could be extended to animals.

In the lower part of Figure 1, it is suggested that there are two major ways in which model predictions of the ecological consequences of land use can be tested. One is to compare model output for particular situations against time series data collected from long-term study sites. Unfortunately, monitoring activity of the kind required has received scant support, and we are now strongly dependent upon those individuals and organisations who, against the odds, have managed to sustain these activities. A second approach to model testing is to conduct manipulative experiments in which changes in land use are applied and records made of the dynamic response of component organisms. Here, as in the utilisation of existing long-term monitoring data sets, the research strategy is to identify discrepancies between model prediction and field reality, and to use these as a basis for further cycles of model refinement and testing.

Using the framework summarised in Figure 1, a wide-ranging discussion ensued and crystallised in the form of seven recommendations, as follows.

1. It was generally agreed that monitoring of change, such as that undertaken in various recent surveys and new permanent plot experiments, was essential and should be encouraged, not merely to test predictions as in Figure 1, but as a valuable activity in its own right. Many important discoveries and ideas owe their origin to unexpected findings in long-term studies.

2. Patterns in spatial distribution and fluctuations through time detected in species are a valuable starting point, but greater ecological inference is possible where there is a functional characterisation of the organisms under study. Life history, reproductive biology, and physiological requirements and tolerances can often provide an excellent basis for interpretation and predictive modelling of phenomena such as resistance to perturbation, resilience, and dispersal.

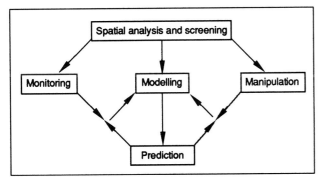

Figure 1. The role of modelling in studies of the ecological consequences of land use changes

3. Some organisms, eg flowering plants, have been used extensively as indicators of land use impacts, whilst others have been neglected. It was agreed that more effort was needed in the UK, to follow the lead of the Scandinavians in using soil micro-organisms in surveys and experiments. Bryophytes are underutilised, and there is further scope to employ pathogens of crops, moths, and dragonflies. Beetles, because they are virtually ubiquitous, and flies, because they are very responsive to land use change, also had strong advocates.

4. It was recognised that land use studies could not usually deal with all the major groups of plants and animals represented in the landscape. Recent studies, such as those relating the characteristics of butterflies to those of their foodplants, may point the way to a survey strategy in which some organisms (or even features of the physical or chemical environment) are used as *surrogates* for particular groups. This approach can only be expected to work for relatively common organisms, and will require further research before it can be recommended with confidence.

5. Led by Professor Mather, there was a lively discussion of the factors currently limiting the use of remote sensing and aerial photography in the documentation and analysis of land use impacts on flora and fauna. It was concluded that ecologists needed to be bolder and more explicit in stating their requirements, and might need to become more directly involved in shaping the technology. With the prospect of a wider range of scanning operations from space, there appears to be a particular need to develop interpretative skills which can understand aggregated signals.

6. Introductions of exotic organisms, the spread of plants and animals following climate change, and more adventurous development of landscape are bringing closer the possibility of an occupation of extensive areas of Britain by entirely new assemblages of plants and animals. It could be argued that this situation already prevails in many urban areas of southern England. There is an urgent need to consider the long-term implications of such developments.

7. Prompted by representatives from the Department of the Environment, the final phase of our discussion turned to the objectives and means of research. It was recognised that research on the effects of land use was more likely to draw public support if the results could be integrated within a broader framework, linking ecology to social and economic issues. In the past, many ecologists had appeared to exist in a world apart from that of 'the man in the street'. Global and regional concerns were now projecting ecology into the foreground of political debate and every-day conversation. There are now excellent opportunities for well-conceived ecological projects to combine good science with service to the community.

REFERENCES

Clutton-Brock, T.H. & Harvey P.H. 1979. Comparison and adaptation. *Proceedings of the Royal Society of London,* **205B**, 547-565.

Grime, J.P. 1965. Comparative experiments as a key to the ecology of flowering plants. *Ecology,* **45**, 513-515.

Keddy, P.A. 1990. The use of functional as opposed to phylogenetic systematics: a first step in predictive community ecology. In: *Biological approaches and biological trends in plants,* edited by S. Kawano, 386-406. London: Academic Press.

Washitani, I. & Masuda, M. 1990. A comparative study of the germination characteristics of seeds from a moist grassland community. Functional *Ecology,* **4**, 543-557.

Hydrological factors

B H Wilkinson

Institute of Hydrology, Maclean Building, Crowmarsh Gifford, Wallingford, Oxfordshire OX10 8BB

The hydrological cycle interacts strongly with the biochemical cycles. Consequently, land use change such as afforestation, deforestation, desertification and urbanisation may have a major impact on hydrology at a continental, regional, river basin, or subcatchment scale. Within a river basin, this impact may lead to such effects as an increase in flood size and frequency, a reduction in river or groundwater flow which imposes a stress on water resources, a deterioration in water quality, or an increase in sediment transport, soil erosion, landslips, etc. At a continental scale, major land use changes may affect global climate and regional hydrology.

In view of the above issues, it was appropriate that one of the discussion sessions should be concerned with predicting the hydrological consequences of land use change through the use of mathematical models.

The discussions were focused on a number of questions, and a summary is presented below.

Which land use changes are of most concern to hydrologists?

Afforestation/deforestation

The importance of land use changes resulting from afforestation or deforestation of a region was fully recognised by the group. Reference was made to Law's 1960's research on the Stocks Reservoir Catchment*. From a series of lysimeter interception studies, he concluded that afforestation of the reservoired catchment would result in some 20% loss of runoff. Subsequently, more detailed work on paired grassland and forested catchments in Plynlimon (Wales) and elsewhere has confirmed these early findings. Thus, in the humid temperate regions, afforestation will generally lead to a reduction in the water supply yield from a catchment.

With respect to the impact of afforestation/ deforestation on floods, it was noted that there is a substantial body of data from the humid temperature regions of the world, which shows that deforestation reduces the time for the peak

*Summarised in Calder, I.R. 1990. *Evaporation in the uplands,* 1-2. Chichester: Wiley.

flood to arrive but increases the size of the peak. In some cases, the increase may be very dramatic. Other detrimental effects of afforestation were noted, such as the increase in sediment loads in rivers which occurs during both planting and timber extraction. There are also measurements to show that coniferous forests will scavenge pollutants from the atmosphere. The pollutants are then carried by rain to the land surface and, if the soil has little buffering capacity, acidification of surface waters may result. Because of these important impacts, there has been a major effort in the hydrological modelling of forests. The use of the Institute of Hydrology's (IH) hydrological rainfall runoff model (HYRROM) to predict the change in the water resources of a Welsh catchment due to proposed afforestation was described.

Agriculture

The impact of agricultural practice on local hydrology was discussed. The drainage of much of eastern England by mole ploughing or tile drains was noted. Such drainage may have a major effect on flood peaks and the time to peak, depending on whether the catchment soil is predominantly clayey or sandy.

Agriculture may have a marked effect on the quality of surface waters and groundwaters. The ploughing of permanent grassland in south-east England during the 1940s and 1950s, and its conversion to arable land have led to a major release of nitrate. The problem has been exacerbated by the use of nitrogen-based fertilizers. Models of both surface waters and groundwaters have been and are being developed to predict future impacts. The problem with pesticides and herbicides was largely unrecognised some 15 years ago, but the substances are now finding their way into drinking water supplies. Advanced hydrological modelling is required to gain an understanding of how such substances move through the soil and into watercourses.

Urbanisation and industrial development

The group discussed ways in which increasing urbanisation and the growth of industry impact on the natural drainage systems, as rural land is

converted to a concrete or bitumen surface and watercourses are channelled and piped. Heavy polluting loads may be carried by rainwater from the urban surface into streams and rivers. In addition, there are associated sewage effluent discharges. There has been a major growth in modelling activity to address the urban problems over the last ten years.

For which land use change situations are suitable hydrological models available?

The group noted the wide range of hydrological models available. They saw the role of the model to predict surface water or groundwater flows within and from a catchment for a given effective rainfall distribution. The models vary from the relatively simple storage types where the catchment is represented by one or more cascading reservoirs to physically based distributed models, such as the systeme hydrologique Europeen (SHE) and the IH distributed model (IHDM) which require detailed representation of the spatial properties within a catchment, eg the distribution of hydraulic properties of the soils, etc.

A wide range of models also exists for predicting water quality, but these were generally a component part of a hydrological flow model. It was accepted that, if it is not possible to develop a reliable flow model for a particular situation, then any attempt to model water quality in this situation will fail.

Are there any hydrological modelling techniques which should be particularly encouraged?

The group first considered those models which use historic records of hydrological data, such as precipitation, river flow, groundwater flow, etc, to establish parameters in statistical or storage type models of catchments (eg HYRROM). Such models will predict runoff for a given rainfall input for the catchment in question, and for the prevailing land use during the period over which the hydrological data used in the parameterisation were collected. Comparison of the model parameters from catchments with the same general hydrological setting but with different land uses enables the sensitivity of the model parameters to land use changes to be identified.

The second approach is to use models which are more physically based. The catchment is usually subdivided into a number of distinct regions, often on a grid pattern, and the appropriate hydrological equations are set and solved numerically by computers. Some of the larger models may demand a major computing facility. As a precursor to running such models, understanding and quantification of the hydrological processes for a variety of land use situations are needed. These processes include interception, evaporation, transpiration, infiltration, surface water runoff,

shallow subsurface runoff, deep groundwater flow, sediment transport, water quality changes, soil water storage, etc. These processes may change during a day, with the season, and through time for a given land use. For example, the closure of the canopy during the growth of a forest may profoundly affect the hydrology within a catchment. Models of this latter type include SHE and IHDM. There was general agreement that the models based on a physical description of the hydrological processes are likely to be more reliable in making predictions in situations where there have been major land use changes. However, the more traditional models still have a role to play where the perturbations to the system are not too extreme. The group reached a consensus that it was healthier to have research workers moving forward with developments on a series of fronts, rather than focusing on one particular area.

Are there problem areas associated with the development of hydrological models for land change assessment?

Several problems in model development were identified. For example, there was discussion over the choice of scale for physically based hydrological models. Too coarse a grid scale may lead to the loss of the description of the spatial inhomogeneity within the catchment, while too fine a grid scale may lead to unacceptably long computer runs. It was recognised that much more computing power would be needed in the future if the hydrological impacts of land use changes over very large catchment basins are to be modelled. Such effects may arise as a result of climate change.

The availability of some data bases was causing concern, in that they were so costly that it took them out of the reach of some research groups. The possibility of digitising remotely sensed satellite data and using them in hydrological models was discussed. This was seen as opening up exciting modelling possibilities, but concern was also expressed that costs may be prohibitive.

It was accepted that geographical information systems have a key role to play in assembling and manipulating data for use in hydrological model development.

How should models be validated?

A number of the participants expressed concern over the proliferation of hydrological models. They were particularly concerned that there was no standard against which the performance of a model could be judged. While this may not pose a problem for the researcher who is able to follow new developments closely, the 'model user' may be making predictions of events tens of years into the future, with no means of assessing the reliability of such predictions. There was a plea for work to be done in establishing a data set and validation procedures against which the reliability of

hydrological models could be tested. There was a tendency among model developers to claim that 'my model is better than your model', with little actual justification.

Is there the need to link hydrological and ecological (biological) models?

The group felt that more needed to be done to improve the representation of biological processes within the hydrological models. The view was also expressed that, in many situations, those working on the ecological impacts of land use change could not develop sound predictive ecological (biological) models, unless there was a reliable hydrological model available as a foundation.

Socio-economic factors

D R Harvey

Dept of Agricultural Economics and Food Marketing, University of Newcastle upon Tyne, Newcastle upon Tyne NE1 7RU

The Conference raised some interesting questions and problems about the appropriate modelling of socio-economic behaviour, which were explored during this discussion period.

During the plenary sessions, Professor Munton referred to a 'weakened' agriculture, which some participants could be forgiven for interpreting as a 'weekend' agriculture, in either case pointing to the obvious fact that agriculture is no longer necessarily either a full-time occupation or the sole and only use/objective of landowners and operators. Agriculture may continue to be the major user, but it is clearly not the major economic or social activity in rural areas. Lowe referred to the substantial variation in farmer, landowner and occupier response to social pressures, economic and policy signals. Such statistically deviant behaviour might also be taken by some to imply deviance of a more general kind. In any event, the variation in individual and household circumstances and motivations, leading to substantial variations in response to external pressures and incentives, is also of major importance to the appearance and characteristics of the countryside, which modellers ignore at their peril. From the policy-makers' and advisers' point of view, the question of whether policy needs are 'bottom-up' or 'top-down' is important. For some aspects of the rural environment (Sites of Special Scientific Interest, Environmentally Sensitive Areas policy, local employment opportunities, and planning concerns), the people and nature on the ground are the primary focus. For other concerns (the Common Agricultural Policy, the General Agreement in Tariffs and Trade, and national agricultural and environmental policy), the primary focus becomes one of national and regional production and land use patterns, and regional employment tendencies – the 'top-down' view. The over-riding conclusion from these observations is that there is no unique modelling approach which can hope to capture all of the interesting and relevant aspects of the socio-economic complex which conditions rural land use, either from a behavioural or from a policy analytic perspective.

Over and above these pragmatic concerns, there emerge three rather more philosophical points. First, there may be a social science equivalent of the Heisenburg Uncertainty Principle, which conditions attempts to discover and understand socio-economic behaviour – the more one knows (observes) the current activities (position) of the system and its participants, the less one can know about the direction and rate of travel of this system and its component parts. Such a characteristic certainly applies to the task of modelling the rural socio-economic system, given our current methodologies and techniques. Accurate model representation of the existing system tends to mitigate against reliable and credible representation of tendencies and behavioural responses, as the accuracy of present representation requires a level of detail about the heterogeneity of circumstance and condition which is extremely difficult to capture in a responsive model system. However, this condition is a reflection of the lack of development of modelling methods, and is not therefore an exact analogue of the Heisenburg Uncertainty Principle. An exact analogue would be that observation of people involved is altering their underlying behaviour patterns, a problem which has not yet received much attention.

Second, there remains some conflict between those who seek to explore and understand individual behaviour and the possible interactions between individuals and their associated groups, and those who seek to model the system on the basis of more or less formal 'behavioural equations' representing a distillation of previous tendencies and theoretical constructs which necessarily abstract from and simplify reality, to a greater or lesser degree. In part, this conflict is reflected in the differences between those who wish to examine present (and historic) conditions in considerable micro-level detail, and those who are more concerned to model the behaviour of the system with the objective of analysing potential responses to changes in market and policy signals.

Third, there remains a considerable difference, at least on the surface, between methodological approaches to socio-economic behaviour. In part,

this is manifested in alternative explanations offered by a Marxian approach *versus* the neo-classical economic approach. While there is little doubt that social and political conditions and ideologies colour, if not determine, individual, household, and group behaviour, neo-classical economics does not yet incorporate these factors and may well be incomplete, at least, as a result.

As a 'straw man' to generate discussion and also to impose a chairman's structure to the debate, participants were asked to consider a 'pipe dream' about the development of socio-economic modelling associated with land use change, briefly outlined as follows. On the basis of, for instance, the Institute of Terrestrial Ecology land classification system, questions are being asked as to how rural land use would change in the event of market and policy changes. As a first attempt to provide answers, partial budgets on 'constructed' input/output (I/O) relationships can be applied, land class by land class, to give projections of cover type changes, based on changes in gross margins of particular agricultural enterprises, either for particular surveyed squares or over the total land class. This approach was then developed at the Centre for Agricultural Strategy (CAS), Reading, into a national farm model, again using constructed rather than estimated enterprise activities. However, this approach gave rise to a number of problems, especially concerned with (i) repeatability, calibration, and validation of input/output relationships; and (ii) the imposition of market constraints. As a result, the CAS land use allocation model (LUAM) is now being developed to incorporate estimated I/O relationships (on the basis of Farm Business Survey (FBS) data) and to include labour and capital use, as well as national market clearing relationships, though still working at a 'national farm' level, on the basis of enterprise use of land of different sorts and at different levels of intensity.

In contrast, the Farm Level Ecological Land Use Relationships project (FLEUR), under the Economic and Social Research Council's (ESRC) Joint Agriculture and Environment Programme at Newcastle, is modelling behaviour at the farm level, using 'archetypal' farms, with the intention of illustrating farm- and field-level consequences for a variety of farm types, sizes, locations, family attitudes and circumstances, in an attempt to capture diversity and individual variation in behaviour. One problem being dealt with under NELUP is the possible integration of these two ('top-down' and 'bottom-up') approaches. Some experimentation with econometric estimation of direct relationships between observed land use and production/price changes has been attempted, but has proved impractical (because of data limitations) and highly dubious as to behavioural response. The alternative is, therefore, a form of simulation modelling. There are three major possibilities:

1. EPIC (erosion productivity impact calculator)-type enterprise models, based on 'known' physical relationships associated with 'known' economic parameters (prices and costs), to generate profit functions as response engines, which can be tested against FBS data;

2. LUAM extensions – more detailed at river basin level, using FBS data, and perhaps modelling the total area on the basis of these farms explicitly (with the model land-using activities comprising farm business rather than enterprise;

3. validated FLEUR models as the basis of explicit aggregation of farm-level models to the river basin level.

As the last option has proved in the past to be particularly cumbersome and difficult, an alternative is to use farm-level models to generate responses of archetypal farms to selected policy scenarios, and to develop reduced-form activities from these to extend the LUAM structure.

Extensions of this framework for modelling socio-economic behaviour with respect to land use include:

i.   the incorporation of *risk* (already being done with the FLEUR models);

ii.   the incorporation of *attitudes and values* through modifications to FLEUR-type models;

iii. the development of an understanding of changing farm *structure*, possibly based on work underway at Newcastle in the ESRC Countryside Change Unit on reduction of size distributions to log normal distributions, which allows for more comprehensive analysis of the history of structural change, possibly using FLEUR-type models of accumulating and selling land, and engaging in 'off-farm' activities, and possibly eventually through the explicit aggregation of these types of models to the regional or national level.

The discussion of this framework revealed considerable scepticism, particularly on the ability of economic maximising models to capture:

● finer-scale impacts and spatially specific concerns;

● policy implementation issues;

● institutional, attitude and value aspects of behaviour.

In contrast to ecological and hydrological modellers, the term 'mechanistic' tends to be used as one of abuse with respect to socio-economic modellers, and economic models are largely mechanistic. However, the discussion did not resolve the question of whether the problem is one of fundamental philosophy – that human behaviour can or cannot *ever* be reduced to a mechanistic or systematic set of relationships; or one of inadequate empirical research – that we simply do not yet know what these relationships are in sufficient detail to be able to model them reliably. Nevertheless, two

important points did emerge from this discussion: first, that policy decisions are being taken as if the relationship between policy instruments and their final effects were known, so that the very existence of policy and policy debates implies some significant belief that human behaviour contains substantial elements of systematic behaviour; second, that, in order to identify the critical areas of ignorance, it is useful to be able to identify the sensitivity of systematic models of behaviour to the underlying assumptions and estimated/constructed relationships. Without trying to build systematic models of behaviour, it is difficult to identify those areas of behaviour for which our current knowledge is critically inadequate. Thus, a major output of modelling activity is, at least potentially, information on social science research priorities. In conclusion, the discussion noted that most of the time had been spent on problems of modelling *causes* of land use change from a socio-economic perspective, while the title of the Conference and of the discussion session emphasised *consequences*. Land use is not the only focus of socio-economic models or research, even from a strictly natural environment perspective. For instance, employment, recreation, and consumption patterns and tendencies will all affect and be affected by changes in land use, while the socio-economic development of rural areas is itself a legitimate area for both policy and research concern, yet increasingly divorced from agricultural or land use questions. The interaction between past and present land use decisions and current and future policy questions and policy processes remains a fascinating field of discussion, with a great deal yet to be done. We remain woefully ignorant, and, even then, knowledge is not the same thing as understanding. Yet policies will continue to be introduced and amended as if we knew all the answers. There is still a large amount of work to be done.

Priorities for research in land use change

W E S Mutch

Forestry and Land Use Consultant (formerly University of Edinburgh),
19 Barnton Grove, Edinburgh EH4 6EQ

This résumé of suggested priorities for research relating to land use change is a free-ranging response to the flow of ideas and material presented in papers and posters at the Conference. It makes no attempt at a detailed review or criticism of the individual papers which are to be reproduced in full in the proceedings, or of the excellent posters which have deserved close attention and examination. In these papers and posters, the Conference has been given evidence, or in some instances glimpses, of exceedingly interesting work, and some important work, which deserves to be carried through to successful conclusion: the criteria of success require to be defined.

In the list of priorities, there stands first the duty of the Research Councils to support projects which may develop new technologies, or methodologies which will apply technologies or test concepts in new areas. The Conference has had examples; several papers at the beginning of the programme described the enhanced capacity for perceiving and measuring environmental change, and many posters relate to those techniques and to the use of the data so obtained to model some aspect of the environment or land use that is particularly sensitive. In research, undoubtedly there must be continuing and enhanced programmes for monitoring environmental change, and progressive upgrading of the modelling founded upon it so that its implications may be interpreted. Professor Grime's summary of the ecological workshop has provided an admirable review and a list of the important research topics in this field of modelling.

There is a *prima facie* case for further international collaboration and for applications within the European Community (EC) to develop joint methodologies and internationally compatible systems. In this regard, I look back, within my own experience, to the considerable initial difficulties, but also to the success and great potential, of the Forest Ecology Research Network of the European Science Foundation, funded by the Natural Environment Research Council on behalf of the UK Government.

In respect of the investigation of global warming, it appears that, while the programme of monitoring change and modelling must proceed, it is still too early to be worth spending money and effort on consideration of possible changes in land use, because the probabilities of changes in wetness, windiness, and the local amplitude of temperature fluctuations are so imperfectly known that the prediction of cropping possibilities would be unrewardingly premature. Data collection, modelling and validation should proceed along the lines of Professor Grime's report; they may rely upon a few well-resourced groups in pure physical science, mostly without biologists and land users at this stage, to predict and interpret climatic trends, while biologists and land users consolidate data and identify the indicators upon which observations of trends may be validly based.

To those who model and predict 'global warming', I would emphasise strongly the need for indications of changes in wetness, windiness, and the amplitude of seasonal fluctuations of temperature, which are required to allow land users to begin forecasting cropping possibilities.

It is useful to recall the general diagram for the justification of research. Research expenditure is made in the expectation of eventual net benefit, that improved understanding will allow applications which will lift the net benefit line from the lower side of cost or disbenefit to the upper, positive benefit area. Professor Harvey, presenting the summary of the socio-economic workshop, referred to the 'chap in the field', and it is he who waits expectantly for the opportunity to benefit from the fruits of the research. The tendency of the researcher is generally to delve, pursue and refine, involving investment even further down the dotted line of increasing cost in the diagram, until he is pulled up by the request to interpret and apply his results; this is particularly relevant for research programmes relating to land use change.

Conference speakers and poster writers have shown wide agreement on a significant and continuing change of objectives in rural land use, broadly away from the production of market goods of food and wood to something more complex. What are the implications of such change for

scientific research? From about 1950 through to 1980 at least, the dominant feature of ecological and agricultural research was interest in autecology and crop ecology. Species after species was subjected to rigorous scrutiny and reported in monograph. The research was largely monospecific.

Two years ago, I, as a member of a Forestry Commission research review group, visited the Cowal peninsula in Scotland, and I use that place and the discussion of the visiting group to demonstrate the change we now face. Cowal is the mountainous peninsula in the Clyde estuary, lying between Loch Long and Loch Fyne. Some 40% of the land is forest, mostly coniferous. The coastal fringe is occupied by people, from high water mark to about 20 m elevation. Above that, to 500 m, is almost completely forested. Above that, in turn, are hill sheep farms and, on the mountains rising to 1000 m or so, an important concentration of golden eagles *(Aquila chrysaetos)* and other birds of prey. Responsibility for the research and protection of the eagles, raven *(Corvus corax)*, and so on, is with the Nature Conservancy Council for Scotland, that for the sheep the Department of Agriculture and Fisheries for Scotland, the Macaulay Land Use Research Institute and the Scottish Agricultural College. The large red deer *(Cervus elaphus)* herd is served, for research and monitoring, by the Red Deer Commission and partly by the Forestry Commission. The Forestry Commission looks after the trees and much of the woodland wildlife.

In this complex situation, there is very little collaborative effort, although there is full respect and communication between most of the people on the ground. No-one is responsible for what has come to be called landscape ecology. If the sheep stocks were withdrawn, as they may well be in impending change to the Common Agricultural Policy (CAP), the eagles would no longer have sheep to prey upon or scavenge. Would the eagles suffer, or would the deer expand to fill the empty grazings and, as an unmanaged grazer, allow the eagles to fare even better? What are the relative merits of running a fenced and an unfenced forest with, in the latter, the red deer able to range from the shelter of the trees in winter to the high pastures in summer? What would be the financial, as well as the ecological, results?

The neglect of landscape ecology is national and I am much less confident of the present position that Professor Wilkinson's report of the hydrological workshop appeared to suggest.

The weakness of our understanding of the integrated systems, such as may come from landscape ecological research, makes me doubtful of the reliability of advice from the commendable NERC/ESRC Land Use Programme (NELUP) for other than very modest marginal changes of input and output levels. The intentions of the integrated ecological/hydrological/economic models

are unquestionably good: my fear is that the knowledge of the realities of the ecological relationship and of the substitution responses at the ecological level is so incomplete that part of the foundation is unreliable, with inevitable consequences for the structure built upon it.

Such understanding is particularly important at present because wildlife conservation and creative conservation are presented as possible income providers for farmers, as an alternative to food production. On the other hand, it might be contended that keeping sheep on the hill would be justified, as in the Cowal example, by the accepted desirability of maintaining eagles and other raptors, so that society should enter into a management agreement with the farmer to maintain an extensive sheep regime. On the other hand, the red deer might achieve that end without a payment. We simply do not know.

In other situations, landscape ecology is equally important, for instance in relation to hydrological research, pesticides, nitrate leakage, and so on.

Landscape ecology would have my highest priority in land use research, although I am aware that a few groups are already engaged in it. Nevertheless, its pursuit is difficult, administratively, technically, and financially: administratively, because departments of Government regard sheep or trees or deer or eagles as their particular preserve, and both resent and seek to frustrate those who have the temerity to encroach upon it; technically, because the research group must deal, of necessity, with much more than one organism or a partial system; financially, because such research is difficult to fund – referees do not like it because most are specialists and highly suspicious of broad research. Furthermore, our whole research educational system is against it, from the honours project to be completed in ten weeks and PhD projects which must be fully completed within three years, and postdoctoral grants which, as I know from experience, appear far more difficult to obtain for broad topics than narrow ones. As a result, most scientists are ill-prepared for landscape ecology through their career development and the structure, even the philosophy, of university science.

Because one of the responsibilities of the Research Councils is to provide for the training of research scientists, I trust they will place higher emphasis than previously on interdisciplinary research and educational breadth. In that respect, particularly, the objective of the NELUP project is admirable.

In the presentation of the NELUP project, however, I was concerned at the implications and limitations of working with the parish data from the Ministry of Agriculture, Fisheries and Food returns. The expression of these as 'an average farmer' for a particular parish might be useful for some purposes, but appears seriously inadequate for the purpose of predicting best decisions and most

suitable strategies. The possible 'decision-takers' in the current situation have widely different aspirations. Politicians at Westminster and in the EC probably aspire to changing the CAP so that payments to farmers are minimised, subject to constraints relating to the political impact upon their electorate. Regional planners have aspirations relating to landscape, public access, nature conservation and social impact. The farmer, however, aspires to none of these; he may want to minimise his labour inputs or to keep his options open for capital gain through planning permission for some building development.

The difficulties of defining the stance and aspirations of 'the decision-taker' are a concern in regard to the important NELUP project and others of a similiar kind. In the area where I have most understanding of farmers' behaviour, it is evident that farmers take decisions that do not come near to matching the expectations even of their agricultural advisers. Virtually all, tenants and owner-occupiers, are in debt to the banks. Most look for minimum labour strategies and devote themselves to an income-earning job off the farm, probably 'moonlighting' to minimise tax liability. For considerations of tax, even the farm adviser may not be informed, and the June returns may be made inaccurately, at least in respect of labour inputs. Furthermore, the owner-occupier farmer's perception of the best management strategy is heavily dependent upon when he bought his farm and with how much borrowing. The charges for servicing mortgages may be vastly different even between neighbours on identical land; consequently, the decisions they take, quite logically, in response to prices and grant incentives may be entirely different.

It was partly for these reasons that the paper by Lowe was so welcome. In the current and impending changes in land use, in the social structure of the countryside, and in the public expectations of what the countryside should provide, more research is required in the relevant social sciences.

One aspect of that arises from what the Minister said at the opening of the Conference about various schemes of creative conservation and community woodlands. In this country, we have miniscule experience of creating community woodlands of any size, and much of that experience has been disastrous. It is alarming to hear that these community woodlands 'are in an advanced stage of planning' and that nine more will be added to the programme almost immediately. It appears predictable that costly disaster will ensue if planners and landscape architects seek to impose absolutist decisions on urban fringe communities. In Britain, we have much to learn about the establishment and management of community woodlands from neighbouring countries in Europe, especially from The Netherlands, and also about methods of consulting and motivating tight communities, which various developing countries are doing very effectively.

With the professional planner and the scientific researcher regarded as belonging to an outside world, much depends for success in urban forestry on identifying and consulting the key opinion-formers in local society. Frequently they are not the locally elected representatives, and they may not even be part of any recognisable organisation, but they have the power to save or to condemn 'community projects'. It is evident, therefore, that research to obtain (and how to obtain) the ideas of local people is vital to the creation of community woodlands, and no pencil should be put on a map until that work has been done.

The change of rural land use strategy from the production of food and wood to multiple use may be seen as bringing a string of consequential issues and problems but, to a great extent, these are subsumed in one: how are the non-market benefits of multiple-use management enjoyed by the public to be translated into an income for those who work the land? In order to obtain the benefits of landscape and nature conservation, the countryside requires to be farmed, albeit gently. In effect, the farmer and forest manager provide a backdrop of scenery and habitats for the enjoyment of visitors, but there are generally no means, or inadequate means, of collecting a fee for that enjoyment. The visitors enjoy a consumer surplus, paying less for their experience than the benefit they perceive in it. The evaluation of non-market benefits and costs of many kinds is a research field that is difficult, neglected, but very relevant to the determination of the causes and consequences of land use change.

It may be that the principal consumer for research on non-market costs and benefits will be the Treasury, because the financial support for multiple use will probably continue to be delivered by payment from the public purse, and the beneficiaries of multiple use will pay through taxation. That does not weaken the case for the work. The programme of research into non-market costs and benefits bears on a very wide field: water quality, pollution control, creative conservation programmes, community woodlands, etc, and the achievement of stable funding for these systems and programmes is particularly desirable.

Finally, there is the other major subject from the Minister's address: sustainable development. This appealing principle derived from the *World conservation strategy*** presents difficulty in definition, but its adoption as an official policy by national and supra-national politicians advances the claim that research will be required to demonstrate how it may be implemented.

*International Union for the Conservation of Nature and Natural Resources. 1980. *World conservation strategy: living resource conservation for sustainable development*. Gland: IUCN.

Whether a harvested system may be held to be ecologically sustainable depends on where the boundary is drawn round the system and the terms on which energy inputs are used. The question arises whether sustention should be achieved within each field, or may the whole farm be self-balancing, or even some larger land unit? More usually, the term 'sustainable development' is interpreted as requiring the acceptance only of uses that do not involve irreversible degradation of ecosystems, a less harsh constraint but a definition that is more readily comprehended. Irrespective of the definition, the research will be demanding and lengthy. It should, however, have one advantage: given the politicians' attraction to the principle of developing sustainable systems, this is at least one research topic of land use change that should command full financial support. If it does not, it seems likely that the words will remain little more than a convenient catchphrase for politicians and journalists.

Postscript

M C Whitby

Countryside Change Unit, Dept of Agricultural Economics and Food Marketing,
University of Newcastle upon Tyne, Newcastle upon Tyne NE1 7RU

Like motherhood, multidisciplinary research has been with us for a long time and has received nominal support both from those who do it and those who do not. However, to take this noble idea beyond the stage of mere enthusiasm has proved difficult in the past, and for that reason it is a genuinely serendipitous result of the current wave of environmental concern that it has positively reinstated multidisciplinarity on the agenda for a number of researchers. The evidence of these proceedings is that appropriate funding of research *can* begin to persuade researchers to emerge from their habitual bunkers and start to share problems, methods and, eventually, results.

Why has this always been so difficult in the past? The system of incentives associated with peer review must bear part of the blame and, no doubt, the inherent conservatism of researchers who seek to offset the uncertainties of their (often lonely) existence by clinging to the certainties of (apparently) well-established disciplinary boundaries. The quest for knowledge is easier when the aim is sharply defined. Indeed, a career in the social or natural sciences is much more securely based on a series of well-received articles in the refereed journals than on a necessarily smaller output of, perhaps faltering, steps based on multidisciplinary research: necessarily smaller because the effort needed to drive multidisciplinary work through to a conclusion is much greater for a given result. Effort is needed to establish a common professional language in which problems are conceptualised and methods described.

Tolerance is needed to surmount the stereotypes in which traditional enemies are clothed. Patience is essential in negotiating a satisfactory consensus as to the new 'rules of the game' which are to operate when decisions are to be made and conclusions reached.

The exigencies of environmental policy, calling for answers to complex questions which can only be satisfactorily attacked by appeal to combinations of both natural and social scientific disciplines, are now beginning to bring about some new collaborations. Most recently, the evidence in this volume of the prospective outcome of the NERC/ESRC Land Use Programme shows that boundaries can be spanned within the separate fields of the natural and social sciences. The final stages of that work will require mingling of the two sciences in the production of a decision support system.

The final message from this volume must, therefore, be that the requirements for productive multidisciplinary research are now being met more effectively. In the types of funding undertaken, the Research Councils have taken a welcome initiative in directing funds to multidisciplinary research. The process has been taken a step further in the establishment of the Land Use Research Coordination Committee, which combines the necessary breadth of scientific disciplines with experience and expertise from the policy machine itself. Meanwhile, having taken such imaginative steps, the research community must now await the results.

Poster Papers

A feature of the Conference was the invited poster papers on display. Of their nature, such papers cannot be reproduced in the written proceedings. Instead, the scope of their coverage is indicated in the abstracts which follow, grouped under four subject areas.

Environment

The influence of peatland afforestation and water quality

H Anderson & J Miller
Macaulay Land Use Research Institute (MLURI)

Afforestation in the peatlands of Caithness and Sutherland has caused considerable controversy. In 1988, the Forestry Commission established experimental plots on a deep peat at Bad a'Cheo, Rumster Forest, to investigate the consequences of current forest practices on water quantity and quality in collaboration with MLURI. The site can be regarded as free from anthropogenic pollution, but with large marine inputs, leading to a high S content in the peat. Cultivation and draining of the organic soil have led to increased outputs of organic matter, in the form of colloidal particles and soluble components. Mineralisation of N and S has led to increases in both ammonium and sulphate in the drainage, but nitrate concentrations have remained small. These changes occurred rapidly, but fertilizer losses have been slower, being dependent on whether drainage is across, or through, the peat.

Growth and utilisation of heather under contrasting managements

J P Byrne, J Wildig & S P Rushton
MAFF/ADAS Redesdale EHF, Pwllpeiran EHF & Dept of Agriculture & Environmental Science, University of Newcastle upon Tyne

The influence of the grazing animal on loss of heather *(Calluna vulgaris)* and its regeneration is being investigated at Redesdale and Pwllpeiran Experimental Husbandry Farms. Trial design at the two sites is similar. The main treatments are Normal Farm Stocking Rate (NSR), contrasted with a reduction of 30% on that figure (RSR). Plot and farm scale experiments are in place.
Results from the first year's studies of the utilisation of heather at Redesdale indicate differences between the two treatments for this factor. However, only at the January assessment date was the difference significant (NSR 26% vs RSR 13.5% utilisation). These preliminary results suggest that regeneration of heather is possible under sensitive management. There is hope, therefore, that in the future environmental and agricultural needs can be integrated successfully. This has relevance to the land use issues being debated at the present time.

The environmental effects of blanket peat exploitation in Northern Ireland

A Cooper, R Murray & T McCann
Dept of Environmental Studies, University of Ulster

Multivariate land classification has been used to assess the extent and rate of change of mechanical peat cutting on blanket peat in Northern Ireland in relation to other land uses in the uplands. Development of the technology for machine cutting and the dependence of farmers on peat for fuel as part of the farm economy are the driving forces for change. The paper will cover these issues and assess the environmental effects and ecological implications of machine cutting.

Establishment of an upland silvopastoral land use system

W R Eason
AFRC Institute of Grassland and Environmental Research

As part of a national network trial, a silvopastoral experiment was established in 1987 at Bronydd Mawr Research Centre in south Wales. The effect of tree species and spacing on animal production is being recorded. This poster also focuses on a number of aspects of tree establishment, including tree protection and weed control.

Managing conifer forests for nature conservation: Kielder Forest case study

J E G Good, T G Williams, A Buse, D Norris & H L Wallace
Institute of Terrestrial Ecology, Bangor Research Unit

Coniferous afforestation disrupts upland ecosystems, altering the range and proportions of different habitats available to plants and animals. A study of the effects of afforestation on flora and fauna at Kielder Forest are described. Proposals for changing forest management to improve plantations for wildlife are discussed.

Sediment and solute delivery from agricultural land: a non-point source of river pollution

A L Heathwaite

Dept of Geography, University of Sheffield

The effect of changing land use practices on water quality at both the long (90 year) and short (single water year) timescales are discussed. Current annual sediment and inorganic nutrient export, from the arable and grassland Slapton catchment in south-west Devon, is of the order: 6 t NH_4–N, 282 t NO_3–N, 2 t PO_4–P and 1440 t suspended sediment. Rainfall simulation experiments for characteristic land uses suggest that overgrazed permanent grassland is an important source of sediment, total nitrogen and total phosphorus, resulting in 12x, 9x and 16x the load of ungrazed grassland. This is due to increased runoff as a result of surface compaction. Permanent grassland forms over 60% of riparian land use, so its contribution to stream sediment and solute loads may be high. The effect of changing land use in accelerating the eutrophication of Slapton Ley, a 0.8 ha freshwater lake which is the sink for catchment inputs, is discussed.

Climate and land use

M N Hough

Meteorological Office

The poster will show the relations of the following to the water balance climate:

1. proportion of farmland under grass
2. the percentage of land sown to winter wheat in autumn

The greatest changes in grassland or wheat areas over the years occur in areas to which they are most climatically suited.

Environmental consequences of changes in arable agriculture

D S Powlson, K W T Goulding, A J Macdonald & P R Poulton

Rothamsted Experimental Station

Changes in arable farming practice can greatly influence the quantity of residual nitrate in soil at risk to leaching or denitrification. A combination of field experiments and mathematical modelling can help in elucidating such effects. Set-Aside can decrease nitrate leaching, but future ploughing up will produce a pulse of nitrate. Afforestation will almost certainly decrease leaching, but leads to acidification of soil.

Nitrate (NO_3–N) loading and agricultural intensity relationships within Grampian Region river systems

G G Wright & A C Edwards

Macaulay Land Use Research Institute

Modern agricultural practices have been strongly linked with increased NO_3–N loadings. Nitrate leaching increases as land use progresses from forest and moorland, through grassland, to arable agriculture. There are, within the UK, few studies on a regional scale capable of displaying a relationship between land cover (agricultural intensity) and water quality. This relationship can be investigated using computer manipulation of spatial geographic information, together with conventional river and agricultural census data.

Measurement and perception of change

Environmentally Sensitive Areas

D Askew

Ministry of Agriculture, Fisheries & Food, Leeds

The display boards give background information on the ESA schemes throughout the country. More detailed information is given on one particular scheme: the Pennine Dales ESA. The ESA schemes provide a vehicle for controlling environmental change and the monitoring of schemes has involved measuring these changes.

Land classification for wide area conservation evaluation in strategic planning

R Aspinall

Macaulay Land Use Research Institute

A range of detailed climatic, topographic, geological, and edaphic maps provide a comprehensive environmental data base within a geographical information system. These data can be summarised into a series of ecological land classes which describe particular combinations of environmental conditions. Land classes are used here to assess the environmental associations of 28 different semi-natural habitat classes mapped across Grampian Region at a scale of 1:50 000. This analysis allows an objective evaluation of strategic level conservation interest to be made, and provides a framework for incorporating conservation interests into regional planning processes.

Countryside Survey 1990

C J Barr, R M Fuller & F T Furse

Institute of Terrestrial Ecology (ITE) & Institute of Freshwater Ecology

The Countryside Survey 1990 project centres on a sample-based field survey of land cover, habitats and species, linked with a land cover map derived from satellite imagery. Other components include freshwater biota sampling and a detailed soil survey of sample sites throughout Great Britain. It is funded by the Department of the Environment and Natural Environment Research Council, with support from the Nature Conservancy Council.

Results from the 1990 survey will be compared with those from earlier surveys by ITE and others, so that both stock and change statistics can be computed for great Britain and for major planning regions. Mapped information will be digitised and handled using geographical information systems. Results will become available over the next 12 months.

National Countryside Monitoring Scheme

J T C Budd, K M Sutherland, G Tudor, A Giblin & P Holden

Nature Conservancy Council, Peterborough & Edinburgh

Changes in the land cover of the 'wider countryside' are quantified for the whole of Scotland, based on a stratified random sample of each Region. Results for the period 1940–70 are now complete, and a pilot exercise for Central Region indicates the continuing trends to the present day.

Landsat mapping of Great Britain

R M Fuller, G B Groom & A R Jones

Environmental Information Centre, Institute of Terrestrial Ecology (ITE), Monks Wood Experimental Station

In the summer of 1990, the Environmental Information Centre of ITE was commissioned by the Department of Trade and Industry and the Department of the Environment to produce a land cover map for the United Kingdom. The aims of this study are:

1. to compile a digital map of land cover in Great Britain, based on a hierarchical classification of important major land cover types

2. to make quantitative assessments of accuracy of end products

3. to integrate the map with the field survey data of Countryside Survey 1990 and with other topographic and thematic data in a geographical information system (GIS) environment

4. to produce demonstrator GIS output in vector format.

This paper describes preliminary aspects of the project and initial results of the survey are presented. The product is an integral part of the Countryside Survey 1990, which aims to provide information on the land use and ecology of Great Britain in 1990, to assess past changes, and is a baseline against which to measure changes in the future.

SDD land cover and look-back projects

J Gauld, J Bell, W Towers, D Miller & R Aspinall

Macaulay Land Use Research Institute

Baseline information on land cover in Scotland is being collected from an aerial photographic census at the 1:24 000 scale. Interpreted land cover types are incorporated into a geographical information system (GIS). These data form the basis for a series of land cover and land cover change monitoring and evaluation projects. For example, land cover data have been photo-interpreted for the Cairngorm area from 1947 and 1966 photography. These historic data sets allow assessment of the extent and nature of land cover change since the late 1940s; changes are evaluated against environmental and land ownership data sets held in the GIS to identify possible policy-related causes of change.

Mapping land cover change in water catchments from satellite imagery

G Griffiths & C Williams

Hunting Land and Environment Ltd

Landsat multispectral scanner (MSS) and thematic mapper (TM) satellite imagery was used to map land cover change over ten years in two water catchments: the river Exe in Devon and the river Hodder in Lancashire. The project, which was funded by the Department of the Environment at the National Remote Sensing Centre, was undertaken for the Institute of Freshwater Ecology, in support of its research programme to investigate the effects of land use change on water quality.

Conflicting trends in Finnish land use policy

A Selby

Finnish Forest Research Institute

An aim of Finland's agricultural policy is to reduce agricultural production to the level of self-sufficiency to avoid ever-increasing export subsidies, and bring agricultural policy closer to the requirements of the General Agreement in Tariffs and Trade (GATT). The means to reduce production have included legislation to encourage land use change via grants, fees, and other payments. The afforestation of arable land has been one such means. Since 1969, some 110 000 ha of fields have been cleared for agricultural expansion, while the intensity of agricultural production has increased unabated. The uneven distribution of measures to reduce the area of arable land under cultivation is beginning to threaten both the environment and the socio-economic stability of certain regions of the country. Agricultural, forestry, and environmental land use policies require integration into a unified policy.

A cost-benefit analysis of farm forestry

R M Willis, C Price & T H T Thomas

School of Agriculture & Forest Sciences, University College of North Wales (UCNW)

Achievement of the objectives of farm forestry programmes is measured by three variables: speed of adoption (and therefore of land use diversification), selectivity of proposed schemes (related to environmental objectives), and expenditure. The UCNW project aims to show the trade-offs between the variables by modelling:

1. the economic comparison between agriculture and forestry

2. the costs of imposing environmental constraints, and of infringing them

3. the effects of farmers' attitudes on the update of forestry programmes.

By relating economic, environmental and attitudinal attributes to the Institute of Terrestrial Ecology land classes, results of case studies can be scaled up to national level, under a variety of price and policy scenarios.

Modelling

Modelling the agricultural and environmental consequences of sheep grazing heather moorland

H Armstrong
Macaulay Land Use Research Institute

A dynamic mechanistic model has been built which describes the changes in vegetation when heather moorland is grazed by sheep. The model encompasses the growth and defoliation consequences for all the significant vegetation communities associated with heather, as well as heather itself, of foraging by sheep among these plant communities, and the productivity of sheep populations. Examples of the various uses to which the model can be put will be illustrated.

Modelling soil erosion under future climates

J Boardman, D T Favis-Mortlock & R Evans
Countryside Research Unit, Brighton Polytechnic & Dept of Geography, University of Cambridge

Data for present-day erosion on agricultural land in Britain are used to predict future rates under 'greenhouse effect' climate, eg +3°C and +10% winter rain. Land use change involving new crops and changed locations for existing crops may lead to increases in erosion.

Hydrology of soil types (HOST)

D B Boorman, J M Hollis & A Lilly
Institute of Hydrology, Soil Survey & Land Research Centre, & Macaulay Land Use Research Institute

The HOST classification presents an integrated model of water movement through the soil and substrate capable of predicting a range of river flow parameters for any catchment within the UK. Based on the three main soil characteristics, hydrogeology and proximity to groundwater, this model is applicable at a wide range of geographical scales.

Modelling land allocation to farm forestry on upland farms

C S Butcher & A R Sibbald
Macaulay Land Use Research Institute

The physical resource base of a farm or estate is used to predict production for a range of crops (arable, livestock and trees), in a series of submodels which generate output as employment opportunities, conservation values, or financial returns. Land is allocated to different patterns through a hierarchy of decision rules which can represent different objectives. These rules are clearly articulated and the order can be changed according to the priorities of the user.

The model will help evaluate the medium- to long-term consequences of changes in land use at the management unit level.

The integration of geographical information systems and process-based water quality models

R Ferrier, D Miller & J Morrice
Macaulay Land Use Research Institute

The sensitivity of water quality models is dependent upon the scale of input information. During an investigation of water quality in the river Feshie, Cairngorm, parameterisation of the MAGIC model used soils information at medium (1:63 360) and small (1:250000) scales. Three spatial analyses were undertaken:

1. soils information weighted by area over the whole catchment

2. proximity analysis of soil units surrounding the stream

3. flow pathway analysis identifying the last soil unit that 100 random point sources of deposition encounter before reaching the stream.

Discussion will centre on model response to parameter selection. Optimum parameterisation has been used to model predictions on the effects of land use change within the catchment.

Modelling the consequences of land use on water resources in part of the Fenland

J Gowing, E O'Connell, J Lingard R Wadsworth
University of Newcastle upon Tyne

Our aim is to present an outline of the interlinked microcomputer-based simulation models that were developed to investigate the impact on water resources of land use and irrigation policy within the Middle Level. We will describe the agrohydrological model, agroeconomic model, and water resources model, and the way in which they were integrated to produce predictions on which policy-making could be based.

Modelling and predicting the effects of land use change on bird distributions

D Hill, D Gibbons & R Fuller
British Trust for Ornithology (BTO)

This new three-year project aims to relate bird distributions (3 BTO Atlas data sets) to land use and environmental factors using generalised linear interactive modelling and ordination/classification to determine changes in distributions over a 20-year period, and to predict effects of proposed land use changes.

A functional interpretation of botanical surveys

J G Hodgson, J P Grime, F Sutton, S Hillier & S Band
NERC Unit of Comparative Plant Ecology

The Unit has pioneered an approach known as FIBS (Functional Interpretation of Botanical Surveys) in an

attempt to understand why areas differ in their species composition. The approach has been used in an analysis of floristic changes between 1965 and 1990 in the semi-natural grassland over a 3000 km² area of central England around Sheffield.
Worked examples for four sites are included on the poster to show how FIBS analyses are actually carried out.

Modelling stream chemistry in response to afforestation/deforestation

A Jenkins
Institute of Hydrology

A model of the combined long-term effects of acidic deposition and forest growth has been developed. The model indicates that afforestation can increase the strong mineral acidity of streams in areas receiving high levels of acidic oxides from the atmosphere. Deforestation promotes a rapid decrease in acidity, although the soil base saturation recovers slowly.

Modelling the impact on water quality of land use change in an agricultural catchment

P J Johnes & T P Burt
School of Geography, University of Oxford

An export coefficient model was applied to the 350 km Windrush catchment, a tributary of the upper Thames, in order to predict nutrient and sediment loads, with particular reference to nitrate. A land use survey was used to calibrate the model, and the results of a three-year field work programme, together with archival material provided by the National Rivers Authority, were used for validation. The model was then used to predict water quality for a range of possible changes in land use; these included the changes in farming practice outlined within the new Nitrate Sensitive Area scheme. The approach allows identification of export zones and evaluation of strategies for control of pollution from agricultural land.

Environmental assessment – landscape impacts of land use change

D Miller & A Law
Macaulay Land Use Research Institute

Objective protocols for assessing impacts of land use change on landscape are presented. Scales of assessment range from Scottish national to observer-based scene analysis using digital terrain and land cover data. Orthogonal measures of terrain variation over a local area are combined with observer-based censuses of land visibility to target the assessment of impact on tourists. Changes in land cover provide a basis for retrospective impact assessment for the district of Badenoch and Strathspey in Scotland.

Macaulay Land Use Information and Modelling System

C Osman
Macaulay Land Use Research Institute

Baseline environmental, biological, and land resource information for Scotland, often collected through detailed field survey, is integrated with planning and other administrative designations, as well as a wide range of socio-economic data from census returns and survey, into a comprehensive information system structured around a geographical information system and relational data base. The information has application to land use issues from local, through regional, to national and international scales, and may be applied to a wide variety of land use questions. The Macaulay Land Use Information and Modelling System provides a highly flexible capability and is currently used for resource management and assessment, scientific research, and land use planning.

A geographical information system (GIS) for Dorset heaths

G L Radford & N R C Webb
Institute of Terrestrial Ecology, Monks Wood Experimental Station & Furzebrook Research Station

Records in the form of maps of the distribution and extent of heathland in Dorset dating back to last century have been brought together in a GIS, using a modern base map. The rate and extent of fragmentation are clearly evident from the map series; the severe reduction in viability of the characteristic ecological communities in the scattered remnant areas points to the need for restoration as well as protection. The results of ecological survey over the last 25 years are being incorporated into a GIS to help identify which of those areas recently lost to heathland are likely to respond best to restoration, and give the best chance of success in terms of extending heathland viability.

Modelling lowland farms and farm forestry decision-making

K J Thomson & J F Atkins
Dept of Agriculture, University of Aberdeen

This paper will outline the farm modelling work being carried out in the Department of Agriculture as part of the Joint Agriculture and Environment Programme. The modelling approach used to assess farm forestry options and the criteria used to evaluate various land use scenarios will also be presented.

Socio-economics

Environmental accounts for the primary land use sector

N Adger, K Brown, D Rimmer, R Shiel & M Whitby
University of Newcastle upon Tyne

Prevalent measures of aggregate welfare, such as Gross National Product, do not accurately reflect the standard of living in an economy because they do not

include those elements of the economy not traded in markets. Neither household production, the use of non-renewable resources nor environmental goods are in conventional accounts. This study produces a framework and attempts to estimate the importance of environmental 'goods' and 'bads' in aggregate welfare produced from the primary land use sectors, with a view to extending this for the whole UK economy.

Forestry planning

R Aspinall and D MacMillan

Macaulay Land Use Research Institute

Planning forestry demands an understanding of tree crop growth in relation to environmental and management conditions, an assessment of the comparative economic position of forestry and alternative land uses, and an appreciation of a wide range of land use and socio-economic constraints which influence decision-making. Here, an economic model of forestry and alternative agricultural land uses, which incorporates a model of tree response to site environmental conditions, is used to calculate forestry investment potential. The analysis is presented within a geographical information system environment, and results are set within the framework provided by a Regional Indicative Forestry Strategy. This provides a model of possible future location and uptake of forestry, the analysis being presented for Grampian Region, north-east Scotland.

Diversification – the potential role of alternative animal enterprises

A J F Russel

Macaulay Land Use Research Institute

To be economically viable, alternative animal enterprises must concentrate on quality products which can command signi   ficant

price premiums. Quality venison production has been shown to be feasible and the prospects for cashmere production are promising. Other enterprises which merit investigation include superfine wool production and fibre production from guanacos. Information will be provided on production systems, their costs and the prices of products required to make such systems profitable.

Environmental valuation

K Willis & G Garrod

Countryside Change Unit, Dept of Agricultural Economics & Food Marketing, University of Newcastle upon Tyne

Examples of environmental valuation using the travel-cost and hedonic-price methods are presented for forestry, inland waterways and countryside characteristics. Such valuations are increasingly being used by agencies such as the Forestry Commission and British Waterways in appraising new projects, and by the Treasury to ensure value for money in public investments.

Gates, pillars and posts

H Gracey

Dept of Agriculture for Northern Ireland, Belfast

Field boundaries, particularly hedgerows and dry stone walls, are outstanding and characteristic of the Northern Ireland countryside. Frequently associated with these are fine examples of gates, pillars and posts.

Such features are a real asset to the landscape and a small but significant part of our farming heritage. They are certainly well worth retaining and maintaining.

List of Conference participants

Ms H Alexander, Imperial College at Silwood Park, Department of Biology, Ascot, Berkshire, SL5 7PY

Dr H A Anderson, Macaulay Land Use Research Institute, Craigiebuckler, Aberdeen, AB9 2QJ

Dr M Anderson, Wye College, Ashford, Kent, TN25 5AH

Mr A Andrews, Institute of Hydrology, Crowmarsh Gifford, Wallingford, Oxfordshire, OX10 8BB

Ms H Armstrong, Macaulay Land Use Research Institute, Pentlandfield, Roslin, Midlothian, EH25 9RF

Mr D R Askew, MAFF Agricultural and Development Advisory Service, Block 2, Government Buildings, Lawnswood, Leeds, LS16 5PY

Dr R Aspinall, Macaulay Land Use Research Institute, Craigiebuckler, Aberdeen, AB9 2QJ

Mr J F Atkins, University of Aberdeen, Department of Agriculture, School of Agriculture Building, 581 King Street, Aberdeen, AB9 1UD

Mr E Audsley, AFRC Institute of Engineering Research, Wrest Park, Silsoe, Bedfordshire, MK45 4HS

Mr C Bancroft, Forestry Commission, Victoria Terrace, Aberystwyth, Dyfed, SY23 2DQ

Mr C J Barr, Institute of Terrestrial Ecology, Merlewood Research Station, Grange-over-Sands, Cumbria LA11 6JU

Mr I Barraclough, National Radiological Protection Board, Chilton, Didcot, Oxfordshire, OX11 0RQ

Mr M Bates, Nature Conservancy Council, Northminster House, Peterborough, PE1 1UA

Mr B G Bell, Institute of Terrestrial Ecology, Bush Estate, Penicuik, Midlothian, EH26 0QB

Dr J R Bevan, Newcastle Polytechnic, Lipman Building, Newcastle upon Tyne, NE1 8ST

Mr J S Bibby, Scottish Agricultural College, 581 King Street, Aberdeen, AB9 1UD

Mr P Bibby, Halcrow Fox & Associates, 44 Brook Green, Hammersmith, London, W6 7BY

Dr J Boardman, Brighton Polytechnic, Countryside Research Unit, Falmer, Brighton, East Sussex, BN1 9PH

Dr D B Boorman, Institute of Hydrology, Crowmarsh Gifford, Wallingford, Oxfordshire, OX10 8BB

Mr R Brand-Hardy, Ministry of Agriculture, Fisheries and Food, Nobel House, Room G15, 17 Smith Square, London, SW1P 3JR

Mr A D Broughall, National Rivers Authority, Severn Trent Region, Hafren House, Welshpool Road, Shelton, Shrewsbury SY3 8BB

Dr A Bullock, Institute of Hydrology, Crowmarsh Gifford, Wallingford, Oxfordshire, OX10 8BB

Dr R G H Bunce, Institute of Terrestrial Ecology, Merlewood Research Station, Grange-over-Sands, Cumbria, LA11 6JU

Dr T P Burt, University of Oxford, School of Geography, Mansfield Road, Oxford, OX1 3TB

Ms C Butcher, Macaulay Land Use Research Institute, Pentlandfield, Roslin, Midlothian, EH25 9RF

Professor J A Catt, AFRC Rothamsted Experimental Station, Harpenden, Hertfordshire, AL5 2JQ

Mr A J Chalmers, MAFF/ADAS, Redesdale Experimental Husbandry Farm, Rochester, Otterburn, Newcastle upon Tyne, NE19 1SB

Dr K Charman, Nature Conservancy Council, Archbold House, Archbold Terrace, Newcastle upon Tyne, NE2 1EG

Dr A Cherrill, University of Newcastle upon Tyne, Centre for Land Use & Water Resources Research, Newcastle upon Tyne, NE1 7RU

Mr J N M Clark, Great North Forest Project, The Grove, Birtley Lane, Chester le Street, Co Durham

Dr A Cooper, University of Ulster, Department of Environmental Studies, Cromore Road, Coleraine, Co Londonderry, BT52 1SA

Ms J Cooper, Scottish Centre of Agricultural Engineering, Bush Estate, Penicuik, Midlothian, EH26 0PH

Mr P W Coppin, South East Regional Research Laboratory, Birkbeck College, Department of Geography, 7-15 Gresse Street, London, W1P 1PA

Dr P Costigan, Ministry of Agriculture, Fisheries and Food, Environmental Protection Division, Nobel House, 17 Smith Square, London, SW1P 3JR

Ms J N Crockford, Nature Conservancy Council, Northminster House, Peterborough, PE1 1UA

Mr R P Cummins, Institute of Terrestrial Ecology, Hill of Brathens, Banchory, Kincardineshire, AB3 4BY

Mr J M Custance, Department of the Environment, Room P1/180, 2 Marsham Street, London, SW1P 3EB

Mr T Davie, University of Bristol, Department of Geography, University Road, Bristol, BS8 3HR

Ms E Davies, Department of the Environment, C15/16, 2 Marsham Street, London, SW1 3EB

Mr S Davies, Scottish Agricultural College, 581 King Street, Aberdeen, AB9 1UD

Mr G Deane, Hunting Technical Services Ltd, Thamesfield House, Boundary Way, Hemel Hempstead, Hertfordshire, HP2 7SR

Professor J B Dent, University of Edinburgh, Institute of Ecology and Resource Management, West Mains Road, Edinburgh, EH9 3JG

Mrs B Doig, Scottish Office, Central Research Unit, Room 5/60, New St Andrews House, Edinburgh, EH1 3SZ

Dr W R Eason, AFRC Institute of Grassland and Environmental Research, Welsh Plant Breeding Station, Plas Gogerddan, Aberystwyth, Dyfed, SY23 3HF

Miss H Edmond, Macaulay Land Use Research Institute, Craigiebuckler, Aberdeen, AB9 2QJ

Ms U Edmunds, Natural Environment Research Council, Polaris House, North Star Avenue, Swindon, Wiltshire, SN2 1EU

Miss N Ellis, Institute of Terrestrial Ecology, Bush Estate, Penicuik, Midlothian, EH26 0QB

Mr G Enders, Cremer & Warner, St Mary's Court, 47c Huntly Street, Aberdeen, AB1 1TH

Professor P R Evans, University of Durham, Department of Biological Sciences, Science Laboratories, South Road, Durham, DH1 3LE

Dr R Evans, University of Cambridge, Department of Geography, Downing Place, Cambridge, CB2 3EN

Mr M D Eyre, University of Newcastle upon Tyne, Centre for Land Use and Water Resources Research, Newcastle upon Tyne, NE1 7RU

Mr M Felton, Nature Conservancy Council, Northminster House, Peterborough, PE1 1UA

Dr S Figiel, University of Agriculture and Technology, 10-718 Olsztyn, Poland

Dr G N Foster, Scottish Agricultural College, Auchincruive, Ayr, KA6 5HW

Mr J R Franks, Postgraduate Student, University of Reading, Whiteknights, Reading, RG6 2AH

Ms J Froud, University of Manchester, Department of Agricultural Economics, Manchester, M13 9PL

Mr G Fry, Norwegian Institute for Nature Research, Box 64, The Agriculture University, N-1432 AAS-NLH, Norway

Mr R M Fuller, Institute of Terrestrial Ecology, Monks Wood Experimental Station, Abbots Ripton, Huntingdon, Cambridgeshire, PE17 2LS

Dr J Gardiner, National Rivers Authority, Technical Services Administration, Kings Meadow House, c/o 8th Floor, Kings Meadow Road, Reading, RG1 8DQ

Dr J H Gauld, Macaulay Land Use Research Institute, Craigiebuckler, Aberdeen, AB9 2QJ

Dr D Gibbons, British Trust for Ornithology, Beech Grove, Tring, Hertfordshire, HP23 5NR

Mr A Giblin, Nature Conservancy Council, Northminster House, Peterborough, PE1 1UA

Miss E Gill, AFRC Institute of Grassland and Environmental Research, Bronydd Mawr Research Centre, Trecastle, Near Brecon, Powys, LD3 8RD

Ms M Gillespie, Institute of Terrestrial Ecology, Merlewood Research Station, Grange-over-Sands, Cumbria, LA11 6JU

Dr J E Good, Institute of Terrestrial Ecology, Bangor Research Unit, University College of North Wales, Deiniol Road, Bangor, Gwynedd, LL57 2UP

Dr H Gracey, Department of Agriculture (NI), Water Drainage and Conservation Division, Hydebank, 4 Hospital Road, Belfast, BT8 8JP

Mr G Griffiths, Hunting Land and Environment Ltd, Thamesfield House, Boundary Way, Hemel Hempstead, Hertfordshire, HP2 7SR

Professor J P Grime, University of Sheffield, Unit of Comparative Plant Ecology, Sheffield, S10 2TN

Mr G B Groom, Institute of Terrestrial Ecology, Monks Wood Experimental Station, Abbots Ripton, Huntingdon, Cambridgeshire, PE18 2LS

Mr R Grove-White, University of Lancaster, Bailrigg, Lancaster, LA1 4YN

Dr R J Haggar, AFRC Institute of Grassland and Environmental Research, Welsh Plant Breeding Station, Plas Gogerddan, Aberystwyth, Dyfed, SY23 3HF

Ms C J Hallam, Institute of Terrestrial Ecology, Merlewood Research Station, Grange-over-Sands, Cumbria, LA11 6JU

Mr J Halley, Centre for Population Biology, Imperial College at Silwood Park, Ascot, Berkshire, SL5 7PY

Dr J F Handley, The Groundwork Trust, 32/34 Claughton Street, St Helens, Lancashire, WA10 2SN

Mr R Harriman, Freshwater Fisheries Laboratory, Faskally, Pitlochry, Perthshire, PH16 5LB

Dr R Harrison, Scottish Office, Central Research Unit, New St Andrew's House, Edinburgh, EH1 3SZ

Professor D R Harvey, University of Newcastle upon Tyne, Department of Agricultural Economics & Food Marketing, Newcastle upon Tyne, NE1 7RU

Professor O W Heal, Institute of Terrestrial Ecology, Bush Estate, Penicuik, Midlothian, EH26 0QB

Ms J Heap, Nature Conservancy Council, Northminster House, Peterborough, PE1 1UA

Dr A L Heathwaite, University of Sheffield, Department of Geography, Sheffield, S10 2TN

Mr D Hickling, National Trust for Scotland, 5 Charlotte Square, Edinburgh, EH2 5DU

Dr D A Hill, British Trust for Ornithology, National Centre for Ornithology, Nunnery Place, Thetford, Norfolk, IP24 2PU

Ms D Hindley, National Remote Sensing Centre Ltd, North Gate Road, Farnborough, Hampshire, GU14 6TW

Dr I Hodge, University of Cambridge, Department of Land Economy, Silver Street, Cambridge, CB3 9EP

Mr P Holden, Nature Conservancy Council, 12 Hope Terrace, Edinburgh, EH9 2AS

Mr A J Hooper, MAFF Agricultural and Development Advisory Service, Room 208, Nobel House, 17 Smith Square, London, SW1P 3JR

Dr M Hornung, Institute of Terrestrial Ecology, Merlewood Research Station, Grange-over-Sands, Cumbria, LA11 6JU

Ms J E Hossell, University of Birmingham, Atmospheric Impacts Research Group, Department of Geography, PO Box 363, Birmingham, B15 2TT

Mr M N Hough, Meteorological Office, London Road, Bracknell, Berkshire, RG12 2SZ

Mr D C Howard, Institute of Terrestrial Ecology, Merlewood Research Station, Grange-over-Sands, Cumbria, LA11 6JU

Mrs B T Jacobsen, Institute of Agricultural Economics, Toftegaards Plads, GL Koege Landoves 1-3, 2500 Valby, Denmark

Mr J M L Jansen, The Winand Staring Centre, Postbox 125, 6700 AC Wageningen, The Netherlands

Professor J N R Jeffers, Ellerhow, Lindale, Grange-over-Sands, Cumbria, LA11 6NA

Mr A Jenkins, Institute of Hydrology, Crowmarsh Gifford, Wallingford, Oxfordshire, OX10 8BB

Dr P J Johnes, University of Liverpool, Department of Environmental and Evolutionary Biology, Liverpool, L69 3BX

Ms J A Johnson, University of Edinburgh, Institute of Ecological Research Management, Darwin Building, King's Buildings, Mayfield Road, Edinburgh, EH9 3JU

Professor B Johnsson, The Swedish University of Agricultural Sciences, Department of Economics, Box 7013, S-750 07 Uppsala, Sweden

Mr A Jones, Kent County Council, Planning Department, Springfield, Maidstone, Kent, ME14 2LX

Ms E Kerrell, Huddersfield Polytechnic, Department of Geography, Queensgate, Huddersfield, HD1 3DH

Mr H S Kingra, c/o AETU, Wolverhampton Polytechnic, Gorway Road, Walsall, West Midlands, WS1 3BD

Professor J L Knill, Natural Environment Research Council, Polaris House, North Star Avenue, Swindon, Wiltshire, SN2 1EU

Mrs K Leitch, University of Newcastle upon Tyne, Centre for Land Use and Water Resources Research, Newcastle upon Tyne, NE1 7RU

Mr P Leonard, Department of the Environment, Room N19/15, 2 Marsham Street, London, SW1P 3EB

Mr A Lilly, Macaulay Land Use Research Institute, Craigiebuckler, Aberdeen, AB9 2QJ

Mr N B Lilwall, Scottish Agricultural College, 42 South Oswald Road, Edinburgh, EH9 2HH

Mr P Lowe, University College London, Department of Geography, 26 Bedford Way, London, WC1H 0AP

Dr M Luff, University of Newcastle upon Tyne, Department of Agricultural and Environmental Science, Centre for Land Use and Water Resources Research, Newcastle upon Tyne, NE1 7RU

Mr R Mackay, University of Newcastle upon Tyne, Department of Civil Engineering, Centre for Land Use and Water Resources Reseach, Newcastle upon Tyne, NE1 7RU

Professor A MacLeary, St Helen's, St Andrew's Road, Ceres, Fife, KY13 5NQ

Mr D Macmillan, Macaulay Lane Use Research Institute, Craigiebuckler, Aberdeen, AB2 4QJ

Professor J S Marsh, University of Reading, Department of Agricultural Economics and Management, 4 Earley Gate, Whiteknights, Reading, RG6 2AR

Mr T Marsters, University of Reading, Farm Management Unit, Department of Agriculture, Earley Gate, Reading, RG6 2AT

Professor P M Mather, University of Nottingham, Department of Geography, Nottingham, NG7 2RD

Dr R McIntosh, Forestry Commission, Eals Burn, Bellingham, Hexham, Northumberland

Dr A Mellor, Newcastle Polytechnic, Department of Environment, Lipman Building, Newcastle upon Tyne, NE1 8ST

Mr D W Merrilees, Scottish Agricultural College, Environmental Sciences Department, Auchincruive, Ayr, KA6 5HW

Ms J Metcalfe, Institute for Terrestrial Ecology, Monks Wood Experimental Station, Abbots Ripton, Huntingdon, Cambridgeshire, PE17 2LS

Dr J Miles, Scottish Office, Central Research Unit, Room 5/54, New St Andrew's House, Edinburgh, EH1 3SZ

Mr D Miller, Macaulay Land Use Research Institute, Craigiebuckler, Aberdeen, AB9 2QJ

Dr J A Milne, Macaulay Land Use Research Institute, Pentlandfield, Roslin, Midlothian, EH25 9RF

Miss M Mitchell, Scottish Agricultural College, Economics Division, Auchincruive, Ayr, KA6 5HW

Mr O Moles, Derwentside District Council, Civic Centre, Consett, Co Durham, DH8 5JA

Mr E Molloy, Institute of Terrestrial Ecology, Merlewood Research Station, Grange-over-Sands, Cumbria, LA11 6JU

Dr M G Morris, Institute of Terrestrial Ecology, Furzebrook Research Station, Wareham, Dorset, BH20 5AS

Dr A Mowle, Nature Conservancy Council, 12 Hope Terrace, Edinburgh, EH9 2AS

Mr W E S Mutch, 19 Barnton Grove, Edinburgh, EH4 6EQ

Professor R J C Munton, University College London, Rural Studies Research Centre, Department of Geography, 26 Bedford Way, London, WC1H 0AP

Professor M D Newson, University of Newcastle upon Tyne, Department of Geography, Newcastle upon Tyne, NE1 7RU

Professor J R O'Callaghan, University of Newcastle upon Tyne, Centre for Land Use and Water Resources Research, Newcastle upon Tyne, NE1 7RU

Ms L O'Carroll, University of Manchester, Department of Agricultural Economics, Faculty of Economics, Manchester, M13 9PL

Mr A M Oliver, Department of the Environment, Room P1/182, 2 Marsham Street, London, SW1P 3EB

Dr D Osborn, Institute of Terrestrial Ecology, Monks Wood Experimental Station, Abbots Ripton, Huntingdon, Cambridgeshire, PE17 2LS

Professor M L Parry, University of Birmingham, School of Geography, Edgbaston, Birmingham, B15 2TT

Mr T Perkins, Edinburgh School of Agriculture, Rural Resource Management Division, Glenbourne, South Oswald Road, Edinburgh, EH9 2HH

Mr J C Peters, Department of the Environment (DRA), Room 917B, Tollgate House, Houlton Street, Bristol, BS2 9DJ

Dr A A C Phillips, Countryside Commission, John Dower House, Crescent Place, Cheltenham, Gloucestershire, GL50 3RA

Dr D S Powlson, AFRC Institute of Arable Crops Research, Rothamsted Experimental Station, Harpenden, Hertfordshire, AL5 2JQ

Professor T M Roberts, Institute of Terrestrial Ecology, Monks Wood Experimental Station, Abbots Ripton, Huntingdon, Cambridgeshire, PE17 2LS

Mr J Robinson, MAFF/ADAS, Trawsgoed, Aberystwyth, Dyfed, SY23 4HT

Mr T J D Rollinson, Forestry Commission, 231 Corstorphine Road, Edinburgh, EH12 7AT

Dr S P Rushton, University of Newcastle upon Tyne, Department of Agricultural and Environmental Science, Centre for Land Use and Water Resources Research, Newcastle upon Tyne, NE1 7RU

Mr R Rysstad, Agricultural University of Norway, Department of Agricultural Economics, PO Box 33, N-1432 AAS-NLH, Norway

Mrs D Salathiel, Department of the Environment, B245 Romney House, 43 Marsham Street, London, SW1P 3PY

Mr R Scarpa, Universitat degli Studie delle Tuscia, Departimento di Scienze, Economiche ed Estimative, 01100 Viterbo, Italy

Dr A Selby, Finnish Forest Research Institute, PO Box 37, SF-00381 Helsinki, Finland

Dr J Shepherd, South East Regional Research Laboratory, Birkbeck College, Department of Geography, 7-15 Gresse Street, London, W1P 1PA

Mr A Sibbald, Macaulay Land Use Research Institute, Pentlandfield, Roslin, Midlothian, EH25 9RF

Mr M J Silverwood, MAFF Agricultural and Development Advisory Service, Block 2, Government Buildings, Lawnswood, Leeds, LS16 5PY

Dr R S Smith, University of Newcastle upon Tyne, Department of Agricultural and Environmental Science, Newcastle upon Tyne, NE1 7RU

Mrs N J Speich, National Rivers Authority, Severn Trent Region, Sapphire East, 550 Streetsbrook Road, Solihull, West Midlands, B91 1QT

Ms A Stokes, University of York, Department of Biology, Heslington, York, YO1 5DD

Dr A Stott, Department of Environment (NI), Countryside and Wildlife Branch, Calvert House, 23 Castle Place, Belfast, BT1 1FY

Ms K Sutherland, Nature Conservancy Council, Northminster House, Peterborough, PE1 1UA

Dr J P Taylor, Royal Society for the Protection of Birds, The Lodge, Sandy, Bedfordshire, SG19 2DL

Dr P B Tinker, Natural Environment Research Council, Polaris House, North Star Avenue, Swindon, Wiltshire, SN2 1EU

Mr G Tudor, Nature Conservancy Council, 12 Hope Terrace, Edinburgh, EH9 2AS

Mrs L A D Turl, Department of Agriculture and Fisheries for Scotland, Pentland House, 47 Robb's Loan, Edinburgh, EH14 1TW

Dr M B Usher, University of York, Department of Biology, Heslington, York, YO1 5DD

Dr H C van Latesteijn, Scientific Council for Government Policy, 2 Plein 1813, PO Box 20004, 2500 EA The Hague, The Netherlands

Mr J Vaughan, Great North Forest Project, The Grove, Birtley Lane, Chester le Street, Co Durham

Mr L Venzi, University of Tuscia-Viterbo, Experimental Farm, Faculty of Agriculture, Strada Riello, 01100 Viterbo, Italy

Mr R A Wadsworth, University of Newcastle upon Tyne, Centre for Land Use and Water Resources Research, Newcastle upon Tyne, NE1 7RU

Mrs P A Ward, Institute of Terrestrial Ecology, Merlewood Research Station, Grange-over-Sands, Cumbria, LA11 6JU

Ms S A Ward, Macaulay Land Use Research Institute, Craigiebuckler, Aberdeen, AB9 2QJ

Dr P J Webber, WK Kellogg Biological Station, Hickory Corners, Michigan 49060, USA

Dr S Webster, Nature Conservancy Council, Northminster House, Peterborough, PE1 1UA

Mr M C Whitby, University of Newcastle upon Tyne, Department of Agricultural Economics and Food Marketing, Newcastle upon Tyne, NE1 7RU

Dr B White, University of Newcastle upon Tyne, Department of Agricultural Economics and Food Marketing, Newcastle upon Tyne, NE1 7RU

Ms S White, University of Newcastle upon Tyne, Department of Civil Engineering, Centre for Land Use and Water Resources Research, Newcastle upon Tyne, NE1 7RU

Mr J Wildig, MAFF Agricultural and Development Advisory Service, Pwllpeiron EHF, Cwmystwyth, Aberystwyth, Dyfed, SY23 4AB

Professor W B Wilkinson, Institute of Hydrology, Crowmarsh Gifford, Wallingford, Oxfordshire, OX10 8BB

Mr R Willis, University College of North Wales, SAFS, Deiniol Road, Bangor, Gwynedd, LL57 2UW

Mr M J Wilson, Macaulay Land Use Research Institute, Craigiebuckler, Aberdeen, AB9 2QJ

Mr R B Wilson, Department of the Environment, Room B352, Romney House, 43 Marsham Street, London, SW1P 3PY

Mr I Woiwood, AFRC Rothamsted Experimental Station, Department of Entomology and Neuratology, Harpenden, Hertfordshire, AL5 2JQ

Mr A Young, Institute of Hydrology, Crowmarsh Gifford, Wallingford, Oxfordshire, OX10 8BB

Printed in the United Kingdom for HMSO.
Dd. 296780, C4, 3/94, 16268.